For Sarah:

Former Teacher, Former Principal,
Current Colleague, Current and Future Spouse

Contents

8 Performance Assessment *157*

9 Portfolio Assessment *181*

10 Affective Assessment *199*

11 Improving Teacher-Developed Assessments *217*

To the Reader

··

This is a book written for teachers and for people who are preparing to become teachers. It's about classroom assessment. The book's subtitle foreshadows its orientation—namely, it is about *What Teachers Need to Know*. It's not a book loaded with measurement minutiae. On the contrary, the book contains mainline material dealing with the day-in and day-out assessment concerns of classroom teachers.

The overriding theme of the book is that *classroom assessment should help teachers make better educational decisions.* If the results of your classroom assessment activities don't improve the quality of the decisions you make about your students, then you're wasting your students' time—and your own.

Actually, this is the second edition of a book I first wrote in the mid-nineties. And, as any astute reader realizes, a second edition ought to be better than its predecessor, which I think this new edition is. But, of course, I'm unashamedly biased.

For one thing, this second edition is more attentive to the *instructional* pay-offs of well-designed classroom tests. I've attempted to highlight the implications testing has on teaching whenever I can. There's even a brand-new chapter (12) entitled Instructionally Oriented Assessment that attempts to make more vivid the integral relationship between teaching and testing. I also realized, after discussing the first edition of the book with many teachers who had read it, that I'd given little attention in the first edition to an important audience for teachers—namely, *parents.* Teachers often need to explain assessment-related topics to parents, such as why a child scored a certain way on a standardized test or the way classroom exams are related to the grades a child receives. So, in every chapter of this new edition, you'll find a feature entitled *Parent Talk.* In these Parent Talk features, I've described a situation in which a teacher needs to explain something about assessment to parents. I then tell you what I would have said to the parents if I had been the teacher in that situation. What I hope you'll do, then, is decide how *you* would respond in that same situation. In fact, you might say *aloud* (in private, if you have any sense) what you'd tell parents. Either paraphrase my words or whip out better words of your own. Teachers who can talk sensibly to parents about assessment-related concerns will find that they're able to establish more effective educational rapport with parents. Such teachers will get along far better with parents than will teachers who convey to parents the idea that "assessment is an exotic measurement mystery, well beyond the perceptive powers of mere parents." As this book will make clear, assessment really involves pretty commonsense stuff. The Parent Talk features will give you some practice in proving it.

Remember, the purpose of the Parent Talk sections in each chapter is to help get you ready to talk to your students' parents about the things you'll be learning in this book. There was a time when teachers weren't called on to explain assessment-related issues to parents. That time has long since passed. Parents have become major players in the educational assessment game. And, in that regard, at the end of Chapter 15, there is an essay written for parents about the misuse of standardized test scores to judge the quality of instruction.

There are 15 chapters designed to take readers on a tour of the key measurement concepts needed by classroom teachers. Each chapter could have been twice as long if the audience had been measurement specialists. Instead, a deliberate effort was made to strip away superfluous information so that you're left with only the need-to-know content, not the nice-to-know content.

I realize all too well that you're not likely to regard the content of a book on assessment as enthralling. For myself, if I had the choice of whether I would read any assessment book or a cracking good espionage novel, I'd shove the assessment book into second place in a millisecond. In recognition of your probable response to the book's content, I've tried to lighten the load with an occasional dash of levity. If you had to write 15 chapters about assessment, I suspect that you would also get whimsical. If you don't find the light style to be acceptable, simply frown during the funny parts. It will teach me a lesson!

Now, here are just a few words about the layout of the book. Every chapter contains several elements intended to foster a stick-to-your-ribs mastery of its content. You'll find the following at the close of each chapter:

- A succinct isolation of *what teachers really need to know* about the chapter's content
- A general *summary* of the chapter's contents
- A set of *self-check* exercises
- A *self-check* key that provides answers to all of the self-check exercises as well as, in a few instances, an elaboration of the concepts addressed by the exercises
- A set of *Pondertime* questions designed to get you thinking about key concepts in the chapter
- *Additional Stuff*—a set of additional books and articles that can extend your understanding of the chapter's content
- *Nonprint Stuff,* such as videotapes or audiotapes that expand on the chapter's concepts

You'll also encounter in each chapter a description of a fictitious teacher in a classroom situation that's related to one or more of the topics treated in the chapter. The insert is concluded with a decision that must be made by the teacher being described. You're then requested to put yourself in the place of the teacher and decide how you'd proceed. These vignettes are intended to set a series of practice problems on your plate, then see how you would munch on them.

I've written books about measurement in the past. All those texts, however, were authored for advanced graduate students nearing the end of their doctoral-degree graduate programs. For that kind of an audience, of course, I had to include all sorts of suitable assessment esoterica. But I've been a classroom teacher and I recall how busy I was. I surely didn't have time for any peripheral material. Thus, for classroom teachers and prospective classroom teachers, I've tried to write a clutter-free book. I hope that, when you've finished this assessment excursion, you'll agree. These days, teachers who don't know most of what this book contains are going into educational battle without suitable weapons.

Good luck in grappling with the assessment topics you'll be greeting on subsequent pages.

I am grateful to Dolly Bulquerin, word-processor nonpareil, who guided the transformation of a first edition into a second.

W. J. P.

1

Why Do Teachers Need to Know about Assessment?

*T*eachers teach students. That hardly constitutes a breakthrough insight. Just as preachers preach and flyers fly—teachers teach. That's why they're called teachers.

But what is a bit less obvious is that teachers teach because they *like* to teach. Primary teachers like to teach little people. High school teachers like to teach bigger people. Most high school teachers like to teach about a particular subject matter. (Have you ever seen how mathematics teachers' eyes get misty when they introduce their students to the raptures of the Pythagorean theorem?) Yes, most teachers love to teach. It is because they enjoy what they do that they waded through a medley of preservice teacher education courses, conquered the challenges of student teaching, and hopped the myriad hurdles of the certification process. Teachers overcame these obstacles in order to earn annual salaries that, particularly during the first few years, are laughably low. Yes, there's little doubt that teachers enjoy teaching.

Although teachers like to *teach*, they rarely like to *test*. Yet, here you are—beginning a book about testing. How can I, the author, ever entice you, the reader, to become interested in testing when your heart has already been given to teaching? The answer is really quite straightforward. Teachers who can test well will be better teachers. Effective testing will enhance a teacher's instructional effectiveness. Really!

If you're willing to suspend any preconceptions about testing while you're reading this book, particularly any negative ones, I'll make a pledge to you. If you tackle this text with even half the enthusiasm you might bring to a teaching assignment, I promise you'll discover how *testing will make you a much better teacher*. And, because I've been a teacher for over 35 years, it's a promise I'll keep. Teachers definitely should not break promises to teachers. Teachers' promises to administrators, on the other hand, should be regarded as eminently renegotiable commitments.

Assessment versus Testing ....

So far, I've been contrasting teaching to testing when, if you'll glance at this book's cover, you'll find that it's supposed to be a book about assessment. If you're alert, you've already started to wonder—What's this author trying to pull off? Am I going to learn about *testing* or *assessment*? Is *assessment* simply a more fashionable word for *testing*? In short, what's he up to? These are reasonable questions, and I'll now try to supply you with a set of compelling, confidence-engendering answers.

Almost everyone knows about the kinds of tests typically encountered in school. Most of today's adults, indeed, were on the receiving end of a hoard of teacher-dispensed tests during their own days in school. There were final exams, midterm exams, end-of-unit tests, pop quizzes, and (in the interest of equity) mom quizzes. All of those tests had one thing in common. They represented the teacher's attempt to get a fix on how much the teacher's students had learned. More accurately, such tests were employed to determine a student's status with respect to the knowledge or skills that the teacher was attempting to promote. That is an altogether praiseworthy endeavor for teachers—to find out how much students know. If teachers are reasonably sure about what their students currently know, then teachers can more accurately tailor instructional activities to what students need to know.

The sorts of tests referred to in the preceding paragraph, such as the quizzes and examinations that most of us took in school, have historically been paper-and-pencil instruments. When I was a student, many years ago, the three most common forms of tests that I encountered were essay tests, multiple-choice tests, and true-false tests. Until the past decade or so, those three kinds of tests were, by far, the most prevalent sorts of tests found in classrooms.

In recent years, however, educators have been urged to broaden their conception of testing so that students' status is determined via a wider variety of measuring devices—a variety extending well beyond traditional paper-and-pencil tests. The reason that teachers have been challenged to expand their repertoire of testing techniques is not merely for the sake of variety. Rather, thoughtful educators have recognized that there are a number of important kinds of student learning that are not measured most appropriately by paper-and-pencil tests. If, for example, a teacher wants to determine how well students can function orally in a job-interview situation, it's pretty clear that a true-false test doesn't cut it.

Thus, because there are many worthwhile learning outcomes that are not best measured by paper-and-pencil tests, and because when most people use the word *test* they automatically think of traditional paper-and-pencil tests, the term *assessment* has been increasingly adopted by many educators and measurement specialists. Assessment is a broader descriptor of the kinds of educational measuring that teachers do—a descriptor that, while certainly including traditional paper-and-pencil tests, covers many more kinds of measurement procedures. Here is a working definition of *assessment* as it is used in an educational context:

> *Educational assessment is a formal attempt to determine students' status with respect to educational variables of interest.*

Lest you be put off by this fairly foreboding definition, let's briefly consider its chief elements. Note that the kind of assessment we're talking about is aimed at determining the status of students regarding "educational variables of interest." *Variables* are merely things that vary. In education, for example, we find that students vary in how much they know about a subject, how skilled they are in performing such operations as long division, and how positive their attitudes are toward school. Those are the sorts of variables with which a teacher is typically concerned, thus they are the "variables of interest" that teachers typically measure. If the teacher's instructional focus is on the industrial revolution, then the teacher may wish to assess how much students know about the industrial revolution. In that case, the variable of interest would be the degree of students' knowledge regarding the industrial revolution. If the teacher is interested in how confident students are regarding their own written composition skills, then students' composition confidence would be a variable of interest. Educational assessment deals with such variables.

Our working definition also indicates that educational assessment constitutes a "formal" attempt to get a fix on students' status. As human beings, we make all sorts of informal determinations regarding people's status. For example, we may conclude that the woman who cut into the supermarket line ahead of us is rude, or that the man who keeps stumbling as he climbs a set of stairs is clumsy. But these are informal status determinations. Teachers, too, make informal judgments about their students. For instance, a teacher might conclude that a student, based on the student's glum demeanor during the first few moments of class, is definitely grumpy. Such informal appraisals, although they may be useful to teachers, should not be regarded as educational assessment.

When I was a high school teacher, for example, I employed informal judgment to conclude that Raymond Gonty, one of the seniors in my U.S. Government class, was not really interested in what I was teaching. I reached this conclusion chiefly because Raymond usually slept during class. I became more firmly convinced, however, when he began arriving at class carrying a pillow!

The kind of educational assessment you'll be reading about in this book is formal—that is, it's a deliberate effort to determine a student's status regarding such variables as the student's knowledge, skills, or attitudes. The kind of educational assessment you'll be considering is more than a teacher's "impressions." Rather, you'll be learning about systematic ways to get a fix on a student's status.

Assessment, therefore, is a broad and relatively nonrestrictive label for the kinds of testing and measuring that teachers must do. It is a label to help remind educators that the measurement of students' status should include far more than paper-and-pencil instruments. Assessment is a word that embraces diverse kinds of tests and measurements. In the remaining pages, you'll find that although I'll use the term *assessment,* I'll often use the words *test* and *measurement.* I'll not be trying to make any subtle distinctions at those times. Instead, I'm probably just tired of using the A-word.

Why Should Teachers Know about Assessment? Yesteryear's Answers ....

Let's play a bit of time travel. Suppose you were magically transported back to the 1950s or 1960s. And, as long as we're in a let's-pretend mode, imagine you're a new teacher taking part in a fall orientation for first-year teachers in a large school district. The thematic topic of the particular session you're attending is Why Should Teachers Know about Testing? The session's lecturer, Professor Tess Tumm, is supplying the audience with a set of traditional answers to that thematic question based on how teachers actually can use classroom tests. Because you are a docile new teacher (remember, this is imaginary), you are compliantly taking notes to help guide you during the coming school year.

What I'm suggesting, as you've probably guessed, is that there are a number of fairly traditional answers to the question of why teachers should learn about assessment. Those answers have been around for several decades. There is also a set of more current answers to the question of why teachers should know about assessment. Let's give tradition its due and, initially, consider four time-honored answers to the question of what teachers should know about testing. Although these reasons for knowing about classroom assessment may have been around for a while, they're still compelling because they are rooted in the realities of what skilled teachers can do with classroom assessment. These four reasons may well have been the major points treated by Professor Tumm during our imaginary orientation session of yesteryear.

Diagnosing Students' Strengths and Weaknesses

One important reason that teachers assess students is to determine an individual student's weaknesses and strengths. If you're an elementary teacher, you need to know how well Giselle is comprehending what she reads so that, if she's having certain difficulties, you can address those problems instructionally. Student weaknesses, once identified via assessment, can be the focus of future instruction.

On the flip side of the issue, teachers need to know what their students' prior accomplishments are. If Jaime is already truly proficient in solving simultaneous equations, it's a waste of Jaime's time to make him plow through practice piles of such equations. When I was growing up, the expression "That's like carrying coal to Newcastle" was used to disparage any scheme that reeked of redundancy. (I always assumed that coal mining was a big deal in Newcastle.) Well, teachers who relentlessly keep instructing students regarding knowledge or skills that the students have already mastered are definitely lugging coal lumps to Newcastle. Assessment can allow teachers to identify students' current strengths and, as a consequence, can help teachers avoid superfluous and wasteful instruction.

Thus, by measuring students' current status, teachers can discern (1) where to put their instructional energies to ameliorate a student's weaknesses and (2) what already mastered skills or knowledge can be instructionally avoided. Such diagnostic assessment is particularly useful for a teacher's planning if the assessment is carried out at the beginning of an instructional sequence. This kind of early diagnosis is often referred to as *preassessment* because it is assessment that takes place prior to the teacher's initiation of instruction.

Monitoring Students' Progress

A second, related answer to the question, Why should teachers assess? is that such assessments help teachers determine whether their students are making satisfactory progress. Sometimes, of course, it's easy for teachers to tell whether their students are or are not progressing satisfactorily. I can still recall, with suitable embarrassment, the absolutely scintillating lesson I provided as a high school English teacher on the topic of Modifying Gerunds with Possessives. It was a lesson designed for a full-class period, and I was confident that at its conclusion my students would not only understand the topic but also be able to explain to others why one of the following sentences contains an appropriate pronoun and one does not:

Improper
Pronoun   *Gerund*
↓   ↓

☹ **Sentence 1:** I really appreciate you sending the brownies.

Proper
Pronoun   *Gerund*
↓   ↓

☺ **Sentence 2:** I really appreciate your sending the brownies.

At the end of a bravura 40-minute lesson, replete with all sorts of real-life examples and a host of on-target practice activities, I was certain I had effectively taught students that because a gerund was a noun-form of a verb, any modifiers of such gerunds, including pronouns, must be possessive. And yet, at the end of the lesson, when I looked into my students' baffled faces, I realized that my optimism was unwarranted. After asking several students to explain to me the essence of what I'd been talking about, I quickly discerned that my lesson about gerund modification was not an award-winning effort. Most of my students couldn't distinguish between a gerund and a geranium.

Although teachers can occasionally discern informally, as I did, that their students aren't making satisfactory progress, more often than not we find teachers' believing that their students are progressing quite well. (Note that in the previous sentence the modifier of the gerund *believing* is the possessive form of *teachers*. Yes, I'm still trying.) It's only human nature for teachers to believe that they're teaching well and that their students are learning well. But unless teachers systematically monitor students' progress via some type of assessment, there's too much chance that teachers will improperly conclude progress is taking place when, in fact, it is not.

A useful function of classroom assessment, therefore, is to determine whether students are moving satisfactorily toward the instructional outcomes the teacher is seeking to promote. If progress for all students is satisfactory, of course, then the teacher need make no instructional changes. If progress for most students is satisfactory, but a few students are falling behind, then some separate doses of remedial assistance would seem to be in order. If progress for most students is inadequate, then the teacher should substantially modify whatever instructional approach is being used because, it is all too clear, that approach is not working. Progress monitoring is a time-honored and altogether sensible use of classroom assessment.

A teacher needs to monitor students' progress via classroom assessment because, more often than you'd think, the teacher can stop instructing on a certain topic well in advance of what the teacher anticipated. Suppose, for instance, you're attempting to get your students to acquire a certain skill, and you've set aside two weeks to promote their mastery of that skill. If you monitor students' progress with an assessment after only a week, however, and discover that your students have already mastered the skill, you should simply scrap your week-two plans and smilingly move on to the next topic.

Assigning Grades

If I were somehow able to carry out an instant nationwide survey of beginning teachers and asked them, "What is the most important function of classroom assessment?" I know what answer I'd get from most of the surveyed teachers. They'd immediately respond: *to give grades.*

That's certainly what I thought testing was all about when I taught in public schools. To be honest (confession, I am told, is good for the soul), the *only* reason I tested my students was to give them grades. Unfortunately, I've talked to hundreds of teachers during the past few years, and I've been dismayed at how many of them continue to regard testing's exclusive function to be grade giving. A third reason, therefore, that teachers assess students is to assemble the evidence necessary to give their students grades. Most school systems are structured so that the end-of-course or end-of-year grades a student earns constitute the beginnings of a record of the student's personal accomplishments—a record destined to follow that student throughout life. Thus, it is imperative that teachers not assign grades capriciously. Whether we like it or not, students' grades are important.

The best way to assign grades properly is to collect evidence of a student's accomplishments so that the teacher will have access to ample information before deciding whether to dish out an A, B, C, D, or F to a student. Some school systems employ less traditional student grading systems—for example, the use of descriptive verbal reports that are relayed to parents or the use of multidimensional checklists. Yet, whatever the reporting system that's used, it is clear that the teacher's assessment activities can provide the evidence necessary to make sensible student-by-student appraisals. The more frequent and varied the evidence of student accomplishments, the more judiciously the teacher can assign to students the grades they deserve.

Determining One's Own Instructional Effectiveness

A fourth and final reason that teachers have traditionally been told they should test students is that students' test performances can help teachers infer how effective their teaching has been. Suppose a teacher sets out to have students attain a set of worthwhile skills and knowledge regarding Topic X during a three-week instructional unit. Prior to instruction, a brief test indicated that students knew almost nothing about Topic X, but after the unit was concluded, a more lengthy test revealed that students had mastered most of the skills and knowledge addressed during the Topic X unit.

Because the comparison of students' pretest and posttest test results indicated that the teacher's students had acquired ample knowledge and skills regarding Topic X, the teacher has a solid chunk of evidence that the instructional approach being used appears to be working. If the teacher's instruction seems to be promoting the desired outcomes, then it probably shouldn't be altered all that much.

On the other hand, let's say a teacher's Topic X pretest-to-posttest results for students suggest that students' progress has been piffling. After comparing results on the end-of-instruction posttest to students' performance on the preinstruction test, it appears that students barely knew more than they knew before the instruction commenced. Such trivial student growth should suggest to the teacher that modifications in the instructional activities seem warranted when teaching Topic X again next term or next year.

I'm not suggesting that students' pretest-to-posttest results are the only way for teachers to tell whether they're flying or flopping, but students' end-of-instruction performances on assessment devices constitute a particularly useful indication of whether teachers should retain, alter, or totally jettison their current instructional procedures.

In review, then, we've considered four fairly traditional answers to the question of why teachers should assess students. Here they are again:

Traditional Reasons That Teachers Assess Students
- To diagnose students' strengths and weaknesses
- To monitor students' progress
- To assign grades to students
- To determine instructional effectiveness

You will notice that each of these four uses of educational assessment is directly related to *helping the teacher make a decision.* When a teacher assesses students' strengths and weaknesses, the teacher uses test results to *decide* what instructional objectives to pursue. When a teacher assesses students' progress, the teacher uses test results to *decide* whether certain parts of the ongoing instructional program need to be altered. When a teacher assesses students to help assign grades, the teacher uses students' performances to *decide* which students get which grades. And, finally, when a teacher uses pretest-to-posttest assessment results to indicate how effective an instructional sequence has been, the teacher is trying to *decide* whether the instructional sequence needs to be overhauled. Teachers should never assess students without a clear understanding of what the decision is that will be informed by results of the assessment. The chief function of educational assessment, you see, is to improve the quality of educational decision making.

Taken in concert, the four reasons we have been discussing should incline teachers to assess up a storm in their classrooms. But these days even more reasons can be given regarding why teachers need to know about assessment.

Why Should Teachers Know about Assessment? Today's Answers ....

In addition to the four traditional reasons that teachers need to know about assessment, there are three new reasons that should incline teachers to take a dip in the assessment pool. Having emerged during the past decade or so, these are compelling reasons why today's teachers dare not be ignorant regarding educational assessment. Let's consider three new roles for educational assessment and see why these new functions of educational testing should incline you to pump up your assessment knowledge.

Influencing Public Perceptions of Educational Effectiveness

When I was a high school teacher a long while ago, teachers were required to give nationally standardized achievement tests. But, to be honest, no one really paid much attention to the test results. My fellow teachers perused the test-score re-

Pressure from "Higher Ups" ·····································

Laura Lund has been teaching second-graders at Horace Mann Elementary School for the past three years. During that period, Laura has become increasingly convinced that "developmentally appropriate instruction" is what she wants in her classroom. Developmentally appropriate instruction takes place when the instructional activities for children are not only matched with the typical developmental level of children in that grade but also matched with the particular developmental level of each child. Because of her growing commitment to developmental appropriateness, and its clear implications for individualized instruction, Laura's students now no longer receive, *in unison,* the same kinds of massed practice drills in reading and mathematics that Laura provided earlier in her career.

Having discovered what kinds of changes are taking place in Laura's second grade, however, the third-grade and fourth-grade teachers in her school have registered great concern over what they regard as less attention to academics, at least less attention of the traditional sort. Because districtwide tests are given to all third- and fourth-grade students each spring, Laura's colleagues are afraid their students will not perform well on those tests because they will not be skilled at the end of the second grade.

A year or so earlier, when Laura was teaching her second grade in a fairly traditional manner, it was widely recognized that most of her students went on to the third grade with a solid mastery of reading and mathematics. Now, however, the school's third- and fourth-grade teachers fear that "Horace Mann's test scores may plummet."

As Laura sees it, she has to decide whether to (1) revert to her former instructional practices or (2) maintain her stress on developmentally appropriate instruction. In either case, she realizes that she has to try to justify her action to her colleagues.

If you were Laura Lund, what would your decision be?

···

ports, but were rarely influenced by them. The public was essentially oblivious of the testing process and altogether disinterested in the results unless, of course, parents received a report that their child was performing below expectations. Testing took place in the fifties and sixties, but it was no big deal.

During the seventies and eighties, however, a modest journalistic wrinkle changed all that. Newspaper editors began to publish statewide educational test results on a district-by-district and even school-by-school basis. Citizens could see how their school or district stacked up in comparison to other schools or districts in the state. Districts and schools were *ranked* from top to bottom.

From a news perspective, the publishing of test results was a genuine coup. The test scores were inexpensive to obtain and readers were really interested in the scores. Residents of low-ranked districts could complain; residents of high-ranked districts could crow. More importantly, because there are no other handy indices of educational effectiveness around, test results became the standard by which citizens reached conclusions about how well their schools were doing. There are many reports of realtors trying to peddle homes to prospective buyers on the basis that a house was located "in a school district with excellent test scores."

Because it is unlikely that the increasingly popular newspaper practice of annually ranking schools and districts on the basis of statewide test scores will disappear, teachers must recognize that the caliber of their collective efforts will often be determined, at least to some extent, by the test performances that are reported in the media. A number of local television stations have also started reporting "high-ranking" and "top-20" school districts. It may not be earthshaking news, but it's definitely news.

Because public perceptions of educational effectiveness these days are dominantly shaped by students' test performances, it is imperative that teachers assess their students accurately. Moreover, teachers also need to learn enough about educational assessment so that they can communicate with parents and other citizens regarding what kinds of test results do, in fact, reflect educational effectiveness and what kinds of test results do not.

These days, students' performances on high-visibility tests (such as statewide administrations of nationally standardized or state-developed achievement tests) constitute the single, most influential determiner of citizens' judgments about an educational system's effectiveness. It is inexcusable for today's teachers to be unfamiliar with assessment approaches that supply legitimate reflections of educational effectiveness and those that foster misleading estimates of educators' effectiveness.

Helping Evaluate Teachers

Teaching skill is coming under increasing scrutiny these days. With the push for more rigorous evaluation of a classroom teacher's performance, we now see many teacher appraisal systems in which students' test performances constitute one key category of evidence being used to evaluate teachers. Typically, teachers are directed to assemble some form of pretest and posttest data that can be used to infer how much learning by students was promoted by the teacher.

Experienced teachers will be quick to tell you that the caliber of students' test performances is dramatically influenced by the caliber of the students being tested. It should be apparent that a teacher who is blessed with a flock of bright students will almost always get better pretest-to-posttest results than a teacher who must work with a less able group of students. Nonetheless, a number of statewide and districtwide teacher evaluation systems now call for teachers to assemble tangible evidence of student accomplishments based on classroom assessment. It is clear, therefore, that today's teachers need to know enough about educational assessment so that they can corral compelling evidence regarding their students' growth.

Clarifying Teachers' Instructional Intentions

For many years, educational tests were regarded as instructional afterthoughts. Once an instructional unit was over, the teacher got busy turning out a test. Tests were rarely created before instruction was initiated. Instead, tests were devised *after* instruction to fulfill some of the traditional functions of educational assessment described earlier in the chapter—for example, the assignment of grades.

Today, however, many educational measuring instruments have become high-stakes tests. A *high-stakes test* is an assessment for which important consequences ride on the test's results. One example of an educational high-stakes tests would be a statewide basic skills test that must be mastered before a student graduates. (Note that the important consequences are for the test taker.) Another example would be a districtwide achievement test whose results are publicized so that local taxpayers' judgments about educational effectiveness are influenced by the test results. (Note that in this second case the important consequences apply to the educators who prepared the students, not the test takers themselves.)

Insofar as important consequences are directly linked to assessment results, the content of such high-stakes tests tends to be emphasized instructionally by teachers. Because teachers want their students to perform well on high-stakes tests (for the students' own good and/or for the teacher's benefit), high-stakes tests tend to serve as the curricular magnet seen in Figure 1.1.

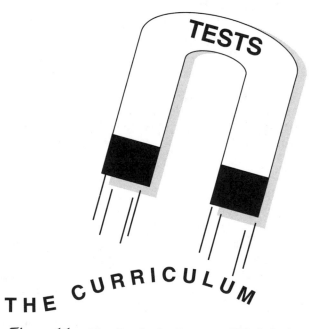

Figure 1.1　**The Curricular Impact of High-Stakes Tests**

On some educational grounds, teachers might prefer that tests did not influence instruction so directly, but the reality is that high-stakes assessment will definitely have an impact on classroom instructional practices. Because this curricular influence is certain to be present, it will be in teachers' and students' best interests if the nature of the upcoming assessment is sufficiently well understood so that the teacher can organize the most effective, on-target instruction possible. (Later in the book, we will consider the deficits of teaching exclusively toward assessment targets.) In a sense, however, the more that teachers understand what the innards of a test are, the more effectively they can use that understanding to clarify what's to be sought instructionally.

Even the low-stakes classroom tests routinely employed by teachers can be used to help teachers clarify their instructional targets. Tests should obviously not, then, be instructional afterthoughts. Rather, classroom assessment instruments should always be prepared *prior* to instruction in order for the teacher to better understand what is being sought of students and, therefore, what to incorporate in instructional activities for students. Assessment instruments prepared prior to instruction concretely exemplify a teacher's instructional intentions and, as a consequence, clarify those intentions. Clarified instructional intentions characteristically lead to more effective instructional decisions by the teacher. The better you understand where you're going, the more efficiently you can get there.

To reiterate, we've now looked at three reasons that today's teachers, unlike their counterparts of a few decades ago, need to know about assessment. These reasons are supplemental to, not in place of, the previously considered traditional reasons that teachers assess students. Here are the three new reasons for teachers' familiarization with educational assessment:

Today's Reasons for Teachers to Know about Assessment

- Test results determine public perceptions of educational effectiveness.
- Students' assessment performances are increasingly seen as part of the teacher evaluation process.
- As clarifiers of instructional intentions, assessment devices can improve instructional quality.

These reasons are also linked to decisions. For instance, when citizens use test results to reach judgments about a school district's effectiveness, those judgments can play a major role in determining what level of taxpayer support will be provided. There are also decisions on the line when students' test scores are used as evidence to evaluate teachers. Such decisions as whether the teacher should be granted tenure or receive merit-pay awards are illustrative of the kinds of decisions that can ride, at least in part, on the results of educational assessments. Finally, from the teacher's perspective, when tests serve as clarifiers of the teacher's instructional intentions, the teacher can make better decisions about how to put together an instructional program that is likely to help students attain the instructional intentions embodied in the assessment. With these three current roles of educational assessment, as was true with the four more traditional roles of educational assessment, test results should contribute to educational *decisions*.

What Do Classroom Teachers Really Need to Know about Assessment? ....

Whether you are already a teacher or are preparing to become a teacher, you really do need to know about educational assessment. But the field of educational assessment contains huge chunks of information. In fact, some educators devote their entire careers to assessment. Clearly, there's more to educational assessment than you probably care to know. The question is, What *should* classroom teachers know about assessment?

The title of this book suggests an answer—namely, *Classroom Assessment: What Teachers Need to Know*. The key word in the title, at least for purposes of this discussion, is *need*. There are oodles of fascinating things about assessment that you might learn. You'd even find a few of them interesting (not all that many, I suspect). But to help your students learn, you really don't *need* to know a host of assessment esoterica. This book about educational assessment is deliberately focused on only those things that you really *must know* in order to promote your students' learning most effectively. I am altogether reluctant to clutter your head with a galaxy of nice-to-know but nonessential knowledge about educational assessment. Such nice-to-know content often crowds out the need-to-know content.

As a preview, I want to describe briefly what you will have learned by the time you reach the book's index. (I have never had much confidence in any book's index as a teaching tool, so if you haven't learned what's needed by that time—it's too late.) It may be easier for you to get a handle on what you'll be reading if you realize you'll be covering topics that deal chiefly with:

1. Constructing your own assessment instruments
2. Using assessment instruments constructed by others
3. Planning instruction based on instructionally illuminating assessments

Creating Classroom Assessment Devices

Let's start with the kinds of classroom assessment devices that you will personally need to create. The chief thing you will learn in this book is how to construct a wide variety of assessment instruments that you can use as part of your day-to-day classroom instruction. You really do need to know how to determine what your students have learned—for example, whether they comprehend what they have read. You really do need to know how to get a fix on your students' educationally relevant attitudes—such as how positively disposed your students are toward the subject(s) you're teaching. Thus, you are going to be learning about how to create classroom assessment approaches to measure students' *achievement* (that is, the knowledge and/or skills students acquire) as well as students' *affect* (that is, the educationally pertinent attitudes and values influenced by school).

As suggested earlier, the kinds of classroom assessment procedures you'll be learning about will extend well beyond traditional paper-and-pencil testing instruments. You may even learn about several assessment approaches with which you are currently unfamiliar.

In a related vein, you will also learn how to judge the quality of the assessment devices *you* create. And, at the same time, you will learn how to judge the quality of assessment devices created by others. Those "others" might be your own colleagues or, perhaps, the folks who devise large-scale assessment instruments. It may seem presumptuous for me to suggest that you, a classroom teacher (in practice or in preparation), could be judging the efforts of folks who create nationally standardized educational tests. But you'll discover from this book that you will, indeed, possess the knowledge and skill necessary to distinguish between tawdry and terrific practices by those who create such large-scale educational tests.

Fundamentally, educational assessment rests on a foundation of common sense. Once you learn the technical vocabulary of assessment, you'll be able to identify departures from commonsensical assessment practices, whether those departures are seen in your own tests, in the tests of a teacher down the hall, or in the tests created by state or national assessment specialists. In short, after you finish this brief text, you really need not be deferent to any so-called measurement experts. You'll know enough to spot serious shortcomings in their work.

In the very next chapter, for example, you will learn about three criteria that should be used to evaluate all educational tests. Those criteria apply with equal force to tests that you might develop as well as to tests that are commercially developed. Once you get the hang of how to evaluate tests, you can apply that skill in many settings.

Interpreting Standardized Test Results

Because your students will often be assessed with nationally standardized or state-developed tests, you will need to know how to interpret the results of such tests. In general, commercially developed educational tests focus either on students' *achievement,* which, as noted earlier, deals with the knowledge and skills that students have acquired, or on *aptitude,* which is a term used to describe a student's learning *potential.* You should know, however, that the term *aptitude* is definitely falling from grace these days. In the old days, when I was a tyke, people talked about intelligence. As a prospective teacher, I learned all about the intelligence quotient (IQ), which was a numerical way of indicating the degree to which a particular individual's intellectual abilities exceeded or fell short of conventional expectations for such individuals.

But "intelligence" has fallen decisively out of favor with educators during the past few decades. The term *intelligence* conveys the notion that students possess an inborn potential that schools can do little to influence. Yet, the so-called intelligence tests, widely used until recently, usually measured what students had learned at school or, more importantly, what students had learned at home. Thus, the term *aptitude* has been increasingly used rather than *intelligence* in order to convey a notion of a student's academic potential. But even the term *aptitude* tends to create the perception that there is some sort of innate cap on one's potential. Because of that perception, we now find that the commercial test makers who formerly created so-called intelligence tests, and then renamed them aptitude tests, are looking for a less negatively loaded descriptor. Interestingly, the tests themselves, although they've been relabeled, haven't really changed all that much.

At any rate, you'll learn how to make sense out of the kinds of reports regarding student performance released by those who conduct large-scale assessments. You will need this knowledge not only to inform your own decisions about classroom instruction but also to interpret students' test performances to parents who may demand answers to questions such as What does my son's standardized test performance at 40th percentile really mean? or If my fifth-grade daughter earned a grade-equivalent score at the eighth-grade level on this year's standardized achievement test, why shouldn't she be promoted?

Instructionally Illuminating Assessment

Earlier, it was suggested that because assessment devices exemplify a teacher's instructional intentions, those assessment instruments can clarify the teacher's instructional decision making. You'll learn more about how the link between testing and teaching can prove beneficial to your students because you can provide more on-target and effective instruction.

On the other hand, you'll also learn how some teachers inappropriately prepare their students for tests, particularly for high-stakes tests. You will learn about ways of judging whether a given test-preparation practice is (1) in students' best interests from an educational perspective and (2) in educators' best interests from an ethical perspective. In short, you'll learn about the increasingly important relationship between instruction and assessment.

Later, you'll learn about a way to build classroom assessments so that they'll have a decisively positive impact on how well you teach. *Tests*, if deliberately created with instruction in mind, *can boost your personal success as a teacher*. We'll dig into that topic in Chapter 12.

Parent Talk ....

Mr. and Mrs. Smothers are attending a back-to-school night at a middle school where their daughter, Cathy, is a fifth-grader. After briefly leafing through Cathy's math portfolio and language arts portfolio, they get around to the real reason they've come to school. Mrs. Smothers, looking more than a little belligerent, says, "Cathy tells us she gets several teacher-made tests in class every week. All that testing can't be necessary. It obviously takes away the time you spend teaching her! Why is there so darn much testing in your class?"

● ● ● *If I were you, here's how I'd respond to Mrs. Smothers:*

"I suppose that it might seem to you there's too much testing going on in my class, and I can understand your concern about testing-time taking away from teaching-time. But let me explain how the time that my students spend doing classroom assessments really leads to much *better* use of instructional time.

"You see, the way I use classroom assessment is to make sure that my instruction is on target and, most importantly, that I don't waste the children's time. Last month, for instance, we started a new unit in social studies and I gave students a short pretest to find out what they already knew. To my delight, I discovered that almost all of the students—including Cathy—knew well over half of what I had been planning to teach.

"Based on the pretest's results, I was able to shorten the social studies unit substantially, and spend the extra time giving students more practice on their map-interpretation skills. You probably saw some of the maps Cathy was interpreting as part of her homework assignments.

"Mr. and Mrs. Smothers, I want Cathy's time in class to be as well spent as possible. And to make *sure* of that, I use formal and informal classroom tests to be certain that I'm teaching her, and her classmates, what they really need to learn."

● ● ● *Now, how would you respond to Mrs. Smothers?*

A Three-Chapter Preview ....

Because the next three chapters in the book are highly related, I'm going to do a little previewing of what you'll be encountering in those chapters. Later in the book, you'll learn all sorts of nifty ways to assess your students. Not only will you learn how to create a variety of traditional paper-and-pencil tests, such as the true-false and multiple-choice instruments, but you'll also discover how to generate

many of the alternative forms of educational assessment receiving so much attention these days. To illustrate, you will learn how to create really demanding performance tests, student portfolios, and assessment devices that can gauge your
students' attitudes and interests. But when you read about these assessment approaches in later chapters, it will make it easier for you to determine their worth *to
you* if you know how to evaluate the quality of educational assessment approaches. The next three chapters give you the concepts you will need to do such
evaluating.

If you're evaluating a test—whether it's your own test, a test developed by
another teacher, or a test distributed by a commercial test publisher—you will
need some criteria to help you decide whether the test should be wildly applauded or, instead, sent swiftly to a paper shredder.

Judging educational tests, in fact, is fundamentally no different from evaluating brownies. If, for example, you are ever called on to serve as a judge in a
brownie bake-off, you'll need some evaluative criteria to use when you appraise
the merits of the contending brownies. I realize that your preferences may differ
from mine, but if I were chief justice in a brownie-judging extravaganza, I would
employ the three evaluative criteria presented in Table 1.1. If you are a brownie
aficionado and prefer other evaluative criteria, I can overlook such preferences.
You may, for example, adore nut-free and high-rise brownies. However, I have no
interest in establishing a meaningful brownie-bond with you.

When we evaluate just about anything, we employ explicit or implicit evaluative criteria to determine quality. And although there may be substantial dis-
agreements among brownie devotees regarding the criteria to employ when appraising their favorite baked goods, there are far fewer disputes when it comes to
judging the quality of educational assessment devices. In the next three chapters,
we're going to look at the three widely accepted criteria that are used to evaluate
educational assessment procedures. Two of the criteria have been around for a
long while. The third is a relative newcomer, having figured in the evaluation of
educational tests only during the last couple of decades.

Table 1.1   **Potential Criteria for Brownie Judging**

Criterion	Optimal Status
• Fudginess	Should reek of chocolate flavor—so much, indeed, as to be considered fundamentally fudgelike.
• Chewiness	Must be so chewy as to approximate munching on a lump of fudge-flavored Silly Putty.
• Acceptable Additives	Although sliced walnuts and extra chocolate chips are praise-worthy, shredded raisins or raw brussels sprouts are not.

Table 1.2   **A Preview of the Three Test-Evaluation Criteria to Be Considered in Chapters 2, 3, and 4**

Criterion	Brief Description
• Reliability	Reliability represents the *consistency* with which an assessment procedure measures whatever it's measuring.
• Validity	Validity reflects the defensibility of the *score-based inference* made on the basis of an educational assessment procedure.
• Absence-of-Bias	Absence-of-bias signifies the degree to which assessment procedures are free of elements that would *offend or penalize* examinees on the basis of examinees' gender, ethnicity, and so on.

In Table 1.2 are the three criteria we'll be considering in the next three chapters. The capsule description of each criterion presented in the table will let you know what's coming. After considering these three criteria, I'll level with you regarding what classroom teachers *really* need to know about each criterion. In other words, I'll toss out my personal opinion regarding whether you should establish an intimate relationship or merely a nodding acquaintance with each criterion.

Of all the things you will learn from reading this book, and there will be lots of them, the topics treated in the next three chapters are regarded by psychometricians as the most important. (*Psychometrician*, by the way, is simply a ritzy descriptor for a measurement specialist.) Chapters 2, 3, and 4 will familiarize you with the pivotal criteria by which assessment specialists tell whether educational assessment procedures are stellar or stupid. Because I've already pledged to keep the treatment of even such important topics mercifully brief, however, you may wish to read further regarding reliability, validity, and absence-of-bias in the references cited at the ends of the three chapters. In educational assessment, it doesn't get much more important than what you'll be dealing with in the next three chapters. Because this book is focused on classroom assessment, we'll be looking at the content of the next three chapters in relation to *educational decisions* that must be made by classroom teachers. I promise not to mess around with psychometric abstractions merely because they induce theoretical thrills (a blatant contradiction).

Chapter Summary ....

In this first chapter, the emphasis was on why teachers really need to know about assessment. *Educational assessment* was defined as a formal attempt to determine students' status with respect to educational variables of interest. Much of the chapter was devoted to a consideration of why teachers must become knowledgeable regarding educational assessment. Based on teachers' classroom activities, four traditional reasons were given for why teachers assess—namely, to (1) diagnose students' strengths and weaknesses, (2) monitor students' progress, (3) assign grades, and (4) determine the teacher's instructional effectiveness. Based on recent uses of educational assessment results, three more current reasons that teachers need to know about instruction were identified. Those more recent functions of educational tests are to (1) influence public perceptions of educational effectiveness, (2) help evaluate teachers, and (3) clarify teachers' instructional intentions. Regardless of the specific application of test results, however, it was emphasized that teachers should use the results of assessments *to make better decisions*. That's really the only excuse for taking up students' time with assessment.

The chapter identified three major outcomes to be attained by those reading the book—namely, becoming more knowledgeable about how to (1) construct and evaluate their own classroom tests, (2) interpret results of standardized tests, and (3) teach students to master what's assessed in classroom and high-stakes tests. The chapter was concluded by a preview of three test-evaluation criteria to be considered in the next three chapters.

Self-Check

This was the book's first chapter. If you're not sure I'm correct, you may wish to check the table of contents. As an initial chapter, it was decisively heavier on pep talk and previewing than on solid assessment-related content. However, to help you get in the groove for the postchapter merriment associated with future chapters, I've included a brief self-check exercise section so you can become familiar with what will be coming up at the end of every chapter. An answer key for all such self-check exercises is provided immediately after the discussion questions (entitled Pondertime to encourage you to ponder) and immediately before the references section (entitled Additional Stuff because it is additional stuff). The answer key will be presented in small type to make you pay careful attention and to make your eyes hurt.

1. Without referring to the text, and using your own words (although, if you're stuck, you can borrow some of mine), how would you define *educational assessment?*

_____

_____

_____

_____

2. An educational *test* is a term that's been around for a long time. Why was it suggested in the chapter that educational *assessment* is the preferred descriptor these days?

_____

_____

_____

_____

3. Review the following list of six fictitious quotes from classroom teachers and decide which four quotations represent the *traditional* reasons that teachers are likely to give in response to the question, Why should you, as a teacher, test your students?
   a. "Because I need to base my students' grades on something other than smiling faces."
   b. "Because I can figure out, before I begin to teach, what my students already know and don't know."
   c. "Because testing takes up classroom time, and I have so many classroom hours to fill and so little content to cover."
   d. "Because I can tell whether my pupils have learned, hence whether I've taught well."
   e. "Because I can see what kinds of progress my students are making, and can give more instruction to those who need it."
   f. "Because I want to learn more about what kinds of pronouns to use when modifying gerunds."

4. (*Note*: The following self-check exercise represents the book's very first multiple-choice item. It will surely not be its last.)

   Which of the following four statements does *not* represent one of the *current* reasons cited in the chapter that today's teacher should either learn about educational assessment or be considered a consummate cluck?
   a. Educational measuring devices, as clarifications for instructional intentions, can improve instructional quality.
   b. Student performances on high-stakes tests substantially influence public perceptions of educational effectiveness.
   c. Today's teacher evaluation systems increasingly incorporate students' performances on educational assessment devices.
   d. Educational assessment devices are now being used to advertise young people's fashionwear.

(Remember, a Self-Check Key is provided following the Pondertime questions.)

Pondertime

Here are a few assessment-related questions for you to ponder. Such pondering can be done in public, as in a class discussion, or in private, as in by yourself. A recent survey of pondering practices in Pennsylvania indicated that public pondering was preferred over private pondering, even by consenting adults, almost two to one. (There was a sampling error for the survey of ±100%.)

1. Why do you think we have witnessed such an increased interest in educational assessment during the past decade or so?

2. In many states, prospective teachers are not required to take any courses dealing with educational assessment. Why do you think this is so?

3. What kind of rights, if any, does the public have regarding educational assessment?

4. Recalling your own days in school, what level of expertise do you think your teachers had regarding educational assessment?

5. Do you think the movement to discourage the use of the terms *intelligence* and *aptitude* is appropriate? Why?

Self-Check Key

1. Any reasonable paraphrase of the following definition, given on page 3, will be acceptable: "Educational assessment is a formal attempt to determine students' status with respect to educational variables of interest."

2. Two related reasons were given—namely, that (1) the phrase *educational test* conjures up notions of only paper-and-pencil instruments and (2) many worthwhile educational outcomes are not best assessed by paper-and-pencil tests.

3. Choices a, b, d, and e are winners. Choices c and f, therefore, are losers.

4. If you did not choose d for this warm-up, giveaway item, you are hereby sentenced to a rereading of the entire first chapter.

Additional Stuff

Airasian, Peter W. *Classroom Assessment* (2nd ed.). New York: McGraw-Hill, 1994.

Arter, Judy. *Assessing Student Performance* (Professional Inquiry Kit, #196214S62). Alexandria, VA: Association for Supervision and Curriculum Development, 1996.

Cizek, Gregory J. "Some Thoughts on Educational Testing: Measurement Policy Issues into the Next Millennium." *Educational Measurement: Issues and Practice*, 12, no. 3 (Fall 1993): 10–16.

Downing, Steven M., and Thomas M. Haladyna. "A Model for Evaluating High-Stakes Testing Programs: Why the Fox Should Not Guard the Chicken Coop." *Educational Measurement: Issues and Practice*, 15, no. 1 (Spring 1996): 5–12.

Linn, Robert L. "Educational Assessment: Expanded Expectations and Challenges." *Educational Evaluation and Policy Analysis*, 15, no. 1 (Spring 1993): 1–16.

McMillan, James H. *Classroom Assessment: Principles and Practice for Effective Instruction.* Boston: Allyn and Bacon, 1997.

Moss, Pamela A. "Enlarging the Dialogue in Educational Measurement: Voices from Interpretive Research Traditions." *Educational Researcher*, 25, no. 1 (January–February 1996): 20–28.

Popham, W. James. "School-Site Assessment: What Principals Need to Know." *Principal*, 75, no. 2 (November 1995): 38–40.

Popham, W. James. *Tests That Help Teaching.* Los Angeles: IOX Assessment Associates, 1995.

Popham, W. James. "Educational Testing in America: What's Right, What's Wrong? A Criterion-Referenced Perspective." *Educational Measurement: Issues and Practice*, 12, no. 1 (Spring 1993): 11–14.

Stiggins, Richard J. *Opening Doors to Excellence in Assessment: A Guide for Using Quality Assessment to Promote Effective Instruction and Student Success.* Portland, OR: Assessment Training Institute, 1997.

Stiggins, Richard J. *Student-Centered Classroom Assessment* (2nd ed.). Upper Saddle River, NJ: Prentice-Hall, 1997.

Stiggins, Richard, and Tanis Knight. *But Are they Learning?* Portland, OR: Assessment Training Institute, 1997.

U.S. Congress, Office of Technology Assessment. *Testing in American Schools: Asking the Right Questions*, OTA-SET-519. Washington, DC: U.S. Government Printing Office, 1992.

Nonprint Stuff

Northwest Regional Laboratory. *A Status Report on Classroom Assessment* (Videotape #NREL-1A). Los Angeles: IOX Assessment Associates.

Northwest Regional Laboratory. *Understanding the Meaning and Importance of Quality Classroom Assessment* (Videotape #NREL-2A). Los Angeles: IOX Assessment Associates.

Northwest Regional Laboratory. *Facing the Challenges of a New Era of Educational Assessment* (Videotape #NREL-14A). Los Angeles: IOX Assessment Associates.

Popham, W. James. *Title I Assessment: What Educators Need to Know* (Videotape #ETVT-21). Los Angeles: IOX Assessment Associates.

2

Reliability of Assessment

*R*eliability is such a cherished commodity. We all want our automobiles, washing machines, and spouses to be reliable. The term *reliability* simply reeks of solid goodness. It conjures up visions of meat loaf, mashed potatoes, and a mother's love. Clearly, reliability is an attribute to be sought.

In the realm of educational assessment, reliability is also a desired attribute. We definitely want our educational assessments to be reliable. In matters related to measurement, however, reliability has a very restricted meaning. When you encounter the term *reliability* in any assessment context, you should draw a mental equal sign between *reliability* and *consistency*, because reliability refers to the consistency with which a test measures whatever it's measuring:

Reliability = Consistency

From a classroom teacher's perspective, there are two important ways that the concept of reliability can rub up against your day-to-day activities. First, there's the possibility that your own classroom assessments might lack sufficient reliability to be doing a good job for you and your students. Second, if your students are obliged to complete any sort of commercially published standardized tests, you're apt to find a parent or two who might want to discuss the adequacy of those standardized tests. And reliability, as noted in the previous chapter's preview, is an evaluative criterion by which commercially published standardized tests are judged. You may need to know enough about reliability's wrinkles so that you'll be able to talk sensibly with parents about the way reliability is employed to judge the quality of standardized tests.

The *Standards for Educational and Psychological Testing,*[1] a joint publication of the American Educational Research Association, the American Psychological Association, and the National Council on Measurement in Education, is generally conceded to be the most important document governing educational assessment procedures because it reflects the opinions of leading assessment experts about educational and psychological testing. As the *Standards* put it, "*Reliability* refers to the degree of which test scores are free from errors of measurement." In other words, the fewer the errors of measurement, the more consistently examinees' scores will accurately reflect examinees' actual status.

But consistency, in educational assessment, appears in three varieties, not merely one. In other words, there are three different ways to think about consistency of measurement. To assume that these three kinds of consistency are interchangeable is erroneous. Let's consider each the three varieties of consistency you're apt to encounter in educational assessment. Table 2.1 previews the three types of reliability evidence you'll be considering in the chapter.

Stability ....

The first kind of reliability we'll be looking at is called *stability*. This conception of reliability often comes to people's minds when someone asserts that reliability equals consistency. Stability, as a form of reliability, refers to consistency of test results over time. We want our educational assessments of students to yield similar results even if the tests were administered on different occasions. For example, suppose you gave your students a midterm exam on Tuesday, but later that afternoon a masked thief (1) snatched your briefcase containing the students' test papers, (2) jumped into a waiting Sherman tank, and (3) escaped to an adjacent state or nation. The next day, after describing to your students how their examinations were purloined by a masked tank-person, you ask them to retake the midterm exam. Because there have been no intervening events of significance, such as more instruction from you on the topics covered by the examination, you would expect your students' Wednesday examination scores to be fairly similar to their Tuesday examination scores. And that's what the *stability* conception of test reliability refers to—consistency over time. If the Wednesday scores aren't comparable to the Tuesday scores, then your midterm exam would be judged to have no stability reliability.

Table 2.1   **Three Types of Reliability Evidence**

Type of Reliability Evidence	Brief Description
• Stability	Consistency of results among different testing occasions
• Alternate Form	Consistency of results among two or more different forms of a test
• Internal Consistency	Consistency in the way an assessment instrument's items function

Quibbling over Quizzes ....

Wayne Wong's first-year teaching assignment is a group of 28 fifth-grade students in an inner-city elementary school. Because Wayne believes in the importance of frequent assessments as motivational devices for his students, he typically administers one or more surprise quizzes per week to his students. Admittedly, after the first month or so, very few of Wayne's fifth-grades are really "surprised" when Wayne whips out one of his unannounced quizzes. Students' scores on the quizzes are used by Wayne to compute each student's six-weeks' grades.

Mrs. Halverson, the principal of Wayne's school, has visited his class on numerous occasions. Mrs. Halverson believes that it is her "special responsibility" to see that first-year teachers receive adequate instructional support.

Mrs. Halverson has recently completed a master's degree from the local branch of the state university. As part of her coursework, she was required to take a class in "educational measurement." She earned an A. Because the professor for that course stressed the importance of "reliability as a crucial ingredient of solid educational tests," Mrs. Halverson has been pressing Wayne to compute some form of reliability evidence for his surprise quizzes. Wayne has been resisting her suggestion because in his view, he administers so many quizzes that the computation of reliability indices for the quizzes would surely be a time-consuming pain. He believes that if he's forced to fuss with reliability estimates for each quiz, he'll reduce the number of quizzes he uses. And, because he thinks students' perceptions that they may be quizzed really stimulates them to be prepared, he is reluctant to lessen the number of quizzes he gives. Even after hearing Wayne's position, however, Mrs. Halverson seems unwilling to bend.

If you were Wayne Wong and were faced with this problem, what would your decision be?

To get a fix on how stable an assessment's results are over time, we usually test students on one occasion, wait a week or two, then retest them with the same instrument. For that reason, stability reliability is sometimes referred to as *test-retest reliability*. It is important, however, that no significant events that might alter students' performances on the second assessment occasion have taken place between the two testing occasions. For instance, suppose the test you are administering assessed students' knowledge regarding World War II. If a widely viewed television mini-series about World War II is presented during the interval between the initial test and the retest, it is likely that the performances of the students who watched the mini-series will be higher on the second test because of their exposure to test-relevant information in the mini-series. Thus, for test-retest results to be interpreted accurately, it is imperative that no significant performance-influencing events occur during the between-assessments interval.

Typically, a *correlation coefficient* is computed between students' test scores on the two assessment occasions—that is, the initial test and the retest. A correlation coefficient reflects the degree of similarity between students' scores on the two tests. If you've already taken a statistics course, you probably know about correlation coefficients. If not, for purposes of this discussion you can think of a correlation coefficient as a numerical indicator (ranging from +1.0 to –1.0) that reflects the degree to which individuals' performances on two sets of test scores are related. A correlation coefficient (signified by r) near 1.0 indicates a strong relationship. A correlation coefficient near 0 indicates a weak relationship. Thus, if the test-retest r for two sets of students' test scores were .84, this would indicate that students' relative test performances on the two testing occasions were quite similar. If the test-retest r were only .23, this would indicate the test yielded performances on the two occasions that weren't all that similar. If there's a high reliability coefficient, it doesn't necessarily signify that examinees' scores on the two tests are identical. Rather, it signifies that students' *relative* performances on the initial test (relative, that is, to the other students' scores) are similar to their relative performances on the retest.

Another procedure for calculating the stability of students' performances on the same test administered on two assessment occasions is to determine the percentage of decisions regarding students that were consistent over time. Such a *decision-consistency* approach to the determination of a test's stability reliability might be used, for instance, when a teacher was deciding which students would be exempted from further study about Topic X. For example, if the teacher establishes an 80% correct level as the degree of proficiency required in order to exempt students from further Topic X study, then on a test-retest basis the teacher would simply determine the percentage of students who were classified the same way on the two assessment occasions. The focus in such an approach would not be on the specific scores a student earned, but only on whether the *same decision* was made about the student. Thus, if Jill Jones earned an 84% correct score on the first testing occasion and a 99% correct score on the second testing occasion, Jill would be exempted from further Topic X study in both cases because she had surpassed the 80% correct standard both times. The teacher's decisions about Jill would be consistent. However, if Harry Harvey received a score of 65% correct on the first testing occasion, and a score of 82% correct on the second testing occasion, different decisions on the two occasions would be made about Harry's need to keep plugging away at Topic X. To determine the percentage of a test's stability decision-consistency, you would simply make the kinds of calculations seen in Table 2.2.

Whether you use a correlational approach or a decision-consistency approach to the determination of a test's consistency over time, it is apparent that you'll need to test students twice in order to determine the test's stability. If a test is yielding rather unstable results between two occasions, it's really difficult to put much confidence in that test's results. Just think about it—if you can't tell whether your students have really performed wonderfully or woefully on a test because their scores might vary depending on the day you test them, how can you proceed to make sensible instructional decisions about those students?

Table 2.2   **An Illustration of How Decision-Consistency Stability Is Determined**

A. Percent of students identified as exempt from further study on both assessment occasions	=	42%
B. Percent of students identified as requiring further study on both assessment occasions	=	46%
C. Percent of students classified differently on the two occasions	=	12%
D. Percentage of the test's decision consistency (A + B)	=	88%

Realistically, of course, why would a sane, nonsadistic classroom teacher administer the identical test to the same students on two different testing occasions? It's pretty tough to come up with a decent answer to that question. What's most important for teachers to realize is that there invariably is a meaningful level of *instability* between students' performances on two different testing occasions, *even if the very same test is used.* And that realization, of course, should disincline teachers to treat a student's test score as though it represents a superscientific reflection of the student's achievement level.

Alternate-Form Reliability ....

The second of our three kinds of reliability evidence for educational assessment instruments focuses on with the consistency between two forms of a test—forms that are supposedly equivalent. *Alternate-form reliability* deals with the question of whether two or more allegedly equivalent test forms are, in fact, equivalent.

In the classroom, teachers rarely have reason to generate two forms of a particular assessment instrument. Multiple forms of educational tests are more commonly encountered in high-stakes assessment situations such as when students must pass basic skills tests before receiving diplomas. In such settings, students who fail an examination when it is initially administered are usually given other opportunities to pass the examination. Clearly, to make the assessment process fair, the assessment hurdle faced by individuals when they took the initial test must be the same as the assessment hurdle faced by individuals when they take the makeup examination. Alternate-form reliability evidence bears on the comparability of two (or more) test forms.

Multiple test forms are apt to be found whenever educators fear that if the same test were simply reused, students who had access to subsequent administrations of the test would be advantaged because those later test takers would have learned about the test's contents, and thus have an edge over the first-time test takers. Typically, therefore, in a variety of high-stakes settings such as (1) those involving high school diploma tests or (2) the certification examinations governing entry to a profession, multiple test forms are employed.

To determine the degree of alternate-form consistency, procedural approaches are employed that are in some ways similar to those used for the determination of stability reliability. First, the two test forms are administered to the same individuals. Ideally, there would be little or no delay between the administration of the two test forms. For example, suppose you were interested in determining the comparability of two forms of a district-developed language arts examination. Let's say you could round up 100 suitable students. Because the examination requires only 20 to 25 minutes to complete, you could administer both forms of the language arts test (Form A and Form B) to each of the 100 students during a single period. To eliminate the impact of the order in which the tests were completed by students, you could ask 50 of the students to complete Form A, then Form B. The remaining students would be directed to take Form B first, then Form A.

Once you obtain each student's scores on the two forms, you could compute a correlation coefficient reflecting the relationship between students' performances on the two forms. As with stability reliability, the closer the alternate-form correlation coefficient is to 1.0, the more agreement there is between students' relative scores on the two forms. Alternatively, you could use the kind of decision-consistency approach for the determination of alternate-form reliability that was described earlier for stability reliability. To illustrate, you could decide on a level of performance that would lead to different decisions for examinees, then simply calculate the percentage of identically classified examinees on the basis of the two test forms. For instance, if a pass/fail cutoff score of 65% correct had been chosen, then you would simply add up (1) the percent of examinees who passed both times (that is, scored 65% or better) and (2) the percent of examinees who failed both times (that is, scored 64% or lower). The addition of those two percentages yields a decision-consistency estimate of alternate-form reliability for the two test forms under consideration.

As you can see, although both species of reliability we've considered thus far are related—in the sense that both deal with consistency—they represent very different conceptions of consistency. Stability reliability deals with consistency over time for a single examination. Alternate-form reliability deals with the consistency of challenge inherent in two or more supposedly equivalent forms of the same examination.

Although classroom teachers will usually have little need for alternate-form reliability for their own tests, primarily because teachers are rarely required to generate two or more versions of the same assessment device, there are a number of educational settings in which teachers should know about the consistency of alternate examination forms used with their students. For instance, if your students' academic future is to be influenced by their performances on multiple forms of an examination that purport to be equally difficult, you really ought to check into the evidence supporting alternate-form reliability for the examination's different forms.

Alternate-form reliability is not established by proclamation. Rather, evidence must be gathered regarding the between-form consistency of the test forms under scrutiny. Accordingly, if you're ever reviewing a commercially published or state-developed test that claims to have equivalent forms available, be sure you inspect the evidence that those claims of equivalence are supported. Determine how the evidence of alternate-form comparability was gathered—that is, under what circumstances. Make sure that what's described makes sense to you.

Later in the book (Chapter 13), we'll consider a procedure known as *item response theory* that, whenever large numbers of students are tested, can be employed to adjust examinees' scores on different forms of tests that are not actually equivalent in difficulty. For purposes of our current discussion, however, simply remember that alternate-form reliability is a special form of consistency dealing with the comparability of two or more test forms.

Internal Consistency Reliability ···························

The final entrant in the reliability sweepstakes is called *internal consistency reliability*. It really is quite a different creature than stability and alternate-form reliability. Internal consistency does not focus on the consistency of examinees' scores on a test. Rather, internal consistency deals with the extent to which the *items* in an educational assessment instrument are functioning in a consistent fashion.

Whereas stability and alternate-form reliability require two administrations of a test, internal consistency reliability can be computed on the basis of only a single test administration. It is for that reason, one suspects, that we tend to encounter internal consistency estimates of reliability far more frequently than we encounter its two reliability partners. Yet, as you will see, internal consistency reliability is quite a different commodity than stability and alternate-form reliability.

Internal consistency reliability reflects the degree to which the items on a test are functioning in a consistent manner—that is, the degree to which the test's items are functioning *homogeneously*. Most educational tests are designed to measure a single variable, such as students' "reading achievement" or their "attitude toward school." If a test's items are all truly measuring a single variable, then each of the test's items ought to be doing fundamentally the same assessment job. To the extent that the test's items are tapping the same variable, of course, the responses to those items by students will tend to be quite similar. For example, if all the items in a 20-item test on problem solving do, in fact, measure one's problem-solving ability, then students who are skilled problem solvers should get most of the 20 test's items right, whereas unskilled problem solvers should miss most of the test's 20 items. The more homogeneous the responses yielded by a test's items, the higher will be the test's internal consistency.

There are several different formulae around for computing a test's internal consistency.[2] Each formula is intended to yield a numerical estimate reflective of the extent to which the assessment procedure's items are functioning homogeneously.

For tests containing items on which a student can be right or wrong, such as a multiple-choice item, the most commonly used internal consistency approaches are the *Kuder-Richardson* procedures (usually referred to as the K-R formulae). For tests containing items on which students can be given different numbers of points, such as essay items, the most common internal consistency approach is called Cronbach's *coefficient alpha* after its originator Lee J. Cronbach. Incidentally, if you want to impress your colleagues with your newfound and altogether exotic assessment vocabulary, you might want to know that test items scored right or wrong (such as true-false items) are called *dichotomous* items, while those that yield multiple scores (such as essay items) are called *polytomous* items. Try to work *polytomous* into a casual conversation around the watercooler. Its intimidation power is awesome.

Incidentally, other things being equal, the more items that there are in an educational assessment device, the more reliable it will tend to be. To illustrate, if you set out to measure a student's mathematics achievement with a 100-item test dealing with various aspects of mathematics, you're apt to get a more reliable fix on an examinee's mathematical prowess than if you asked students to solve only 1 lengthy mathematical word problem. The more times you dip into a pot of soup, the more accurate will be your estimate of what the soup's ingredients are. One spoonful might fool you. Twenty spoonsful will give you a much better idea of what's in the pot. In general, then, more items on educational assessment devices will yield more reliable estimates than will fewer items.

Three Coins in the Reliability Fountain ....

You've now seen that there are three different ways of conceptualizing the manner in which the consistency of a test's results are described. Consistency of measurement is a requisite for making much sense out of a test's results. If the test yields inconsistent results, of course, how can teachers make sensible decisions based on what appears to be a capricious assessment procedure? Yet, as we have seen, reliability evidence comes in three flavors. It is up to you to make sure that the reliability evidence supplied with a test is consonant with the use to which the test's results will be put—that is, the decision linked to the test's results. Although there is surely a relationship among the three kinds of reliability evidence we've been discussing, the following is true:

Stability Reliability	$\neq$	Alternate-Form Reliability	$\neq$	Internal Consistency Reliability

To illustrate, suppose that you were a teacher in a school district where a high school diploma test had been developed by an assistant superintendent in collaboration with a committee of district teachers. The assistant superintendent has claimed that the test's three different forms are essentially interchangeable because each form, when field-tested, yielded a Kuder-Richardson coefficient of .88 or higher. "The three test forms," claimed the assistant superintendent at a recent school board meeting, "are reliable and, therefore, equivalent." You now know better.

If the assistant superintendent really wanted to know about between-form comparability, then the kind of reliability evidence needed would be alternate-form reliability, not internal consistency. (Incidentally, I do not recommend that you rise at the school board meeting to publicly repudiate the assistant superintendent's motley mastery of reliability. Simply send him or her a copy of this book, designating the pages to be read. And send it anonymously.)

Yet, even those educators who know something about reliability and its importance will sometimes unthinkingly mush the three brands of reliability together. They'll see a K-R reliability coefficient of .90 and assume that the test is not only internally consistent but that it will also produce stable results. That's not necessarily so.

The Standard Error of Measurement ....

Before bidding adieu to reliability and all its raptures, there's one other thing you need to know about consistency of measurement. So far, the kinds of reliability evidence we've been considering deal with the reliability of a *group* of examinees' scores. For a few paragraphs, I want to turn your attention to the consistency with which we measure an *individual's* performance. The index used in educational as-

Parent Talk ....

> One of your strongest students, Raphael Hobbs, has recently received his scores on a nationally standardized achievement test used in your school district. Raphael's subtest percentile scores (in comparison to the test's norm group) were the following:

Subject	Percentile
Language Arts	85th
Mathematics	92nd
Science	91st
Social Studies	51st

> Raphael's father, a retired U.S. Air Force colonel, has called for an after-school conference with you about the test results. He has used his home computer and the internet to discover that the internal consistency reliabilities on all four subtests, as published in the test's technical manual, are higher than .93. When he telephoned you to set up the conference, he said he couldn't see how the four subtests could all be reliable when Raphael's score on the social studies subtest was so "out of whack" with the other three subtests. He wants you to explain how this could happen.

• • • If I were you, here's how I'd respond to Colonel Hobbs:

"First off, Colonel Hobbs, I'm delighted that you've taken the time to look into the standardized test we're using in the district. Not many parents are willing to expend the energy to do so.

"I'd like to deal immediately with the issue you raised on the phone regarding the reliability of the four subtests, then discuss Raphael's social studies result. You may already know some of what I'll be talking about because of your access to the Internet, but here goes.

"Assessment reliability refers to the *consistency* of measurement. But there are very different ways that test developers look at measurement consistency. The reliability estimates that are supplied for Raphael's standardized test, as you pointed out, are called internal consistency correlation coefficients. Those correlations tell us whether the items on a particular subtest are performing in the same way—that is, whether they seem to be measuring the same thing.

"The internal consistency reliability for all four subtests is quite good. But that kind of reliability evidence doesn't tell us anything about how Raphael would score if he took the test again or if he took a different form of the same test. We don't know, in other words, whether his performance would be stable across time or would be consistent across different test forms.

"What we do see in Raphael's case is a social studies performance that is decisively different than his performance on the other three subtests. I've checked his grades for the past few years and I've seen that his grades in social studies are routinely just as high as his other grades. So those grades do cast some doubt on the meaningfulness of the lower test performance in social studies.

"Whatever's measured on the social studies subtest seems to be measured by a set of homogeneous items. That doesn't mean, however, that the content of the social studies subtest meshes with the social studies Raphael's been taught here in our district. To me, Colonel Hobbs, I think it's less likely to be a case of measurement unreliability than it is to be a problem of content mismatch between what the standardized examination tests and what we try to teach Raphael.

"I recommend that you, Mrs. Hobbs, and I monitor Raphael's performance in social studies during the school year so that we can really see if we're dealing with a learning problem or with an assessment inaccuracy."

• • • *Now, how would you respond to Colonel Hobbs?*

sessment to describe the consistency of a particular person's performance is referred to as the *standard error of measurement*.

You should think of the standard error of measurement as a reflection of the consistency of an individual's scores if a given assessment procedure were administered to that individual again, and again, and again. However, as a practical matter, it is impossible to readminister the same test innumerable times to the same students because such students would revolt or, if exceedingly acquiescent, swoon from exhaustion. Accordingly, we need to *estimate* how much variability there would be if we were able to readminister a given assessment procedure many times to the same individual. The standard error of measurement is much like the plus or minus "sampling errors" that are so frequently given in the media these days for various sorts of national polls. We are told that "89% of telephone interviewees indicated that they would consider broiled brussels sprouts in brownies to be repugnant" (±3% margin of error).

Other things being equal, the higher the reliability of a test, the smaller the standard error of measurement will be. For all commercially published tests, a technical manual is available that gives you the standard error of measurement for that test. Sometimes, if you ever have an occasion to check out a test's standard error, you'll find that it's much larger that you might have suspected. As is true of sampling errors for surveys, what you'd prefer to have is small, not large, standard errors of measurement.

The standard error of measurement is an important concept because it reminds teachers about the *imprecision* of the test scores that an individual student receives. Novice teachers all too often ascribe unwarranted precision to a student's test results. I can remember all too vividly making this mistake myself when I began teaching. While getting ready for my first group of students, I saw when inspecting student files that one of my students, Sally Palmer, had taken a group intelligence test. (Such tests were popular in those days.) Sally had earned a score of 126. For the next year, I was absolutely convinced that Sally was not merely above average in her intellectual abilities. Rather, I was certain that her IQ was *exactly* 126. I was too ignorant about assessment to realize that there may have been a sizeable standard error of measurement associated with the intelligence test that Sally had taken. Her "true" IQ score might have been substantially lower or higher. I doubt if Sally had retaken the same intelligence test 10 different times that she'd ever get another score of precisely 126. But, in my naivete, I blissfully assumed that Sally's intellectual ability was dead-center 126. The standard error of measurement helps remind teachers that the scores earned by students on commercial *or* classroom tests are not all that exact.

What Do Classroom Teachers Really Need to Know about Reliability? ....

What do you, as a teacher or teacher in preparation, truly need to know about reliability? Do you, for example, need to gather data from your own classroom assessment procedures so you can actually calculate reliability coefficients? If so, do you need to collect all three varieties of reliability evidence? My answers may surprise you. I think you need to know what reliability is, but I don't think you'll have much call to use it with your own tests—you won't, that is, unless certain of your tests are extraordinarily significant. And I haven't run into classroom tests, even rocko-socko final examinations, that I would consider sufficiently significant to warrant your whipping up a reliability extravaganza. In general, if you construct your own classroom tests with care, those tests will be sufficiently reliable for the decisions you will base on the tests' results.

You need to know about what reliability is because you may be called on to explain to parents the meaning of a student's standardized test scores, and you'll want to know how reliable the test is. You need to know what the test manual's authors are talking about and to be wary of those who secure one type of reliability evidence—for instance, a form of internal consistency evidence (because it's the easiest to obtain)—then try to proclaim that form of reliability evidence provides an indication of the test's stability or the comparability of its multiple forms. In short, you need to be at least knowledgeable about the fundamental meaning of reliability, but I do not suggest you make your own classroom tests pass any sort of reliability muster.

Reliability is a central concept in measurement. As you'll see in the next chapter, if an assessment procedure fails to yield consistent results, it is almost impossible to make any accurate inferences about what an examinee's score signifies. Inconsistent measurement is, at least some of the time, bound to be inaccurate measurement. Thus, you should realize that as the stakes associated with an assessment procedure become higher, there will typically be more attention given to establishing that the assessment procedure is, indeed, reliable. If you're evaluating an important test developed by others and you see that only skimpy attention has been given to the establishment of reliability, you should be critical of the test because evidence regarding an essential attribute of an educational test is missing.

The other thing that you should know about reliability is that it comes in three flavors—three kinds of evidence about a test's consistency *that are not interchangeable*. Don't let someone foist a set of internal consistency results on you and suggest that these results tell you anything of importance about stability. Don't let anyone tell you that a stability reliability coefficient indicates anything about the equivalence of a test's multiple forms. Although the three types of reliability evidence are related, they really are fairly distinctive kinds of creatures, something along the lines of second or third cousins.

What I'm trying to suggest is that classroom teachers, as professionals in the field of education, need to understand that an important attribute of educational assessment procedures is reliability. The higher the stakes associated with a test's use, the more the educators should attend to the assessment procedure's reliability. Reliability is such a key criterion by which psychometricians evaluate tests that you really ought to know what it is, even if you don't use it on a daily basis.

The situation regarding your knowledge about reliability is somewhat analogous to a health professional's knowledge about blood pressure and how blood pressure influences one's health. Even though only a small proportion of health professionals work directly with patients' blood pressure on a day-by-day basis, there are few health professionals who don't know at least the fundamentals of how one's blood pressure can influence a person's health.

Although I don't think you should devote a great deal of time to calculating the reliability of your own classroom tests, I think you should have a general knowledge about what it is and why it's important. Besides, computing too many reliability coefficients for your own classroom tests might give you high blood pressure.

Chapter Summary

This chapter focused on the reliability of educational assessment procedures. *Reliability* refers to the consistency with which a test measures whatever it's measuring—that is, the absence of measurement errors that would distort an examinee's score.

There are three distinct types of reliability evidence. *Stability reliability* refers to the consistency of examinees' scores over time. Stability reliability is usually represented by a test-retest coefficient of correlation between examinees' scores on two occasions, but can be indicated by the degree of decision consistency displayed for examinees on two measurement occasions. *Alternate-form reliability* refers to the consistency of results between two or more forms of the same test. Alternate-form reliability is usually represented by the correlation of examinees' scores on two different test forms, but can also be reflected by decision-consistency percentages. *Internal consistency* represents the degree of homogeneity in an assessment procedure's items. Common indices of internal consistency are the Kuder-Richardson formulae as well as Cronbach's coefficient alpha. The three forms of reliability evidence should *not* be used interchangeably, but should be sought for the educational purpose to which an assessment procedure is being put—that is, the kind of educational decision linked to the assessment's results.

The standard error of measurement supplies an indication of the consistency of an individual's score by estimating person-score consistency from evidence of group-score consistency. The standard error of measurement is interpreted in a manner similar to the plus or minus sampling-error estimates often provided with national surveys. Classroom teachers are advised to become generally familiar with the key notions of reliability, but not to subject their own classroom tests to reliability analyses unless the tests are unusually important.

Self-Check

For this chapter's first set of self-check exercises, you can see how well you've mastered the distinctions among the three kinds of reliability evidence that were described in the chapter. Please consider each of the reliability situations described here, then decide whether the question following the description is best answered by stability reliability (S), alternate-form reliability (AF), or internal consistency reliability (IC). There are 10 exercises. See if you can answer all 10 correctly.

S AF IC   **1.** An obsessive-compulsive teacher, having read this chapter and dismissed its recommendation that classroom teachers not gather reliability evidence regarding their own tests, routinely computes a K-R coefficient for all his quizzes and major exams. What brand of reliability evidence is he trying to get?

S AF IC   **2.** A commercially developed science achievement test has been recently published. The test's publishers produce evidence to show that if examinees score well on one of the test's three forms, they will also tend to score well on the other two forms. What kind of reliability evidence is this?

S AF IC   **3.** A state-developed composition test for tenth-grade students requires students to write four short essays. Cronbach's coefficient alpha has been applied because each of the essays is to be scored on a 1, 2, 3, 4, 5, or 6 basis. What sort of reliability evidence is being sought here?

S   AF   IC   **4.** A self-report inventory focusing on students' vocational interests was field-tested by being administered to 1,000 students in late March and again in mid-April. The inventory's developers wanted to see if students' vocational interests shifted over a three-week period. What brand of reliability evidence was the focus of the field-test?

S   AF   IC   **5.** A committee of teachers and central office administrators have been developing a basic skills test that the district's high school students will need to pass if they are to receive an "endorsed" diploma. The test is computer administered and can be taken any time students wish during their senior year. What kind of reliability evidence would be most important because of the different times that students can take the test?

S   AF   IC   **6.** Suppose you were trying to show that the items constituting an educational assessment procedure all measured the same underlying trait. What sort of reliability evidence should you attempt to secure?

S   AF   IC   **7.** A chemistry teacher has created four new versions of her final exam because she believes that some students may have "gained access" to her old single-version exam. She decides that she wants to see if all four new versions of the examination are providing students with the same kind of challenge. What sort of reliability evidence should she gather?

S   AF   IC   **8.** Suppose a commercial test developer wanted to see if students' scores on a new "oral communication" assessment procedure remained the same irrespective of when the student completed the assessment. What kind of reliability evidence would be most pertinent in this instance?

S   AF   IC   **9.** Although a university professor has developed three forms of the same attitudinal inventory, the professor is most interested in the extent to which each set of items on each of the three forms are measuring the same attitudinal dimension. What kind of reliability evidence should the professor be securing for each of the forms?

S   AF   IC   **10.** A new nationally standardized reading achievement test for junior high school students has been created, but the test's developers want to make sure that the three forms of the new test are performing in essentially the same way. What sort of reliability evidence should they snare?

Now that you've displayed your ability to distinguish among the three varieties of reliability evidence, let's see how you do with a pair of tougher exercises. These are open-ended exercises, so use your own words in responding.

Chapter 2

11. What is the purpose of the standard error of measurement?

_____

_____

_____

12. Before the era of electronic computers, a common technique for calculating a test's reliability was the "split-half" procedure. To determine a test's split-half reliability, the test was typically divided into two halves (usually odd-numbered items and even-numbered items). Examinees' scores on the two half-tests were then computed and compared, usually via a correlation coefficient. If examinees' relative performances (that is, relative to the performance of other examinees) on one half-test were similar to their relative performances on the other half-test, the test was deemed to be reliable. Thinking back over the three types of reliability evidence you now know so well, which of these three types best describes split-half reliability?

_____

_____

_____

(A Reminder: A Self-Check Key follows the Pondertime questions. You'd be wise to review the Self-Check Key because for many chapters—this one, for instance—there's neat new stuff presented there. Please note this subtle motivational ploy to get you to snuggle up to the Self-Check Keys.)

Pondertime

1. Why do you think that, although reliability is such a central concept in the appraisal of educational assessment devices, I've recommended that classroom teachers generally not mess around with the determination of reliability for the tests they personally develop?

2. If an educational assessment procedure has a relatively small standard error of estimate, it's likely that the assessment procedure is relatively reliable. Why do you think that is so?

3. What kinds of educational assessment procedures do you think should definitely require the assembly of reliability evidence? Why?

4. Should an educator have a favorite kind of reliability evidence among the three varieties we've considered? Why?

Self-Check Key

1. IC
2. AF
3. IC
4. S
5. S
6. IC
7. AF
8. S
9. IC
10. AF

11. The standard error of measurement provides an estimate of how much variability there would be if an examinee took an examination on another occasion. In a sense, therefore, the standard error of measurement offers test users a notion of the confidence that can be put in the accuracy of an individual's test performance. Unlike the three kinds of reliability evidence that deal with *group* test performances, the standard error of measurement focuses on the consistency of an *individual's* performance on a test.

12. Split-half reliability is a variant of internal consistency reliability. Because shorter tests tend to yield lower reliability than larger tests (shorter tests sample students' status less extensively), a correction is usually applied to boost the size of the split-half correlation between the two half-tests. The correction is referred to as the *Spearman-Brown Prophecy Formula*. The formula works like this:

$$\text{Reliability on full test } = \frac{2 \times \text{reliability on half-test}}{1 + \text{reliability on half-test}}$$

So, if you calculated a correlation coefficient of .60 on the half-test, the Spearman-Brown approach would boost the reliability estimate for the whole test to .75. In passing, I should note that the Spearman-Brown Prophecy Formula is *not* used by tabloids such as *The National Enquirer* to predict future events. At least not yet.

Endnotes

1. *Standards for Educational and Psychological Testing*. Washington, DC: American Psychological Association, 1985. As I was revising this assessment book, a multiyear revision of the 1985 *Standards* was slowly winding its way toward a conclusion. It seems unlikely, however, that any dramatic shift will be seen in the way that the revisers of the *Standards* regard reliability.

2. Please note the use of the Latin plural for formula. Because I once completed two years of Latin in high school and three years in college, I have vowed to use Latin at least once per month to make those five years seem less wasted. Any ninny could have said *formulas*.

Additional Stuff

Airasian, Peter W. *Classroom Assessment* (2nd ed.). New York: McGraw-Hill, 1994.

Linn, Robert L., and Norman E. Gronlund. *Measurement and Assessment in Teaching* (7th ed.). Upper Saddle River, NJ: Prentice Hall, 1995.

McMillan, James H. *Classroom Assessment: Principles and Practice for Effective Instruction.* Boston: Allyn and Bacon, 1997.

Popham, W. James. *Modern Educational Measurement: A Practitioner's Perspective* (2nd ed.). Englewood Cliffs, NJ: Prentice Hall, 1990.

Standards for Educational and Psychological Testing. Washington DC: American Psychological Association, 1985.

Wainer, Howard, and David Thissen. "How Is Reliability Related to the Quality of Test Scores? What Is the Effect of Local Dependence on Reliability?" *Educational Measurement: Issues and Practice,* 15, no. 1 (Spring 1996): 22–29.

3

Validity

*W*e'll be looking at validity in this chapter. Validity is, hands down, the most significant concept in assessment. In order to appreciate the reasons that validity is so all-fired important, however, one first needs to understand why it is that educators carry out assessments in the first place. Thus, let's set the stage a bit for your consideration of validity by explaining why educators frequently find themselves obliged to mess around with measurement.

A Quest for Defensible Inferences

As noted in Chapter 1, we assess students because we want to determine a student's status with respect to an educationally relevant variable. One kind of variable of relevance to teachers is a variable that can be altered as a consequence of instruction. Such a variable would be how much students have learned about world history. Another educationally relevant variable is one that can influence the way a teacher instructs students. Such a variable would be students' attitudes toward the study of whatever content the teacher is dealing with.

The more teachers know about their students' status with respect to educationally relevant variables, the better will be the educational decisions that are made regarding those students. To illustrate, if a junior high school teacher knows that Lee Lacey is a weak reader and has truly negative attitudes toward reading, the teacher will probably decide *not* to send Lee trotting off to the school library to tackle an independent research project based on self-directed reading. Similarly, if a mathematics teacher discovers early in the school year that her students know much more about mathematics than she had previously suspected, the teacher is apt to decide that the class will tackle more advanced topics than originally planned. Teachers use the results of assessments to make decisions about students. But appropriate educational decisions depend on the *accuracy of educational assessment* because, quite obviously, accurate assessments will improve the quality of decisions, whereas inaccurate assessments will do the opposite. And that's what validity is about.

When we try to determine the status of students with respect to an educationally relevant variable, such as how well students can comprehend what they have read, it is obviously impractical to find out how well students can read *everything.* There's too much out there to read. Nonetheless, teachers would like to get an accurate fix on how well a particular student can handle the full array of relevant reading tasks that might be encountered by students of that age. The "full array of relevant reading tasks" is referred to as an *assessment domain.* Because it is impossible to see how well students can perform with respect to an entire assessment domain, we have to fall back on a *sampling* strategy. Thus, when we measure students, we try to sample the contents of an assessment domain in a representative manner so that, based on their performance on the sampled assessment domain, we can infer what the students' status is with respect to the entire assessment domain. In Figure 3.1, this relationship is portrayed graphically. Note that we start with an assessment domain of interest. In Figure 3.1, that's the oval at the left. The left-hand oval represents, for illustration purposes, an assessment domain in reading consisting of a student's ability to comprehend the main ideas of written passages. The oval at the right in Figure 3.1 represents an educational assessment approach—in this instance a 10-item test—that we use to make an *inference* about a student. If you prefer, think of a test-based inference simply as an *interpretation* of what the test results mean. The inference concerns the student's status with respect to the entire assessment domain (the oval at the left). If this inference is accurate, then the resultant educational decisions are likely to be more defensible because those decisions will be based on a correct estimate regarding the student's actual status.

It is the *validity of a score-based inference* that is at issue when measurement folks deal with validity. Tests, themselves, do not possess validity. Educational

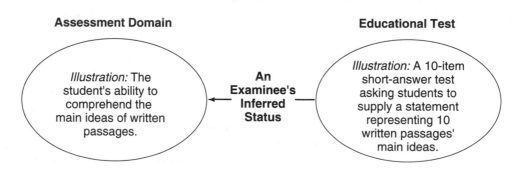

Figure 3.1   **An Illustration of How We Infer an Examinee's Status Regarding An Assessment Domain from the Examinee's Performance on an Educational Test that Samples the Domain**

Group–Influenced Grading ································

A junior high school English teacher, Cecilia Celina, has recently installed coopera-tive learning groups in all five of her classes. The groups are organized so that al-though there are individual grades earned by students based on each student's spe-cific accomplishments, there is also a group-based grade that is dependent on the average performance of a student's group. Cecilia determines that 60% of a student's grade will be based on the student's individual effort and 40% of the student's grade will be based on the collective efforts of the student's group. This 60–40 split is used when she grades students' written examinations as well as when she grades a group's oral presentation to the rest of the class.

Several of Cecilia's fellow teachers have been interested in her use of coopera-tive learning because they are considering the possibility of employing it in their own classes. One of those teachers, Fred Florie, is uncomfortable about Cecilia's 60–40 split of grading weights. Fred believes that Cecilia cannot arrive at a valid esti-mate of an individual student's accomplishment when there's 40% of the student's grade based on the efforts of other students. Cecilia responds that this aggregated grading practice is one of the key features of cooperative learning because it is the contribution of the group grade that motivates the students in a group to help one another learn. In most of her groups, for example, she finds that students help other group members prepare for important examinations.

As she considers Fred's concerns, Cecilia concludes that he is most troubled about the validity of the inferences she makes about her students' achievements. In her mind, however, she separates an estimate of a student's accomplishments from the grade she gives that student.

Cecilia believes she has three decision options facing her. As she sees it, she can (1) leave matters as they are, (2) delete all group-based contributions to an indi-vidual student's grade, or (3) modify the 60–40 split.

If you were Cecilia, what would your decision be?

tests are used so that educators can make inferences about a student's status. If high scores lead to one kind of inference, low scores typically lead to an opposite inference. Moreover, because validity hinges on the accuracy of our inferences about students' status with respect to an assessment domain, it is technically inac-curate to talk about "the validity of a test." A well-constructed test, if used with the wrong group of examinees or if administered under unsuitable circumstances, can lead to a set of unsound and thoroughly invalid inferences. Test-based infer-ences may or may not be valid. It is the test-based inference with which teachers ought to be concerned.

In real life, however, you'll find a fair number of educators talking about the "validity of a test." Perhaps they really do know it's the validity of score-based in-ferences that are at issue, and they're simply using a short-cut descriptor. Based on my experience, it's more likely that they really don't know the focus of validity should be on test-based inferences, not on tests themselves.

Now that you know what's really at issue in the case of validity, if you ever hear a colleague talking about "a test's validity," you'll have to decide whether you should preserve that colleague's dignity by letting such psychometric short-comings go unchallenged. I suggest that, unless there are really critical decisions on the line—decisions that would have an important educational impact on students—you keep your insights regarding validation to yourself. (When I first truly comprehended what was going on with the validity of test-based inferences, I shared this knowledge rather aggressively with several fellow teachers and, thereby, meaningfully miffed them. No one, after all, likes a psychometric smart aleck.)

Validity Evidence ....

Teachers make dozens of decisions, almost on an hourly basis. They decide whether to ask questions of their students and, if questions are to be asked, which student gets which question. Most of a teacher's *instructional* decisions are based to a large extent on the teacher's judgment about students' achievement levels. For instance, if a third-grade teacher concludes that most of her students are able to read independently, then the teacher may decide to use independent reading as a key element in a social studies lesson. The teacher's judgment about students' reading abilities is based on evidence of some sort—gathered either formally or informally.

The major contribution of classroom assessment to a teacher's decision making is that it provides reasonably accurate evidence about students' status. Although teachers are often forced to make inferences about students' knowledge, skills, or attitudes on the basis of informal observations, such unsystematic observations sometimes lead teachers to make invalid inferences about a particular student's status. I'm not knocking teachers' informal observational skills, mind you, for I certainly relied on my own informal observations when I was in the classroom. Frequently, however, I was off the mark! More than once, I saw what I wanted to see by inferring that my students possessed knowledge and skills they really didn't have. Later, when students tackled a midterm or final exam, I discovered that the conclusions I drew from my observation-based judgments were far too generous.

Classroom assessments, if they're truly going to help teachers make solid instructional decisions, should allow a teacher to arrive at valid inferences about students. And, more often than not, because a classroom assessment can be carefully structured, an assessment-based inference is going to be more valid than an inference made while the teacher is focused on other concerns.

The only reason that teachers should assess students is to make better educational decisions about those students. Thus, when you think about validity, remember that it is not some abstruse measurement mystery, knowable only to those who've labored in validity vineyards for eons. Rather, validity centers on the accuracy of the inferences that teachers make about their students. And inferences, unless they contribute to a teacher's decision making, shouldn't even be made.

In recent years, the measurement specialists who write about validity increasingly regard it as a *unitary* concept—that is, a concept concerned with the accuracy of inferences (or interpretations) based on an assessment's results. So, even though there are different ways of determining whether test-based inferences are apt to be valid, the overriding focus is on the *accuracy of an assessment-based inference*. It usually helps to think about validity as an overall evaluation of the degree to which a specific interpretation of a test's results are supported. In a sense, people who develop important tests, such as college admissions exams, try to build a *validity argument* in which they assemble evidence and analyses to show that their tests permit the inferences (interpretations) that the test developers claim.

The inferences that big-time test developers make, or that you'll make in your own classes, always hinge on the *construct* the test is intended to measure. The assessment domain you saw illustrated in Figure 3.1 is an illustration of such a construct. Other examples of assessable constructs would be a student's ability to spell or to compose poetry, or a student's self-esteem as a learner. What you want to do with your own classroom tests is to represent the constructs you're trying to assess so that any inferences based on your students' assessment results will be valid.

One source of assessment invalidity is *construct underrepresentation*. This occurs when an assessment fails to capture important aspects of a construct. Suppose you had developed a test of your students' reading comprehension that was intended to measure the children's ability to read and accurately interpret reading passages. If your test didn't contain a sufficient variety of reading passages, or if a common kind of reading passage had been omitted, inferences about students' reading comprehension abilities would be less valid because of construct underrepresentation.

A second common source of assessment invalidity is *construct irrelevance.* This arises when an assessment measures more than its intended construct. Suppose that the reading comprehension test you developed for your students called for them to write brief essays in order to show what they comprehended. If the students' ability to write plays a major role in the test score you award them, then inferences about the students' reading ability would be less valid because of construct irrelevance. Weak writers, even though they were good readers, might appear to be weak readers.

As a teacher or a teacher in preparation, you may wonder why you have to devote any time at all to different kinds of validity evidence. I appreciate that concern, but I think it's important that you understand at least chief kinds of evidence that bear on the validity of a score-based inference. I promise to give most attention to the sort of validity evidence with which classroom teachers need be concerned.

In the last chapter, we saw that there are three kinds of reliability evidence that can be used to help us decide how consistently a test is measuring what it's measuring. Well, and this should come as no surprise, there are also three kinds of evidence that can be used to help educators determine whether their score-based inferences are valid. Rarely will one set of evidence be so compelling that, all by itself, the evidence assures us that our score-based inference is truly accurate. More commonly, several different sets of validity evidence and several different kinds of validity evidence are needed for educators to be really comfortable about the test-based inferences they make.

When I was preparing to be a high school teacher, many years ago, my teacher education classmates and I were told that "validity refers to the degree to which a test measures what it purports to measure." (I really grooved on the definition because it gave me an opportunity to use the word *purport*. Prior to that time, I didn't have too many occasions to do so.) Although, by modern standards, that traditional definition of validity is pretty antiquated, it contains a solid dose of truth. If a test *truly* measures what it sets out to measure, then it's likely the inferences that we make about students based on their test performances will be valid because we will interpret students' performances according to what the test's developers set out to measure.

Let's take a look, now, at the three kinds of evidence you may encounter in determining whether the inference one makes from an educational assessment procedure is valid. Having looked at the three varieties of validity evidence, I'll give you my opinion about what classroom teachers *really* need to know about validity and what kinds of validity evidence, if any, teachers need to gather regarding their own tests. Table 3.1 previews the three types of validity evidence we'll be considering in the remainder of the chapter.[1]

Table 3.1   **Three Types of Validity Evidence**

Type of Validity Evidence	Brief Description
• Content Related	The extent to which an assessment procedure adequately represents the content of the assessment domain being sampled
• Criterion Related	The degree to which performance on an assessment procedure accurately predicts the examinee's performance on an external criterion
• Construct Related	The extent to which empirical evidence confirms that an inferred construct exists and that a given assessment procedure is measuring the inferred construct accurately

Content–Related Evidence of Validity ....

Remembering that the more evidence of validity we have, the better we'll know how much confidence to place in our score-based inferences, let's look at the first variety of validity evidence—namely, content-related evidence of validity.

Content-related evidence of validity (often referred to simply as *content validity*) refers to the adequacy with which the content of a test represents the content of the assessment domain about which inferences are to be made. When the idea of content representatives was first dealt with by educational measurement folks several decades ago, the focus was dominantly on achievement examinations such as a test of students' knowledge of history. If educators thought that eighth-grade students ought to know 124 specific facts about history, then the more of those 124 facts represented in a test, the more evidence there was of content validity.

These days, however, the notion of *content* refers to much more than factual knowledge. The content of assessment domains in which teachers are interested can embrace knowledge (such as historical facts), skills (such as higher-order thinking competencies), or attitudes (such as students' dispositions toward the study of science). Content, therefore, should be conceived of broadly. When we determine the content representativeness of a test, the content in the assessment domain being sampled can consist of whatever is in that domain.

But what is adequate content representativeness and what isn't? Although this is clearly a situation in which more representativeness is better than less representativeness, let's illustrate varying levels with which an assessment domain can be represented by a test. Take a look at Figure 3.2 where you see an illustrative assessment domain (represented by the shaded rectangle) and the items from different tests (represented by the dots). As the test items coincide less adequately with the assessment domain, the weaker is the content-related evidence of validity.

For example, in Illustration A of Figure 3.2, we see that the test's items effectively sample the full range of assessment-domain content represented by the shaded rectangle. In Illustration B, however, note that some of the test's items don't even coincide with the assessment domain's content, and that those items falling in the assessment domain don't cover it all that well. Even in Illustration C, where all the test's items measure content included in the assessment domain, the breadth of coverage for the domain is insufficient.

Trying to put a bit of reality into those rectangles and dots, think about an Algebra I teacher who is trying to measure his students' mastery of a semester's worth of content by creating a truly comprehensive final examination. Based chiefly on students' performances on the final examination, he will assign grades that will influence whether his students can advance to Algebra II. Let's assume the content the teacher addressed instructionally in Algebra I—that is, the algebraic skills and knowledge taught during the Algebra I course—are truly prerequisite to Algebra II. Then, if the assessment domain representing the Algebra I

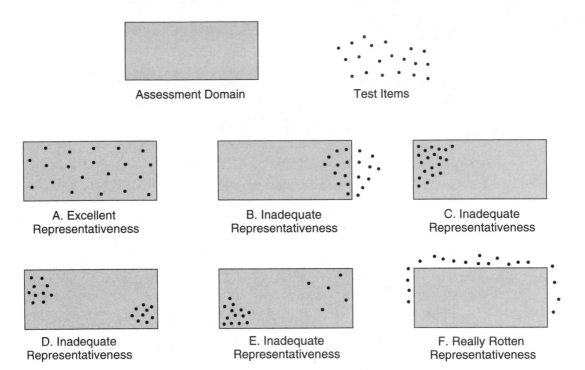

Figure 3.2   **Varying Degrees to Which a Test's Items Represent the Assessment Domain about Which Score-Based Inferences Are to Be Made**

content is *not* satisfactorily represented by the teacher's final examination, the teacher's score-based inferences about students' end-of-course algebraic capabilities and his resultant decisions about students' readiness for Algebra II are apt to be in error. If teachers' educational decisions hinge on students' status regarding an assessment domain's content, then those decisions are likely to be flawed if inferences about students' mastery of the domain are based on a test that doesn't adequately represent the domain's content.

How do educators go about gathering content-related evidence of validity? Well, there are generally two approaches to follow. I'll describe each briefly.

Developmental Care

One way of trying to make sure that a test's content adequately taps the content in the assessment domain the test is representing is to employ a set of test-development procedures carefully focused on assuring that the assessment domain's content is properly reflected in the assessment procedure itself. The higher the stakes associated with the test's use, the more effort is typically devoted to making certain the assessment procedure's content properly represents the content in the assessment domain. For example, if a commercial test publisher were trying to develop an important new nationally standardized test measuring high school students' knowledge of chemistry, it is likely that there would be much effort during the development process to make sure that the appropriate sorts of skills and knowledge were being measured by the new test.

Listed here, for example, are the kinds of activities that might be carried out during the test-development process for an important chemistry test to assure that the content covered by the new test properly represents "the content that high school students ought to know about chemistry."

Possible Developmental Activities to Enhance a High-Stakes Chemistry Test's Content Representativeness

- A panel of national content experts, individually by mail or during extended face-to-face sessions, recommend the knowledge and skills that should be measured by the new test.
- The proposed content of the new test is systematically contrasted with a list of topics derived from a careful analysis of the content included in the five leading textbooks used in the nation's high school chemistry classes.
- A group of high school chemistry teachers, each judged to be a "teacher of the year" in his or her own state, provides suggestions regarding the key topics (that is, knowledge and skills) to be measured by the new test.
- Several college professors, conceded to be international authorities regarding the teaching of chemistry, having independently reviewed the content suggestions of others for the new test, offer recommendations for additions, deletions, and modifications.
- State and national associations of secondary school chemistry teachers provide reviews of the proposed content to be measured by the new test.

With lower-stakes tests, such as the kind of quiz that a high school chemistry teacher might give after a one-week unit, less elaborate content reviews are obviously warranted. Even classroom teachers, however, can be attentive to the content representativeness of their tests. For openers, teachers can do so by *giving deliberate consideration* to whether the content on their classroom tests reflects the assessment domain that is supposedly being measured by those tests. For instance, whatever the test is, a teacher can deliberately try to identify the nature of the assessment domain that the test is supposed to represent. Remember, the test itself should not be the focus of the teacher's concern. Rather, the test should be regarded as simply a "stand in" for an assessment domain.

To illustrate, if a teacher of tenth-grade English wants to create a final examination for her one-semester course, the teacher should first try to identify all the important skills and knowledge that were taught during the semester. An outline of such content, or even a simple listing of topics, will usually suffice. Then, after identifying the content of the assessment domain covering the English course's key content, she can create an assessment instrument that attempts to represent the identified content properly.

The key idea here is that one strives to have the content of a test *represent* the content of the assessment domain about which the teacher will make score-based inferences. It is not necessary for the content of the test to completely coincide with the content of the assessment domain. Tests can adequately represent assessment domains even though they only sample the content of the assessment domain. After all, that's why pollsters can gather responses from only a small sample of citizens, yet derive reasonably accurate estimates regarding the status of citizens' preferences for an entire nation. Another way to assemble content-related evidence of validity for a classroom test that's under development is to see the extent to which the content that is contained in widely used textbooks is, in fact, properly represented in that test. This procedure, of course, assumes that the content contained in textbooks is reasonably appropriate because it has been thoughtfully put together by subject-matter whizbangs.

As you can see, the important consideration here is that the teacher makes a careful effort to conceptualize an assessment domain, then tries to see if the test being constructed actually contains content that is appropriately representative of the content in the assessment domain. Unfortunately, many teachers generate tests without any regard whatsoever for assessment domains. Rather than trying to figure out what domains of knowledge, skills, or attitudes should be promoted instructionally, hence what kinds of domains should be formally assessed, many teachers simply start churning out test items. Before long, a test is born—a test that, more often than not, does a pretty poor job of sampling the assessment domain about which the teacher should be making inferences. Unfortunately, a test whose content-related evidence of validity suggests that the test doesn't properly represent an assessment domain is a test from which no inferences about students' status with respect to the domain should be made. Any educational decisions based on students' performances on the test are also apt to be unsound.

We have seen, then, that one way of supplying content-related evidence of validity is to deliberately incorporate test-development activities that increase the likelihood of representative content coverage. Having done so, these procedures should be carefully documented. It is this documentation, in fact, that constitutes an important form of content-related evidence of validity.

External Reviews

A second form of content-related evidence of validity for educational assessment procedures involves the assembly of judges who rate the content appropriateness of a given test in relationship to the assessment domain the test allegedly represents. For high-stakes test, such as a state-developed examination that must be passed before a student receives a high school diploma, these content reviews are typically quite systematic. For run-of-the-mill classroom tests, such external reviews are usually far more informal. For instance, when one teacher asks a colleague to scrutinize the content coverage of a midterm exam, that's a version of this second approach to reviewing a test's content. Clearly, the care with which external reviews of an assessment procedure's content are conducted depends on the consequences associated with students' performances. The more significant the consequences, the more elaborate the external content-review process. Let's look at a couple of examples to illustrate this point.

Suppose that state department of education officials decide to construct a statewide assessment program in which all sixth-grade students who fail to achieve a specified level of competence in language arts or mathematics must take part in state-designed, but locally delivered, after-school remediation programs. Once the items for the new assessment program are developed (and those items might be fairly traditional or quite innovative), a panel of 20 content reviewers for language arts and a panel of 20 content reviewers for mathematics then consider the test's items. Such reviewers, typically, are subject-matter experts who have substantial familiarity with the content involved.

Using the mathematics portion of the test for illustrative purposes, the 20 members of the Mathematics Content Review Panel might be asked to render a yes/no judgment for *each* of the test's items in response to a question such as this:

An Illustrative Item-Judgment Question for Content-Review Panelists

Does this item appropriately measure mathematics knowledge and/or skill(s) that, because of the content's significance to the student's further study, should, if unmastered, result in after-school remedial instruction for the student?

Note that the illustrative question is a two-component question. Not only should the mathematical knowledge and/or skill involved, if unmastered, require after-school remedial instruction for the student but also the item being judged must "appropriately measure" that knowledge and/or skill. In other words, the knowledge and/or skill must be sufficiently important to warrant remedial instruction on the part of the student *and* the knowledge and/or skill must be properly measured by the item. If the content of an item is important *and* if the content of the item is also properly measured, the content review panelists should supply a *yes* judgment for the item. If either an item's content is not significant, or if the content is badly measured by the item, then the content review panelists should supply a *no* judgment for the item.

By calculating the percentage of panelists who rate each item positively, an index of content-related evidence of validity can be obtained for each item. To illustrate the process, suppose we had a five-item test whose five items received the following positive per-item ratings from a content-review panel: Item One, 72%; Item Two, 92%; Item Three, 88%; Item Four, 98%; and Item Five, 100%. The average positive content per-item ratings for the entire test, then, would be 90%. The higher the average per-item ratings provided by a test's content reviewers, the stronger the content-related evidence of validity.

This first kind of item-by-item judgment for reviewers deals, in part, with *construct irrelevance,* a concept described earlier in the chapter. The judgment by reviewers represents an attempt to isolate (and eliminate) items that are construct irrelevant.

In addition to the content-review panelists' ratings of the individual items, the panel can also be asked to judge how well the test's items represent the domain of content that *should* be assessed in order to determine whether a student is assigned to the after-school remediation extravaganza. This second kind of judgment by panelists relates to the possibility of *construct underrepresentation,* also described earlier in the chapter. Presented here is an example of how such a question for content-review panelists might be phrased.

An Illustrative Content-Coverage Question for Content-Review Panelists

First, try to identify mentally the full range of mathematics knowledge and/or skills you believe to be so important that, if not mastered, should result in a student's being assigned to after-school remediation classes. Then, having mentally identified that content domain of mathematics knowledge and/or skills, please estimate the percent of the content domain that is represented by the set of test items you just reviewed. What percent is it? _____%

If a content panel's review of a test's content coverage yields an average response to such a question of, say, 85%, that's not bad. If, however, the content-review panel's average response to the content coverage question is only 45%, this indicates that there is a solid chunk of important content not being measured by the test's items. For high-stakes tests, external reviewers' average responses to an item-by-item content question for all items and their average responses to a content coverage question for the whole test constitute solid indicators of judgmentally derived content-related evidence of validity. The more positive the evidence, the greater confidence one can have in making score-based inferences about a student's status with respect to the assessment domain being measured.

Although it would be possible for classroom teachers to go through the same content-review machinations just described for their own classroom assessments, I know of no sane teacher who would want to expend that much energy to review the content of a typical classroom test. Instead, a teacher might ask another teacher to look over a test's items and to render judgments akin to those asked of a content-review panel. Because it takes time to provide such judgments, however, a pair of teachers might trade the task of reviewing the content of each other's classroom assessments. ("You scratch my back/review my test, and I'll scratch/review yours.")

One of the significant dividends resulting from having a fellow teacher review the content of your classroom tests is that the prospect of having such a review will usually lead to more representative content coverage in your tests. The more carefully you consider your test's content coverage, the more likely the test's content coverage will be appropriate.

In review, we have considered one kind of validity evidence—namely, content-related evidence of validity—that can be used to support the defensibility of score-based inferences about a student's status with respect to an assessment domain. We've discussed this form of validity evidence in some detail because, as you will see, it is the most important form of validity evidence that classroom teachers need to be concerned with when they judge their own classroom assessment procedures.

Criterion-Related Evidence of Validity ....

The second form of validity evidence you're apt to encounter when working with educational tests is referred to as *criterion-referenced evidence of validity*. As was true with content-related evidence of validity, this kind of evidence helps educators decide how much confidence can be placed in a score-based inference about a student's status with respect to an assessment domain. Yet, a decisively different evidence-collection strategy is used when we gather criterion-related evidence of validity. Moreover, criterion-related evidence of validity is collected only in situations where educators are using an assessment procedure to *predict* how well students will perform on some subsequent criterion.

The earliest way to understand what this second kind of validity evidence looks like is to describe the most common educational setting in which it is collected—namely, the relationship between students' scores on (1) an aptitude test and (2) the grades those students subsequently earn. An *aptitude test* is an assessment device that is used in order to predict how well an examinee will perform at some later point. For example, many high school students complete a scholastic aptitude test when they're still in high school. The test is supposed to be predictive of how well those students are apt to perform in college. More specifically, students' scores on the aptitude test are employed to predict students' grade-point averages (GPAs) in college. It is assumed that those students who score well on the aptitude test will earn higher GPAs in college than those students who score poorly on the aptitude test.

In Figure 3.3, we see the classic kind of relationship between a predictor test and the criterion that it is supposed to predict. As you can see, a test is used to predict examinees' subsequent performance on a criterion. The criterion could be GPAs, on-the-job proficiency ratings, annual income, or some other performance

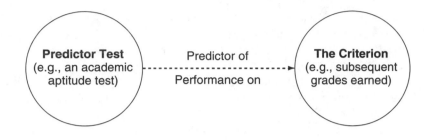

Figure 3.3   **The Typical Setting in Which Criterion-Related Evidence of Validity Is Sought**

variable in which we are interested. Most of the time in the field of education, we are concerned with a criterion that deals directly with educational matters. Thus, grades earned in later years are often employed as a criterion. Teachers could also be interested in such "citizenship" criteria as the number of times that students vote after completing high school (a positive criterion) or the number of misdemeanors or felonies that are subsequently committed by students (a negative criterion).

If we know a predictor test is working pretty well, we can use its results to help us make educational decisions about students. For example, if you discovered that Cliff Carver scored very poorly on a scholastic aptitude test while in high school, but that Cliff's heart is set on attending college, you could devise a set of supplemental instructional activities so that he could try to acquire the needed academic skills and knowledge before he leaves high school. Test results, on predictor tests as well as on any educational assessment procedures, should be used to make better educational decisions.

In some cases, however, psychometricians can't afford to wait the length of time that's needed between the administration of the predictor test and the gathering of the data regarding the criterion. For example, if the staff of a commercial testing company is developing a new academic aptitude test to predict high school students' GPAs at the end of college, the company's staff members might administer the new *high school* aptitude test to *college seniors* a month or so before they earned their baccalaureate degrees. The correlation between the aptitude test scores and the students' final college GPAs would be referred to as *concurrent* criterion-related evidence of validity. Clearly, such evidence is far less compelling than properly gathered *predictive* criterion-related evidence of validity (that is, when a meaningful length of time has elapsed between the predictor test and the collection of the criterion data).

What teachers need to realize about the accuracy of scholastic predictor tests such as the ones we've been discussing is that they are far from perfect. Sometimes the criterion that's being predicted isn't all that reliable itself. (How accurate were *your* college grades, for example?) For instance, the correlations between

Parent Talk ....

> *Mrs. Billings, the mother of one of your students, is this year's president of your school's parent-teacher organization (PTO). As a consequence of her office, she's been reading a variety of journal articles dealing with educational issues. After every PTO meeting, or so it seems to you, Mrs. Billings asks you to comment on one of the articles she's read. Tonight, she asks you to explain what is meant by the phrase* content standards *and to tell her how your classroom tests are related, if at all, to content standards. She says that the author of one article she read argued that "if teachers' tests didn't measure national content standards, the tests wouldn't be valid."*

• • • *If I were you, here's how I'd respond to Mrs. Billings:*

"You've really identified an important topic for tonight, Mrs. Billings. Content standards are regarded by many of the country's educators as a key factor in how we organize our national education effort. Put simply, a *content standard* describes the knowledge or skill that we want our students to master. You might think of a content standard as today's label for what used to be called an instructional objective. What's most imperative, of course, is that teachers focus their instructional efforts on *appropriate* content standards.

"As you may know, our state has already established a series of content standards at all grade levels in language arts, mathematics, social studies, and science. Each of these state-approved sets of content standards is based, more or less, on a set of content standards originally developed by the national subject-matter association involved, for example, the National Council of Teachers of Mathematics. So, in a sense, teachers in our school can consider both the state-sanctioned standards as well as those devised by the national content associations. Most of the school's teachers have looked at both sets of content standards.

"Teachers look over these content standards when they engage in an activity we call *test-sharing.* Each teacher has at least one other colleague look over all the teacher's major classroom assessments to make sure that most of the significant content standards have been addressed. It's really an attempt to gather content-related evidence of validity for the tests we use here.

"Those teachers whose tests do not seem to address the content standards satisfactorily are encouraged to revise their tests so that the content standards are more suitably covered. It really seems to work well for us. We've used the system for a couple of years now, and the teachers uniformly think our assessment coverage of key skills and knowledge is far better."

• • • *Now, how would you respond to Mrs. Billings?*

students' scores on academic aptitude tests and their subsequent grades rarely exceed .50. A correlation coefficient of .50 indicates that, although the test predicts to some degree how students will subsequently perform, there are many other factors (such as motivation, study habits, and interpersonal skills) that play a major role in the grades that a student earns. In fact, the best predictor of students' future grades is not their scores on aptitude tests; it is students' earlier grades. Previous grades more accurately reflect the full range of important grade-influencing factors, such as perseverance, that are not directly assessable via aptitude assessment devices.

As a classroom teacher, you'll frequently encounter students' scores on scholastic aptitude tests. If there is criterion-related evidence of validity provided with such tests, you need to know how compelling the evidence is. And even if such evidence is exceptionally solid, you need to remember that a student's school success in school is governed by many important variables that aren't even touched on by the typical scholastic aptitude test.

Construct-Related Evidence of Validity ....

The last of our three varieties of validity evidence is the most esoteric, yet the most comprehensive. It is referred to as *construct-related evidence of validity*. Construct-related evidence of validity was originally used when psychologists were trying to measure such elusive and covert constructs as individuals' "anxiety" and "perseveration tendencies." Because these variables were clearly hypothetical constructs, if a test was created that could accurately be used to get a fix on a person's level of anxiety, then evidence could also be assembled that (1) the inferred construct was sensible and (2) the test measured that construct with some accuracy.

But most of the variables that educators try to assess are every bit as covert as anxiety and perseveration tendencies. When we talk about a student's "mathematical competence" or a student's "reading comprehension capabilities," there's nothing overt about those variables. Based on the student's observed behavior in class or on tests, we make judgments about what the student's mathematical skills and reading prowess are. Although routine educational variables are less exotic than one's anxiety and perseveration tendencies, a student's knowledge of history and scientific thinking skills are every bit as covert.

The way that construct-related evidence is assembled for a test is, in some sense, quite straightforward. First, based on our understanding of how the hypothetical construct that we're measuring works, we make one or more formal hypotheses about students' performances on the test for which we're gathering construct-related evidence of validity. Second, we gather empirical evidence to see whether the hypothesis (or hypotheses) is confirmed. If it is, we have assembled evidence that the test is measuring what it's supposed to be measuring. As a consequence, we are more apt to be able to draw valid score-based inferences when students take the test.

Construct-related evidence of validity for educational tests is typically gathered by way of a series of studies, not one whopper "it-settles-the-issue-once-and-for-all" investigation. There are three types of strategies most commonly used in construct-related evidence studies. (Have you noticed how often psychometricians toss things into three categories? It's unsettling.) We'll take a brief look at all three approaches to the collection of construct-related evidence of validity.

Intervention Studies

One kind of investigation that provides construct-related evidence of validity is an *intervention study*. In an intervention study, we hypothesize that students will respond differently to the assessment instrument after having received some type of treatment (or intervention). For example, let's say that a group of teachers developed an essay examination that they believed tapped students' "higher-order mathematical skills." It would be hypothesized that students would receive markedly higher scores on the examination after a six-week intensive summer workshop on the topic Messing about with Higher-Order Mathematical Thinking than the scores those same students earned before the workshop. If the hypothesis is confirmed—in other words, if students' postworkshop scores are higher than their preworkshop scores—then this constitutes one chunk of construct-related evidence of validity for the examination under consideration.

Differential-Population Studies

A second kind of investigation that can be used to provide construct-related evidence of validity is a *differential-population study*. In this kind of study, based on our knowledge of the construct being measured, we hypothesize that individuals representing distinctly different populations will score differently on the assessment procedure under consideration. To illustrate, suppose a new oral test of students' bilingual proficiency in English and Spanish had been created. If we would locate three groups of students who were (1) fluent in English but not Spanish, (2) fluent in Spanish but not English, and (3) fluent in Spanish and English, we could predict that the bilingually fluent speakers ought to decisively outperform their monolingual counterparts. If our hypothesis is confirmed when we carry out an actual study, that's more construct-related evidence to support an inference about students' status based on their test performances.

Related-Measures Studies

A third kind of empirical investigation providing construct-related evidence of validity is referred to as a *related-measures study*. In a related-measures study, we hypothesize that a given kind of relationship will be present between students' scores on the assessment device we're scrutinizing and their scores on a related assessment device. To illustrate, if we churned out a brand new test of students' ability to comprehend what they read, we could hypothesize that students' scores on the new reading test would be positively correlated with their scores on an already established and widely used reading achievement test. To the extent that our hypothesis is confirmed, we have assembled more construct-related evidence of validity that will support the validity of our score-based inference (using the new test's results) about a student's reading skill.

When it is hypothesized that two sets of test scores *should* be related, and evidence is collected to show that positive relationship, this is referred to as *convergent evidence* of validity. For example, suppose you were a U.S. history teacher and you used a final exam to cover the period from the Civil War to the present. If another teacher of U.S. history in your school also had a final exam covering the same period, you'd predict the students who scored well on your final exam would also do well on your colleague's final exam. (Your dazzling students should dazzle on his exam and your clunky students should clunk on his exam.) If you went to the trouble of actually doing this (and, of course, why would you?), this would be a form of convergent validity evidence.

In contrast, suppose as a test-crazed U.S. history teacher you tried to compare your students' final exam scores to their scores on a final exam in an algebra class. You'd predict a weaker relationship between your students' final exam scores in your history class and their final exam scores in the algebra class. This lower relationship is referred to as *discriminant evidence* of validity. It simply means that if your test is assessing what you think it is, then scores on your test ought to relate weakly to results of tests designed to measure other constructs.

As indicated earlier, a number of construct validation studies are needed before one can place great confidence in score-based inferences about students. The more elusive the construct being assessed, the more numerous and varied will be the validation studies that are needed. For example, it's much easier to marshall relevant evidence to support score-based interpretations about a student's spelling abilities than it is to support inferences about the student's real-life decision-making capabilities. The more unsure we are about the construct we're interested in, and the more unsure we are about how to go about measuring a student's status regarding that construct, the more construct-related evidence of validity we need to assemble.

An increasing number of psychometricians believe that construct-related evidence of validity actually encompasses other forms of validity evidence. Remember, construct-related evidence of validity draws on empirical evidence to support the proposition that an inferred, unobservable construct exists and, moreover, is measured by the assessment instrument under consideration. Well, *criterion-related* evidence of validity is certainly empirical, and deals with the existence of a predictor construct. Therefore, such evidence would seem to be subsumed as a form of construct-related evidence. Similarly, to the extent that empirical *content-related* evidence of validity is gathered, as is the case when measurement specialists obtain quantifiable content ratings from review panelists, this too constitutes a form of support for the contention that the unobservable construct under consideration (for example, a set of basic skills needed by high school graduates) has been suitably measured. In short, depending on how you look at the first two forms of validity evidence we treated, they might well be regarded as special instances of construct-related evidence of validity.

Whether you consider the three forms of validity evidence to be genuinely distinctive or collapsible into one category, the more evidence that can be assembled regarding validity, the better. Gathering evidence of validity is like building one's case in a hotly contested courtroom struggle. There's often no single piece of evidence that, in and of itself, carries the day. Rather, each side tries to build a cumulatively persuasive case by piling on pertinent evidence until the jury is sufficiently swayed. Similarly, in attempting to help educators decide how much confidence they can place in score-based inferences about a student's status regarding the assessment domain ostensibly measured by a test, more validity evidence wins out over less validity evidence.

Sanctioned and Unsanctioned Forms of Validity Evidence ....

Validity, as implied in the outset of the chapter, is the linchpin of educational measurement. If teachers can't draw valid score-based inferences about students, there's simply no reason to measure students in the first place. However, because validity is such a central notion in educational assessment, some folks have attached specialized meanings to it that, although helpful at some level, also may introduce confusion.

One of these is *face validity,* a notion that has been around for a number of decades. All that is meant by face validity is that the *appearance* of a test seems to coincide with the use to which the test is being put. To illustrate, if an assessment procedure is supposed to measure a student's actual ability to function collaboratively with a group of other students, then a true-false test that focused exclusively on abstract principles of group dynamics would not appear to be face valid. But, appearance can be deceiving, as has been noted in a variety of ways, such as "not being able to judge a book by its cover." Thus, even though an assessment procedure may *appear* to be consonant with the assessment procedure's mission, we must still assemble evidence that inclines us to put confidence in the score-based inference we arrive at by using the test. If an assessment procedure has no face validity, we're less inclined to assume that the assessment procedure is doing its job. Yet, even in those circumstances, we still need to assemble one or more of the three sanctioned varieties of validity evidence to help us know how much confidence, if any, we can put in a score-based inference derived from using that assessment procedure.

Another more recently introduced variant of validity is something known as consequential validity. *Consequential validity* refers to whether the *uses* of test results are valid. If, for example, a test's results are inappropriately employed to deny students a reasonable expectation, such as progressing to the next grade level, the test may be said to be consequentially invalid because its results had been used improperly. Yet, whereas educators should obviously be attentive to the consequences of test use, the notion of consequential validity is apt to confuse the central thrust of validity—namely, to confirm or disconfirm the defensibility of score-based inferences we make about our students. If we make accurate inferences about students' status based on a test, yet rely on those inferences to make terrible educational decisions, our test will have negative consequences. But it was the use to which we put our valid score-based inferences that is deplorable. The score-based inference was right on the mark. Consequential validity might be a decent way to remind educators of the importance of consequences when tests are used; it isn't a *bona fide* form of validity evidence.

The safest course of action for an educator who wants to remain clearheaded about validity is to rely on the most current version of the *Standards for Educational and Psychological Testing* referred to in the previous chapter. The most recent version of those important *Standards,* at this writing, is the 1985 revision. A new revision of the *Standards* is scheduled to be published very soon. I've tried to keep abreast of the key revisions in the new *Standards* by reviewing draft revision chapters. Insofar as possible, I've attempted to keep this second edition of my classroom assessment book absolutely *au courant.* (This is either a French phrase for up-to-date or a scone with small raisins.) Educators who want to keep current with what's officially happening in educational assessment will want to familiarize themselves with the new *Standards* as soon as that important document is published.

The Relationship between Reliability and Validity ·······························

If convincing evidence is gathered that a test is permitting valid score-based inferences, we can be assured that the test is also yielding reasonably reliable scores. In other words, valid score-based inferences almost certainly guarantee that consistent test results are present. The reverse, however, is not true. If a test yields reliable results, it may or may not yield valid score-based inferences. A test, for example, could be measuring with remarkable consistency a construct that the test developer never even contemplated measuring. For instance, although the test developer thought that an assessment procedure was measuring students' punctuation skills, what is actually measured is students' general intellectual ability which, not comprisingly, splashes over into how well students can punctuate. Inconsistent results will invariably preclude the validity of score-based inferences. Evidence of valid score-based inferences almost certainly requires that consistency of measurement is present.

What Do Classroom Teachers Really Need to Know about Validity? ....

Well, we've spent a fair number of words worrying about the validity of score-based inferences. How much, if anything, do classroom teachers really need to know about validity? Do classroom teachers need to collect validity evidence for their own tests? If so, what kind(s)?

As with reliability, I think a classroom teacher needs to understand what the essential nature of the three kinds of validity evidence is, but I don't think that classroom teachers need to go into a frenzy of evidence gathering regarding validity. Clearly, if you're a teacher or a teacher in preparation, you'll be far too busy in your classroom trying to keep ahead of the students to spend much time in assembling validity evidence. I do recommend, however, that for your more important tests, you devote at least some attention to content-related evidence of validity. As suggested in the chapter, giving serious thought to the content of an assessment domain being represented by a test is a good first step. Having a colleague review your tests' content is also an effective way to help make sure that your classroom tests represent satisfactorily the content you're trying to promote, and that your score-based inferences about your students' status are not miles off the mark.

Regarding the other two forms of validity evidence, however, I urge little more than a reasonable understanding of what those kinds of evidence are like. If you're ever asked to help scrutinize a high-stakes educational test, you'll want to know enough about such versions of validity evidence so that you're not intimidated when measurement specialists start reciting their "odes to validity."

Chapter Summary ....

The focus of Chapter 3 was on three forms of validity evidence. *Content-related evidence* provides a picture of the extent to which an assessment procedure suitably samples the content of the assessment domain it represents. *Criterion-related evidence* of validity deals with the degree to which an exam accurately predicts an examinee's subsequent status. *Construct-related evidence* of validity deals with the assembly of empirical evidence that a hypothetical construct, such as a student's ability to generate written compositions, is accurately assessed.

The relationship between validity evidence and reliability evidence was considered, as were certain unsanctioned forms of validity. It was suggested that, in general, more validity evidence is better than less, but that classroom teachers need to be realistic in how much evidence of validity to secure for their own tests. A recommendation was given to have teachers become familiar with all three forms of evidence, but to focus only on content-related evidence of validity for their own classroom assessment procedures.

Self-Check

For the first five self-check exercises, you'll be given four-option multiple-choice items in which you're asked to identify the kind of validity evidence that's described or to indicate that "None of the above" is the best response. Notice that the inclusion of the None-of-the-above option increases the difficulty of the items because, had there only been three evidence categories, you could simply choose the *best* answer from the three. With the None-of-the-above option, you have to decide whether there's any validity evidence there at all. After the first five multiple-choice items, you'll be getting five short-answer items.

1. A fifth-grade classroom teacher is concerned about whether he's measuring the appropriate content in his end-of-the-year final examination. Accordingly, he decides to see how well his students' end-of-the-year exam scores predict students' grades earned *at the end of the sixth grade.* He waits one year, then computes a correlation coefficient between his students' fifth-grade final exam scores and the end-of-year grades supplied by their sixth-grade teachers. What kind of evidence is the teacher assembling?
   a. Content-related evidence of validity
   b. Criterion-related evidence of validity
   c. Construct-related evidence of validity
   d. None of the above

2. Having created two forms of a final examination for her physics course, a teacher wishes to verify that the two forms are presenting equidifficult challenges to her students. She has her students take one form of the examination on a Wednesday and the second form of the examination on a Friday. She then correlates students' scores on the two forms. What kind of evidence is the teacher assembling?
   a. Content-related evidence of validity
   b. Criterion-related evidence of validity
   c. Construct-related evidence of validity
   d. None of the above

3. A school district measurement specialist has been studying a newly developed test of children's thinking skills as a potential assessment instrument to be used in the district. Because effective thinkers are supposed to be flexible, the developers of the new test provide evidence that there is a negative

relationship between students' test scores and their scores on a rigidity test. (The higher the scores on the rigidity test, the less flexible the examinee is supposed to be.) What kind of evidence are the developers of the thinking skills test providing?

   a. Content-related evidence of validity
   b. Criterion-related evidence of validity
   c. Construct-related evidence of validity
   d. None of the above

4. For all of his major classroom assessments, a history teacher asks the district's social studies supervisor to review the draft assessment instruments to make sure that they're covering the right knowledge and skills. Although most of the time the supervisor approves the proposed tests as is, on a few occasions the supervisor has identified content-coverage gaps. What kind of evidence is the teacher assembling?

   a. Content-related evidence of validity
   b. Criterion-related evidence of validity
   c. Construct-related evidence of validity
   d. None of the above

5. A third-grade teacher is concerned that her language arts tests are covering content that is too heterogenous. Accordingly, she computes an internal consistency correlation coefficient for each test so that she can establish the degree of content homogeneity represented in those tests. The resultant coefficients tend to range between .80 and .90. What kind of evidence is the teacher assembling?

   a. Content-related evidence of validity
   b. Criterion-related evidence of validity
   c. Construct-related evidence of validity
   d. None of the above

6. In your own words, describe the essence of *content-related evidence of validity*.

7. In your own words, describe the essence of *criterion-related evidence of validity*.

8. In your own words, describe the essence of *construct-related evidence of validity.*

_____

_____

_____

9. What, in a nutshell, is the essential relationship between validity and reliability?

_____

_____

_____

10. Why is it incorrect to say that "a test is valid" or to say that "a classroom assessment procedure is valid"?

_____

_____

_____

Pondertime

1. Why do you think validity is such a central concept in educational assessment?

2. It was suggested that some measurement specialists regard all forms of validity evidence as construct-related validity evidence. Do you agree? If so, or if not, why?

3. What, if anything, do you think school board members need to know about assessment validity?

4. What, if anything, do you think run-of-the-society citizens need to know about assessment validity?

5. What is your own view regarding the kinds of validity evidence that classroom teachers need to assemble regarding these classroom assessment devices?

6. What is your opinion of "consequential validity"?

Self-Check Key

Here are the correct answers for the first five self-check exercises: 1:b, 2:d (it's alternate-form reliability evidence she's gathering), 3:c, 4:a, 5:d (this is a quest for reliability evidence, not validity evidence).

6. You should have said something that resembles the brief description provided in Table 3.1.

7. You should have done what it says in number 6 above.

8. You should have done what it says in number 7 above that it says you should have done in number 6 above.

9. In a walnut shell (walnuts go great in brownies), if a test is reliable, it may or may not yield valid score-based inferences; if the test yields valid score-based inferences, it is almost certainly reliable.

10. Validity, in the case of classroom assessment procedures or any kind of test, refers not to the measurement itself, but to the validity of score-based inferences. More technically, we are trying to see if our test-based inferences about students' status with respect to a specific assessment domain are valid.

Endnote

1. As noted in the previous chapter, the *Standards for Educational and Psychological Testing* (Washington, DC: American Psychological Association, 1985) are soon to be revised. That revision may modify to some extent the three-part nature of validity evidence described here.

Additional Stuff

Linn, Robert L. "Evaluating the Validity of Assessments: The Consequences of Use." *Educational Measurement: Issues and Practice*, 16, no. 2 (Summer 1997): 14–15.

Linn, Robert L., and Norman E. Gronlund. *Measurement and Assessment in Teaching* (7th ed). Upper Saddle River, NJ: Prentice Hall, 1995.

Mehrens, William A. "The Consequences of Consequential Validity." *Educational Measurement: Issues and Practice*, 16, no. 2 (Summer 1997): 16–18.

Messick, Samuel. "Standards of Validity and the Validity of Standards in Performance Assessment." *Educational Measurement: Issues and Practice*, 14, no. 4 (Winter 1995): 5–8.

Moss, Pamela A. "Themes and Variations in Validity Theory." *Educational Measurement: Issues and Practice*, 14, no. 2 (Summer 1995): 5–13.

Popham, W. James. "Consequential Validity: Right Concern—Wrong Concept." *Educational Measurement: Issues and Practice*, 16, no. 2 (Summer 1997): 9–13.

Shepard, Lorrie A. "The Centrality of Test Use and Consequences for Test Validity." *Educational Measurement: Issues and Practice*, 16, no. 2 (Summer 1997): 5–8, 13, 24.

Standards for Educational and Psychological Testing. Washington DC: American Psychological Association, 1985.

Stiggins, Richard J. *Student-Centered Classroom Assessment* (2nd ed.). Upper Saddle River, NJ: Prentice-Hall, 1997.

Nonprint Stuff

American Educational Research Association. *Invited Address: Evaluating Test Validity* (Cassette Recording No. RA 3-20.25). Chicago: Teach 'Em, April 13, 1993.

4

Absence-of-Bias

*T*he last of the "big three" criteria for evaluating educational assessment devices is, in contrast to reliability and validity, a new kid on the block. During the past couple of decades, educators have increasingly recognized that the tests they use are often biased against particular groups of students. As a consequence, students in those groups do not perform as well on a test, not because the students are less able, but because there are features in the test that distort the nature of the students' performances.

Assessment bias refers to qualities of an assessment instrument that offend or unfairly penalize a group of examinees because of examinees' gender, ethnicity, socioeconomic status, religion, or other such group-defining characteristics. Most teachers are sufficiently familiar with the idea of test bias these days that, at least in a general way, they recognize what's being talked about when someone says, "That test was biased." In this chapter, however, we'll take a deeper look at what test bias is—and what it isn't. Moreover, we'll consider some procedures that can help classroom teachers recognize whether bias is present in assessment procedures and, as a consequence, can help reduce or eradicate bias in teachers' own classroom tests.

Because the other two criteria for evaluating educational tests—reliability and validity—are "good things," we're going to use the expression *absence-of-bias* to describe the third evaluative criterion. When bias is absent in tests, that also is a "good thing." Before looking at procedures to promote the absence-of-bias in educational assessment procedures, let's first look more directly at what we're trying to eliminate. In other words, let's look at assessment bias.

The Nature of Assessment Bias

As indicated earlier, assessment bias is present when there are elements in an assessment procedure that distort an examinee's performance merely because of the examinee's personal characteristics such as gender, ethnicity, and so on. Most of the time, we think about distortions that tend to lower the scores of examinees because those examinees are members of particular subgroups. For example, suppose that officials in State *X* installed a high-stakes mathematics test to be passed before students receive an "honors" diploma. If the mathematics test contained many word problems based on competitive sports examples about which boys were more familiar than girls, then girls might perform less well on the test than boys. The lower performance by girls would not occur because girls were less skilled in mathematics, but because they were less familiar with the sports contexts in which the word problems were placed. The mathematics test, therefore, appears to be biased against girls. On the other hand, it could also be said that the mathematics test is biased in favor of boys. In the case of assessment bias, what we're worried about is distortions of students' test performances—either unwarranted increases or unwarranted decreases.

Let's try another illustration. Suppose that a scholastic aptitude test featured test items based on five lengthy reading selections, two of which were based on content that was more likely to be known to members of a particular religious group. If, because of familiarity with the content of the two selections, members of the religious group outperformed others, this would be a distortion in their test performances. There would be an assessment bias in their favor.

If you think carefully about the issue we're considering, you'll realize that assessment bias, because it distorts examinees' performances, interferes with the validity of the score-based inferences we draw from our assessment procedures. But, because assessment bias constitutes such a distinctive threat to the validity of test-based inferences, and a threat that can be directly addressed, it is usually regarded as a separate criterion when evaluating educational tests. To the extent that bias is present, we can be quite sure that for the groups of students against whom the test is biased, valid score-based inferences are not apt to be forthcoming.

Let's look, now, at two forms of assessment bias—that is, two ways in which the test performances of individuals in particular groups can be distorted. It was noted earlier in the chapter that assessment bias is present if an educational assessment procedure offends or unfairly penalizes students because of their membership in a gender, ethnic, religious, or similar subgroup. We'll consider both of these forms of assessment bias.

Offensiveness

An assessment procedure is biased if its content (for example, its items) *offends* a subgroup of examinees. Such offensiveness often occurs when negative stereotypes of certain subgroup members are presented in a test. For instance, suppose that in all of an exam's items we saw males portrayed in high-paying and prestigious positions (e.g., attorneys and physicians) and we saw women portrayed in low-paying and unprestigious positions (e.g., housewives and clerks). Because at least some female examinees will, quite appropriately, be offended by this gender inequality, their resultant distress may lead to less than optimal performances on the exam and, as a consequence, scores that do not accurately represent their capabilities. (Angry women, or angry men, aren't the best test takers.)

Other kinds of offensive content includes slurs, blatant or implied, based on stereotypic negatives about how members of particular ethnic or religious groups behave. This kind of offensive content, of course, can distract examinees in the offended group so that they end up focusing more on the offensiveness of a given item than on accurately displaying their own abilities on subsequent items.

Although most of the nation's major test-development agencies now employ item-writing and item-review procedures designed to eliminate such offensive content, one encounters far too many examples of offensive content in the less carefully developed teacher-made tests. It is not that teachers deliberately set out to offend any of their students. Rather, many teachers have simply not thought carefully about whether the content of their classroom assessment procedures might cause distress for any of their students. Later in the chapter, we'll consider some procedures for eradicating offensive content in teacher's classroom assessment procedures.

Unfair Penalization

A second factor contributing to assessment bias is content in a test that may *unfairly penalize* a student based on the student's ethnicity, gender, socioeconomic status, religion, and so on. Let's consider for a moment what an "unfair" penalty really is.

Unfair penalization arises when a student's test performance is distorted because of content that, although not offensive, disadvantages the student because of the student's group membership. The previously cited example about girls' unfamiliarity with certain competitive sports would be an illustration of what an unfair penalty would be. As another example, suppose that an assessment procedure includes content apt to be known only to children from affluent families. Let's say that an assessment procedure is installed to see how well students can "collaboratively problem solve" in groups, and that the assessment activity culminates when the teacher gives students a new problem to analyze collaboratively in a group discussion. If the content of the new problem deals with a series of locally presented operas and symphonies likely to have been attended only by those who can afford such performances' hefty ticket prices, then students from less affluent families will be unfairly penalized because there was probably much less dinner conservation about the local operas and symphonies. Students from lower socioeconomic strata might perform less well on the "collaborative problem solving" assessment enterprise not because they are less skilled at collaborative problem solving, but because they are unfamiliar with the upper-crust content of the particular assessment procedure being employed to gauge students' collaborative problem-solving skills.

Choose Your Language, Children! ··································

Jaime Jemez teaches mathematics in Wilson Junior High School. He has done so for the past 10 years and is generally regarded as an excellent instructor. In the past few years, however, the student population at Wilson Junior High has been undergoing some dramatic shifts. Whereas there were relatively few Hispanic students in the past, almost 30% of the student population is now Hispanic. Moreover, almost half of those students arrived in the United States less than 2 years ago. Most of the newly arrived students in Jaime's classes came from Mexico and Central America.

Because English is a second language for most of these Hispanic students, and because many of the newly arrived students still have a difficult time with written English, Jaime has been wondering if his mathematics examinations are biased against many of the Hispanic students in his classes. Because Jaime reads and writes Spanish fluently, he has been considering whether he should provide Spanish-language versions of his more important examinations. Although such a decision would result in some extra work for him, Jaime believes that language-choice tests would reduce the bias in his assessment procedures for students whose initial language was Spanish.

Jaime is also aware that the demographics of the district are still shifting and that an increasing number of Southeast Asian students are beginning to show up in his classes. He is afraid that if he starts providing Spanish-language versions of his tests, perhaps he will need to provide the tests in other languages as well. However, he is fluent only in Spanish and English.

If you were Jaime, what would your decision be?

Some penalties, of course, are as fair as they can be. If you're a classroom teacher who's generated a test on a unit you've been teaching, and some students perform poorly because they didn't pay attention in class or didn't do their homework assignments, their lousy performance on your test is eminently fair. Their "penalty," in fact, simply reeks of fairness. Poor performances on an assessment procedure need not signify that the resultant penalty to the student (such as a low grade) is unfair. Many of the students I taught in high school and college richly deserved the low grades I gave them.

Unfair penalization arises only when it is not the student's ability that leads to poor performance but, rather, the student's group membership. If, because of the student's gender, ethnicity, and so on, the content of the test distorts how the student would otherwise have performed, then a solid case of assessment bias is at hand. As was true in the case of offensiveness of test content, we sometimes find classroom teachers who haven't thought carefully about whether their assessment procedures' content gives all students an equal chance to perform well. We'll soon consider some ways for classroom teachers to ferret out test content that might unfairly penalize certain of their students.

Disparate Impact and Assessment Bias ....

It is sometimes the case that when a statewide, high-stakes test is originally installed, its impact on different ethnic groups will be disparate. For example, African American students or Hispanic students may perform less well than non-Hispanic White students. Does this mean that the test is biased? Not necessarily. However, if a test has a disparate impact on members of a particular ethnic, gender, or religious subgroup, this disparate impact certainly warrants further scrutiny to see if the test is biased. Disparate impact does not equal assessment bias.

Let me tell you about an experience I had in the late seventies that drove this point home so I never forgot it. I was working in a southern state to help its state officials develop a series of statewide tests that, ultimately, would be used to deny diplomas to students who failed to pass the twelfth-grade level of the test. Having field-tested all of the potential items for the tests on several thousand children in the state, we had assembled a committee of 25 teachers from throughout the state, roughly half of whom were African American, to review the field-test results. The function of the committee was to see if there were any items that should be discarded. For a number of the items, the African American children in the statewide tryout had performed significantly less well than the other children. Yet, almost any time it was proposed that such items be jettisoned because of such a disparate

impact, it was the African American teachers who said, "Our children need to know what's in that item. It deals with important content. Don't you *dare* toss that item out!"

Those African American teachers were saying, in no uncertain terms, that African American children, just as non-African American children, *should* know what was being tested by those items, even if a disparate impact was currently present. The teachers wanted to make sure that if African American youngsters could not correctly perform well enough on those items, the presence of the items in the test would allow such deficits to be identified and, as a consequence, to be remediated. The teachers wanted to make sure that *future* disparate impacts would be eliminated.

If an assessment procedure leads to a differential impact on a particular group of students, then it is imperative to discern if the assessment procedure is biased. But if the assessment procedure does not offend or unfairly penalize any student subgroups, then the most likely explanation of disparate impact is prior instructional inadequacies for the low-performing group. In other words, there's nothing wrong with the test, but there was definitely something wrong with the quality of education previously provided to the subgroup of students who scored poorly on the examination.

It is well known, of course, that genuine equality of education has not always been present in every locale. Thus, it should come as no surprise that some tests will, in particular settings, have a disparate impact on certain subgroups. But this does not necessarily signify that the tests are biased. It may well be that the tests are helping identify prior inequities in instruction that should be ameliorated.

Let's conclude our consideration of assessment bias by dealing with two strategies for eliminating or, at least, markedly reducing the extent to which unsuitable content on assessment devices can distort certain students' scores. Such distortions, of course, erode the validity of the score-based inference that educators arrive at by using such assessment devices. And rotten inferences about students' status, of course, usually lead to rotten decisions about those students.

Judgmental Approaches ....

One particularly useful way to identify any aspects of an assessment procedure that may be biased is to call on content-knowledgeable reviewers to *judgmentally scrutinize* the assessment procedure, item by item, to see if any items offend or unfairly penalize certain subgroups of examinees. When any important, high-stakes test is developed these days, it is customary to have a bias review panel consider its items in order to isolate and discard any that may contribute to assessment bias. After seeing how such a procedure is implemented for high-stakes tests, we'll consider how classroom teachers can carry out the essential features of judgmental bias-detection reviews for their own assessment procedures.

Bias Review Panels

For high-stakes tests, a bias review panel of, say, 15 to 25 reviewers, is typically as-sembled. Each of the reviewers is conversant with the content of the test being re-viewed. For example, if a sixth-grade language arts test were under development, the bias review committee might be comprised mostly of sixth-grade teachers along with a few district-level language arts curriculum specialists or university professors. The panel should be composed exclusively, or almost exclusively, of individuals from the subgroups who might be adversely impacted by the test. In other words, if the test is to be administered to minority students who are Asian American, Native American, African American, and Hispanics, there should be representatives of each group on the panel. There should also be a mix of male and female panelists so that panelists can attend to possible gender bias in items.

After the bias review panel is assembled, its members should be given a thorough orientation regarding the meaning of assessment bias—perhaps along the lines of the discussion earlier in this chapter. Ideally, panelists should be given some guided practice in reviewing a few assessment items that have been deliber-ately designed to illustrate specific deficits—for instance, content that is offensive or content that unfairly penalizes certain subgroups. Discussions of such illustra-tive items usually help clarify the panel's understanding of assessment bias.

An Individual Item Absence-of-Bias Judgment

After the orientation, the bias review panelists should be asked to respond to a question such as the following for *each* of the test's items:

> ### An Illustrative Absence-of-Bias Item Question for Bias Review Panelists
>
> Might this item offend or unfairly penalize any group of examinees on the basis of personal characteristics such as gender, ethnicity, reli-gion, or socioeconomic status?

Panelists are to respond *yes* or *no* to each item using this question. Note that the il-lustrative question does not ask panelists to judge whether an item *would* offend or unfairly penalize. Rather, the question asks whether an item *might* offend or unfairly penalize. In other words, if there's a *chance* that the item might be biased, bias review panelists are to answer *yes* to the absence-of-bias question.

The percentage of *no* judgments per item is then calculated so that an average per-item absence-of-bias index (for the whole panel) can be computed for each item and, thereafter, for the entire test. The more *no* judgments that panelists supply, the less bias they think is present in the items. If the test is still under development, items are generally discarded that are judged to be biased by several panelists. Because panelists are usually encouraged to indicate (via a brief written comment) why an item appears to be biased, it is often the case that an item will be discarded because of a *single* panelist's judgment if it is apparent that the panelist spotted a deficit in the item that had been overlooked by other panelists.

An Overall Absence-of-Bias Judgment

Although having a bias review panel scrutinize the individual items in an assessment device is critical, there's always the chance that the *items in aggregate* may be biased, particularly with respect to the degree to which they might offend certain students. For instance, as the bias review panelists consider the individual items, they may find few problems. Yet, when considered as a collectivity, the items may prove to be offensive. Suppose, for example, that in an extensive series of mathematics word problems, the individuals depicted were almost always females. Although this gender disproportion was not apparent from panelists' reviews of individual items, it could be discerned from panelists' responses to an overall absence-of-bias question such as the following:

> ### An Illustrative Overall Absence-of-Bias Question for Bias Review Panelists
>
> Considering all of the items in the assessment device you just reviewed, do the items, taken as a whole, offend or unfairly penalize any group of examinees on the basis of personal characteristics such as gender, ethnicity, religion, or socioeconomic bias?

As with the item-by-item judgments of panelists, the percent of *no* responses by panelists to this overall absence-of-bias question can provide a useful index of whether the assessment procedure is biased. As with the individual item judgments, bias review panelists who respond *yes* to an overall absence-of-bias question are usually asked to indicate why. Typically, the deficits identified in response to this overall question can be corrected rather readily. For instance, in the previous example about too many females being described in the mathematics word problems, all that needs to be done is a bit of gender changing (verbally rather than surgically).

In review, then, judgmental scrutiny of an assessment procedure's items, separately or *in toto*, can prove effective in identifying items that contribute to assessment bias. Such items should be modified or eliminated.

Empirical Approaches ....

If a high-stakes educational test is to be administered to a large number of students, it is typically possible to gather evidence regarding the performance of different groups of students on individual items, then review any items for potential bias for which there are substantial disparities between the performances of different groups. There are a number of different technical procedures for identifying items on which subgroups perform differently. Generally, these procedures are characterized as *differential item functioning* procedures because the analyses are used to identify items that function differently for one group (for example, girls) than for another (for example, boys).

Even after an item has been identified as a differentially functioning item, this does not automatically mean that the item is biased. Recalling our discussion of the difference between assessment bias and disparate impact, it is still necessary to scrutinize a differentially functioning item to see if it is biased or, instead, is detecting the effects of prior instructional inadequacies for a particular group of students. In most large-scale test-development projects these days, even after all items have been subjected to the judgmental scrutiny of a bias review panel, items identified as functioning differentially are "flagged" for a second review by bias reviewers (for example, the earlier bias review panel or perhaps a different panel). Only those items that are, at this point, judgmentally identified as biased are excised from the test.

To reiterate, large numbers of students are required in order for empirical bias-reduction approaches to work. Several hundred responses per item for each subgroup under scrutiny are needed before a reasonably accurate estimate of an item's differential functioning can be made.

Bias Detection in the Classroom ....

If you're an experienced teacher or are preparing to be a teacher, what can you do about assessment bias in your own classroom? I have a deceptively simple but, I believe, accurate answer to that question. The answer is: *become sensitive to the existence of assessment bias and the need to eliminate it.*

You'll remember that there are three big-bopper evaluative criteria you've been urged to use in evaluating any kind of educational assessment—namely, reliability, validity, and absence-of-bias. Bias really can be a serious shortcoming of your own tests. As indicated earlier, a test that's biased won't allow you to make valid inferences about your students' learning levels, and if your inferences are invalid, who cares if you're making those inferences reliably? Absence-of-bias, in short, is significant stuff.

Okay, let's assume you've made a commitment to be sensitive to the possibility of bias in your own classroom assessments. How do you go about it? I recommend that you always review your own assessments, insofar as you can, from the perspective of the students you have in your classes—students whose experiences will frequently be decisively different from your own. Even if you're a Hispanic American and you have a dozen Hispanic American students, this does *not* mean that their backgrounds parallel yours.

What you need to do is *think seriously* about the impact that differing experiential backgrounds will have on the way students respond to your classroom assessments. You'll obviously not always be able to "get inside the heads" of the many different students you have, but try to.

My first teaching job was in a rural high school in an eastern Oregon town with a population of 1,500 people. I had grown up in a fairly large city and had no knowledge about farming or ranching. To me, a "range" was a kitchen appliance on which one cooked meals. In retrospect, I'm certain that many of my classroom tests contained "city" content that might have confused my students. I'll bet anything that some of my early test items unfairly penalized some of the boys and girls who had rarely, if ever, left their farms or ranches to visit more metropolitan areas. And, given the size of our tiny town, almost anyplace on earth was "more metropolitan." But assessment bias was something I simply didn't think about. I hope you will.

Some of the newer forms of assessment that you'll be reading about in later chapters, particularly performance assessment (in Chapter 8) and portfolio assessment (in Chapter 9), because teachers are less familiar with those types of assessment, contain serious potential for assessment bias. To illustrate, most performance assessments call for students to respond to a fairly elaborate task of some sort (such as researching a social issue and presenting an oral report to the class). Because these tasks sometimes require students to draw heavily on their own experiences, it is imperative to select tasks that present the cherished "level playing field" to all students. You'd certainly not wish to use a performance assessment that gave an up-front advantage to students of more affluent parents.

Then there's the problem of how to evaluate students' responses to performance assessments or how to judge the student-generated products in students' portfolios. All too often I have seen teachers evaluate students' responses on the basis of whether those responses displayed "good thinking ability." What those teachers were doing, unfortunately, was creating their own, off-the-cuff version of a group intelligence test—an assessment approach now repudiated. Students' responses to performance and portfolio assessments are too often judged on the basis of factors that are more background dependent than instructionally promotable. Assessment bias applies to *all* forms of testing, not just traditional paper-and-pencil tests.

Parent Talk ....

Assume that you are White and were raised in a middle-class environment. During your fourth year of teaching, you've been transferred to an inner-city elementary school in which you teach a class of 27 fifth-graders, half of whom are African Americans. Suppose that Mrs. Johnson, a mother of one of your students, calls you after school to complain about her son's test results in your class. Mrs. Johnson says, "George always got good grades until he came to your class. But on your tests, he always scores low. I think it's because your tests are biased against Black children!"

• • • *If I were you, here's how I'd respond to Mr. Johnson:*

"First, Mrs. Johnson, I really appreciate your calling about George's progress. We both want the very best for him, and now that you've phoned, I hope we can work together in his best interest.

"About George's test performance, I realize that he hasn't done all that well on most of the tests. But I'm afraid it isn't because of test bias. Because this is my first year in this school, and because about half of my fifth-graders are African American, I was really worried that, as a White person, I *might* be developing tests that were biased against some of my students.

"So, during my first week on the job, I asked Ms. Fleming—another fifth-grade teacher who's African American—if she'd review my tests for possible bias. She agreed and she's been kind enough to review every single test item I've used this year. I try to be careful myself about biased items, and I'm getting pretty good at it, but Ms. Fleming helped me spot several items, particularly at the start of the year, that might have been biased against African American children. I removed or revised all those items.

"What I think is going on in George's case, Mrs. Johnson, is the instruction he's received in the past. I think George is a very bright child, but I know your family transferred to our district this year from another state. I really fear that where George went to school in the past, he may not have been provided with the building-block skills he needs for my class.

"What I'd like to do, if you're willing, is to set up a conference either here at school or in your home, if that's more convenient, to discuss the particular skills that George is having difficulty with. I'm confident we can work out an approach, with your assistance, that will help George acquire the skills he needs."

• • • *Now, how would you respond to Mrs. Johnson?*

If you want to expunge bias from your own assessments, try to review *every* item in *every* assessment from the perspective of whether there is anything present in the item that will *offend* or *unfairly penalize* any of your students. If you ever find such bias in any of your items, then patch them up or plow them under without delay.

You'll probably never be able to remove *all* bias from your classroom assessments. Biased content has a nasty habit of slipping past even the most bias-conscious classroom teacher. But if you show me 100 teachers who are seriously sensitized to the possibility of assessment bias in their own tests and 100 teachers who've not thought all that much about assessment bias, there's little doubt in my mind regarding which 100 teachers will create less biased assessments.

What Do Classroom Teachers Really Need to Know about Absence-of-Bias? ....

Classroom teachers need to know that assessment bias exists. Assessment bias in educational tests is probably less prevalent than it was a decade or two ago because most measurement specialists, having been sensitized to the presence of assessment bias, now strive to eliminate such biases. However, for the kinds of teacher-developed assessment procedures seen in typical classrooms, systematic attention to bias eradication is much less common.

All classroom teachers *routinely* need to use absence-of-bias as one of the three evaluative criteria by which they judge their own assessments and those educational assessments developed by others. For instance, if you are ever called on to review the quality of a high-stakes test such as a district-developed or district-adopted examination whose results will have a meaningful impact on students' lives, be sure that suitable absence-of-bias procedures, both judgmental and empirical, were employed during the examination's development.

But what about your own tests? How much effort should you devote to making sure that your tests don't offend or unfairly penalize any of your students because of personal characteristics such as ethnicity or gender? My answer is that you really do need to devote attention to absence-of-bias for *all* of your classroom assessment procedures. For the least significant of your assessment procedures, I suggest that you simply heighten your consciousness about bias eradication as you generate the test items or, having done so, as you review the completed test.

For more important examinations, try to enlist the assistance of a colleague to review your assessment instruments. If possible, attempt to secure the help of colleagues from the same subgroups as those represented in your students. For instance, if many of your students are Hispanics (and you aren't), then try to get a Hispanic colleague to look over your test's items to see if there are any that might offend or unfairly penalize Hispanic students. When you enlist a colleague to help you review your tests for potential bias, try to carry out a mini-version of the bias review panel procedures described in the chapter. Briefly describe to your co-workers how you define assessment bias, give them a succinct orientation to the review task, and structure their reviews with absence-of-bias questions such as those seen earlier in the chapter.

Most importantly, if you personally realize how repugnant all forms of assessment bias are, and how it can distort certain students' performances even if the assessment bias was inadvertently introduced by the test's developer, you'll be far more likely to eliminate assessment bias in your own tests. In education, as in any other field, assessment bias should definitely be *absent*.

Chapter Summary ....

This chapter on absence-of-bias was, quite naturally, focused on how educators make bias absent. Assessment bias was described as any element in an assessment procedure that offends or unfairly penalizes examinees because of personal characteristics such as their gender and ethnicity. Assessment bias, when present, was seen to distort certain examinees' performances on educational tests, hence reduce the validity of score-based inferences about those examinees. The two chief contributors to assessment bias were identified as offensiveness and unfair penalization. The essential features of both of these factors were considered. It was contended that an examination having a disparate impact on a particular subgroup was not necessarily biased, although such a differential impact certainly would warrant further scrutiny of the examination's content to discern if assessment bias was present. In many instances, disparate impact from an examination simply indicates that certain groups of students have previously received inadequate instruction.

Two procedures for identifying biased segments of educational assessment devices were described. A *judgmental* approach relies on the considered opinions of properly oriented bias reviewers. Judgmental approaches to bias detection can be formally employed with high-stakes tests or less formally used by classroom teachers. An *empirical* approach that relies chiefly on differential item functioning can also be used, although its application requires large numbers of examinees. It was recommended that classroom teachers be vigilant in the identification of bias, whether in their own tests or in the tests of others. For detecting bias in their own tests, classroom teachers were urged to adopt a judgmental review strategy consonant with the importance of the assessment procedures being involved.

Self-Check

For this set of self-check exercises, you are to review five test items, then decide whether you think there are elements in each item that are biased and, if so, why. Supply your response in your own words. If your response is *no* (that is, if you don't think there's bias present), you can respond with any form of that word you wish.

1. Here's a reading comprehension item for openers:

   In certain Christian religions, there are gradients of sinful acts. For example, in the Roman Catholic Church, a *venial* sin need not be confessed whereas a *mortal* sin must be confessed.

Based on the context clues contained in the reading selection above, which of the following statements is most accurate?
a. For Catholics, there is no difference in the gravity of mortal or venial sins.
b. For Catholics, a mortal sin is more serious than a venial sin.
c. For Catholics, a venial sin is more serious than a mortal sin.
d. Priests are required to forgive mortal sins that are confessed.

Do you believe this item to be biased? If so, why?

_____

_____

_____

2. Here's a mathematics item for you to review:

Heinrich Homborg collects World War II mementos. His original collection of official swastikas numbered 49. Recently, he sold 12 of his swastikas to another collector. How many swastikas does Heinrich have left? (Show your work.)

   Number of swastikas remaining:_____

Do you believe this item to be biased? If so, why?

_____

_____

_____

3. And now for a language arts item:

In which of the following three statements are all pronouns used properly?
a. I truly enjoyed his telling of the joke.
b. We watched him going to the cafe.
c. We listened to them singing the song.

Do you believe this item to be biased? If so, why?

_____

_____

_____

4. Next, here's an item designed to measure students' composition skills.

> Write a short essay of at least 500 words on the topic *Soccer in the United States.* Be sure to engage in prewriting activities, draft an initial response, and revise your draft. You have 60 minutes to complete this task.

Do you believe this item to be biased?

_____

_____

_____

5. For the last potentially biased item, let's swing back to mathematics for a moment.

> Ramon Ruiz is sorting out beans. He has four piles based on different groups of beans. He thinks he has made a mistake in adding up how many beans are in each pile. Pick the addition that is in error.
> a. 20 beans plus 32 beans = 52 beans
> b. 43 beans plus 18 beans = 61 beans
> c. 38 beans plus 39 beans = 76 beans

Do you believe this item to be biased?

_____

_____

_____

6. What is a persuasive argument that if an educational test has a disparate impact, it need not be biased?

_____

_____

_____

7. What is one very practical impediment to a classroom teacher's use of *empirical* methods to excise biased items from a teacher-developed test?

_____

_____

_____

8. Which of the two factors that were identified in the chapter as contributing to the bias of assessment procedures do you consider to be more difficult to detect? Why?

_____

_____

_____

Pondertime

1. If you were asked to support a high school graduation test that you knew would result in more minority than majority youngsters being denied a diploma, could you do it? If so, under what circumstances?

2. Only in the past decade or so have we seen measurement specialists and commercial test developers become really attentive to assessment bias. Why do you think it took so long for people to become exercised about this form of bias?

3. Which, if either, of the two approaches to bias detection discussed in the chapter (judgmental and empirical) do you think yields the most compelling evidence of assessment bias? Why?

4. Have you ever taken a test that you believed was biased? If you did, what features of the test do you think were biased?

5. What is your view about how much effort a classroom teacher should devote to bias detection and bias elimination?

6. What kind of overall strategy for educational assessment can you think of that might reduce the bias found in educational assessment devices?

7. Can bias in educational assessment devices be totally eliminated? Why or why not?

Self-Check Key

Remembering that the detection of bias, at least for these exercises, is a judgmental game, and that your answers may not coincide perfectly with mine, here's what I think about the first five items.

1. I think this item is biased in favor of Catholics and, conversely, biased against non-Catholics. Catholics who already had been taught about a difference between mortal and venial sins would clearly have an advantage over non-Catholics or Catholics who'd forgotten such a distinction. Incidentally, if you messed up on this item, I am told it was barely a venial sin.

2. This fairly simple subtraction problem is surely apt to offend a number of students such as those children whose family members were killed in World War II as a consequence of Nazi actions in Germany. In particular, many Jewish students would (should) be upset by such an insensitive choice of swastikas as commodities for a subtraction problem.

3. I don't think this item is biased, even though it might be tough for many students to answer correctly. Difficulty does not equal bias. Oh yes, the item is based on my personal hang-up involving modifiers of gerunds. The correct answer is a.

4. This composition task clearly appears to be biased against those students who don't know that much about soccer, and particularly those who know little of soccer in the United States. The item unfairly penalizes such students and thus is almost certainly biased.

5. This item is apt to offend Hispanics because it appears that an Hispanic (Ramon Ruiz) is portrayed as a bean counter, and beans have often been used as part of ethnic slurs against Hispanics. Moreover, the item implies that counting beans is, for a Hispanic, a reasonable activity. The item, in my view, is definitely insensitive and biased.

6. I think that the best argument to be mounted regarding this issue is that a test which results in disparate impact may be completely unbiased, yet could be detecting instructional inadequacies for those who perform poorly.

7. The most compelling reason that classroom teachers shouldn't mess around with empirical bias-detection techniques is that there are too few students to yield reliable estimates about differentially functioning items.

8. This is a judgment call, but I think unfair penalization is tougher to spot. Although there are exceptions, offensiveness needs to be fairly blatant if many folks are truly apt to be offended. As a consequence, it's usually fairly easy to identify. It's often more difficult to identify content that will unfairly disadvantage particular groups unless you understand the culture of those groups awfully well.

Additional Stuff

Bond, Lloyd. "Unintended Consequences of Performance Assessment: Issues of Bias and Fairness." *Educational Measurement: Issues and Practice,* 14, no. 4 (Winter 1995): 21–24.

Burton, Nancy. "Have Changes in the SAT Affected Women's Mathematics Performance?" *Educational Measurement: Issues and Practice,* 15, no. 4 (Winter 1996): 5–9.

Camilli, Gregory, and Lorrie A. Shepard. *Methods for Identifying Biased Test Items.* Thousand Oaks, CA: Sage, 1994.

Geisinger, K. F. "Psychological Testing of Hispanics." *Journal of Educational Measurement,* 30, no. 4 (Winter 1993): 351–356.

Holland, P. W., and H. Wainer (Eds.). *Differential Item Functioning: Theory and Practice.* Hillsdale, NJ: Erlbaum, 1993.

Keenan, Jo-Anne Wilson, and Anne Wheelock. "The Standards Movement in Education: Will Poor and Minority Students Benefit?" *Poverty & Race,* 6, no. 3 (May/June 1997): 1–3, 7.

Klein, Stephen P., Jasna Jovanovic, Brian M. Stecher, Dan McCaffrey, Richard J. Shavelson, Edward Haertel, Guillermo Solano-Flores, and Kathy Comfort. "Gender and Racial/Ethnic Differences on Performance Assessments in Science." *Educational Evaluation and Policy Analysis*, 19, no. 2 (Summer 1997): 83–97.

Langenfeld, Thomas E. "Test Fairness: Internal and External Investigations of Gender Bias in Mathematics Testing." *Educational Measurement: Issues and Practice*, 16, no. 1 (Spring 1997): 20–26.

Popham, W. James. *Educational Evaluation* (3rd ed.). Boston: Allyn and Bacon, 1993.

Rumberger, William F., and J. Douglas Willms. "The Impact of Racial and Ethnic Segregation on the Achievement Gap in California High Schools." *Educational Evaluation and Policy Analysis*, 14, no. 4 (Winter 1992): 377–396.

Singham, Mano. "Race and Intelligence: What Are the Issues? *Phi Delta Kappan*, 77, no. 4 (December 1995): 271–278.

5

**Deciding What to Assess
and How to Assess It**

*N*ow that you've struck up at least a nodding acquaintance with three criteria that can be used to evaluate tests, it's time to focus on what sorts of things a classroom teacher should be assessing in the first place. Because almost all classroom assessment procedures can accurately be described as teacher-made tests, in this chapter you'll learn how to answer two whopper questions about tests that you'll be making. The two whopper questions, suitably highlighted in upper-case type, are presented below:

1. WHAT SORTS OF THINGS SHOULD A CLASSROOM TEACHER TRY TO ASSESS?
2. HAVING DECIDED ON WHAT TO ASSESS, HOW SHOULD A CLASSROOM TEACHER GO ABOUT ASSESSING IT?

Let's tackle the first of these two questions—that is, the what-to-assess question. Having given you some ways to answer it, we'll then figure out how to respond to the how-to-assess-it question.

What to Assess

Far too many teachers simply stumble into an assessment pattern without giving serious consideration to why they're assessing what they're assessing. Typically, teachers test students in order to dispense grades in a manner that somehow resembles the levels of academic performance that students have displayed. Students who score well on the teacher's tests are given good grades; low-scoring students get the other kind. Traditionally, the need to dole out grades to students has been the chief factor spurring teachers to assess their students.

Yet, as suggested in Chapter 1, there are a number of other significant reasons these days that teachers construct and use assessment instruments. For example, results of classroom assessments may be employed to identify certain students' areas of deficiency so that the teacher can more effectively target additional instruction at those content or skill areas where there's the greatest need. Another important function of classroom assessment is to help teachers, *prior* to the design of an instructional sequence, understand more clearly what their end-of-instruction targets really are. This clarification occurs because properly constructed assessment procedures can illuminate the nature of instructional targets for teachers.

Decision-Driven Assessment

Teachers use tests to get information about their students. As we've already seen, teachers typically make score-based inferences about their students' status with respect to whatever assessment domains are being represented by the tests. Based on these inferences, teachers then make decisions. Sometimes the decisions are as straightforward as whether to give Sue Smith an A or a B. Sometimes the decisions are more difficult, such as how to modify an instructional unit based on students' performances on an end-of-unit exam. But, whatever the decisions are, classroom assessment should be unequivocally focused on the *action options* that teachers have at their disposal. The information garnered from assessing students is then used to help a teacher make the specific decision that's at issue. Because the nature of the decision to be serviced by the test results will usually influence the kind of assessment approach that the teacher selects, it is important to clarify, *prior to the creation of a test,* just what the decision or decisions are that will be influenced by students' test performances.

I realize that it may seem silly to you, or at least somewhat unnecessary, to identify *in advance* what decisions are linked to your classroom assessments, but it really does make a difference in determining what you should assess. For instance, suppose that the key decisions riding on a set of test results is how to structure a series of remedial instructional activities for those students who performed poorly on a teaching unit about a higher-order thinking skill. In that sort of situation, the teacher would definitely need some fine-grained diagnostic information about the *en route* skills or knowledge that each student did or didn't possess. Thus, instead of designing a test so that it merely assessed students' mastery of the overall thinking skill being taught, there would also need to be a sufficient number of items assessing students' *en route* skills. Based on the pattern of diagnostic data derived from the test, a sensible set of remedial instructional activities could then be designed for the low performers.

If, on the other hand, the key decision linked to test results is a simple determination of whether the teacher's instruction was sufficiently effective, a pretest-posttest assessment of more global (and less diagnostic) outcomes would suffice. It's also likely, by the way, that for purposes of judging the effectiveness of a teacher's instruction, the assessment device should often contain items intended to assess students' attitudes about what was being taught, not merely the knowledge and/or skills being taught.

In short, the decisions to be serviced by the assessment results should always influence the nature of classroom assessment. Teachers should, therefore, routinely consider the decision(s) at issue prior to creating a classroom assessment device.

A fairly easy way to decide if a test's results will really influence a classroom teacher's decision is to imagine that the test results turn out in two opposite ways—for example, a set of excellent student test performances versus a set of inferior student test performances. If the teacher would be apt to make a *different* decision based on those disparate sets of performances, then the teacher truly has a test that can help inform decisions. If the teacher's decision would be pretty much the same, no matter what the test results were, there's a strong likelihood that the assessment procedure is more ritual than genuine help for the teacher.

The Role of Instructional Objectives

Most classroom assessment takes place after an instructional sequence has been completed. There are exceptions, of course, such as diagnostic preassessment or the pretesting that a teacher might use as part of a pretest-posttest appraisal of the teacher's instructional effectiveness. Yet, most testing in the classroom occurs at the close of instruction. And, because much classroom instruction is intended to help students achieve specified instructional objectives, it is quite reasonable to think that if teachers consider the content of their instructional objectives, those teachers can more readily answer the what-to-assess question. What teachers should assess will, in most instances, stem directly from the teacher's instructional objectives because it will be those objectives that influence what the teacher will be teaching and, in all probability, what the students will be learning.

Consideration of your instructional objectives, therefore, is one action you can take to help get a fix on what you should assess. The more clearly you state your objectives, the more useful they will be to you in answering the what-to-assess question. In the 1960s and 1970s, there was widespread advocacy of *behavioral objectives*—that is, educational objectives stated in terms of the postinstruction behavior of learners. The push for behavioral objectives was fueled, at least in part, by dissatisfaction with the traditional form of general and ambiguous instructional objectives often used by educators. An example of such general objectives would be the following: "At the end of the course, students will understand the true function of our federal government." My favorite gunky instructional objective of that era was one I ran across in a state-level language arts syllabus: "The student will learn to relish literature." After that time, I kept on the lookout for an objective such as "The student will mayonnaise mathematics." I haven't encountered one—yet.

Still, in their attempt to move from unclear general objectives toward superclear behavioral objectives, the proponents of behavioral objectives (and I was right in there proponing up a storm) made a serious mistake. We failed to realize that if we encouraged teachers to use instructional objectives that were *too* specific, the result would be an abundance of small-scope behavioral objectives. The resulting piles of hyperspecific instructional objectives would so overwhelm teachers that they would end up paying attention to no objectives at all.

If you are currently a classroom teacher, you know that you can't realistically keep track of whether your students are achieving hundreds of instructional objectives. If you are preparing to be a classroom teacher, you'll soon discover that dozens and dozens of instructional objectives will overwhelm you. The trick in conceptualizing instructional objectives that help rather than hinder is to frame those objectives broadly enough so that you can sensibly organize instruction around them while making sure that the objectives are still measurable. The degree of *measurability* is clearly a key in the way you should state your objectives. The broader the objective is, while still measurable, the more useful the objective will be because you can be guided by an intellectually manageable set of instructional intentions. If you can conceptualize your instructional objectives so that one broad, measurable objective subsumes a scad of lesser, smaller-scope objectives, you'll have an objective that will guide your instruction more effectively and, at the same time, that will be a big help in deciding what to assess.

In language arts instruction, for example, when teachers set out to have their students become good writers, an instructional objective focused on the students' ability to author an original composition is an objective that, although still measurable (by simply having students churn out an original essay), incorporates a number of smaller-scope objectives such as the students' ability to employ appropriate syntax, word choice, and proper spelling.

Here's an example of two small-scope objectives in language arts:

* When presented with reading passages containing unfamiliar words, students can employ context clues to infer the unfamiliar words' meanings.
* The student will be able to write sentences in which verbs agree in number with relevant nouns and pronouns.

Now let's look at a broad-scope language arts objective that subsumes these small-scope objectives plus a load of similar small-scope objectives:

* After reading an age-appropriate nonfiction essay, the student will be able to compose two paragraphs, the first of which summarizes the essay's central message and the second of which provides the student's personal reaction to the essay's message.

Strive to come up with a half dozen or so truly salient, broad, yet measurable, instructional objectives for your own classroom. Too many small-scope, hyperspecific objectives will be of scant value to you because, if you're at all normal, you'll soon disregard an overwhelming array of superspecific instructional objectives. On the other hand, a small number of intellectually manageable, broad, yet measurable objectives will not only prove helpful to you instructionally but will also help you answer the what-to-assess question. Simply put, you'll want to create assessments that help you determine whether your students have, as you hoped, achieved your instructional objectives.

Cognitive, Affective, and Psychomotor Assessment

In thinking about what to assess, classroom teachers can often be helped by considering potential assessment targets according to whether they are chiefly focused on cognitive, affective, or psychomotor targets. *Cognitive* assessment targets are those that deal with the student's intellectual operations—for instance, when the student displays acquired knowledge or demonstrates a thinking skill such as decision making or problem solving. *Affective* assessment targets are those that deal with students' attitudes and values, such as a student's self-esteem, risk-taking tendencies, or attitudes toward learning. *Psychomotor* assessment targets are those that deal with students' large-muscle or small-muscle skills. Examples of psychomotor assessments that take place in schools would include tests of students' keyboarding skills in a computer class or their prowess in shooting a basketball in gym class.

On Demand Assessment ....

Dolly Davis is a fourth-grade teacher who has set up her social studies activities on a mastery learning basis. Students are allowed to work through most of their social studies assignments at their own speed. Much of the social studies program in Dolly's class is based on reading assignments, so that students can move at their own pace. When students believe that they are ready to demonstrate mastery of the social studies skills and knowledge that Dolly has described in written documents she distributes early in the school year, students set up an oral assessment. Dolly then spends 10 to 15 minutes presenting a series of short-answer items that students must answer orally. So that students do not discover from previously assessed students what the items on the assessment are, Dolly selects items at random from a pool of nearly 50 items for each of the four major social studies assessments during the year.

Although most students seem to appreciate Dolly's willingness to let them be assessed when they're ready, several students have complained that they "got a harder test" than some of their classmates. The dissatisfied students have encouraged Dolly to retain her mastery learning model, but to assess all students at the same time.

Dolly is deciding whether to maintain her on-call oral assessments or to revert to her former practice of written examinations administered to the entire class at the same time.

If you were Dolly, what would your decision be?

The distinction among cognitive, affective, and psychomotor educational outcomes was first introduced in 1956 when Benjamin Bloom and his colleagues (Bloom et al., 1956) proposed a classification system for educational objectives organized around those three categories. While recognizing that there are usually admixtures of all three domains of behavior in most things that teachers ask students to do on tests, the 1956 *Taxonomy of Educational Objectives* made it clear that there was typically a dominant kind of student behavior sought when teachers devised educational objectives for their students. For example, if a student is completing an essay examination in a social studies class, the student may be using a pencil (*psychomotor*) to write the essays and may be feeling remarkably confident (*affective*) about the emerging quality of the essay, but the chief domain of behavior involved is *cognitive* because it is the student's intellectual analysis of the test's items and the student's intellectual organization of a response that account mostly for what the student's essay contains.

Because the bulk of most teachers' classroom assessments will deal with the cognitive domain rather than the other two domains, here is a terse summary of the six levels of cognitive objectives that Bloom and his colleagues cranked out near midcentury.

Knowledge. Knowledge is the lowest level of the cognitive taxonomy. Because it describes the student's recall of factual information, this level of taxonomy is dependent chiefly on the student's memory.

Comprehension. Comprehension, the cognitive taxonomy's second level, represents the lowest nonrote form of understanding. A student knows what information is being communicated and can make some use of it without necessarily seeing it in its fullest implications or its relationship to other information.

Application. At the application level of the cognitive taxonomy, the student uses abstractions in concrete situations. This taxonomic level, as its title implies, signifies that the student can intellectually apply what he or she has learned to new situations.

Analysis. When a student engages in analytic behavior, he or she breaks down a complex communication into its constituent parts in such a way that the relationships among those parts are made clear.

Synthesis. Synthesis occurs when a student blends elements and parts in order to form a coherent structural pattern that was not previously present.

Evaluation. The highest level of Bloom's cognitive taxonomy is evaluation. Evaluation, in this context, means that the student makes qualitative or quantitative judgments about phenomena using the student's own evaluative criteria or evaluative criteria supplied by others.

In the 1960s and 1970s, when there was so much attention being given to instructional objectives, many educators spent endless hours classifying their educational objectives according to Bloom's six-level cognitive hierarchy. Hindsight suggests that this was typically time not well spent. The cognitive taxonomy is likely to be of most use to teachers if they shrink it down to only two categories: (1) knowledge and (2) anything higher than knowledge. This distinction is illustrated in Figure 5.1, where it can be seen that the lowest of Bloom's six levels is shaded differently than the highest five levels. In view of the many "Knowledge-only" items I've encountered in teachers' classroom tests, I'm now willing to describe as "higher order" any assessments calling for higher than the *lowest* of Bloom's six levels.

Because many teachers' focus their instruction almost exclusively on the lowest level of cognitive taxonomy (that is, knowledge) and because knowledge calls for nothing but memorized facts, it can clearly be helpful for teachers to see that little assessment attention in their class is being given to higher-level cognitive process. Beyond the isolation of a teacher's excessive emphasis on memorized facts, however, taxonomic analyses at higher levels of the cognitive taxonomy have proven to be of limited value to busy classroom teachers. They have better things to do with their time.

In much the same vein, although the affective domain of educational objectives was carved into five levels in 1964 by David Krathwohl and his colleagues (Krathwohl et al., 1964), classroom teachers have found almost no utility in differentiating among various kinds of affective objectives. It is, unfortunately, the case that genuine affective objectives are so rarely encountered in our classrooms that, just as with other truly scarce species, it's sometimes not worth categorizing them. It *is* useful, however, for classroom teachers to employ the general notion of the affective domain to determine if they're focusing their instructional activities exclusively on cognition. If such is the case, it may be a signal to add a dollop of affect to what one teaches and what one assesses.

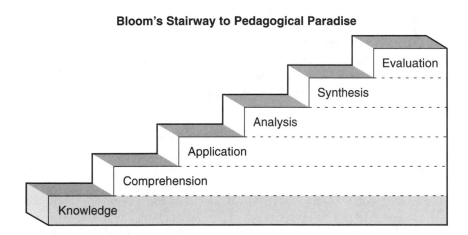

Bloom's Stairway to Pedagogical Paradise

Figure 5.1   **The Six Levels of the Cognitive Taxonomy with the Lowest Level, Knowledge, Distinguished from the Five Higher Levels**

Turning to the psychomotor domain, most teachers understand fairly well whether they are responsible for psychomotor kinds of skills. In certain subjects—for example, woodshop or auto mechanics—it would take a truly catatonic teacher not to realize that there are significant psychomotor outcomes to be promoted. Although the psychomotor domain has also been subdivided into hierarchical levels by several different authors, none of those classification schemes has been widely adopted by the nation's educators. In fact, taxonomic attention to psychomotor objectives has been fairly dormant for a number of years now.

To review, as classroom teachers consider potential assessment content while wrestling with the what-to-assess question, a potentially helpful framework to apply consists of the three domains of educational objectives first differentiated in 1956—namely, the cognitive, affective, and psychomotor domains. There is nothing wrong, of course, with having a teacher's assessment targets focus exclusively on a single domain if that kind of unidimensional focus stems from the teacher's considered judgment. In too many instances these days, however, we find teachers measuring students in only one domain (guess which one) and at one level in that domain (guess which level). Reliance on Bloom's taxonomies, at a fairly gross level, can help classroom teachers avoid unthinking unidimensionality in their classroom assessments.

Standards-Based Classroom Assessment

Whether you are an elementary teacher who has instructional responsibility for a number of subject areas, or a secondary teacher who has instructional responsibility for one or two subject areas, you should be concerned that your instruction and your assessment address appropriate content. Fortunately, in the last decade or so, various national organizations have attempted to isolate the most important content to teach in their respective subject areas. These content-delineation efforts can prove quite helpful to teachers who are trying to "teach the right things." These national content-delineation efforts are part of the 1990s *educational standards movement*.

First off, let's define what an educational *standard* actually is. Unfortunately, you'll find that different educators use the term all too loosely and often incorrectly. Actually, there are three types of educational standards you need to know about:

- A *content standard* describes the knowledge or skills that educators want students to learn.
- A *performance standard* identifies the desired level of proficiency at which educators want a content standard mastered.
- An *opportunity-to-learn standard* describes the amount of instruction that students should be given so they have a fair chance of mastering a content standard at the level determined in that content standard's associated performance standard.

It should be apparent that although we might refer to all of the above as "standards," they are very different creations. Just as cowboys in a western movie might loosely refer to "cattle," those cowpokes know that boy-cattle and girl-cattle perform decisively different functions.

From a classroom teacher's perspective, the most useful kind of standards, without question, will be content standards because those standards set forth what the standards identifiers regard as the most important content for children to learn. Years ago, when I was a high school teacher, we had a district "curriculum guide" and a state "scope and sequence" manual, both of which attempted to identify the most important knowledge and skills that students should learn in each subject area. Too be honest, those documents weren't all that wonderful. My fellow teachers and I found those curriculum materials to be vague, ambiguous, and altogether unhelpful.

During the 1990s, however, there have been major attempts on the part of national organizations, led by the National Council of Teachers of Mathematics (NCTM) 1989 publication of *Curriculum and Evaluation Standards for School Mathematics.* In that publication, NCTM made a major effort to reconceptualize how mathematics should be taught by identifying a set of important new content standards. Those content standards defined the chief aim of mathematics education as the promotion of students' mathematical power—that is, students' ability to use mathematical thinking and understanding to solve problems and communicate the results of those solutions mathematically.

Soon thereafter, other national subject-matter associations began to bring forth their own sets of content standards and, in some instances, performance standards as well. There even were a few subject-matter associations whose members attempted to identify opportunity-to-learn standards for their content areas.

I have had a chance to review many of these standards documents. (I suspect this means I took advantage of my "opportunity to learn.") Most of the standards documents are very impressive. All of the standards documents represent the efforts of top-flight subject-area specialists who devoted enormous time to circumscribing the knowledge and skills that students should learn.

I think it would be great if *you* spent some time reviewing these standards documents and skills that you should be teaching (and, therefore, testing). But I do *not* believe you should meekly succumb to the curricular preferences expressed in those standards collections. The reason for my warning is straightforward. These standards documents were produced by subject-matter *specialists*. And subject-matter specialists really adore their subject matters. Subject-matter specialists would like to see students master almost *everything* in their field.

Subject specialists usually approach their standards-identification tasks not from the perspective of a busy classroom teacher, but from the perch of a content devoteé. Content devoteés and classroom teachers, just like steers and cows, are different members of the cattle crowd. If teachers tried to teach students to do *all* the things set forth in the 1990s standards documents, there'd be no time left for food, sleep, or movies! So, what I recommend that you do is *consult* the national standards document(s) relevant to your own teaching responsibilities, then see which of the content standards you have time to address. Without question, you'll get some wonderful ideas from the standards documents. But select your own content standards judiciously; don't try to stuff the whole wad of standards into your students' skulls. They won't all fit.

I've listed here a series of standards collections that, depending on your content preferences, you may wish to consult. These are not *all* of the potentially relevant collections of content standards. There are more extensive listings of such collections available that you may wish to consult.[1] But here are many of the most important national collections of content standards:

The Arts

- Consortium of National Arts Education Associations. (1994). *National Standards for Arts Education: What Every Young American Should Know and Be Able to Do in the Arts.* Reston, VA: Music Educators National Conference.

Civics

- Center for Civic Education. (1994). *National Standards for Civics and Government.* Calabasas, CA: Author.
- National Council for the Social Studies. (1994). *Expectations of Excellence: Curriculum Standards for Social Studies.* Washington, DC: Author.

Economics

- National Council for the Social Studies. (1994). *Expectations of Excellence: Curriculum Standards for Social Studies.* Washington, DC: Author.
- Saunders, P., & Gilliard, J. (Eds.). (1995). *A Framework for Teaching Basic Economic Concepts with Scope and Sequence Guidelines, K–12.* New York: National Council on Economic Education.

English Language Arts

- National Assessment of Educational Progress Reading Consensus Project. (1990). *Reading Assessment Framework for the 1992 National Assessment of Educational Progress.* Washington, DC: National Assessment Governing Board.
- National Council of Teachers of English and the International Reading Association. (1996). *Standards for the English Language Arts.* Urbana, IL: National Council of Teachers of English.
- New Standards. (1995, June). *Draft Performance Standards for English Language Arts.* Washington, DC: Author.

Foreign Language

- National Standards in Foreign Language Education Project. (1996). *Standards for Foreign Language Learning: Preparing for the 21st Century.* Lawrence, KS: Allen Press.

Geography

- Geography Education Standards Project. (1994). *Geography for Life: National Geography Standards.* Washington, DC: National Geographic Research and Exploration.
- National Assessment of Educational Progress Geography Consensus Project. (1992). *Geography Assessment Framework for the 1994 National Assessment of Educational Progress.* (Draft). Washington, DC: National Assessment Governing Board.

Health

- Joint Committee on National Health Education Standards. (1995). *National Health Education Standards: Achieving Health Literacy.* Reston, VA: Association for the Advancement of Health Education.

History

- Crabtree, C., Nash, G. B., Gagnon, P., & Waugh, S. (Eds.). (1992). *Lessons from History: Essential Understandings and Historical Perspectives Students Should Acquire.* Los Angeles: National Center for History in the Schools.
- National Center for History in the Schools. (1994). *National Standards for History: Basic Edition.* Los Angeles: Author.
- National Center for History in the Schools. (1994). *National Standards for History for Grades K–4: Expanding Children's World in Time and Space.* Los Angeles: Author.
- National Center for History in the Schools. (1994). *National Standards for United States History: Exploring the American Experience.* Los Angeles: Author.
- National Center for History in the Schools. (1994). *National Standards for World History: Exploring Paths to the Present.* Los Angeles: Author.
- National Council for the Social Studies. (1994). *Expectations of Excellence: Curriculum Standards for Social Studies.*

Mathematics

- National Assessment of Educational Progress. (1992, March 31). Framework for the 1994 National Assessment of Educational Progress Mathematics Assessment. Washington, DC: Author.
- National Council of Teachers of Mathematics. (1989). *Curriculum and Evaluation Standards for School Mathematics.* Reston, VA: Author.
- New Standards. (1995, June). *Draft Performance Standards for Mathematics.* Washington, DC: Author.

Physical Education

- National Association for Sport and Physical Education. (1992). *Outcomes of Quality Physical Education Programs.* Reston, VA: Author.
- National Association for Sport and Physical Education. (1995). *Moving into the Future, National Standards for Physical Education: A Guide to Content and Assessment.* St. Louis: Mosby.

Science

- Aldridge, B. G. (Ed.). (1995). *Scope, Sequence, and Coordination of Secondary School Science: Vol. 3. A High School Framework for National Science Education Standards.* Arlington, VA: National Science Teachers Association.
- Aldridge, B. G., & Strassenburg, A. A. (Eds.). (1995). *Scope, Sequence, and Coordination of National Science Education Content Standards: An Addendum to the Content Core Based on the 1994 Draft National Science Education Standards.* Arlington, VA: National Science Teachers Association.
- National Assessment of Educational Progress Science Consensus Project. (1993). *Science Assessment and Exercise Specifications for the 1994 National Assessment of Educational Progress.* Washington, DC: National Assessment Governing Board.

Social Studies

- National Council for the Social Studies. (1994). *Expectations of Excellence: Curriculum Standards for Social Studies.* Washington, DC: Author.

Of Standards and Emperors

Then a small voice called out from the crowd, "But the emperor's not wearing new standards at all; he's wearing old objectives!"

According to a classic but uncorroborated fairy tale, a ruler can be persuaded to parade around in the buff if he's made to believe he's wearing wonderful but invisible garments. The moral of "The Emperor's New Clothes" fable, of course, is that a ruler is not apt to redress his state of undress unless someone informs him he's naked as a jaybird.

Standards, of course, is a warmth-inducing word. Although perhaps not in the same league with *motherhood, democracy,* and *babies,* I suspect that *standards* ranks right up there with *oatmeal, honor,* and *excellence.* It's really tough not to groove on *standards,* especially if those standards are *high.* Everyone wants students to reach high standards. And, because high standards are so intrinsically praiseworthy, if teachers pursue such standards, then teachers can sleep tranquilly at night. Teachers are clearly questing after that which, like the Holy Grail, warrants such questing.

If by the expression *content standards* we refer to the knowledge and skills that we want our students to achieve as a consequence of education, how is a content standard different from an instructional objective? The answer (all emperors and emperors-in-training take heed) is that there really is *no* difference between instructional objectives and content standards. Both phrases describe the educational intentions we have for our students.

One reason that content standards is much more appealing to almost everyone than instructional objectives, as noted earlier, is that content *standards* is warmth-inducing phrase. Instructional objectives is not. What right-minded politician or educational policymaker would not leap with enthusiasm to be "in solid support of high content standards!" It's far less exciting for someone to applaud instructional objectives.

So, for both of these reasons, I foresee continued widespread support for the identification and promotion of defensible content standards. As I listen, however, to today's enthusiastic endorsements of content standards and their pivotal role in educational improvement, I find myself doing a bit of mental transformation, so I guess I'm still covertly thinking about instructional objectives.

Assessment Blueprints

Some teachers find it helpful, especially when constructing major examinations, to develop what's called an *assessment blueprint* or a *test blueprint*. These blueprints are essentially two-way tables in which one dimension represents the content standards (or objectives) the teacher wants to assess, while the other dimension represents the levels of cognitive functioning being sought. For instance, the example below from a teacher's assessment blueprint will illustrate how these sorts of organizational schemes work:

	Number of Items	
Objective No.	*Cognitive Level*	
	Knowledge	*Above Knowledge*
1	3	1
2	1	4
3	2	2
etc.	etc.	

Assessment blueprints can help teachers identify content standards or objectives that are not being measured with sufficient items or with sufficient items at an appropriate level of cognitive demand.

Collar a Colleague

Too many classroom teachers carry out their professional chores in isolation. If you're trying to figure out what to assess in your own classroom, one straightforward scheme for tackling that task is to seek the counsel of a colleague, particularly one who teaches the same sort of class and/or grade level that you teach.

Always keeping in mind that what you assess should be governed by the decisions that will be influenced by your students' assessment results, simply solicit the advice of a respected colleague regarding what sorts of things you should be assessing in your class. If you're uncomfortable about making such a request, simply read (with feeling) the following scripted question: "If you were I, what would you assess?" I admit that the phrasing of the question isn't all that exotic, but it will get the job done. What you're looking for is some sensible advice from a nonpartisan co-worker.

If you've already devoted a chunk of thought to the what-to-assess question, you might simply ask your colleague to review your answers so that you can discern whether your planned assessment targets seem reasonable to another teacher. A second pair of eyes can frequently prove useful in deciding whether you've really staked out a defensible set of emphases for your planned classroom assessments.

What-to-Assess Considerations

In review, then, we've looked at several considerations that can help classroom teachers in deciding what they should measure in their classroom assessment procedures. From the discussion of those points, five possible ways of addressing the what-to-assess question can be derived:

1. Focus all class assessment procedures on clearly explicated decision options.
2. A small number of significant instructional objectives can provide a useful framework for deciding what to assess.
3. An analysis of whether assessments should focus on cognitive, affective, or psychomotor behavior (and, if cognitive, at what taxonomic level) can prove helpful.
4. A review of relevant collections of content standards can help identify key knowledge and skills to be pursued.
5. Advice from a colleague about what to assess can prove beneficial.

How to Assess It ....

Let's assume that you've decided what you're going to measure in your classroom assessments. Now the task turns to how you're going to assess it. In the remainder of the chapter, we'll look at several choices to consider when deciding how to answer the how-to-assess-it question. More specifically, we'll be dealing with the following choices:

1. Whether to adopt a norm-referenced or a criterion-referenced assessment approach
2. Whether to emphasize selected-response or constructed-response assessment schemes
3. What kind of item type(s) to select from such alternatives as multiple-choice, short-answer, or performance tests

Norm-Referenced versus Criterion-Referenced Interpretations

There are two rather distinctive, yet widely used, assessment strategies available to educators these days: norm-referenced measurement and criterion-referenced measurement. The most fundamental difference between these two approaches to educational assessment is the nature of the interpretation that is used to make sense out of students' test performances.

With a *norm-referenced test*, educators interpret a student's performance in relation to the performances of students who have previously taken the same examination. That previous group of test takers is referred to as the *norm group*. Thus, when educators try to make sense out of a student's tests score by "referencing" that score back to the norm group's performances, it is apparent why these sorts of interpretations are characterized as norm referenced.

To illustrate, when a teacher asserts that a student "scored at the 90th percentile on a scholastic aptitude test," the teacher means that the student's test performance has exceeded the performance of 90% of students in the test's norm group. In education, norm-referenced interpretations are most frequently encountered when reporting students' results on academic aptitude tests, such as the Scholastic Assessment Test, or on widely used standardized achievement tests such as the Iowa Tests of Basic Skills, the Metropolitan Achievement Tests, or the California Assessment Tests. In short, norm-referenced test interpretations are *relative* interpretations of students' performances because such interpretations focus on how a given student's performance stacks up in relation to the performances of other students.

In contrast, a *criterion-referenced test* interpretation is an *absolute* interpretation because it hinges on the extent to which the criterion assessment domain represented by the test is actually possessed by the student. Once an assessment domain is defined, the student's test performance can be interpreted according to the degree to which the domain has been mastered. For instance, instead of a norm-referenced interpretation such as the student "scored better than 85% of the students in the norm group," a criterion-referenced interpretation might be that the student "mastered 85% of the test's content and can be inferred to have mastered 85% of the assessment domain being represented by the test." Note that a criterion-referenced interpretation doesn't depend at all on how other students performed on the test. The focus is on the domain of content represented by the test.

As you can see, the meaningfulness of criterion-referenced test interpretations is directly linked to the clarity with which the test's assessment domain is described. Clearly described assessment domains can yield crisp, understandable criterion-referenced interpretations. Ambiguously defined assessment domains are certain to yield fuzzy criterion-referenced interpretations that are of little utility.

Although loads of educators refer to "criterion-referenced tests" and "norm-referenced tests," there are, technically, no such creatures. Rather, there are criterion- and norm-referenced *interpretations* of students' test performances. For example, educators in a school district might have built a criterion-referenced test, used the test for several years, and, in the process, gathered substantial data regarding the performances of district students. As a consequence, the district's educators could build normative tables that would permit norm-referenced interpretations of the test that, although born as a criterion-referenced device, can still permit meaningful norm-referenced interpretations.

Because most of the assessment-influenced decisions faced by classroom teachers are benefited by the teacher's understanding of what it is that students can and cannot do, not merely their relative standing in relationship to one another, classroom teachers will generally want to make criterion-referenced rather than norm-referenced interpretations. A teacher's instructional choices, for example, are better serviced by evidence about particular students' skills and knowledge than by evidence about how those students compare with one another.

About the only instance in which classroom teachers will need to employ norm-referenced interpretations occurs when there are fixed-quota settings—that is, when there are insufficient slots for all of the teacher's students to be assigned to a given educational experience. For example, suppose that there were five students to be chosen for a special outside-of-class enrichment program in mathematics, and that the teacher had been directed by the school principal to choose the "best" mathematics students for the program. In such a situation, because *best* is, by definition, a relative descriptor, norm-referenced interpretations would be warranted. A teacher might try to build a test that helped spread students out according to their mathematics skills so that the top students could be identified. Barring those rare situations, however, most classroom teachers would be better off using tests that yield criterion-referenced interpretations. Criterion-referenced interpretations provide a far more lucid idea of what it is that students can and can't do. Teachers need that clarity if they're going to make solid instructional decisions.

In a later chapter, you'll be considering standardized, norm-referenced achievement tests. At that time, the appropriate and inappropriate uses of test results from such commercially distributed assessment instruments will be identified. For most classroom assessment, however, the measurement strategy should almost always be criterion referenced rather than norm referenced.

Selected Responses and Constructed Responses

Assuming that a classroom teacher has come up with a reasonable answer to the what-to-assess question, an important point in determining how to assess it arises when the teacher must choose between assessment strategies that elicit selected responses or constructed responses from students. If you think for a moment about the way educators assess students' educational status, you'll realize that there are really only two kinds of responses students can make. Students select their responses from alternatives we present to them—for example, when we give students multiple-choice tests and their responses must be selected from each item's available options. Other examples of selected-response assessment procedures are binary-choice tests such as the true-false tests where, for each item, students must select either a true or a false answer.

In contrast to selected-response sorts of tests, students construct all kinds of responses. In an English class, for instance, students construct original essays. In a woodshop class, students construct end tables. In a speech class, students construct five-minute oral speeches. In a drama class, students construct their responses while they present a one-act play. In a homemaking class, students construct soufflés and upside-down cakes. Constructed-response tests lead either to student *products,* such as the end tables or soufflés, or *behaviors,* such as the speeches and the one-act plays. When the students' constructed responses take the form of tangible product, classroom teachers have the luxury of judging the quality of the product at their leisure. For instance, once students create an original essay, the teacher can take that product home on the weekend and, while relaxing in the jacuzzi, either grade or immerse the essays.

When the students' constructed responses are in the form of behavior, however, such as when students are asked in a physical education class to run a mile in less than 12 minutes, the teacher must somehow make a record of the behavior or else it disappears. The record might be created by the teacher's completion of written records or be captured electronically via an audio or video recording. For example, when students in a speech class give a series of impromptu speeches, the teacher typically fills out some sort of evaluation form for each speech. Similarly, physical education teachers use their stopwatches to note how much time it takes for students to run a mile, then note the elapsed time in a record book.

It used to be thought that although selected-response tests were difficult to create, they were easy to score. Similarly, it was believed that constructed-response tests were just the opposite—simple to create but tough to score. These days, however, as educators have become more sophisticated about constructed-response tests and are employing many more types of constructed-response assessment procedures than only essay tests or short-answer tests, it is generally conceded that both selected-response and constructed-response tests require considerable care when being created. It is still true, however, that the scoring of selected-response tests is substantially easier than the scoring of constructed-response tests.

If, as a classroom teacher, you're really considering these two assessment schemes, you need to focus less on the ease of scoring students' responses than on the nature of the score-based inference you wish to make. Some score-based inferences simply shriek out for selected-response assessment schemes. For instance, if you want to make inferences about how many historical facts your students know, a selected-response procedure will fill the bill and be simple to score. Other

Parent Talk •••

Suppose that Ms. Collins, a parent of one of your students, has cornered you after school and asked for a few minutes of your time. She wants to know what all the talk about "new, challenging standards" really means. She's read an article about educational standards in the local newspaper, and she wonders whether the "new" standards are really new. Her question to you is, "Why is there all this fuss about educational standards these days when it seems that teachers in this school are still teaching pretty much what they've always taught and testing what they've always tested?"

••• *If I were you, here's how I'd respond to Ms. Collins:*

"I really understand your concern about educational standards, Mrs. Collins. They've certainly been receiving plenty of attention from educators during recent years. But, regrettably, there's still a fair amount of confusion about standards, even among educators.

"Actually, there are two kinds of educational standards that you and I need to consider. A *content standard* simply identifies the skills and knowledge we want students to acquire in school. For example, your daughter has recently been improving her composition skills quite dramatically. She can now write narrative and persuasive essays that are quite wonderful. An example of a content standard would be *written communication skills.*

"A *performance standard,* on the other hand, indicates *how well* a content standard should be mastered. We score students' essays on a four-point scale, and the school's teachers have agreed that a student should achieve at least a three in written communication to be considered satisfactory.

"What we now call *content standards,* we used to describe as goals, objectives, or outcomes. What we now call *performance standards,* we used to describe as passing levels or cut scores. So some of the descriptive labels may be new, but the central idea of trying to teach children important skills and knowledge—that hasn't really changed very much.

"What is new, at least to me, is a much greater concern about the *defensibility* of our content and performance standards. All across the nation, educators are being urged to adopt more challenging standards—standards that demand more of our children. This has been taking place in our school, as well. So if you look more closely at what we're teaching and testing here, I think you'll see important differences in the kinds of skills and knowledge we're pursuing—and the levels of excellence we expect of our students."

••• *Now, how would you respond to Ms. Collins?*

score-based inferences you might wish to make really require students to display complex behavior, not merely choose among options. If, for example, you want to make inferences about how well students can compose sonnets, then selected-response assessment schemes just won't get the job done. To see if students can churn out a sonnet, you need to have them construct sonnets. Reliance on a selected-response test in such a situation would be psychometrically silly. It is, as usual, the *test-based inference* the teacher needs to make that should guide the choice between selected-response and constructed-response assessment strategies.

It is always possible, of course, for teachers to rely on both of these two assessment strategies in their classrooms. A given assessment, for instance, might represent a blend of both selected- and constructed-response approaches. As always, the assessment procedure should be employed to help the teacher get a fix on the students' status with respect to an otherwise unobservable variable in which the teacher is interested.

A Profusion of Item Types

Beyond the basic constructed-response versus selected-response distinction just considered, there are numerous types of items available for inclusion in classroom assessment procedures. Certain of these item types have been employed for many, many years. The essay test, for example, has probably been around since Socrates was strutting his instructional stuff. Multiple-choice tests have been with us for more than a century. True-false tests were probably used, at least in oral form, by prehistoric teachers who might have put such true-false toughies to their students as "True or False: Today's dinosaur was a leaf-munching brontosaurus rather than a people-munching tyrannosaurus rex."

During the recent years, however, there have been some significant advances in educational measurement procedures so that, for example, many educational measurement specialists now advocate wider use of *portfolio assessment* and *performance assessment*. These significant new item types must now be added to the menu of assessment alternatives open to today's classroom teacher. In the next several chapters I'll be describing how to create classroom assessments using all of the major item types now available in the classroom teacher's assessment arsenal.

We're going to start off with the more traditional sorts of selected- and constructed-response types of tests because, quite frankly, you're more likely to be familiar with those item types and you'll have less difficulty in learning about how to crank out, for instance, a simply splendid short-answer test item. Thereafter, in separate chapters, we'll be considering portfolios and how they can be used for classroom assessment, as well as performance tests and how they can be employed. After that, we'll deal with the special kinds of item types to be used when you're trying to get a fix on students' affective status.

As a preview, then, in the next few chapters, you'll be encountering the following types of items that can be employed in classroom assessments:

- Binary-choice items (Chapter 6)
- Multiple binary-choice items (Chapter 6)
- Multiple-choice items (Chapter 6)
- Matching items (Chapter 6)
- Short-answer items (Chapter 7)
- Essay items (Chapter 7)
- Observational approaches (Chapter 8)
- Performance tests (Chapter 8)
- Portfolios (Chapter 9)
- Affective assessment procedures (Chapter 10)

As you can see, there are plenty of options open to classroom teachers when it comes to item types. When I was preparing to be a classroom teacher in the 1950s, my professors familiarized me with several different item types (all as traditional as they could be), then encouraged me to employ different types of items "for variety's sake." That, to be honest, was dumb advice. Classroom assessment is not like a fashion show where you need to change styles in your examinations simply to maintain students' interest.

When you're choosing among item types, select the one (or ones) that best allows you to make the test-based inference in which you're interested and the decision that's linked to it. Sometimes it won't make all that much difference which type of item you choose. I suspect that in many instances it really isn't the case that a batch of multiple-choice items is vastly superior to a set of matching items. In other cases, however, there will be substantial differences in the suitability of differing item types. To make your own choice, simply ask yourself the question, Will my students' responses to this type of item allow me to reach a defensible inference that I need to help me make the educational decision facing me?

As we consider various types of items in the next five chapters, you'll become more conversant with the particulars of each item type, and thus more skilled in differentiating their utility to you in your own classroom assessment.

What Do Classroom Teachers Really Need to Know about What to Assess and How to Assess It? ....

What is the main message of this chapter for classroom teachers who must decide what to assess and how to assess it? The answer is rather straightforward. All you need to do is to think seriously about both questions. Any experienced teacher will, if pressed, confess that instructional inertia plays a key role in what usually goes on in the teacher's classroom. Classroom teachers find it far easier to engage in activities this year than they engaged in last year simply because it takes less effort to employ "same-old, same-old" instructional procedures than to install new instructional procedures. There's also assessment inertia that inclines teachers to rely on whatever assessment schemes they've previously utilized. It's so much simpler to massage last year's true-false exams than to whip out a brand new performance test.

In recognition of these all-too-human tendencies to adopt the path of least resistance, it becomes more important to try to "get it right the first time" or, putting it in more pedantic parlance, to "eschew egregiously inferior initial assessment conceptualizations." In other words, the more up-front thought that teachers give to answering the what-to-assess and how-to-assess-it questions, the more likely they'll be to avoid the kind of serious assessment errors that, because of practical pressures, may plague them for years.

You really do need to acquire some familiarity with the three taxonomic domains. Many educators pepper their language with references to cognitive, psychomotor, or affective educational outcomes. Just so you don't look like a ninny at faculty meetings when folks use such terms, a little knowledge about the three domains will prove useful. (And knowledge, of course, is only at the lowest level of the cognitive domain.)

You also need to know that a small number of broad-scope instructional objectives can prove useful to you in deciding what to assess, but that a litany of small-scope objectives won't help you much in your instruction or your assessment because you're apt to be overwhelmed by them. And a review of documents containing relevant content standards is almost always going to be of some help to you. Most importantly, however, is the idea that you need to devote serious up-front thought to the decisions that you want your classroom assessment to inform, then assess your students in accord with those decision options.

Chapter Summary ....

Two major questions guided the content of this chapter—namely, what should a classroom teacher assess and, having answered that question, how should it be assessed? It was contended that both of these decisions must be primarily influenced by the decisions that the teacher hopes to illuminate by gathering assessment data from students.

In determining what to assess, it was suggested that instructional objectives could play a prominent role in the teacher's choice of assessment emphases. In particular, broad-scope measurable objectives were recommended as helpful vehicles for identifying potential assessment targets. The three domains of student outcomes contained in Bloom's *Taxonomies of Educational Objectives* were also suggested as a helpful framework to decide whether there are instructional and assessment overemphases on cognitive outcomes and, if so, whether too much instruction and assessment attention was being given to the lowest level of that taxonomy. Two other considerations recommended when teachers set out to answer the what-to-assess question were (1) the content standards recommended by national organizations and (2) the views of colleagues.

When addressing the how-to-assess-it question, the chapter dealt with three topics. First, a distinction was drawn between norm-referenced and criterion-referenced assessment approaches. It was suggested that the bulk of a classroom teacher's assessment needs will be better served by criterion-referenced rather than norm-referenced interpretations because criterion-referenced interpretations tend to provide teachers with a clearer picture of what it is that students can or can't do. A discussion of selected-response and constructed-response test options was concluded with a listing of the numerous types of assessment items that classroom teachers have at their disposal. It was suggested that because descriptions of how these various types of test items should be constructed will be provided in the book's next five chapters, the reader hold off on deciding which item types for which decisions until those five chapters have been read.

Self-Check

We'll set off this chapter's self-check exercises with several binary-choice items. Look over the following five instructional objectives, then decide whether each is small scope (S S) or broad scope (B S).

1. Students will be able to select, from four options, the correct answer to any double-digit multiplication problem. (S S or B S?)

2. At the end of the Australasia unit, students will write, without prompting, 10 new facts learned about the geography of Australia or New Zealand. (S S or B S?)

3. When presented with descriptions of educational research situations requiring statistical analyses, students will be able to choose the appropriate analytic technique from any of the 40 statistical procedures treated during the statistics course. (S S or B S?)

4. The student will correctly spell aloud any 10 of the words the teacher identifies from the 50-word "spelling terrors" test. (S S or B S?)

5. The student will be able to write an original essay that suitably synthesizes any three related but dissimilar newspaper articles on the same general topic. (S S or B S?)

Let's turn now to a little taxonomic tussling. For the next five exercises, decide whether the assessment activity described is primarily affective, psychomotor, or cognitive. And, if it's cognitive, whether it's at the lowest level of that taxonomy (that is, knowledge) or at a higher than lowest level of taxonomy (that is, at any of the other five cognitive levels). These questions will be followed with three short-answer items.

6. The teacher observes how students seat themselves in the cafeteria as a reflection of their feelings about members of ethnic groups other than their own. What is the chief focus of this assessment activity?
   a. Affective
   b. Psychomotor
   c. Cognitive—lowest level
   d. Cognitive—higher than lowest level

7. Students are given previously unencountered examples of student compositions, then asked to classify them according to whether each composition is an example of narrative, persuasive, expository, or descriptive writing. What is the chief focus of this assessment task?
   a. Affective
   b. Psychomotor
   c. Cognitive—lowest level
   d. Cognitive—higher than lowest level

8. A business teacher is checking students' word-entry speed on microcomputers. What is the chief focus of this assessment task?
   a. Affective
   b. Psychomotor
   c. Cognitive—lowest level
   d. Cognitive—higher than lowest level

9. Students are asked by their chemistry teacher to name the chemical ingredients in 25 widely used chemical compounds. What is the chief focus of this assessment task?
   a. Affective
   b. Psychomotor
   c. Cognitive—lowest level
   d. Cognitive—higher than lowest level

10. Students must solve a complex word problem in mathematics and show their work to indicate that one of three acceptable solution analyses has been employed. What is the chief focus of this assessment task?
    a. Affective
    b. Psychomotor
    c. Cognitive—lowest level
    d. Cognitive—higher than lowest level

11. What are the key differences among the following three kinds of educational standards: content, performance, and opportunity-to-learn?

_____

_____

_____

12. Supply at least two examples of constructed-response test tasks and at least two examples of selected-response test tasks.

_____

_____

_____

13. What is the critical difference between norm-referenced and criterion-referenced approaches to educational measurement?

_____

_____

_____

Pondertime

1. It was argued in the chapter that most classroom assessment tasks call for criterion-referenced approaches to measurement. Do you agree? Why or why not?

2. Why should/shouldn't classroom teachers simply teach toward the content standards isolated by national groups? If teachers don't, are they unpatriotic?

3. Are there any educational settings you can think of in which the teacher should never wish to assess higher-level cognitive outcomes? How about never assessing affect? Explain.

4. Suppose you were asked to give your best answer to the question, How should a classroom teacher decide what to assess? How would you respond?

5. Suppose you were asked to give your best answer to the question, How should a classroom teacher decide to assess whatever has been determined to be assessed? How would you respond?

Self-Check Key

The answers for the first five self-check exercises should have been these: 1: S S, 2: S S, 3: B S, 4: S S (although, as the number of words on the list gets longer, the objective becomes more broad in its scope), 5: B S.

For the next five taxonomic teasers, you should have come up with these answers: 6:a, 7:d, 8:b, 9:c, 10:d.

11. Your answer should have approximated the distinctions drawn among the three standards that was provided on page 92.

12. You might have supplied examples such as these:

    Constructed-response test tasks: Compose a sonnet; give an impromptu speech; create a watercolor; or produce and direct a major motion picture.

    Selected-response test tasks: Choose from multiple-choice options; select true or false for each statement; from three choices select the most (or least) plausible solution for the problem presented; or select from three major motion pictures that would be most likely to get universal "thumbs up" from film critics.

13. At bottom, norm-referenced assessment approaches require *interpretations* of test scores based on the examinee's performance relative to that of other examinees. In contrast, criterion-referenced assessment approaches require *interpretations* of test scores according to the degree of a clearly defined assessment domain that the examinee has mastered.

Endnote

1. See, for example, *Designing a Comprehensive Guide to Standards-Based Districts, Schools, and Classrooms* by Robert J. Marzano and John S. Kendall (Aurora, CO: McREL, 1996).

Additional Stuff

Bloom, B. S. et al. *Taxonomy of Educational Objectives: Handbook I: Cognitive Domain*. New York: David McKay, 1956.

Burz, Helen L., and Kit Marshall. *Performance-Based Curriculum for Language Arts: From Knowing to Showing*. Thousand Oaks, CA: Corwin Press, 1997.

Burz, Helen L., and Kit Marshall. *Performance-Based Curriculum for Science: From Knowing to Showing*. Thousand Oaks, CA: Corwin Press, 1997.

Burz, Helen L., and Kit Marshall. *Performance-Based Curriculum for Social Studies: From Knowing to Showing*. Thousand Oaks, CA: Corwin Press, 1997.

Burz, Helen L., and Kit Marshall. *Performance-Based Curriculum for Mathematics: From Knowing to Showing*. Thousand Oaks, CA: Corwin Press, 1996.

Frisbie, David A., Diane U. Miranda, and Kristin K. Baker. "An Evaluation of Elementary Textbook Tests as Classroom Assessment Tools." *Applied Measurement in Education*, 6, no. 1 (1993): 21–36.

Harp, Bill (Ed.). *Assessment and Evaluation in Whole Language Programs*. Norwood, MA: Gordon Publishers, 1993.

Jervis, Kathe, and Joseph McDonald. "Standards: The Philosophical Monster in the Classroom." *Phi Delta Kappan*, 77, no. 8 (April 1996): 563–569.

Krathwohl, D. R. et al. *Taxonomy of Educational Objectives: Handbook II: Affective Domain.* New York: David McKay, 1964.

Lewis, Anne C. "An Overview of the Standards Movement." *Phi Delta Kappan,* 76, no. 10 (June 1995): 744–750.

Marzano, Robert J., and John S. Kendall. *A Comprehensive Guide to Designing Standards-Based Districts, Schools, and Classrooms.* Aurora, CO: McREL (Mid-Continent Regional Educational Laboratory), 1996.

Martin, Jane Roland. "There's Too Much to Teach: Cultural Wealth in an Age of Scarcity." *Educational Researcher,* 25, no. 2 (March 1996): 4–10, 16.

McMillan, James H. *Classroom Assessment: Principles and Practice for Effective Instruction.* Boston: Allyn and Bacon, 1997.

Rhodes, Lynn K. (Ed.). *Literacy Assessment: A Handbook of Instruments.* Portsmouth, NH: Heinemann, 1993.

Rothman, Robert. *Measuring Up: Standards, Assessments, and School Reform.* San Francisco: Jossey-Bass, 1995.

Stiggins, Richard J. *Student-Centered Classroom Assessment* (2nd ed.). Upper Saddle River, NJ: Prentice Hall, 1997.

Wainer, Howard, and David Thissen. "Combining Multiple-Choice and Constructed-Response Test Scores Toward a Marxist Theory of Test Construction." *Applied Measurement in Education,* 6, no. 2 (1993): 103–118.

Nonprint Stuff

American Educational Research Association. *Criterion-Referenced Measurement: A 30-Year Retrospection* (Cassette Recording No. RA 3-3230). Chicago: Teach 'Em, April 14, 1993.

Dusewicz, Russel A. *How to Make a Better Test: Part I* (Videotape #906-1A). Livingston, NJ: NASSP InService Video Network.

Dusewicz, Russel A. *How to Make a Better Test: Part II* (Videotape #906-2A). Livingston, NJ: NASSP InService Video Network.

Northwest Regional Laboratory. *Measuring Thinking in the Classroom* (Videotape #NREL-5A). Los Angeles: IOX Assessment Associates.

Northwest Regional Laboratory. *Assessing Reading Proficiency* (Videotape #NREL-6A). Los Angeles: IOX Assessment Associates.

Northwest Regional Laboratory. *Assessing Mathematical Power* (Videotape #NREL-11A). Los Angeles: IOX Assessment Associates.

Northwest Regional Laboratory. *Assessment in the Science Classroom* (Videotape #NREL-12A). Los Angeles: IOX Assessment Associates.

Popham, W. James, and Sarah J. Stanley. *Norm-Referenced Tests: Uses and Misuses* (Videotape #ETVT-32A). Los Angeles: IOX Assessment Associates.

Popham, W. James, and Sarah J. Stanley. *Criterion-Referenced Measurement: Today's Alternative to Traditional Testing* (Videotape #ETVT-35A). Los Angeles: IOX Assessment Associates.

6

···

Selected-Response
Tests

*I*n this and the following four chapters, you will learn how to construct almost a dozen different kinds of test items that you might wish to use for your own classroom assessments. As suggested in the preceding chapter, you really need to choose item types that mesh properly with the inferences you want to make about students—and to be sure that those inferences are directly linked to the educational decisions you need to make. Just as the child who's convinced that vanilla is ice cream's only flavor won't benefit from a 36-flavor ice cream emporium, the more item types you know about, the more appropriate your selection of item types will be. In this chapter and the next four, you'll be learning about blackberry-ripple exams and mocha-mango assessment devices.

Let me level with you regarding what you can really expect after wading through the exhilarating exposition about item construction contained in the next five chapters. Unless you're a remarkably quick study, you'll probably finish the chapters and *not* be instantly transformed into a consummately skilled test constructor. It takes more than reading a set of fairly brief chapters to turn someone into a capable item developer. But just as the journey of a thousand miles begins with a single toe wiggle, you'll have initiated a tentative trot toward the Test Construction Hall of Fame. You'll have learned the essentials of how to construct the most common kinds of classroom assessments.

What you'll need after you complete the five test-construction chapters is tons of practice in churning out classroom assessment devices. And, if you remain in teaching for a while, such practice opportunities will surely come your way. Ideally, you'll be able to get some feedback about the quality of your classroom assessment procedures from a supervisor or colleague who is clearheaded and/or conversant with educational measurement. If a competent cohort critiques your test-construction efforts, you'll profit by being able to make needed modifications in how you create your classroom assessment instruments.

Ten (Divided by Two)
Item–Writing Commandments . . . .

As you can discern from this chapter's title, it's going to describe how to construct selected-response kinds of test items. You'll learn how to create four different varieties of selected-response test items—namely, binary-choice items, multiple binary-choice items, multiple-choice items, and matching items. All four of these selected-response kinds of items can be used effectively by teachers to derive defensible inferences about students' cognitive status—that is, the knowledge and skills that teachers typically try to promote in their students.

But no matter whether you're developing selected-response or constructed-response kinds of test items, there are several general guidelines that, if adhered to, will lead to better assessment procedures. And, because the original Ten Commandments were stated in fairly stern "Thou shall not" form and have proved successful in shaping many folks' behavior, I shall now dish out five general item-writing commandments structured along the same lines. If followed, these commandments won't get you into heaven, but they will make your assessment schemes slightly more divine. All five commandments are presented in the box below. (I had requested the use of stone tablets, but the publisher instantly dismissed such whimsy.) A subsequent discussion of each commandment will help you understand how to adhere to the five item-writing mandates being discussed. It will help if you refer to each of the following item-writing commandments before reading the discussion of that commandment.

Five General Item–Writing Commandments

1. Thou shall not provide opaque directions to students regarding how to respond to your assessment instruments.
2. Thou shall not employ ambiguous statements in your assessment items.
3. Thou shall not provide students with unintentional clues regarding appropriate responses.
4. Thou shall not employ complex syntax in your assessment items.
5. Thou shall not use vocabulary that is more advanced than required.

Opaque Directions

The first item-writing commandment deals with a topic most teachers haven't thought seriously about—the directions for their classroom tests. Teachers who have been laboring to construct a collection of test items typically know those items very well. Thus, because of the teacher's intimate knowledge not only of the items but also how students are supposed to respond to those items, it is often the case that only sketchy directions are provided to students regarding how to respond to a test's items. Yet, of course, unclear test-taking directions can lead to confused test takers. And the responses of confused test takers don't lead to very accurate inferences about those test takers.

Flawed test directions are particularly problematic when students are being introduced to forms of assessment with which they're not all that familiar, such as the performance tests I'll be describing in Chapter 8 or the multiple binary-choice tests to be discussed later in this chapter. It is useful to create directions for examinees early in the game when you're developing an assessment instrument. When generated as a last-minute afterthought, test directions typically turn out to be tawdry.

Ambiguous Statements

The second item-writing commandment deals with ambiguity. In all kinds of classroom assessments, ambiguous writing is to be avoided. If your students aren't really sure about what you mean in the tasks you present to them, the students are apt to misinterpret what you're saying and, as a consequence, come up with incorrect responses even though they might really know how to respond correctly. For example, sentences in which pronouns are used can frequently be unclear about the individual or individuals to whom the pronoun refers. Suppose, in a true-false test item, you asked your students to indicate whether the following statement was true or false: "Leaders of developing nations have tended to distrust leaders of developed nations because of their imperialistic tendencies." Because it is ambiguous regarding whether the pronoun *their* refers to the "leaders of developing nations" or to the "leaders of developed nations," and because the truth or falsity of the statement depends on the pronoun's referent, students are likely to be confused.

Because you will typically be writing your own assessment items, *you* will know what you mean. At least you ought to. However, try to slide yourself, at least figuratively, into the shoes of your students. Reread your assessment items from the perspective of the students, and modify any statements that might be ambiguous to those less well-informed students.

Unintended Clues

The third of our item-writing commandments calls for you to *intentionally* avoid something *unintentional*. Well, nobody said that commandment following was going to be easy! What this commandment is trying to sensitize you to is the tendency of test-development novices to inadvertently provide clues to students about appropriate responses. As a consequence, students come up with correct responses even if they don't possess the knowledge or skill being assessed.

For example, inexperienced item writers often tend to make the correct answer to multiple-choice items twice as long as the incorrect answers. Even clucko students will opt for the lengthy response; they get so many more words for their choice. As another example of how inexperienced item writers unintentionally dispense clues, absolute qualifiers such as *never* and *always* are sometimes used for the false items in a true-false test. Because even uninformed students know that there are few absolutes in this world, they gleefully (and often unthinkingly) indicate that such items are false. One of the most blatant examples of unintended clue giving occurs when writers of multiple-choice test items initiate those items with incomplete statements such as "The bird in the story was an . . ." then offer answer options in which only the correct answer begins with a vowel. For instance, even though you never read the story referred to in the previous incomplete statement, if you encountered the following four response options, I bet you'd know the correct answer: A. Falcon, B. Hawk, C. Robin, D. Owl. The article *an* gives the game away.

Unintended clues are seen more frequently with selected-response items than constructed-response items, but even in supplying background information to students for complicated constructed-response items, the teacher must be wary of unintentionally pointing even unknowledgeable students down the correct-response trail.

Complex Syntax

Complex syntax, although it sounds like an exotic surcharge on cigarettes and alcohol, is often encountered in the assessment items of neophyte item writers. Even though some teachers may regard themselves as Steinbecks-in-hiding, assessment procedures are no setting in which to wax eloquent. This fourth item-writing commandment directs you to avoid complicated sentence constructions and, instead, use very simple sentences. Although esteemed writers such as Thomas Harding and James Joyce are known for their convoluted and clause-laden writing styles, I'll wager they would have been mediocre item writers. Too many clauses, except at Christmas-time, mess up test items. (For readers needing a clue to the previous sentence's cryptic meaning, think of a red-garbed guy who brings presents.)

Difficult Vocabulary

Our fifth and final item-writing commandment is fairly straightforward. It indicates that when writing educational assessment items, *you should eschew obfuscative verbiage.* In other words, in almost *any* other words, use vocabulary suitable for the students who'll be taking your tests. Assessment time is not the occasion for you to trot out your best collection of polysyllabic terms or to secure thesaurus-induced thrills. The more advanced the vocabulary level is in your assessment devices, the more likely you'll fail to get a good fix on your students' status. They will have been laid low by the overblown vocabulary. In the case of the terminology to be used in classroom assessment instruments, simple wins.

In review, you've now seen five item-writing commandments that apply to any kind of classroom assessment device you develop. They certainly apply to tests containing selected-response items. And that's what we'll be looking at in the rest of the chapter. More specifically, you'll be encountering a series of item-writing guidelines that should be followed when constructing particular kinds of selected-response items. The guidelines are based either on empirical research evidence or on decades of teachers' experience in using such items. If you opt to use any of the item types to be described, try to follow the guidelines for that kind of item. Your tests will typically turn out to be better than if you hadn't.

Binary-Choice Items ....

A *binary-choice item* gives students only two options from which to select. The most common form of binary-choice item is the true-false item. Educators have been using true-false tests probably as far back as Socrates. (True or False: Plato was a type of serving-dish used by Greeks for special meals.) Other variations of binary-choice items would be those in which students must choose between yes-no, right-wrong, correct-incorrect, fact-opinion, and so on.

The virtue of binary-choice items is they are typically so terse that students can answer many items in a short time. Therefore, it is possible to cover a large amount of content in a brief assessment session. The greatest weakness of binary-choice items is that, because there are only two options, students have a 50-50 chance of guessing the correct answer even if they don't have the foggiest idea of what's correct. If a large number of binary-choice items are used, however, that weakness tends to evaporate. After all, although students might guess their way correctly through a few binary-choice items, they would need to be extraordinarily lucky to guess their way correctly through 30 such items.

Here are five item-writing guidelines for binary-choice items. A brief discussion of each guideline is provided in the following paragraphs.

Item-Writing Guidelines for Binary-Choice Items

1. Phrase items so that a superficial analysis by the student suggests a wrong answer.
2. Rarely use negative statements, and never use double negatives.
3. Include only one concept in each statement.
4. Have an approximately equal number of items representing the two categories being tested.
5. Keep item length similar for both categories being tested.

Phrasing Items to Elicit Thoughtfulness

Typically, binary items are quite brief, but brevity need not reflect simplistic choices for examinees. In order to get the most payoff from binary-choice items, you'll want to phrase items so that students who approach the items superficially will answer them incorrectly. Thus, if you were creating the items for a true-false test, you would construct statements for your items that were not blatantly true or blatantly false. Blatancy in items rarely leads to accurate inferences about students. Beyond blatancy avoidance, however, you should phrase at least some of the items so that if students approach them unthinkingly, they'll choose false for a true statement and vice versa. What you're trying to do is to get students to *think* about your test items, and thereby give you a better idea about how much good thinking they can do.

Minimizing Negatives

With binary-choice items, many students have a really difficult time responding to negatively phrased items. For instance, suppose that in a true-false test you were asked to decide about the truth or falsity of the following statement: "The League of Nations was not formed immediately after the conclusion of World War II." What the item is looking for as a correct answer to this statement is *true*, because the League of Nations was in existence prior to World War II. Yet, the existence of the *not* in the item really will confuse some students. They'll be apt to answer *false* even if they know that the League of Nations was functioning before World War II commenced.

Because I've churned out my share of true-false items over the years, I know all too well how tempting it is to simply insert a *not* into an otherwise true statement. But don't yield to the temptation. Only rarely succumb to the lure of the nagging negative in binary-choice items. Items containing double negatives or triple negatives (if you could contrive one) are obviously to be avoided.

Avoiding Double-Concept Items

The third guideline for binary-choice items directs you to focus on only a single concept in each item. If you were creating a statement for a right-wrong test, and had an item in which half of the statement was clearly right and the other half was clearly wrong, you make it mighty difficult for students to respond correctly. The presence of two concepts in a single item, even if both are right or both are wrong, tends to confuse students and, as a consequence, yields test results that are apt to produce inaccurate inferences about those students.

Balancing Response Categories

If you're devising a binary-choice test, try to keep an approximately equal number of items representing the two response categories. For example, if it's a true-false test, make sure that you have somewhat similar proportions of true and false statements. It's not necessary to have exactly the same number of true and false items. The proportion of true and false items, however, should be roughly the same. This fourth guideline is quite easy to follow if you simply keep it in mind when creating your binary-choice items.

Maintaining Item-Length Similarity

The fifth guideline is similar to the fourth because it encourages you to structure your items so that there are no give-away clues associated with item length. If your two response categories are *accurate* and *inaccurate*, make sure that the length of the accurate statements is approximately the same as the length of the inaccurate statements. When creating true-false tests, there is a tendency to toss in qualifying clauses for the true statements so that those statements, properly qualified, are truly true—but also long! As a result, there's a systematic pattern wherein long statements are true and short statements are false. As soon as students catch on to this pattern, they can answer items correctly without even referring to an item's contents.

In review, we've considered five item-writing guidelines for binary-choice items. If you'll follow those guidelines and keep your wits about you when creating binary-choice items, you'll often find that this type of test will prove useful in the classroom. And that's true, not false.

Multiple Binary-Choice Items ....

A *multiple binary-choice item* is one in which a cluster of items is presented to students, requiring a binary response to *each* of the items in the cluster. Typically, but not always, the items are related to an initial statement or set of statements. Multiple binary-choice items are formatted so that they look like traditional multiple-choice tests. In a multiple-choice test, the student must choose one answer from several options, but in the multiple binary-choice test the student must make a response for each statement in the cluster. Figure 6.1 is an example of a multiple binary-choice item.

David Frisbie (1992) has reviewed the available research regarding such items and has concluded that multiple binary-choice items are (1) highly efficient for gathering student achievement data, (2) more reliable than other selected-response items, (3) able to measure the same skills and abilities as multiple-choice items dealing with comparable content, (4) a bit more difficult for students than multiple-choice tests, and (5) perceived by students to be more difficult but more efficient than multiple-choice items. Frisbie believes that when teachers construct

Figure 6.1   **An Illustrative Multiple True-False Item**

• • • Suppose that a dozen of your students completed a 10-item multiple-choice test and earned the following number of correct scores:

5, 6, 7, 7, 7, 7, 8, 8, 8, 8, 9, 10

9. The median for your students' scores is 7.5.   (True)
10. The mode for the set of scores is 8.0.   (False)
11. The range of the students' scores is 5.0.   (True)
12. The median is different than the mean.   (False)

multiple binary-choice items, they must be attentive to all of the usual considerations in writing regular binary-choice items. However, he suggests the following two additional guidelines.

> ### *Item-Writing Guidelines for Multiple Binary-Choice Items*
>
> 1. Separate item clusters vividly from one another.
> 2. Make certain that each item meshes well with the cluster's stimulus material.

Separating Clusters

Because many students are familiar with traditional multiple-choice items, and because each of those items is numbered, there is some danger that students may become confused by the absence of numbers where such numbers are ordinarily found. Thus, be sure to use some kind of formatting system to make it clear that a new cluster is commencing. In the illustrative item seen in Figure 6.1, notice that three dots (• • •) have been used to signify the beginning of a new cluster of items. You can use asterisks, lines, boxes, or some similar way of alerting students to the beginning of a new cluster.

Coordinating Items with Their Stem

In multiple-choice items, the first part of the item—the part preceding the response options—is called the *stem*. For multiple binary-choice items, we refer to the first part of the item cluster as the cluster's stem or stimulus material. The second item-writing guideline for this item type suggests that you make sure all items in a cluster are, in fact, linked in a meaningful way to the cluster's stem. If they're not, then you might as well use individual binary-choice items rather than multiple binary-choice items.

There's another compelling reason that you should consider adding multiple binary-choice items to your classroom assessment repertoire. Unlike traditional binary-choice items, for which it's likely students will need to rely on *memorized* information, that's rarely the case with multiple binary-choice items. It is rare, that is, *if* the stimulus materials contain content that's not been encountered previously by students. In other words, if the stem for a subset of multiple binary-choice items contains material that's new to the student, and if each binary-choice item depends directly on the previously unencountered content, it's dead certain the student will need to function above the knowledge level of Bloom's taxonomy. So, if you make certain your stimulus material for multiple-binary-choice items contains new content, those items will surely be more intellectually demanding than the run-of-the-memory true-false item.

In review, we've considered an item type that's not widely used but that has some special virtues. The major advantage of multiple binary-choice items is that students can respond to two or three such items in the time that it takes them to respond to a single multiple-choice item. Other things being equal, the more items that students respond to, the more reliably we can gauge their abilities.

I must confess to a mild bias toward this often overlooked item type because for over 20 years I used such tests as the final examinations in an introductory educational measurement course I taught in the UCLA Graduate School of Education. I'd give my students 20 one- or two-paragraph descriptions of previously unencountered educational measurement situations, then follow up each description with five binary-choice items. In all, then, I ended up with a 100-item final exam that really seemed to sort out those students who knew their stuff from those who didn't. The five items in each cluster were simply statements to which students were to respond *accurate* or *inaccurate.* I could just as appropriately have asked for *true* or *false* responses, but I tried to add a touch of suave to my exams. After all, I was teaching in a *Graduate* School of Education. (In retrospect, it seems a mite silly.) Nonetheless, I had pretty good luck with my 100-item final exams. I used a 50-item version for my midterm exams, and they worked well too. For certain kinds of purposes, I think you'll find that multiple binary-choice items will prove useful.

Multiple-Choice Items ....

For a number of decades, *multiple-choice test items* have dominated achievement testing in the United States and many other nations. Multiple-choice items can be used to measure a student's possession of knowledge or a student's ability to engage in higher levels of thinking. A strength of multiple-choice items is they can contain several answers that differ in their *relative* correctness. Thus, the examinee can be called on to make subtle distinctions among answer options, several of which may be somewhat correct. A weakness of multiple-choice items, as is the case with all selected-response items, is that examinees need only *recognize* a correct answer. They need not *generate* a correct answer. Although a fair amount of criticism has been heaped on multiple-choice items, particularly in recent years, properly constructed multiple-choice items can tap a rich variety of student skills and knowledge and can thus be a useful tool for classroom assessment.

The first part of a multiple-choice item, as noted earlier, is referred to as the item's *stem*. The potential answer options are described as an item's *alternatives*. Incorrect alternatives are typically referred to as the item's *distractors*. Two common ways of creating multiple-choice items are to use an item stem that is either a direct question or an incomplete statement. With younger students, the direct-question approach is preferable. Using either direct-question stems or incomplete-statement stems, a multiple-choice item can ask students to select either a correct answer or, instead, to select a best answer.

Figure 6.2   **Illustrative Multiple-Choice Items**

Direct-Question Form (best-answer version)

Which of the following modes of composition would be most effective in explaining to someone how a bill becomes a law in this nation?

    A. Narrative
 * B. Expository
    C. Persuasive
    D. Descriptive

Incomplete-Statement Form (correct-answer version)

Mickey Mouse's nephews are named

    A. Huey, Dewey, and Louie.
    B. Mutt and Jeff.
    C. Larry, Moe, and Curly.
 * D. Morty and Ferdie.

In Figure 6.2 there are examples of a direct-question item requesting a best-answer response and an incomplete-statement item requesting a correct-answer response.

Let's turn now to a consideration of item-writing guidelines for multiple-choice items. Because of the widespread use of multiple-choice items over the past half-century, there are quite a few experience-sired suggestions regarding how to create such items. Below, you'll find five of the more frequently cited recommendations for constructing multiple-choice items.

Item-Writing Guidelines for Multiple-Choice Items

1. The stem should consist of a self-contained question or problem.
2. Avoid negatively stated stems.
3. Do not let the length of alternatives supply unintended clues.
4. Randomly assign correct answers to alternative positions.
5. Never use "all-of-the-above" alternatives, but do use "none-of-the-above" alternatives to increase item difficulty.

Stem Stuffing

A properly constructed stem for a multiple-choice item will present a clearly described task to the student so that the student can then get to work on figuring out which of the item's options is best (if it's a best-answer item) or correct (if it's a correct-answer item). A poorly constructed stem for a multiple-choice item will force the student to read one or more of the alternatives in order to figure out what the item is getting at. In general, therefore, it's preferable to load as much of the item's content as possible into the stem. Lengthy stems and terse alternatives are, as a rule, much better than skimpy stems and long alternatives. You might try reading the stems of your multiple-choice items without any of the alternatives to see if the stems (either direct questions or incomplete statements) make sense all by themselves.

Knocking Negatively Stated Stems

It has been alleged, particularly by overly cautious individuals, that "one robin does not spring make." Without debating the causal relationship between seasonal shifts and feathered flyers, in multiple-choice item writing we could say with confidence that "one negative in an item stem does not confusion unmake." Negatives are strange commodities. A single *not*, tossed casually into a test item, can make students crazy. Besides, because *not* is such a tiny word, and might be overlooked by students, there's a chance that a number of students (who didn't see the *not*) will be trying to ferret out the best alternative for a positively stated stem that, in reality, is negative.

 For example, let's say you wanted to do a bit of probing of your students' knowledge of U.S. geography and phrased the stem of a multiple-choice item such as this: "Which one of the following cities is located in a state west of the Mississippi River?" If your alternatives were: A. San Diego, B. Pittsburgh, C. Boston, and D. Atlanta, students would have little difficulty in knowing how to respond. Let's say, however, that you decided to add a little difficulty by using the same alternatives but tossing in a *not*. Now your item's stem might read something like this: "Which one of the following cities is not located in a state east of the Mississippi River?" For this version of the item, the student who failed to spot the *not* (this, in psychometric circles, is known as not-spotting) would be in big trouble.

 By the way, note that in both stems, the student was asked to identify which *one* of the following answers was correct. If you leave the *one* out, a student might have interpreted the question to mean that there were two or more cities being sought.

 If there is a compelling reason for using a negative in the stem of a multiple-choice item, be sure to highlight the negative with italics, boldface type, or underscoring so that students who are not natural not-spotters will have a fair chance to answer the item correctly.

Attending to Alternative Length

Novice item writers often fail to realize that the length of a multiple-choice item's alternatives can give away what the correct answer is. Let's say choices A, B, and C say blah, blah, blah, but choice D says blah, blah, blah, blah, blah, and blah. The crafty student will be inclined to opt for choice D not simply because one gets

Multiple-Guess Test Items? ....

For all six years that he has taught, Leroy Larson has worked with fifth-graders. Although Leroy enjoys all content areas, he takes special pride in his reading instruction because he believes that his students enter the sixth grade with dramatically improved comprehension capabilities. Leroy spends little time trying to promote his students' isolated reading skills but, instead, places great emphasis on having students "construct their own meanings" from what they have read.

All of Leroy's reading tests consist exclusively of four-option, multiple-choice items. As Leroy puts it, "I can put together a really mean multiple-choice item when I put my mind to it." Because he has put his mind to it many times during the past six years, Leroy is quite satisfied that his reading tests are as good as his reading instruction.

At the most recent open house night at his school, however, a group of five parents registered genuine unhappiness with the exclusive multiple-choice makeup of Leroy's reading tests. The parents had obviously been comparing notes prior to that time, and Mrs. Jenkins (the mother of one of Leroy's fifth-graders) acted as their spokesperson. In brief, Mrs. Jenkins argued that multiple-choice tests permitted even weak students to "guess their way to good scores." "After all," Mrs. Jenkins pointed out, "do you want to produce good readers or good guessers?"

Surprised and somewhat shaken by this incident, Leroy has been rethinking his approach to reading assessment. He concludes that he can (1) stick with his tests as they are, (2) add some short-answer or essay items to his tests, or (3) replace all of his multiple-choice items with open-ended items. As he considers these options, he realizes that he has given himself a multiple-choice decision!

If you were Leroy, what would your decision be?

---

many more blahs for one's selection, but because the student will figure out the teacher has given so much attention to choice D that there must be something special about it.

Thus, when you're whipping up your alternatives for multiple-choice clues, try either to keep all the alternatives about the same length or, if that isn't possible, to have at least two alternatives be of approximately equal length. For instance, if you were using four-alternative items, you might have two fairly short alternatives and two fairly long alternatives. What you want to avoid, of course, is having the correct alternative be one length (either short or long) while the distractors are all another length.

Incidentally, the number of alternatives is really up to you. Most frequently, we see multiple-choice items with four or five alternatives. Because students can guess correct answers more readily with fewer alternatives, three alternatives are not seen all that often except with younger students. Having more than five alternatives puts a pretty heavy reading load on the student. I've usually employed four alternatives on my own multiple-choice tests, but in a few instances, the nature of the test's content has led me to use five alternatives.

Assigning Correct Answer Positions

A fourth guideline for writing multiple-choice items is to make sure that you scatter your correct answers among your alternatives so that students don't "guess their way to high scores" simply by figuring out that your favorite correct answer spot is, for instance, choice D or perhaps choice C. Many novice item writers are reluctant to put the correct answer in the choice-A position because they believe it gives away the correct answer too early. Yet, the choice-A position deserves its share of correct answers too. Absence-of-bias should also apply to answer-choice options.

As a rule of thumb, if you have four-alternative items, try to assign roughly 25% of your correct answers to each of the four positions. It may be necessary to do some last-minute shifting of answer positions in order to achieve what is essentially a random assignment of correct answers to the available positions. But always do a last-minute check on your multiple-choice tests to see that you haven't accidentally overbooked your correct answers too heavily in a particular answer-choice position.

Dealing with "of-the-above" Alternatives

Sometimes a beginning item writer who's trying to come up with four (or five) reasonable alternatives will toss in a none-of-the-above or an all-of-the-above alternative simply as a "filler" alternative. But both of these options must be considered more carefully.

The fifth guideline for this item type says quite clearly that you should never use the all-of-the-above alternative. Here's the reason why. Let's say you're using a five-option type of multiple-choice item and you want to set up the item so that the fifth option (choice E), "all of the above," would be correct. This means that the first four answers, choices A through D, would all have to be correct. The problem with such an item is that even a student who only knows that two of the first four alternatives are correct will be able to select the all-of-the-above response because if any two responses are correct, choice E is the only possible best answer. Even worse, some students will read only the first alternative, see that it is correct, mark choice A on their response sheet, and move on to the next test item without going over the full array of alternatives for that item. For either of these reasons, you should never use an all-of-the-above alternative in your multiple-choice items.

What about the none-of-the above alternative? The guideline indicates that it should be used when you wish to increase an item's difficulty. You should do so only when the presence of the none-of-the-above alternative will help you make the kind of test-based inference you want to make. To illustrate, let's say you wanted to find out how well your students could perform basic mathematical operations such as multiplying and dividing. Moreover, you want to be confident that your students can really perform the computations either "in their heads," by using scratch paper, or by employing a hand-held calculator. Now, if you use only four-alternative multiple-choice items, there's a real likelihood that certain

Parent Talk ·····································

Assume that you've been using a fair number of multiple-choice items in your classroom examinations. Benito's parents, Mr. and Mrs. Olmedo, have set up a 15-minute conference with you during a Back-to-Classroom Night to talk about Benito's progress.

When they arrive, they soon get around to the topic in which they are most interested—namely, your multiple-choice test items. As Mr. Olmedo puts it, "We want our son to learn to use his mind, not his memory. Although my wife and I have little experience with multiple-choice tests because almost all of our school exams were of an essay nature, we believe that multiple-choice tests measure only what Benito has memorized. He has a good memory, as you've probably found out, but we want more for him. Why are you using such low-level test items?"

• • • *If I were you, here's how I'd respond to Mr. Olmedo's question:*

"I appreciate your coming in to talk about Benito's education and, in particular, the way he is being assessed. And I also realize that recently there has been a good deal of criticism of multiple-choice test items. More often than not, such criticism is altogether appropriate. In far too many cases, because multiple-choice items are easy to score, they're used to assess just about everything. And, all too often, those kinds of items do indeed ask students to do little more than display their memorization skills.

"But this doesn't need to be the case. Multiple-choice items, if they are carefully developed, can assess a wide variety of truly higher-order thinking skills. In our school, all teachers have taken part in a series of staff-development workshop sessions in which every teacher learned how to create *challenging* multiple-choice items that require students to display much more than memory. (At this point, I'd whip out a few examples of demanding multiple-choice items used in my own tests, then go through them, from stem to alternatives, showing Mr. and Mrs. Olmedo what I meant. If I *didn't* have any examples of such items from my tests, I'd think seriously about the legitimacy of Benito's parents' criticism.)

"So, although there's nothing wrong with Benito's acquiring more memorized information, and a small number of my multiple-choice items actually do test for such knowledge, the vast majority of the multiple-choice items that Benito will take in my class call for him to employ that fine mind of his.

"That's what you two want. That's what I want."

• • • *Now, how would you respond to Mr. and Mrs. Olmedo's concerns?*

students won't be able to perform the actual mathematical operations, but may be able to select by estimation the answer that is most reasonable. After all, *one* of the four options *has* to be correct. Yet, simply by adding the none-of-the-above option (as a fourth or fifth alternative), students can't be sure that the correct answer is sitting there among the item's alternatives. To determine whether the correct answer is *really* one of the alternatives for the item, they'll be obliged to perform the required mathematical operation and come up with the actual answer. In essence, when the none-of-the-above option is added, the task presented to the student more closely approximates the task that the teacher is interested in. A student's chance of guessing the correct answer to a multiple-choice item is markedly less likely when a none-of-the-above option shows up in the item.

In review, we've taken a cursory look at five guidelines for the creation of multiple-choice items. There are other more subtle suggestions for creating such items, but if you combine these guidelines with the five item-writing commandments discussed earlier in the chapter, you'll have a good set of ground rules for devising decent multiple-choice items. As with all of the item types we've been describing, there's no substitute for oodles of practice in item writing followed by collegial or supervisorial reviews of your item-writing efforts. It is said that Rome wasn't built in a day. Similarly, in order to become a capable constructor of multiple-choice items, you'll probably need to develop more than one such test— or even two.

Matching Items ....

A *matching item* consists of two parallel lists of words or phrases that require the student to match entries on one list with appropriate entries on the second list. Entries in the list for which a match is sought are referred to as *premises*. Entries in the list from which selections are made are referred to as *responses*. Usually, students are directed to match entries from the two lists according to a specific kind of association that is described in the test directions. Figure 6.3 is an example of a matching item.

Figure 6.3   **An Illustrative Matching Item**

Directions: On the line to the left of each military conflict listed in column A, write the letter of the U.S. president in column B who was in office when that military conflict was concluded. Each name in Column B may be used no more than once.

Column A

___ 1. World War I
___ 2. World War II
___ 3. Korea
___ 4. Vietnam
___ 5. Persian Gulf

Column B

A. Bush
B. Clinton
C. Eisenhower
D. Johnson
E. Nixon
F. Roosevelt
G. Truman
H. Wilson

Notice in the illustrative matching item that both lists are *homogeneous*—that is, all of the entries in the column at the left (the premises) are U.S. military conflicts and all of the entries in the column at the right (the responses) are names of U.S. presidents. Homogeneity is an important attribute of properly constructed matching items.

An advantage of matching items is that their compact form takes up little space on a printed page, thus making it easy to tap a good deal of information efficiently. Matching items can also be easily scored by simply holding a correct-answer template next to the list of premises where students are to supply their selections from the list of responses. A disadvantage of matching items is that, as with true-false items, they sometimes encourage students' memorization of low-level factual information that, in at least some instances, is of debatable utility. The illustrative matching item is a case in point. Although it's relatively easy to create matching items such as this, is it really important to know which U.S. chief executive was in office when a military conflict was concluded? That's the kind of issue you'll be facing when you decide what kinds of items to include in your classroom assessments.

Typically, matching items are used as *part* of a teacher's assessment instruments. It's pretty difficult to imagine a major classroom examination that would consist exclusively of matching items. Matching items don't work well when teachers are trying to assess relatively distinctive ideas, because matching items require pools of related entries to insert into the matching format.

Let's consider a half-dozen guidelines that you should think about when creating matching items for your classroom assessment instruments. The guidelines are presented here.

Item-Writing Guidelines for Matching Items

1. Employ homogeneous lists.
2. Use relatively brief lists, placing the shorter words or phrases at the right.
3. Employ more responses than premises.
4. Order the responses logically.
5. Describe the basis for matching and the number of times responses may be used.
6. Place all premises and responses for an item on a single page.

Employing Homogeneous Entries

As noted earlier, each list in a matching item should consist of homogeneous entries. If you really can't create a homogeneous set of premises and a homogeneous set of responses, you shouldn't be mucking about with matching items.

Going for Relative Brevity

From the student's perspective, it's much easier to respond to matching items if the entries on both lists are relatively few in number. About 10 or so premises should be the upper limit for most matching items. The problem with longer lists is that students spend so much time trying to isolate the appropriate response for a given premise that they may forget what they're attempting to find. Very lengthy sets of premises or responses are almost certain to cause at least some students difficulty in responding because they'll lose track of what's being sought. It would be far better to take a single matching item with 24 premises and split it into three 8-premise matching items.

In addition, to cut down on the reading requirements of matching items, be sure to place the list of shorter words or phrases at the right. In other words, make the briefer entries the responses. In this way, when students are scanning the response lists for a matching entry, they'll not be obliged to read too many lengthy phrases or sentences.

Loading Up on Responses

A third guideline for the construction of matching items is to make sure that there are at least a few extra responses. Otherwise, if the number of premises and responses are equal, the student who knows, say, 80% of the matches to the premises may be able to figure out the remaining matches by a process of elimination. A few extra responses reduce that likelihood substantially. Besides, they're inexpensive.

Ordering Responses

So that you'll not provide unintended clues to students regarding which responses go with which premises, it's a good idea in matching items to order the responses in some sort of logical fashion—for example, alphabetical or chronological sequence. Notice that in the illustrative matching item in Figure 6.3, the names of the U.S. presidents are listed alphabetically.

Describing the Task for Students

The fifth guideline for the construction of matching items suggests that the directions for an item always make explicit the basis on which the matches are to be made and, at the same time, the number of times a response can be used. The more clearly students understand how they're supposed to respond, the more accurately they'll respond, and the more validly you'll be able to make score-based inferences about your students.

Formatting Items to Avoid Page Flipping

The final guideline for this item type suggests that you make sure all premises and responses for a matching item are on a single page. Not only does this eliminate the necessity for massive, potentially disruptive page turning by students but it will also decrease the likelihood that students will overlook correct answers merely because they were on the "other" page.

In review, matching items, if employed judiciously, can efficiently assess your students' knowledge. The need to employ homogeneous lists of related content tends to diminish the applicability of this type of selected-response item. Nonetheless, if you are dealing with content that can be addressed satisfactorily by such an approach, you'll find matching items a useful member of your repertoire of item types.

What Do Classroom Teachers Really Need to Know about Selected-Response Tests? ....

If you engage in any meaningful amount of assessment in your own classroom, it's quite likely you'll find that selected-response items will be useful. Selected-response items can typically be used to ascertain students' mastery of larger domains of content than is the case with constructed-response kinds of test items. Although it's often thought that selected-response items must, of necessity, measure only lower-order kinds of cognitive capabilities, inventive teachers can create selected-response options that elicit higher levels of cognitive skills from students.

As for the four types of items treated in the chapter, you really need to understand enough about each kind to help you decide whether one or more of those item types would be useful for a classroom assessment task you have in mind. If you do decide to use binary-choice, multiple binary-choice, multiple-choice, or matching items in your own tests, then you'll find that the sets of item-writing guidelines for each item type will come in handy.

Yet, in honesty, even if you adhere to the chapter's five general item-writing commandments and the set of guidelines for a particular type of item, you'll still need practice in constructing selected-response items such as those considered here. As was suggested several times in the chapter, it is exceedingly helpful if you can find someone with measurement moxie, or at least an analytic mind, to review your test-development efforts. It's difficult in any realm to improve if you don't get feedback about the adequacy of your efforts. That's surely true with classroom assessment. Try to entice a colleague or supervisor to look over your selected-response test items to see what needs to be strengthened. However, even without piles of practice, if you adhere to the item-writing guidelines provided in the chapter, your selected-response tests won't be all that shabby.

The most important thing to learn from this chapter is that there are four useful *selected*-response procedures for drawing valid inferences about your students' status. The more assessment options you have at your disposal, the more appropriately you'll be able to assess those student variables in which you're interested.

Chapter Summary ·······································

The chapter was initiated with a presentation of five item-writing commandments that pertain to both constructed-response and selected-response items. The five admonitions directed teachers to avoid unclear directions, ambiguous statements, unintentional clues, complex syntax, and hypersophisticated vocabulary.

In turn, then, consideration was given to the four most common kinds of selected-response test items—namely, binary-choice items, multiple binary-choice items, multiple-choice items, and matching items. For each of these four item types, after a brief description of the item type and its strengths and weaknesses, a set of item-writing guidelines was presented. These four sets of guidelines were presented on pages 116, 119, 121, and 127. Each guideline was briefly discussed. Readers were encouraged to consider the four item types when deciding on an answer to the how-to-assess-it question.

Self-Check

For this chapter's self-check exercises, you'll be asked to evaluate a series of selected-response items. The items deal with content about assessment that was addressed in earlier sections of this book. Therefore, you should regard this chapter's self-check as an instructionally reinforcing experience. Specifically, you'll be asked to evaluate a series of selected-response items. In considering each item, think back to the five general item-writing commandments that apply to all the items you'll write. In addition, recall the specific item-writing guidelines associated with the type of item you're being asked to evaluate. To evaluate these *selected*-response items, you'll be asked to supply *constructed* (short-answer) responses. This requirement will either increase your item-writing flexibility or initiate a bit of psychometric schizophrenia.

1. Here are two binary-choice items. In the lined spaces below the items, please evaluate the quality of the two items. Be sure to note any particular item-writing deficits you discern.

   Directions: For each of the following statements, indicate whether the statement is right (R) or wrong (W).

   R or W ____ (1) The most important attribute of validity evidence is content coverage, whereas the most important attribute of reliability evidence is consistency of results.

R or W   ____ (2) Absence-of-bias determinations are not best made only by judgmental procedures.

_____

_____

_____

2. Now look over the following two multiple-choice items and make an evaluation of their intrinsic virtues.

   Directions: Choose the best answer from the alternatives for each of the following items.

   (1) Which of the following kinds of validity evidence, when analyzed carefully, is the most comprehensive descriptor for supportive information regarding the validity of test-based inference?
      a. Content-related evidence of validity
      b. Predictive criterion-related evidence of validity
      c. Concurrent criterion-related evidence of validity
      d. Construct-related evidence of validity

   (2) If you were a classroom teacher who wished to improve your students' higher-order thinking skills, in which of the following taxonomic domains should you be most interested?
      a. The cognitive domain
      b. The affective domain
      c. The psychomotor domain
      d. None of the domains given above

   _____

   _____

   _____

3. Here's a multiple binary-choice item for you to consider. See what you think of it.

   Directions: For *each* statement in the cluster of statements, indicate whether the statement is true (T) or false (F).

   ****In an elaborate effort to ascertain the reliability of a new high-stakes test developed in their district, central-office administrators have calculated the following types of reliability evidence based on a tryout of the test with 2,400 students:

   - Internal consistency $r = .82$
   - Test-retest $r = .78$
   - Standard Error of Measurement $= 4.3$

_____ (1) The three types of reliability evidence calculated by the central-office staff are essentially interchangeable.

_____ (2) The minor difference between the stability and internal consistency coefficients constitutes no cause for alarm.

_____ (3) The test-retest r should never be smaller than an internal consistency reliability coefficient.

_____ (4) The standard error of measurement is derived chiefly from the test's reliability indices.

_____

_____

_____

4. Let's close out this practice scrutiny of selected-response items with a quick look at the following matching item that grabs its content from this very chapter.

Directions: Choose the best match between the item types in List X and the strengths/weaknesses in List Y.

List X

_____ (1) matching
_____ (2) binary choice
_____ (3) multiple binary choice
_____ (4) multiple choice

List Y

a. Can efficiently cover much informational content

b. Can measure students' higher-order cognitive skills if properly constructed

c. Often encourages low-level recall of information

d. Assesses what students can recognize rather than create

_____

_____

_____

Pondertime

1. If you were asked to take part in a mini-debate about the respective virtues of selected-response items versus constructed-response items, what do you think would be your major points if you were espousing the use of selected-response test items?

2. During your lifetime you've probably completed all, or most all, of the item types described in the chapter. Which types were your most favorite and least favorite? Why?

3. Why do you think that multiple-choice tests have been so widely used in nationally standardized norm-referenced achievement tests during the past half-century?

4. How do you think that classroom teachers can become truly effective writers of selected-response test items?

5. If you had to build your classroom assessments exclusively using selected-response test items, which item types would you prefer to use? Why?

Self-Check Key

1. The first of the two items violated the third item-writing guideline for binary-choice items: Don't include two concepts in one statement. An examinee may not be able to keep separate the part of the item dealing with validity evidence from the part that deals with reliability evidence. Incidentally, although the segment of the item dealing with reliability is accurate, the segment about validity is off the mark because not all validity evidence is content related.

   The second of the two items violates Guideline 2: Avoid negative statements. Because the descriptive phrase being used is *absence-of-bias*, the item already has a negative notion built into it. By the time the student reads the *not* and the *only*, full-bodied confusion is apt to be present.

2. The first multiple-choice item isn't all that bad. There don't seem to be any major deficits in the item (the correct answer to which is choice d).

   The second multiple-choice isn't all that bad either, except choice d (a version of "none of the above") is pretty much of a throw-away choice. It would be better to have only three alternatives or to split the cognitive domain based on whether the cognitive behavior deals with lowest level cognition (knowledge) or higher than the lowest level cognition (all other kinds of cognitive behavior). The correct answer, of course, is choice a.

3. Although it's surely possible to improve the phrasing of items such as these, in general, this multiple binary-choice item looks fairly acceptable in that it has violated neither the guidelines for multiple binary-choice items nor the guidelines for binary-choice items. The correct answers, by the way, are (1) F, (2) T, (3) F, and (4) T.

4. This is a genuinely cruddy item. There are almost more mistakes in the item than the words used to create it. First off, the directions are too sloppy and violate Guideline 5 for matching items by giving neither the basis for matching nor the number of times responses can be used. In addition, there are identical numbers of premises and responses, a violation of Guideline 3. The response list isn't homogeneous (Guideline 1) because it contains advantages *and* disadvantages. Guideline 2 also is violated because the shorter phrases are at the left rather than the right. About the only good thing you can say about the item is that it all fits on a single page. Regarding the correct answers—who knows?

Additional Stuff

Airasian, Peter W. *Classroom Assessment* (2nd ed.). New York: McGraw-Hill, 1994.

Crocker, Linda. "Assessing Content Representativeness of Performance Assessment Exercises." *Applied Measurement in Education,* 10, no. 1 (1997): 83–95.

Downing, Steven M. "True-False, Alternate-Choice, and Multiple-Choice Items." *Educational Measurement: Issues and Practice,* 11, no. 3 (Fall 1992): 27–30.

Downing, Steven M., and Thomas M. Haladyna. "Test Item Development: Validity Evidence from Quality Assurance Procedures." *Applied Measurement in Education,* 10, no. 1 (1997): 61–82.

Ebel, R. L., and D. A. Frisbie. *Essentials of Educational Measurement* (5th ed.). Englewood Cliffs, NJ: Prentice Hall, 1991.

Frary, Robert B. "The None-of-the-Above Option: An Empirical Study." *Applied Measurement in Education,* 4, no. 2 (1991): 115–124.

Frisbie, David A. "The Multiple True-False Format: A Status Review." *Educational Measurement: Issues and Practice,* 11, no. 4 (Winter 1992): 21–26.

Frisbie, David A., and Douglas F. Becker. "An Analysis of Textbook Advice about True-False Tests." *Applied Measurement in Education,* 4, no. 1 (1991): 67–83.

Harasym, P. H., M. L. Doran, R. Brant, and F. L. Lorscheider. "Negation in Stems of Single-Response Multiple-Choice Items." *Evaluation & the Health Professionals,* 16, no. 3 (September 1993): 342–357.

Linn, Robert L., and Norman E. Gronlund. *Measurement and Assessment in Teaching* (7th ed.). Upper Saddle River, NJ: Prentice-Hall, 1995.

McMillan, James H. *Classroom Assessment: Principles and Practice for Effective Instruction.* Boston: Allyn and Bacon, 1997.

Mehrens, W. A., and I. J. Lehmann. *Measurement and Evaluation in Education and Psychology* (4th ed.). New York: Holt, Rinehart and Winston, 1991.

Nonprint Stuff

Northwest Regional Laboratory. *Paper-and-Pencil Test Development* (Videotape #NREL-4A). Los Angeles: IOX Assessment Associates.

Popham, W. James. *Creating Challenging Classroom Tests: When Students SELECT Their Answers* (Videotape #ETVT-23). Los Angeles: IOX Assessment Associates.

7

Constructed-Response Tests

You're going to learn about constructed-response tests in this chapter. To be really truthful, you're going to learn about only two kinds of *paper-and-pencil* constructed-response items—namely, short-answer items and essay items (including students' written compositions). Although I suspect you already know that "you can't tell a book by its cover," now you've discovered that a chapter's title doesn't always describe its contents accurately. Fortunately, as far as I know, there are no state or federal "truth-in-chapter-entitling" laws.

You might be wondering why your ordinarily honest, never-fib author has descended to this act of blatant mislabeling. Actually, it's just to keep your reading chores more manageable. In an earlier chapter, you learned that student-constructed responses can be obtained from a wide variety of item types. In this chapter, we'll be looking at two rather traditional forms of constructed-response items, both of them paper-and-pencil in nature. In the next chapter, the focus will be on *performance tests,* such as those that arise when we ask students to make oral presentations or supply comprehensive demonstrations of skills in class. After that, in Chapter 9, we'll be dealing with portfolio assessment and how portfolios are used for assessment purposes.

Actually, all three chapters could be lumped under the single description of *performance assessment* or *constructed-response measurement* because any time you assess your students by asking them to respond in other than a selected-response manner, the students are *constructing;* that is, they are *performing.* It's just that if I'd loaded all of that performance assessment stuff in a single chapter, you'd have thought you were experiencing a month-long TV mini-series. The self-check exercises would have been as long as a short novel, and you'd have been pondering the pondertime questions for years. Yes, it was my inherent kindness and concern for readers that led me to disregard accuracy when entitling this chapter.

The major payoff of all constructed-response items is that they elicit student responses more closely approximating the kinds of behavior students must display in real life. After students leave school, for example, their demands of daily living almost never require them to choose responses from four nicely arranged alternatives. And when was the last time, in normal conversation, that you were obliged to render a flock of true-false judgments about a set of statements? Yet, you may well be asked to make a brief oral presentation to your fellow teachers or to a parent group, or you may be asked to write a brief report for the school newspaper about your students' field trip to City Hall. Constructed-response tasks unquestionably coincide more closely with nonacademic tasks than do selected-response tasks.

As a practical matter, if the nature of a selected-response task is sufficiently close to what might be garnered from a constructed-response item, then you may wish to consider a selected-response assessment tactic to be a reasonable surrogate for a constructed-response assessment tactic. Selected-response tests are clearly much more efficient to score. And, because almost all teachers I know are busy folks, time-saving procedures are not to be scoffed at. Yet, there will be situations when you'll want to make inferences about your students' status when selected-response tests just won't fill the bill. For instance, if you wish to know what kind of a cursive writer Jamal is, then you'll have to let Jamal write cursively. A true-false test about *i* dotting and *t* crossing just doesn't cut it.

Short-Answer Items ....

The first kind of constructed-response item we'll look at is the *short-answer item*. Short-answer items call for students to supply a word, a phrase, or a sentence in response to either a direct question or an incomplete statement. If an item asks students to come up with a fairly lengthy response, it would be considered an essay item, not a short-answer item. If the item asks students to supply only a single word, then it's a *really* short-answer item.

Short-answer items are suitable for assessing relatively simple kinds of learning outcomes such as those focused on students' acquisition of knowledge. If crafted carefully, however, short-answer items can measure substantially more challenging kinds of learning outcomes. The major advantage of short-answer items is that students need to *produce* a correct answer, not merely recognize it from a set of selected-response options. The level of partial knowledge that might allow a student to respond correctly to a choose-the-best-response item won't be sufficient when the student is required to produce a correct answer to a short-answer item.

The major drawback with short-answer items, as is true with all constructed-response items, is that students' responses are difficult to score. The longer the responses sought, the tougher it is to score them accurately. And inaccurate scoring, as we saw in Chapter 2, leads to reduced reliability, which, in turn, reduces the validity of the test-based inferences we make about students, which, in turn, reduces the quality of the decisions we base on those inferences. Educational measurement is much like the rest of life—it's simply loaded with trade-offs. When classroom teachers choose constructed-response tests, they must be willing to trade some scoring accuracy (that comes with selected-response approaches) for greater congruence between constructed-response assessment strategies and the kinds of student behaviors about which inferences are to be made.

Here, you will find five straightforward item-writing guidelines for short-answer items. Please look them over, then I'll briefly amplify each guideline and describe how it works.

Item-Writing Guidelines for Short-Answer Items

1. Usually employ direct questions rather than incomplete statements, particularly for young students.
2. Structure the item so that a response should be concise.
3. Place blanks in the margin for direct questions or near the end of incomplete statements.
4. For incomplete statements, use only one or, at most, two blanks.
5. Make sure blanks for all items are equal in length.

Using Direct Questions Rather than Incomplete Statements

For young children, the direct question is a far more familiar format than the incomplete statement. Accordingly, such students will be less confused if direct questions are employed. Another reason short-answer items should employ a direct-question format is that the use of direct questions typically forces the item writer to phrase the item so less ambiguity is present. With incomplete-statements formats, there's often too much temptation simply to delete words or phrases from statements the teacher finds in textbooks. To make sure that there isn't more than one correct answer to a short-answer item, it is often helpful if the item writer first decides on the correct answer, then builds a question or incomplete statement designed to elicit a *unique* correct response from knowledgeable students.

Nurturing Concise Responses

Responses to short-answer items, as might be inferred from what they're called, should be *short*. Thus, no matter whether you're eliciting responses that are words, symbols, phrases, or numbers, try to structure the item so that a brief response is clearly sought. Suppose you conjured up an incomplete statement item such as this: "An animal that walks on two feet is _____." There are all sorts of answers that a student might legitimately make to such an item. Moreover, some of those responses could be fairly lengthy. Now note how a slight restructuring of the item constrains the student: "An animal that walks on two feet is technically classified as _____." By the addition of the phrase "technically classified as," the item writer has restricted the appropriate responses to only one—namely, "biped." If your short-answer items are trying to elicit students' phrases or sentences, you may wish to place word limits on each, or at least indicate in the test's directions that only a *short* one-sentence response is allowable for each item.

Always try to put yourself, mentally, inside the heads of your students and try to anticipate how they are apt to interpret an item. What this second guideline suggests is that you massage an item until it truly lives up to its name—that is, until it becomes a *bona fide* short-answer item.

Positioning Blanks

If you're using direct questions in your short-answer items, place the students' response areas for all items near the right-hand margin of the page, immediately after the item's questions. By doing so, you'll have all of a student's responses nicely lined up for scoring. If you're using incomplete statements, try to place the blank near the end of the statement, not near its beginning. A blank positioned too early in a sentence tends to confuse the students. For instance, notice how this too-early blank can lead to confusion: "The _____ is the governmental body which, based on the United States Constitution, must ratify all U.S. treaties with foreign nations." It would be better to use a direct question or to phrase the item as follows: "The governmental body which, based on the United States Constitution, must ratify all U.S. treaties with foreign nations is the _____."

Limiting Blanks

For incomplete-statement types of short-answer items, you should use only one or two blanks. Any more blanks and the item is labeled a "swiss-cheese item," or an item with holes galore. Here's a swiss-cheese item to illustrate how confusing a profusion of blanks can make what is otherwise a decent short-answer item: "After a series of major conflicts with natural disasters, in the year ____, the explorers _____ and _____, accompanied by their _____, discovered _____." The student who could supply correct answers to such a flawed short-answer item should also be regarded as a truly successful explorer.

Inducing Linear Equality

Too often in short-answer items, a beginning item writer will give away the answer by varying the length of the answer blanks so that short lines are used when short answers are correct and long lines are used when lengthier answers are correct. This practice tosses unintended clues to students and so should be avoided. In the interest of linear egalitarianism, not to mention decent item writing, keep all blanks for short-answer items equal in length. Be sure, however, that the length of the answer spaces provided is sufficient for students' responses—in other words, not so skimpy that students have to cram their answers in an illegible fashion.

In review, short-answer items are the most simple form of constructed-response items, but they can help teachers measure important skills and knowledge. Because such items seek students' constructed rather than selected responses, they can be employed to tap some genuinely higher-order skills. Although students' responses to short-answer items are more difficult to score than are their answers to selected-response items, the scoring of such items isn't all that difficult. That's because short-answer items, by definition, should elicit only *short* answers.

Essay Items: Development ....

The essay item is surely the most commonly used form of constructed-response assessment item. Any time teachers ask their students to churn out a paragraph or two on what the students know about Topic *X* or to compose an original composition describing their "Favorite Day," an essay item is being used. Essay items are particularly useful in gauging a student's ability to synthesize, evaluate, and compose. Such items have a wide variety of applications in most teachers' classrooms.

A special form of the essay item is the *writing sample*—when teachers ask students to generate a written composition in an attempt to measure students' composition skills. Because the procedures employed to construct items for such writing samples and, thereafter, for scoring students' compositions are so similar to the procedures employed to create and score responses to any kind of essay item, we'll treat writing samples and other kinds of essay items all at one time in this chapter. You'll find it helpful, however, to remember that the requirement to have students generate a writing sample is, in reality, a widely used type of *performance test*. We'll dig more deeply into performance tests in the following chapter.

For assessing certain kinds of complex learning outcomes, the essay item is the hands-down winner. It clearly wins out when you're trying to see how well students can create original compositions. Yet, there are a fair number of drawbacks associated with essay items, and if you're going to consider using essay items in your own classroom, you have to know the weaknesses as well as the strengths of this item type.

One difficulty with essay items is that they're more difficult to write—at least write properly—than is generally thought. I must confess that as a first-year high school teacher, I sometimes conjured up essay items while walking to school, then slapped them up in the chalkboard so that I created almost instant essay exams. At the time, I thought my essay items were pretty good. Such is the pride of youth and the product of ignorance. I'm glad that I have no record of those items. In retrospect, I assume they were pretty putrid. I now know that generating

Forests or Trees? ....

Allison Allen is a brand-new English teacher assigned to work with seventh-grade and eighth-grade students at Dubois Junior High School. Allison has taken part in a state-sponsored summer workshop that emphasizes "writing as a process." Coupled with what she learned while completing her teacher education program, Allison is confident that she can effectively employ techniques such as brainstorming, outlining, early drafts, peer critiquing, and multiple revisions. She assumes that her students will acquire not only competence in their composition capabilities but also confidence about their possession of those capabilities. What Allison's preparation failed to address, however, was how to grade her students' compositions.

Two experienced English teachers at Dubois Junior High have gone out of their way to help Allison get through her first year as a teacher. Mrs. Miller and Ms. Stovall have both been quite helpful during the early weeks of the school year. However, when Allison asked them one day during lunch how she should judge the quality of her students' compositions, two decisively different messages were given.

Ms. Stovall strongly endorsed *holistic* grading of compositions—that is, a general appraisal of each composition as a whole. Although Ms. Stovall bases her holistic grading scheme on a set of explicit criteria, she believes a single "gestalt" grade should be given so that "one's vision of the forest is not obscured by tree-counting."

Arguing with equal vigor, Mrs. Miller urged Allison to adopt *analytic* appraisals of her students' compositions. "By supplying your students with a criterion-by-criterion judgment of their work," she contended, "each student will be able to know precisely what's good and what isn't." (It was evident during the fairly heated interchanges that Mrs. Miller and Ms. Stovall had disagreed about this topic in the past.) Mrs. Miller concluded her remarks by saying, "Forget about that forest-and-trees metaphor, Allison. What we're talking about here is clarity!"

If you were Allison, how would you decide to judge the quality of your students' compositions?

a really good essay item is a tough task—a task that could not be accomplished in an instant. You'll see that from the item-writing rules to be presented shortly. It takes time to create a solid essay item. You'll need to find time to create suitable essay items for your own classroom assessments.

The most serious problem with essay items, however, is the difficulty that teachers have in scoring students' responses reliably. Let's say you use a six-item essay test to measure your students' ability to solve certain kinds of problems in social studies. Suppose that, by some stroke of measurement magic, all your students' responses could be transformed into typed manuscript form so you could not tell which response came from which student. Let's say that you were asked to score the complete set of responses twice. What do you think is the likelihood your two sets of scores would be consistent? Well, experience suggests that most teachers aren't able to produce very reliable results when they score students' essay responses. The task in this instance, of course, is to *increase* the reliability of your scoring efforts so that you're not distorting the validity of the score-based inferences you want to make on the basis of your students' responses.

Creating Essay Items

Because the scoring of essay responses (and students' compositions) is such an important topic, you'll soon be getting a separate set of guidelines on how to score responses to such items. The more complex the nature of students' constructed responses become, as you'll see in the next two chapters, the more attention you'll need to lavish on scoring. You can't score responses to items that you haven't written, however, so let's look at the five guidelines for the construction of essay items.

Item-Writing Guidelines for Essay Items

1. Convey to students a clear idea regarding the extensiveness of the response desired.
2. Construct items so that the student's task is explicitly described.
3. Provide students with the approximate time to be expended on each item as well as each item's value.
4. Do not employ optional items.
5. Precursively judge an item's quality by composing, mentally or in writing, a possible response.

Communicating the Desired Extensiveness of Students' Responses

It is sometimes thought that if teachers decide to use essay items, students have total freedom of response. On the contrary, teachers can structure essay items so that students produce (1) barely more than they would for a short-answer item or, in contrast, (2) extremely lengthy responses. The two types of essay items reflecting this distinction in the desired extensiveness of student's responses are described as restricted-response items and extended-response items.

Restricted-response items decisively limit the form and content of students' responses. For example, a restricted-response item in a health education class might ask students the following: "Describe the three most common ways that HIV, the AIDS virus, is transmitted. Take no more than 25 words to describe each method of transmission." In this example, the number of HIV transmission methods was specified, as was the maximum length for each transmission method's description.

In contrast, an *extended-response item* provides students with far more latitude in responding. Here's an example of an extended-response item from a social studies class: "Identify the chief factors contributing to the enormous U.S. government's financial deficit of the 1980s and 1990s. Having identified those factors, decide which factors, if any, have been explicitly addressed by the U.S legislative and/or executive branches of government in the last five years. Finally, critically evaluate the likelihood that any currently proposed remedies will bring about significant reductions in the U.S. national debt." A decent response to such an extended-response item not only should get high marks from the teacher but might also be the springboard for a successful career in politics.

One technique that teachers commonly use to limit students' responses is to provide a certain amount of space on the test paper or in their students' response booklets. For instance, the teacher might direct students to "Use no more than two sheets (both sides) in your blue books to respond to each test item." Although the space-limiting ploy is an easy one to implement, it really disadvantages students who write in a large-letter, scrawling fashion. Whereas such large-letter students may only be able to cram a few paragraphs onto a page, those students who write in a small, scrunched-up style may be able to produce a short novella in the same space.

This first guideline asks you to think carefully about whether the inference at issue that you wish to make about your students is best serviced by students' responses to (1) more essay items requiring shorter responses or (2) fewer essay items requiring extensive responses. Having made that decision, then be sure to convey to your students a clear picture of the degree of extensiveness you're looking for in their responses.

Describing Students' Tasks

Students will find it difficult to construct responses to tasks if they don't understand what the tasks are. Moreover, students' responses to badly understood tasks are almost certain to yield flawed inferences by teachers. The most important part of an essay item is, without question, the description of the *assessment task*. It is the assessment task that students respond to when they generate essays. Clearly, then, poorly described assessment tasks will yield many off-target responses that, had the student truly understood what was being sought, might have been more appropriate.

There are numerous labels used to represent the assessment task in an essay item. Sometimes it's simply called the *task,* the *charge,* or perhaps the *assignment.* In essay items that are aimed at eliciting student compositions, the assessment task is often referred to as the *prompt.* No matter how the assessment task is labeled, if you're a teacher who is using essay items, you must make sure that the nature of the task is really set forth clearly for your students. Put yourself, at least hypothetically, in the student's seat and see if, with the level of knowledge possessed by most of your students, the nature of the assessment task is really apt to be understood.

To illustrate, if you wrote the following essay item, there's little doubt that your students' assessment task would have been badly described: "In 500 words or less, discuss democracy in Latin America." In contrast, notice in the following item how much more clearly the assessment task is set forth: "Describe how the checks and balances provisions in the U.S. Constitution were believed by the Constitution's framers to be a powerful means to preserve democracy (300–500 words)."

Providing Time-Limit and Item-Value Guidance

When teachers create an examination consisting of essay items, they often have an idea regarding which items will take more of the students' time. But students don't know what's in the teacher's head. As a consequence, some students will lavish loads of attention on items that the teacher thought warranted only modest effort, yet devote little time to items that the teacher thought deserved substantial attention. Similarly, sometimes teachers will want to weight certain items more heavily than others. Again, if students are unaware of which items count most, they may toss loads of rhetoric at the low-value items and have insufficient time to give more than a trifling response to the high-value items.

To avoid these problems, there's quite a straightforward solution—namely, letting students in on the secret. If there are any differences among items in point value or in the time students should spend on them, simply provide this information in the directions or, perhaps parenthetically, at the end of each item. Students will appreciate such clarifications of your expectations.

Avoiding Optionality

It's fairly common practice among teachers who use essay examinations to provide students with a certain number of items, then let each student choose to answer fewer than the number of items presented. For example, the teacher might allow students to "choose any five of the seven essay items presented." Students, of course, really groove on such an assessment procedure because they can respond to items for which they're well prepared and avoid those items for which they're inadequately prepared. Yet, other than inducing student glee, this optional-items classroom assessment scheme has little going for it.

When students select different items from a menu of possible items, they are actually responding to different examinations. As a consequence, it is impossible to judge their performances on some kind of common scale. Remember, as a classroom teacher you'll be trying to make better educational decisions about your students by relying on test-based inferences regarding those students. It's tough enough to make a decent test-based inference when you have only one test to consider. It's infinitely more difficult to make such inferences when you are faced with a medley of different tests because you allow your students to engage in a mix-and-match measurement procedure.

In most cases, teachers rely on an optional-items procedure with essay items when they're uncertain about the importance of the content measured by their examinations' items. Such uncertainty gives rise to the use of optional items because the teacher is not clearheaded about the inferences for which the examination's results will be used. If you spell out those inferences crisply, prior to the examination, you will usually find you'll have no need for optional item selection in your essay examinations.

Previewing Students' Responses

After you've constructed an essay item for one of your classroom assessments, there's a quick way to get a preliminary fix on whether the item is a winner or loser. Simply toss yourself, psychologically, into the head of one of your typical students, then anticipate how such a student would respond to the item. If you have time, and are inclined to do so, you could try writing a response that the student might produce to the item. More often than not, because you'll be too busy to conjure up such fictitious responses in written form, you might try to compose a mental response to the item on behalf of the typical student you've selected. An early mental run-through of how a student might respond to an item can often help you identify deficits in the item, because when you put yourself, even hypothetically, on the other side of the teacher's desk, you'll sometimes discover shortcomings in items that you otherwise wouldn't have identified. Too many times I've seen teachers give birth to a set of essay questions, send them into battle on examination day, and only then discover that one or more of the items suffers severe genetic deficits. Mental previewing of likely student responses can help you detect such flaws while there's still time for repairs.

In review, we've looked at five guidelines for creating essay items. If you'll remember that all of these charming little collections of item-specific recommendations should be adhered to *in addition to* the five general item-writing commandments set forth in Chapter 6 (see page 112), you'll probably be able to come up with a pretty fair set of essay items. Then, perish the thought, you'll have to score your students' responses to those items. That's what we'll be looking at next.

Essay Items: Scoring Students' Responses ....

If you'll recall what's to come in future chapters (and, of course, recall is the *lowest* level of Bloom's cognitive taxonomy), you'll be looking at how to evaluate students' responses to performance assessments in Chapter 8 and how to judge students' portfolios in Chapter 9. In short, you'll be learning much more about how to evaluate your students' performances in constructed-response assessments.

Thus, to spread out the load a bit, in this chapter we'll be looking only at how to score students' responses to essay items (including tests of students' composition skills). You'll find that many of the suggestions for scoring students' constructed responses that you will encounter in the following two chapters will also be applicable when you're trying to judge your students' essay responses. But just to keep matters simple, let's look now at recommendations for scoring students' responses to essay items.

Guidelines for Scoring Responses to Essay Items

1. Score responses holistically and/or analytically.
2. Prepare a tentative scoring key in advance of judging students' responses.
3. Make decisions regarding the importance of the mechanics of writing prior to scoring.
4. Score all responses to one item before scoring responses to the next item.
5. Insofar as possible, evaluate responses anonymously.

Choosing an Analytic and/or Holistic Scoring Approach

During the past decade or two, the measurement of students' composition skills by having students generate actual writing samples has become widespread. As a consequence of all this attention to students' compositions, educators have become far more skilled regarding how to evaluate students' written compositions. Fortunately, classroom teachers can use many of the procedures that have been identified and refined while educators scored thousands of students' compositions during statewide assessment extravaganzas. (In Texas, over a million students' essays were scored annually. Even for Texas, pardner, that's a pile of essays.)

A fair number of the lessons learned about scoring students' writing samples apply quite nicely to the scoring of responses to any kind of essay item. One of the most important of the scoring insights picked up from those large-scale scoring of students' compositions is that almost any type of student-constructed response can be scored either *holistically* or *analytically*. That's why the initial guideline in the following box suggests you make an early-on decision whether you're going to score your students' responses to essay items using a holistic approach, an analytic approach or, perhaps, using a combination of the two scoring approaches. Let's look at how each of these two scoring strategies works.

A *holistic* scoring strategy, as its name suggests, focuses on the essay response (or written composition) as a whole. At one extreme of scoring rigor, the teacher can, in a fairly unsystematic manner, supply a "general impression" overall grade to each student's response. Or, in a more systematic fashion, the teacher can isolate, in advance of scoring, those evaluative factors that should be attended to in order to arrive at a single, overall score per essay. Generally, a score range of four to six points is used for each response. (Some scoring schemes have a few more points, some a few less.) A teacher, then, after considering whatever factors should be attended to in a given item, will give a score to each student's response. Here is a set of evaluative criteria that teachers might use in holistically scoring a student's written composition.

> ## Illustrative Evaluative Criteria That Could Be Considered When Scoring Students' Essay Responses Holistically
>
> **For scoring a composition intended to reflect students' writing prowess:**
>
> - Organization
> - Communicative Clarity
> - Adaptation to Audience
> - Word Choice
> - Mechanics (spelling, capitalization, punctuation)

And now, here are four evaluative factors that a speech teacher might employ in holistically scoring a response to an essay item used in a debate class.

> ## Potential Evaluative Criteria That Could Be Used When Scoring Students' Essay Responses in a Debate Class
>
> **For scoring a response to an essay item dealing with rebuttal preparation:**
>
> - Anticipation of Opponent's Positive Points
> - Support for One's Own Points Attacked by Opponents
> - Isolation of Suitably Compelling Examples
> - Preparation of a "Spontaneous" Conclusion

When teachers score students' responses holistically, they do *not* dole out points-per-criterion for a student's response. Rather, the teacher keeps in mind evaluative criteria such as those set forth in the previous two boxes. The speech teacher, for instance, while looking at the student's essay response to a question regarding how someone should engage in effective rebuttal preparation, will not necessarily penalize a student who overlooks one of the four evaluative criteria. The response as a whole may lack one point, yet otherwise represent a really wonderful response. Evaluative criteria such as those illustrated simply dance around in the teacher's head when the teacher scores students' essay responses holistically.

In contrast, an *analytic* scoring scheme strives to be a fine-grained, specific point-allocation approach. Suppose, for example, that instead of using the holistic method of scoring students' compositions, a teacher chose to employ an analytic method of scoring students' compositions. Under those circumstances, a scoring guide such as the example in Figure 7.1 might be used by the teacher. Note that, for each evaluative criterion in the guide, the teacher must award 0, 1, or 2 points. The lowest overall score for a student's composition, therefore, would be 0, whereas the highest overall score from a student's composition would be 10 (that is, 2 points times 5 criteria).

The advantage of an analytic scoring system is that it can help you identify the specific strengths and weaknesses of your students' performances and therefore communicate such diagnoses to students in a pinpointed fashion. The downside of analytic scoring is that a teacher sometimes becomes so attentive to the subpoints in a scoring system that, almost literally, the forest (overall quality) can't be seen because of a focus on individual trees (the separate scoring criteria). In less metaphoric language, the teacher will miss the communication of the student's response "as a whole" because of excessive attention to a host of individual evaluative criteria.

Figure 7.1   **An Illustrative Guide for Analytically Scoring a Student's Written Composition**

Factor	Unacceptable (0 points)	Satisfactory (1 point)	Outstanding (2 points)
1. Organization	___	✓	
2. Communicative Clarity	___		✓
3. Audience Adaptation	___	✓	
4. Word Choice	___		✓
5. Mechanics	___	✓	

Total Score = __7__

One middle-of-the-road scoring approach can be seen when teachers initially grade all students' responses holistically, then return for an analytic scoring of only those responses that were judged, overall, to be unsatisfactory. After the analytic scoring of the unsatisfactory responses, the teacher then relays more fine-grained diagnostic information to those students whose unsatisfactory responses were analytically scored.

This initial guideline for scoring students' essay responses applies to the scoring of responses to all kinds of essay items. As always, your decision about whether to opt for holistic or analytic scoring should flow directly from the use to which you'll be putting the test results. Putting it another way, your choice of scoring approach will depend on the educational decision linked to the test's results.

Devising a Tentative Scoring Key

No matter what sort of approach you opt for in scoring your students' essay responses, you'll find that it will be useful to develop a tentative scoring key for responses to each item *in advance* of actually scoring students' responses. Such tentative scoring schemes are almost certain to be revised on the basis of your scoring of actual student papers, but that's to be anticipated. If you wait until you commence scoring your students' essay responses, there's too much likelihood that you'll be unduly influenced by the responses of the first few students whose papers you grade. If those papers are atypical, the resultant scoring scheme is apt to be unsound. It is far better to think through, at least tentatively, what you really hope students will supply in their responses, then modify the scoring key if unanticipated responses from students suggest that alterations are requisite.

If you don't have a tentative scoring key in place, there's a great likelihood that you'll be influenced by such factors as a student's vocabulary or writing style even though, in reality, such variables may be of little importance to you. Advance exploration of the evaluative criteria you intend to employ, either holistically or analytically, is a winning idea when scoring responses to essay items.

Deciding Early about the Importance of Mechanics

Few things influence scorers of students' essay responses as much as the mechanics of writing employed in the response. If the student displays subpar spelling, chaotic capitalization, and poor punctuation, it's pretty tough for a scorer of the student's response not to be influenced adversely. In some instances, of course, mechanics of writing certainly do play a meaningful role in scoring students' performances. For instance, suppose you're scoring students' written responses to a task of writing an application letter for a position as a reporter for a local newspaper. In such an instance, it is clear that mechanics of writing would be pretty important when judging the student's response. But in a chemistry class, perhaps the teacher cares less about such factors when scoring students' essay responses to a problem-solving task. The third guideline simply suggests that you make up your mind about this issue early in the process so that, if mechanics aren't all that important to you, you don't let your students' writing mechanics subconsciously influence the way you score their responses.

Scoring One Item at a Time

If you're using an essay examination with more than one item, be sure to score all of your students' responses to one item, then score all of their responses to the next item, and so on. Do *not* score all responses of a given student, then go on to the next student's paper. There's too much danger that a student's responses to early items will unduly influence your scoring of responses to subsequent items. If you score all responses to item number 1, then move on to the responses to item number 2, you can eliminate this tendency. In addition, the scoring will actually go a bit quicker because you won't need to shift evaluative criteria between items. Adhering to this fourth guideline will invariably lead to more consistent scoring, hence to more accurate response-based inferences about your students. There'll be more paper shuffling than you might prefer, but the increased accuracy of your scoring will be worth it. (Besides, you'll be getting a smidge of psychomotor exercise.)

Striving for Anonymity

Because I've been a teacher, I know all too well how quickly teachers can identify their students' writing styles, particularly those students who have especially distinctive styles such as the "scrawlers," the "petite letter-size crew," and those who dot their *i*s with half-moons or cross their *t*s with lightning bolts. Yet, insofar as you can, try not to know whose responses you're scoring. One simple way to help in that effort is to ask students to write their names on the reverse side of the last sheet of the examination in the response booklet. Try not to peek at the students' names until you've scored all of the exams.

I used such an approach for three decades of scoring graduate students' essay examinations at UCLA. It worked fairly well. Sometimes I was really surprised because students who had appeared to be knowledgeable during class discussions displayed just the opposite on the exams, while several Silent Sarahs and Quiet Quentins came up with really solid exam performances. I'm sure that if I had known whose papers I had been grading, I would have been improperly influenced by my classroom-based perceptions of different students' abilities. I am not suggesting that you shouldn't use students' classroom discussions as part of your evaluation system. Rather, I'm advising you that classroom-based perceptions of students can sometimes cloud your scoring of essay responses. That's one strong reason for you to strive for anonymous scoring.

In review, we've considered five guidelines for scoring students' responses to essay examinations. If your classroom assessment procedures involve any essay items, you'll find that these five practical guidelines will go a long way in helping you come up with consistent scores for your students' responses. And

Parent Talk ···

The mother of one of your students, Jill Jenkins, was elected to your district's school board two years ago. Accordingly, any time Mrs. Jenkins wants to discuss Jill's education, you are understandably "all ears."

Mrs. Jenkins recently stopped by your classroom to say that three of her fellow board members have been complaining that there are too many essay tests being given in the district. The three board members contend that such tests, because they must be scored "subjectively," are neither reliable or valid.

Because many of the tests you give Jill and her classmates are essay tests, Mrs. Jenkins asks you if the three board members are correct.

• • • ***If I were you, here's how I'd respond to Jill's mom.*** *(Oh yes, because Mrs. Jenkins is a board member, I'd simply ooze politeness and professionalism while I responded.)*

"Thanks for giving me an opportunity to comment on this issue, Mrs. Jenkins. As you've already guessed, I side with you on the importance of constructed-response examinations such as essay tests. The real virtue of essay tests is that they call for students to *create* their responses, not merely *recognize* correct answers, as students must with other types of tests such as multiple-choice exams.

"The three school board members are correct when they say it is more difficult to score constructed-response items consistently than it is to score selected-response items consistently. And that's a shortcoming of essay tests. But it's a shortcoming that's more than compensated for by the far greater *authenticity* of the tasks presented to students in almost all constructed-response tests. When Jill writes essays during my major exams, that's much closer to what she'll be doing in later life than choosing the best answer from four options. In real life, people aren't given four-choice options. Rather, they're required to generate a response that reflects their views. Essay tests give Jill and her classmates a chance to do just that.

"Now, let's talk briefly about consistency and validity. Actually, Mrs. Jenkins, it is important for tests to be scored consistently. We refer to the consistency with which a test is scored as its *reliability*. And if a test isn't reliable, then the interpretations about students we make based on test scores aren't likely to be valid. It's a technical point, Mrs. Jenkins, but it isn't a *test* that's valid or invalid, it's a score-based inference about students that may or may not be valid. As your board colleagues pointed out, some essay tests are not scored all that reliably. But essay tests *can* be scored reliably and they *can* yield valid inferences about students.

"I hope my reactions have been helpful. I'll be happy to show you some of the actual essay exams I've used with Jill's class. And I'm sure the District Superintendent, Dr. Stanley, can supply you with additional information."

• • • ***Now, how would you respond to Mrs. Jenkins?***

consistency, as you learned in Chapter 2, is something that makes psychometricians mildly euphoric.

Now, after you've completed this chapter's usual end-of-chapter stuff, in the next two chapters you'll learn about two less common forms of constructed-response items. You'll learn how to create and score performance assessments and to use students' portfolios in classroom assessments. You'll find that what we've been dealing with in this chapter will serve as a useful springboard to the content of the next two chapters.

What Do Classroom Teachers Really Need to Know about Constructed-Response Tests? ....

At the close of a chapter dealing largely with the nuts and bolts of creating and scoring written constructed-response tests, you probably expect to be told that you really need to internalize all those nifty little guidelines so that, when you spin out your own short-answer and essay items, you'll elicit student responses that you can score accurately. Well, that's not a terrible aspiration, but there's really a more important insight you need to walk away with after reading the chapter. That insight, not surprisingly, derives from the central purpose of classroom assessment—namely, to draw accurate inferences about students' status so that you can make more appropriate educational decisions. What you really need to know about short-answer items and essay items is that you should use them as part of your classroom assessment procedures if you want to make inferences about your students that those students' responses to such items would support.

Putting it another way, if you, as a classroom teacher, want to determine if your students have the skill and/or knowledge that can be best measured by short-answer or essay items, then you need to refresh your memory regarding how to avoid serious item construction or response scoring errors. A review of the guidelines presented on pages 137, 141, and 145 should give you the brushup that you need. Don't believe that you are obligated to use short-answer or essay items simply because you now know a bit more about how to crank them out. If you're interested in the extensiveness of your students' *knowledge* regarding Topic Z, it may be far more efficient to employ fairly low-level selected-response kinds of items. If, however, you really want to make inferences about your students' abilities to perform the kinds of tasks represented by short-answer and essay items, then the guidelines provided in the chapter should be consulted.

Chapter Summary ....

After a fairly elaborate, guilt-induced apology for the chapter's mislabeling, the chapter started off with a description of short-answer items accompanied by a set of guidelines (page 137) regarding how to write short-answer items. The chapter then took up essay items and indicated that, although students' written compositions constitute a particular kind of essay response, most of the recommendations for constructing essay items and for scoring students' responses were the same, whether measuring students' composition skills or skills in subject areas other than language arts. Guidelines were provided for writing essay items (page 141) and for scoring students' responses to essay items (page 145). The chapter was concluded with the suggestion that much of the content to be treated in the following two chapters, because those chapters also focus on constructed-response assessment schemes, will relate to the creation and scoring of short-answer and essay items.

Self-Check

This chapter's self-check exercises will start off with a brief set of illustrative short-answer and essay items. Your task is to identify whether any of the chapter's item-writing guidelines have been violated. If so, you are to indicate what the violated guideline was or, if two or more guidelines have been flaunted, which ones those were. If not, indicate that no guidelines have been violated. Because you'll be responding with brief constructed responses, what kind of test items do you suppose you're about to mess with?

Oh yes, if you want to, you might like to engage in a quick review of the item-writing guidelines on pages 137 and 141. It's not necessary, but some people are compulsive when they think their self-worth is going to be under scrutiny.

1. (The following item was written for fifth-graders.) Before the United States became an independent nation, most of the men and women who had come to settle were from which European nation or nations?

   _____   _____   _____

   Any violation(s)? _____

   _____

   _____

2. (This item is for high school students.) You have just viewed a videotape containing three widely seen television commercials. What is the one classic propaganda technique present in all three commercials? _____

   Any violation(s)? _____

   _____

   _____

3. (This item is for eighth-grade students.) If a friend has asked you to engage in the use of alcohol or _____ , and you wish to decline, you should _____ and _____ without delay.

   Any violation(s)? _____

   _____

   _____

4. (This item was written for eleventh-grade English students.) In the space provided below and on the attached sheet, please compose a brief 200-word editorial in favor of the school district's expanded after-school tutorial program. The intended audience for your position statement consists of those people who read the local newspaper's editorial page. Because you have the entire class period to prepare your response, please use the scratch paper provided for a first draft, then revise your editorial before copying it on these sheets. The editorial will contribute 40 percent to your six-week's Persuasive Writing grade.

   Any violation(s)? _____

   _____

   _____

5. (This item was written for sixth-graders.) Thinking back over the mathematics lesson and homework assignments you had during the past 12 weeks, what conclusions can you draw? Take no more than one page for your response.

   Any violation(s)? _____

   _____

   _____

6. For the chapter's final self-check exercise, please read the description of how a fictitious teacher went about scoring an essay examination in a high school class called U.S. Government Service. Then evaluate how well the teacher carried out the scoring.

   "I was using a four-item essay examination on which my students were to spend 10 to 15 minutes per item. Before scoring students' papers, I worked up a tentative analytic scoring guide for each item. I identified two evaluative criteria that *had* to be satisfied in each response in order for it to receive full credit. If a student satisfied a criterion fairly well, the response earned 5 points; if the criterion was satisfied well, the response earned 10 points. In all, then, with two criteria per item, and 0 to 10 points per criterion, I could give a student 0 points up to 80 points. My scoring keys, which placed no emphasis on a student's use of mechanics, worked so well that I didn't have to revise them.

"I scored each student's response to all four items at a single sitting, and I found that I could interpret students' responses more sensitively because, from the student's name on the first page of the response booklet, I could tell whose responses I was grading. The entire scoring operation for the 29 students in my class took somewhat less than 90 minutes."

What is your evaluation of this teacher's scoring procedures?

_____

_____

_____

Pondertime

1. What do you think has been the *instructional* impact, if any, of the increasingly wide incorporation of student writing samples in the high-stakes educational achievement tests used in numerous states?

2. How would you contrast short-answer items and essay items with respect to the levels of cognitive behavior set forth in Bloom's taxonomy? Are there differences in the kinds of cognitive behavior elicited by the two item types? If so, what are they?

3. What do you see as the major weaknesses of short-answer and essay items? What are their major strengths?

4. What would influence you in deciding whether to use selected-response items or the kinds of constructed-response items treated in this chapter?

5. What kinds of student outcomes could not be assessed properly with short-answer items but could be assessed properly with essay items?

Self-Check Key

1. This item really doesn't violate any of the guidelines listed on page 137, but it's a weak item because it violated one of the general-purpose item-writing commandments cited in Chapter 6. The item presents an ambiguous task to students insofar

as it asks for a nation (or nations) from which "most" of the settlers came, then provides three blank spaces, thereby indicating that three, not one, response is sought, even though, by definition, there is only one "most." An astute answer from you for this self-check item would have been something along these lines: "No violations, but cruddy nonetheless."

2. This item violates no guidelines and isn't really all that shabby.

3. This item violates a pair of guidelines. It uses too many blanks and the blanks are unequal in length. It would be difficult for students, given the nearly total ambiguity introduced by the initial blank, to know how to respond to that item. It is, in short, a loser item.

4. This item violates none of the chapter's item-writing guidelines for essay items. As you can note, the first three guidelines on page 141 have all been specifically followed in the item. It's a fairly decent prompt for a persuasive writing task.

5. This item violates several of the chapter's guidelines for writing essay items. Although it limits the student's response to one page, there is substantial ambiguity about the nature of the task that the teacher wants the students to undertake. Twelve weeks' worth of mathematics can add up (a mathematical operation) to a pretty hefty pile of math. The number of conclusions that the student can legitimately draw are myriad. Thus, Guideline 2 is clearly violated because the student doesn't know what to do. Guideline 3 is also violated because there's no indication given regarding time limit or point value for the item. This item needs a good deal of refurbishing.

6. This fictitious teacher adhered to one of the guidelines on page 145 when a tentative analytic scoring key was used that dealt with the importance of a student's written mechanics. There were two serious guideline violations, however, in that the teacher didn't score items one at a time and also failed to score students' responses anonymously. On balance, therefore, you should have given a "thumbs-down" to this teacher's essay-scoring effort. The two serious violations are too likely to threaten the validity of any score-based inferences the teacher might wish to draw.

Additional Stuff

Airasian, Peter W. *Classroom Assessment* (2nd ed.). New York: McGraw-Hill, 1994.

Linn, Robert L., and Norman E. Gronlund. *Measurement and Assessment in Teaching* (7th ed.). Upper Saddle River, NJ: Prentice Hall, 1995.

McMillan, James H. *Classroom Assessment: Principles and Practice for Effective Instruction.* Boston: Allyn and Bacon, 1997.

Mehrens, W. A., and I. J. Lehmann. *Measurement and Evaluation in Education and Psychology* (4th ed.). New York: Holt, Rinehart and Winston, 1991.

Page, Ellis B., and Nancy S. Petersen. "The Computer Moves into Essay Grading: Updating the Ancient Test." *Phi Delta Kappan,* 76, no. 7 (March 1995): 561–565.

Stiggins, Richard J. *Student-Centered Classroom Assessment* (2nd ed.). Upper Saddle River, NJ: Prentice Hall, 1997.

Nonprint Stuff

Northwest Regional Laboratory. *Writing Assessment: Issues and Answers* (Videotape #NREL-7A). Los Angeles: IOX Assessment Associates.

Northwest Regional Laboratory. *Writing Assessment: Training in Analytical Scoring* (Videotape #NREL-8A). Los Angeles: IOX Assessment Associates.

Popham, W. James. *Creating Challenging Classroom Tests: When Students CONSTRUCT Their Responses* (Videotape #ETVT-24). Los Angeles: IOX Assessment Associates.

8

Performance Assessment

*D*uring the early 1990s, a good many educational policymakers became enamored with performance assessment. *Performance assessment* is an approach to measuring a student's status based on the way that the student completes a specified task. Theoretically, of course, when the student chooses between *true* and *false* for a binary-choice item, the student is completing a task, although an obviously modest one. But the proponents of performance assessment have measurement schemes in mind that are meaningfully different from binary-choice or multiple-choice tests. Indeed, it was a dissatisfaction with traditional paper-and-pencil tests that caused many educators to scurry down the performance-testing trail.

What Is a Performance Test?

Before digging into what makes performance tests tick and how you might use them in your own classroom, we'd best explore the chief attributes of such an assessment approach. Even though all educational tests, as noted earlier, require students to perform in some way, when most educators talk about performance tests, they are thinking about assessments in which the student is required to construct an original response. More often than not, an examiner (such as the teacher) *observes* the process of construction so that observation of the student's performance and judgment of that performance are required. Close to three decades ago, Fitzpatrick and Morrison (1971) observed that "there is no absolute distinction between performance tests and other classes of tests." They pointed out that the distinction between performance assessments and more conventional tests is chiefly the degree to which the examination simulates the criterion situation—that is, the examination approximates the domain of student behaviors about which we wish to make inferences.

Suppose, for example, that a teacher who had been instructing students in the process of collaborative problem solving wanted to see whether students had acquired that collaborative skill. The *inference* at issue centers on the extent to which each student has mastered the skill. The *educational decision* on the line might be whether particular students need additional instruction or, instead, whether it's time to move on to other instructional objectives. The teacher's real interest, then, is in how well students can work with other students to arrive collaboratively at solutions to problems. In Figure 8.1, you will see there are several assessment procedures that could be used to get a fix on a student's collaborative problem-solving skills. Yet, note that the two selected-response assessment options (numbers 1 and 2) don't really ask students to construct anything. For the other three constructed-response assessment options (numbers 3, 4, and 5), however, there are clear differences in the degree to which the task presented to the student coincides with the class of tasks called for by the teacher's instructional objective. Assessment Option 5, for example, is obviously the closest match to the behavior called for in the objective. Yet, Assessment Option 4 is surely more of a "performance test" than is Assessment Option 1.

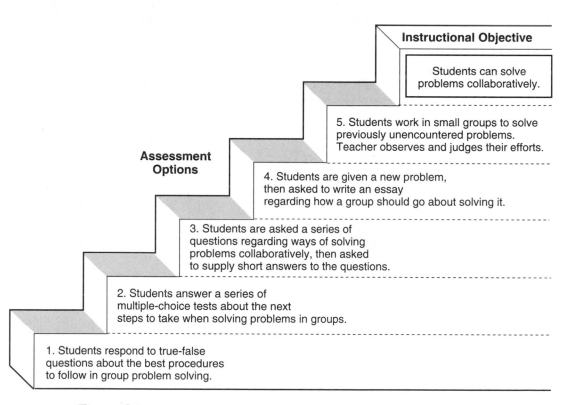

Instructional Objective

Students can solve problems collaboratively.

Assessment Options

5. Students work in small groups to solve previously unencountered problems. Teacher observes and judges their efforts.

4. Students are given a new problem, then asked to write an essay regarding how a group should go about solving it.

3. Students are asked a series of questions regarding ways of solving problems collaboratively, then asked to supply short answers to the questions.

2. Students answer a series of multiple-choice tests about the next steps to take when solving problems in groups.

1. Students respond to true-false questions about the best procedures to follow in group problem solving.

Figure 8.1 **A Set of Assessment Options That Vary in the Degree to Which Student's Task Approximates the Desired Criterion Behavior**

It should be apparent to you, then, that different educators will be using the phrase *performance assessment* to refer to very different kinds of assessment approaches. Many teachers, for example, are willing to consider short-answer and essay tests a form of performance assessment. In other words, they essentially equate performance assessment with any form of constructed-response assessment. Other teachers establish more stringent requirements in order for a measurement procedure to be described as a performance assessment. For example, some performance assessment proponents contend that genuine performance assessments must possess at least three features:

- *Multiple evaluative criteria.* The student's performance must be judged using more than one evaluative criterion. To illustrate, a student's ability to speak Spanish might be appraised on the basis of the student's accent, syntax, and vocabulary.
- *Prespecified quality standards.* Each of the evaluative criteria on which a student's performance is to be judged is clearly explicated in advance of judging the quality of the student's performance.
- *Judgmental appraisal.* Unlike the scoring of selected-response tests in which electronic computers and scanning machines can, once programmed, carry on without the need of humankind, genuine performance assessments depend on human judgments to determine how acceptable a student's performance really is.

Looking back to Figure 8.1, it is clear that if the foregoing three requirements were applied to the five assessment options supplied, Assessment Option 5 would qualify as a performance test, and Assessment Option 4 probably would as well, but the other three assessment options wouldn't qualify under a definition of performance assessment that requires the incorporation of multiple evaluative criteria, prespecified quality standards, and judgmental appraisals.

A good many advocates of performance assessment would prefer that the tasks presented to students represent real-world rather than school-world kinds of problems. Other proponents of performance assessment would be elated simply if more school-world measurement was constructed response rather than selected response in nature. Still other advocates of performance testing want the tasks in performance tests to be genuinely *demanding*—that is, way up the ladder of Bloom's taxonomy. In short, proponents of performance assessment often advocate different approaches to measuring students on the basis of how they perform.

You'll sometimes encounter educators who use other phrases to describe performance assessment. For example, they may use the phrase *authentic assessment* (because the assessment tasks more closely coincide with real-life, nonschool tasks) or *alternative assessment* (because such assessments constitute an alternative to traditional, paper-and-pencil tests). In the next chapter, we'll be considering *portfolio assessment*, which is a particular type of performance assessment and should not be considered a synonymous descriptor for the performance assessment approach to educational measurement.

Why Performance Assessment? ....

Advocates of performance assessment, and there are many, base their support of performance assessment on a number of factors. Mehrens (1992), a prominent educational measurement specialist, has identified a series of reasons that educators advocate performance assessment. Presented here are descriptions of three influences that Mehrens believes contribute to the support for performance assessment.

- *Dissatisfaction with selected-response tests.* Proponents of performance assessment tend to believe that because multiple-choice and binary-choice tests call only for *recognition* on the part of the student, those tests fail to tap higher-order thinking skills such as whether students can solve problems, synthesize, or think independently. Although selected-response tests are sometimes criticized as being biased or as dealing with unimportant content, the most frequently voiced criticism of selected-response tests is, not surprisingly, that the student need only *select* a response.
- *The influence of cognitive psychology.* Cognitive psychologists believe that students must acquire both content knowledge and procedural knowledge. Such psychologists argue that all cognitive tasks require both kinds of knowledge, but for certain kinds of tasks, there are different emphases on the two kinds of knowledge (Snow and Lohman, 1989). Because particular types of procedural knowledge are not assessable via selected-response

tests, many cognitive psychologists have been calling for increased use of performance assessment in education to accompany what they believe should be an increased instructional emphasis on students' acquisition of procedural knowledge.

- *The sometimes harmful instructional impact of conventional tests.* As the stakes associated with an educational test rise, teachers tend to emphasize instructionally the content embodied in the test. Consequently, particularly if the instruction coincides too directly with the test, students' scores on the test may rise although their mastery of the domain of skills or knowledge represented by the test does not. Because many educators recognize that high-stakes tests will most likely continue to influence what a teacher teaches, they argue that performance assessments will constitute more praiseworthy instructional targets than traditional paper-and-pencil tests. As a consequence of more appropriate high-stakes assessment targets, it is believed teachers' instructional activities will shift in appropriate directions.

   Suppose, for example, that an important statewide multiple-choice achievement test were given to students in your state at the grade level (or in the subject fields) of the students you teach. If you believed that your *personal* instructional competence was being judged, at least in part, according to how well your students performed on the test, there would be a meaningful temptation to align your classroom assessments and classroom instruction with the statewide test's multiple-choice assessment targets. Recognizing the likely instructional impact of high-stakes assessment, proponents of performance testing want to install more suitable assessment targets.

There are other arguments that can be mustered in favor of performance assessment, but Mehrens (1992) has nicely captured the major motivations of those who advocate the widespread installation of performance assessments. Mehrens, incidentally, is highly supportive of the use of performance tests by classroom teachers because he believes significant instructional improvement will flow from such assessments. He is skeptical, however, about the use of performance tests for purposes of educational accountability—that is, for determining how effectively teachers (individually or aggregated at the school/district level) are providing instruction for their students.

We now turn to the twin issues that are at the heart of performance assessments: *selecting appropriate tasks* for students and, once the students have tackled those tasks, *judging the adequacy of students' responses.*

Identifying Suitable Tasks for Performance Assessment ....

Performance assessment typically requires students to respond to a small number of more significant tasks rather than respond to a large number of less significant tasks. Thus, rather than answering 50 multiple-choice items on a conventional

Grow, Plants, Grow! ....

Francine Floden is a third-year biology teacher in Kennedy High School. Because she has been convinced by several of her colleagues that traditional paper-and-pencil examinations fail to capture the richness of the scientific experience, Francine has decided to base almost all of her students' grades on a semester-long performance test. As Francine contemplates her new assessment plan, 90% of the students' grades will stem from the quality of their responses to the performance test's task; 10% of the grades will be linked to classroom participation and a few short true-false quizzes administered throughout the semester.

The task embodied in Francine's performance test requires each student to design and conduct a two-month experiment to study the growth of three identical plants under different conditions, then prepare a formal scientific report describing the experiment. Although most of Francine's students carry out their experiments at home, several students use the shelves at the rear of the classroom for their experimental plants. A number of students vary the amount of light or the kind of light received by the different plants, but most students modify the nutrients given to their plants. After a few weeks of the two-month experimental period, all of Francine's students seem to be satisfactorily underway with their experiments.

Several of the more experienced teachers in the school, however, have expressed their reservations to Francine about what they regard as "overbooking on a single assessment experience." The teachers suggest to Francine that she will be unable to draw defensible inferences about her students' true mastery of biological skills and knowledge based on a single performance test. They urged her to reduce dramatically the grading weight for the performance test so that, instead, additional grade-contributing examinations can be given to the students.

Other colleagues, however, believe that Francine's performance test approach is precisely what is needed in courses such as biology. They recommend she "stay the course" and alter "not one whit" of her new assessment strategy.

If you were Francine, what would your decision be?

chemistry examination, students who are being assessed via performance tasks may find themselves asked to perform an actual experiment in their chemistry class, then write an interpretation of the experiment's results and an analytic critique of the procedures they used. From the chemistry teacher's perspective, instead of seeing how students respond to the 50 "mini-tasks" represented in the multiple-choice test, an estimate of each student's status must be derived from a student's response to a single, complex task. Given the significance of each task that is used in a performance-testing approach to classroom assessment, it is apparent that great care must be taken in the selection of such tasks. Generally speaking, classroom teachers will either have to (1) generate their own performance test tasks or (2) select performance test tasks from the increasing number of tasks that are available from educators elsewhere.

Inferences and Tasks

Consistent with the frequently asserted message of this bundle-of-fun book about classroom assessment that you are currently reading, the chief determinants of how you assess your students are (1) the inference you want to make about those students and (2) the decision that will be based on that inference. For example, suppose you're a history teacher and you've spent a summer at a lakeside cabin meditating about curricular matters (which, in one lazy setting or another, is the public's perception of how most teachers spend their vacations). After three months of heavy curricular thought, you have concluded that what you really want to teach your students is to be able to apply historical lessons of the past to the solution of current and future problems that, at least to some extent, parallel the problems of the past. You have decided to abandon your week-long, 1,500-item true-false final examination that your stronger students refer to as a "measurement marathon" and your weaker students refer to by using a rich, if earthy, vocabulary. Instead of true-false items, you are now committed to a performance assessment strategy and wish to select tasks for your performance tests that will help you infer how well your students can draw on the lessons of the past to illuminate their approach to current and/or future problems.

In Figure 8.2, you will see a graphic depiction of the relationships among (1) a teacher's key educational objective, (2) the inference that the teacher wishes to draw about each student, and (3) the task for a performance test intended to secure data to support the inference that the teacher wants to make. As you will note, the teacher's instructional objective provides the source for the inference, and the assessment tasks yield the evidence needed for the teacher to arrive at defensible inferences regarding the extent to which students can solve current or future problems using historical lessons. To the degree that students have mastered the instructional objective, the teachers will make a decision about how much more instruction, if any, is needed.

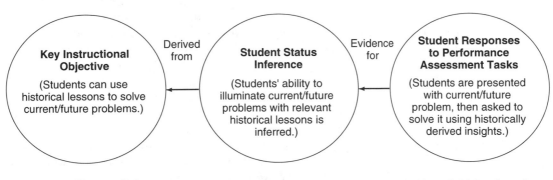

Figure 8.2 **Relationships among a Teacher's Key Instructional Objective, the Assessment-Based Inference Derivative from the Objective, and the Performance Assessment Task That Will Provide Evidence for the Inference**

The Generalizability Dilemma

One of the most serious difficulties with performance assessment is that because students respond to fewer tasks than would be the case with conventional paper-and-pencil testing, it is often more difficult to generalize accurately about what skills and knowledge are possessed by the student.

To illustrate, let's say you're trying to get a fix on your students' ability to multiply pairs of double-digit numbers. If, because of your instructional priorities, you can devote only a half hour to assessment purposes, you could require the students to respond to 20 such multiplication problems in the 30 minutes available. (That's probably more problems than you'd need, but I'm trying to draw a vivid contrast for you.) From a student's responses to 20 multiplication problems, you can get a pretty fair idea about what kind of double-digit multiplier the student is. As a consequence of the student's performance on a *reasonable sample* of items drawn from the assessment domain, you can conclude that "Javier really knows how to multiply those sorts of problems," or that "Fred really couldn't multiply double-digit multiplication problems if his life depended on it." It is because you have sampled well the domain of student performance (to which you wish to make an inference) that you can confidently make inferences about your students' abilities to solve similar sorts of multiplication problems. With only a 30-minute assessment period available, however, if you moved to a more elaborate kind of performance test, you might only be able to have students respond to one big-bopper item. ("Big-bopper," incidentally, is not a psychometrically sanctioned descriptor of classroom assessments.) For example, if you presented a multiplication-focused mathematics problem involving the use of manipulatives, and wanted your students to derive an original solution and then describe it in writing, you'd be lucky if your students could finish the task in a half hour. Based on this single task, how confident would you be in making inferences about your students' abilities to perform comparable multiplication tasks?

And that, as you now see, is the rub with performance testing. Because students respond to fewer tasks, the teacher is put in a trickier spot when it comes to deriving inferences about students' general abilities. If you use only one performance test, and a student does well on the test, does this signify that the student *really* possesses the category of skills that the test was designed to measure, or did the student just get lucky? On the other hand, if a student messes up on a single-performance test, does this signify that the student *really* doesn't possess the assessed skill, or was there a feature in this particular performance test that misled the student who, given other tasks, might have performed wonderfully?

As a classroom teacher, you're faced with two horns of a classic measurement dilemma. Although performance tests often measure the kinds of student abilities that you'd prefer to assess (because those abilities are in line with really worthwhile instructional aims), the inferences that you make about students on the basis of their responses to performance tests must be made with increased caution. As with many dilemmas, there may be no perfect way to hop the dilemma's two horns. But there is, at least, a way of dealing with the dilemma as sensibly as you can. In this instance, the solution strategy is to devote great care to the selection of the tasks embodied in your performance tests. Among the most important considerations in selecting such tasks is to choose tasks that optimize the likelihood of accurately generalizing about your students' capabilities. If you really keep generalizability at the forefront when you select/construct performance-test tasks, you'll be able to make the strongest possible performance-based inferences about your students' capabilities.

Factors to Consider When Evaluating Performance-Test Tasks

We've now considered what many measurement specialists regard as the most important factor that you can consider when judging potential tasks for performance assessments—*generalizability*. Let's look at a list of seven such factors you might wish to consider, whether you select a performance test task from existing tasks or, in contrast, create your own performance test tasks.

Evaluative Criteria for Performance-Test Tasks

- *Generalizability.* Is there a high likelihood that the students' performance on the task will generalize to comparable tasks?
- *Authenticity.* Is the task similar to what students might encounter in the real world as opposed to encountering only in school?
- *Multiple foci.* Does the task measure multiple instructional outcomes instead of only one?
- *Teachability.* Is the task one that students can become more proficient in as a consequence of a teacher's instructional efforts?
- *Fairness.* Is the task fair to all students—that is, does the task avoid bias based on such personal characteristics as students' gender, ethnicity, or socioeconomic status?
- *Feasibility.* Is the task realistically implementable in relation to its cost, space, time, and equipment requirements?
- *Scorability.* Is the task likely to elicit student responses that can be reliably and accurately evaluated?

Whether you're developing your own tasks for performance tests or selecting such tasks from an existing collection, you may wish to apply some but not all of the factors listed here. Personally, I would usually try to apply all seven factors, although I can see how one might, on occasion, dump the *authenticity* criterion or the *multiple foci* criterion. In some instances, for example, school tasks rather than real-world tasks might be suitable for the kinds of inferences that a teacher wishes to reach, hence the authenticity criterion may not be relevant. And even though it is economically advantageous to measure more than one outcome at one time, particularly considering the time and effort that goes into almost any performance test, there may be instances in which a single educational outcome is sufficiently important so that it warrants a solo performance test. More often that not, though, a really good task for a performance test will satisfy all seven of the evaluative criteria presented here.

Performance Tests and Teacher Time

Back in Chapter 1, I promised that if you completed this book with a reasonable degree of attentiveness, you'd become a better teacher. Now I have another promise for you. I promise to be *honest* about the measurement mysteries we're probing together. And that brings me to an important consideration regarding performance testing. In brief, it takes time!

Think for a moment about the time that you, as the teacher, need to give to (1) the selection of suitable tasks, (2) the development of an appropriate scheme for scoring students' responses, and (3) the actual scoring of students' responses. Talk to any teacher who's already used many classroom performance tests and you'll learn it takes a ton of time to use performance assessment.

So what I want to suggest to is that there's one additional factor that you should throw into your decision making about performance assessment. It is the *significance of the skill* that you're using the performance test to assess. Because you'll almost certainly have time for only a handful of such performance tests in your teaching, make sure that every performance test you use is linked to a truly significant skill that you're trying to have your students acquire. If performance assessments aren't based on genuinely demanding skills, you'll soon stop using them because, to be truthful, they'll be more trouble than they're worth.

Identifying Scoring Criteria ....

Performance assessments invariably are based on constructed-response measurement procedures in which students generate rather than select their responses. Student-constructed responses must be scored, however, and it's clearly much tougher to score constructed responses than to score selected responses. The scoring of constructed responses centers on the *evaluative criteria* that one calls on to determine the adequacy of students' responses. Let's turn our attention now to the evaluative criteria that are used to decide whether students' responses to performance tests are splendid or sucko.

A *criterion*, according to *Webster's Dictionary,* is "a standard on which a judgment or decision may be based." In the case of scoring students' responses to a performance test's task, you're clearly trying to make a judgment regarding the adequacy of the student's constructed response. The specific criteria to be used in making that judgment will obviously influence the way that you score a student's response. For instance, if you were scoring a student's written composition on the basis of organization, word choice, and communicative clarity, you might arrive at very different scores than if you scored the composition on the basis of spelling, punctuation, and grammar. The evaluative criteria that are used when scoring students' responses to performance tests (or their responses to any kind of con-structed-response item) really control the whole evaluative enterprise.

In passing, having completed five years of Latin in high school and college, I feel compelled to use a word or two of Latin at least on a semi-annual basis. Thus, be aware that the Latin word *criterion* is singular and the Latin word *criteria* is plural. Unfortunately, so many educators mix up these two terms that I don't even become distraught about it anymore. However, now that you know the difference, if you find any of your colleagues erroneously saying "the criteria is" or the "the criterion were," you can display an ever so subtle yet altogether condescending smirk.

The scoring procedures for judging students' responses to performance tests are usually referred to these days as *scoring rubrics* or, more simply, *rubrics*. A rubric that's used to score students' responses to a performance assessment has, at minimum, three important features:

- *Evaluative criteria.* These are the factors to be used in determining the quality of a student's response.
- *Descriptions of qualitative differences for the evaluative criteria.* For each evaluative criterion, a description must be supplied so that qualitative distinctions in students' responses can be made using the criterion.
- *An indication of whether a holistic or analytic scoring approach is to be used.* The rubric must indicate whether the evaluative criteria are to be applied collectively in the form of *holistic* scoring or on a criterion-by-criterion basis in the form of *analytic* scoring.

The identification of a rubric's evaluative criteria, as might be guessed, is probably the most important task for rubric developers. If you're creating a rubric for a performance test you wish to use in your own classroom, be careful not to come up with a lengthy laundry list of the evaluative criteria that a student's response should satisfy. Personally, I think that when you isolate more than three or four evaluative criteria per rubric, you've identified too many. If you find yourself facing more than a few evaluative criteria, simply *rank each criterion in order of importance,* then chop off those listed lower than three or four.

The next job you'll have is deciding how to *describe in words* what a student's response must be in order to be judged wonderful or woeful. The level of descriptive detail that you apply needs to work *for you.* Remember, you're devising a scoring rubric for your own classroom, not a statewide or national test. Keep the aversiveness of the work down by employing brief descriptors of quality differences that you can use and, if you're instructionally astute, your students can use as well.

Finally, you'll need to decide whether you'll make a single, overall judgment about a student's response by considering all of the rubric's evaluative criteria (holistic scoring) or, instead, award the response points on a criterion-by-criterion basis (analytic scoring). The virtue of holistic scoring, of course, is that it's quicker to do. The downside of holistic scoring is that it fails to communicate to students, especially low-performing students, what their shortcomings are. Clearly, analytic scoring yields a greater likelihood of diagnostically pinpointed scoring and sensitive feedback than does holistic scoring. Some classroom teachers have attempted to garner the best of both worlds by scoring all responses holistically, then analytically rescoring (for feedback purposes) all responses of low-performing students.

Because most performance assessments call for fairly complex responses from students, there will usually be more than one evalautive criterion employed to score students' responses. For each of the evaluative criteria chosen, a numerical scale is typically employed so that for each criterion, a student's response might be assigned a specified number of points—for instance, 0 to 6 points. Usually, these scale points are accompanied by verbal descriptors; sometimes they aren't. For instance, in a 5-point scale, the following descriptors might be used: 5 = Exemplary, 4 = Superior, 3 = Satisfactory, 2 = Weak, 1 = Inadequate. If no verbal descriptors are used for each score point on the scale, a scheme such as the following might be employed:

In some cases, the scoring scale for each criterion is nonnumerical; that is, it consists only of verbal descriptors such as "exemplary," "adequate," and so on. Although such verbal scales can be useful with particular types of performance tests, their disadvantage is that scores from multiple criteria cannot be added together in order to produce a meaningful overall score.

The heart of the intellectual process in isolating suitable evaluative criteria is to get to the essence of what the most significant factors are that distinguish acceptable from unacceptable responses. In this instance, as in many others, less is more. A few truly important criteria are preferable to a plethora of trifling criteria. Go for the big ones. If you need help in deciding what criteria to employ in conjunction with a particular performance test, don't be reluctant to ask colleagues to toss in their ideas regarding what factors to use (for a given performance test) in order to discriminate between super and subpar responses.

Both in this chapter and, later, in Chapter 12, you'll be presented with scoring rubrics that can serve as useful models for your own construction of such rubrics. In those illustrative scoring rubrics, you'll see that great care has been taken to isolate a small number of instructionally addressable evaluative criteria. As Chapter 12 points out, the greatest payoff from a well-formed scoring rubric is in its contribution to improved instruction.

Two Illustrative Performance-Test Tasks and a Scoring System ....

To give you a better idea about the kinds of tasks that might be used in a performance test and the way that you might score a student's responses, let's take a look at two tasks for performance tests. The first one, presented in Figure 8.3, is intended to assess students' mastery of an oral communications skill. The second task, presented in Figure 8.4, is designed to measure the kind of higher-level skill in history described earlier in the chapter (see Figure 8.2). The skill is entitled *Using History's Lessons.*

A rubric for scoring students' oral communication skills—that is, for scoring their responses to the performance task given in Figure 8.3—is presented later in Chapter 12. A rubric for scoring students' responses to the *Using History's Lessons* performance test in Figure 8.4 is provided in Figure 8.5.

Figure 8.3   **Task Description and Sample Tasks for a One-on-One Oral Communication Performance Assessment**

An Oral Communications Performance Test

Introduction

There are numerous kinds of speaking tasks that students must perform in everyday life, both in school and out of school. This performance assessment focuses on some of these tasks—namely, describing objects, events, and experiences; explaining the steps in a sequence; providing information in an emergency; and persuading someone.

In order to accomplish a speaking task, the speaker must formulate and transmit a message to a listener. This process involves deciding what needs to be said, organizing the message, adapting the message to the listener and situation, choosing language to convey the message and, finally, delivering the message. The effectiveness of the speaker may be rated in terms of how well the speaker meets the requirement of the task.

Sample Tasks

Description Task: Think about your favorite class or extracurricular activity in school. Describe to me everything you can about it so that I will know a lot about it. (How about something like a school subject, a club, or a sports program?)

Emergency Task: Imagine that you are home alone and you smell smoke. You call the fire department and I answer your call. Talk to me as if you were talking on the telephone. Tell me everything I would need to know to get help to you. (Talk directly to me; begin by saying hello.)

Sequence Task: Think about something you know how to cook. Explain to me, step by step, how to make it. (How about something like popcorn, a sandwich, or scrambled eggs?)

Persuasion Task: Think about one change you would like to see made in your school, such as a change in rules or procedures. Imagine I am the principal of your school. Try to convince me that the school should make this change. (How about something like a change in the rules about hall passes or the procedures for enrolling in courses?)

Source: Based on assessment efforts of the Massachusetts Department of Education.

Figure 8.4 **Skill and Task Descriptions Plus One Sample Task** for the Skill of *Using History's Lessons*

Using History's Lessons

Skill Description

Students will be able to draw on the lessons of history to predict the likely consequences of current-day proposals. More specifically, students will be presented with a current problem setting and a proposed solution. The student must then (1) identify one or more historical events that are particularly relevant to the problem setting and proposed solution, (2) justify those selected, (3) make a history-based prediction regarding the likely consequences of the proposed solution, and (4) defend that prediction on the basis of historical parallels.

Nature of Tasks

Students will be given a description of a real or fictitious problem situation in which a course of action is being proposed as a solution to the problem. Students will be asked to write an essay in which they (1) identify, from a prespecified time line of major events in U.S. history, one or more historical events that are relevant to the proposed solution; (2) justify the relevance of the identified event(s); (3) make a defensible prediction of the probable consequences of the proposed solution based on the identified historical event(s); and (4) defend the prediction on the basis of parallels between the problem situation, the proposed solution, and the identified historical event(s).

Sample Task

Read the fictitious situation described below, then follow the directions that appear after the description.

War or Peace

Nation A is a large, industrialized country whose population is almost 100,000,000. Nation A has ample natural resources and is democratically governed. Nation A also owns two groups of territorial islands that, although quite distant, are rich in iron ore and petroleum.

Nation B is a country with far fewer natural resources and a population of only 40,000,000. Nation B is about one-third the size of Nation A. Although much less industrialized than Nation A, Nation B is as technologically advanced as Nation A. Nation B is governed by a three-member council of generals.

Recently, without any advance warning, Nation A was ruthlessly attacked by Nation B. As a consequence of this attack, more than half of Nation A's military equipment was destroyed.

After its highly successful surprise attack, Nation B's rulers have proposed a "peace agreement" calling for Nation A to turn over its two groups of islands to Nation B.

> If the islands are not conceded by Nation A, Nation B's rulers have threatened all-out war.
>
> Nation A's elected leaders are fearful of the consequences of the threatened war because their military equipment is now much weaker than that of Nation B. Nation A's leaders are faced with a choice of (1) peace obtained by giving up the islands or (2) war with a militarily stronger nation.
>
> Nation A's leaders decide to declare that a state of war exists with Nation B. They believe that even though Nation B is now stronger, in the long term, Nation A will win the war because of its greater industrial capability and richer natural resources.
>
> *Directions:* Compose a well-written essay. In that essay, drawing on your knowledge of U.S. history, select one or more important historical events that are especially relevant to the fictitious situation described above. Then justify the relevance of your selection(s). Next, make a reasonable history-based prediction about the likely consequences of the decision by Nation A's leaders to go to war. Finally, defend your prediction on the basis of the historical event(s) you identified.

Source: Based on assessment efforts of the U.S. Department of Defense Dependents' Schools, Hessen, Germany.

Ratings and Observations ....

Once you've selected your evaluative criteria, you then need to apply them reliably to the judgment of students' responses. If the nature of the performance test task calls for students to create some sort of *product,* such as a written report of an experiment carried out in a biology class, then at your leisure you can rate the product's quality in relation to the criteria you've identified as important. For example, if you had decided on three criteria to use in evaluating students' reports of biology experiments, and could award from 0 to 4 points for each criterion, then you could leisurely assign from 0 to 12 points for each written report. The more clearly you understand what each criterion is, and what it means to award a different number of points on whatever scale you've selected, the more accurate your scores will be. Performance tests that yield student products are easier to rate because you can rate students' responses when you're in the mood.

It is often the case with performance tests, however, that the student's performance takes the form of some kind of *behavior.* With such performance tests, it will usually be necessary for you to observe the behavior as it takes place. To illustrate, suppose that you are an elementary school teacher whose fifth-grade students have been carrying out fairly elaborate social studies projects that are to culminate in 15-minute oral reports to classmates. Unless you have the equipment to videotape your students' oral presentations, you'll have to observe the oral

Figure 8.5   **A Rubric for Scoring Students' Responses**
to *Using History's Lessons*

Scoring Rubric: *Using History's Lessons*

The quality of students' responses to any task will be evaluated according to three evaluative criteria: (1) the selection and justification of relevant historical events, (2) the quality and defensibility of the history-based prediction regarding the consequences of the proposed problem solution, and (3) the written presentation of the analysis. Each of these criteria will be described in terms of the key elements constituting a criterion. Four levels of quality (Distinguished: 4 points, Proficient: 3 points, Apprentice: 2 points, and Novice: 1 point) will be described for each criterion according to that criterion's key elements. A zero will be given to students who make no response or whose responses are illegible or in a foreign language. Although responses will be scored analytically, on a criterion-by-criterion basis, a single overall score will be assigned to each student's response.

Criterion One: Historical Event Selection/Justification
(identifying relevant historical events, then justifying those events effectively)

Key Elements:

- *Event Selection:* Choosing one or more appropriate events from the *U.S. History Time Line: Major Events*—that is, those events sufficiently parallel to the described problem situation and the proposed solution to permit a defensible prediction regarding the proposed solution's likely consequences

U.S. History Time Line
Major Events*
(For 11th-Grade U.S. History)

Constitution	Depression
Territorial Expansion	New Deal
Civil War	World War II
Reconstruction	Cold War
Industrial Revolution	Civil Rights
Imperialism	Vietnam
World War I	Communication
	Revolution

*A different time line would be used at lower grade levels.

- *Event Justification:* Supporting the relevance of the historical event(s) selected to the proposed solution by identifying features of the historical event and the proposed solution that are sufficiently similar to warrant a history-based prediction about the proposed solution's consequences

Quality Levels:

Distinguished (4 points): The selection of historical events is completely accurate—that is, all appropriate historical events are selected and no inappropriate events are selected.* The selection of all those events is well justified.

Proficient (3 points): The selection of historical events is satisfactorily accurate—that is, at least one appropriate historical event is selected and any inappropriate historical events selected are justified at least adequately. In addition, all appropriate historical events are justified at least adequately.

Apprentice (2 points): Not all appropriate historical events are selected, but those inappropriate events selected are justified at least adequately.

Novice (1 point): No appropriate historical events are selected, and those inappropriate events selected are inadequately justified.

Criterion Two: Prediction Defensibility
(making a sound history-based prediction and defending it strongly)

Key Elements:

- **Prediction Quality:** Predicting the consequences of the proposed solution in a manner that is reasonably derivative from the historical event(s) selected

- **Strength of Defense:** Defending the history-based prediction by identifying those features of any selected historical events that bear on the likelihood of the prediction's accuracy

Quality Levels:

Distinguished (4 points): The prediction of the consequences of the proposed solution is reasonably based on the historical event(s) selected and is strongly defended by the citation of pertinent aspects of the historical event(s) selected.

Proficient (3 points): The prediction of the consequences of the proposed solution is adequately based on the historical event(s) selected and is at least adequately defended by pertinent aspects of the historical event(s) selected.

Apprentice (2 points): *Either* the prediction of the consequences of the proposed solution is adequately based on the historical event(s) but inadequately defended *or* the prediction is inadequate even though its historically based justification is strong.

Novice (1 point): The prediction of the consequences of the proposed solution is inadequate and the defense of the prediction is only adequate or worse.

*The appropriately relevant historical event(s) for each task will be determined by the examiners.

(continued)

Figure 8.5   **Continued**

> *Criterion Three: Written Communication*
> (communicating effectively in writing)
>
> **Key Elements:**
> * *Organization:* Structuring the essay appropriately
> * *Mechanics:* Employing suitable spelling, punctuation, and grammar
> * *Voice:* Incorporating effective usage and word choice
>
> **Quality Levels:**
>   *Distinguished* (4 points): All three key elements are well developed.
>   *Proficient* (3 points): All three key elements are at least adequately developed.
>   *Apprentice* (2 points): Only one or two key elements are adequately developed.
>   *Novice* (1 point): No key elements are adequately developed.
>
> **Overall Score:** Derived analytically or holistically, each student should be assigned an overall score of 0 to 4.

Source: Based on assessment efforts of the U.S. Department of Defense Dependents' Schools, Hessen, Germany.

reports and make judgments about the quality of a student's performance as it occurs. As was true when scores were given to student products, in making evaluative judgments about students' behavior, you will apply whatever criteria you've chosen and assign what you consider to be the appropriate number of points on the scales you are using.

For some observations, you'll find it sensible to make instant, on-the-spot quality judgments. For instance, if you are judging students' social studies reports on the basis of (1) content, (2) organization, and (3) presentation, you might make observation-based judgments on each of those three criteria as soon as a report is finished. In other cases, your observations might incorporate a delayed evaluative approach. For instance, let's say that you are working with students in a speech class on the elimination of "filler words and sounds," two of the most prominent of which are starting a sentence with "well" and interjecting frequent "uh"s into a presentation. In the nonevaluative phase of the observation, you could simply count the number of "well"s and "uh"s uttered by a student. Then, at a later time, you could decide on a point allocation for the criterion "avoids filler words and sounds." Putting it another way, systematic observations may be set up so that you make immediate or delayed allocations of points for the evaluative criteria you've chosen. If the evaluative criteria involve qualitative factors that must be appraised more judgmentally, then on-the-spot evaluations and point assignments are typically the way to go. If the evaluative criteria involve more quantitative factors, then a "count now and judge later" approach usually works better.

Sources of Error in Scoring
Student Performances ·····································

When scoring student performances, there are three common sources of error that can contribute to inaccurate inferences. First, there is the *scoring scale*. Second, there are the *scorers* themselves who may bring a number of bothersome biases to the enterprise. Finally, there are errors in the *scoring procedure*—that is, the process by which the scorers employ the scoring scale.

Scoring-Instrument Flaws

The major defect with most scoring instruments is the lack of descriptive rigor with which the evaluative criteria to be used are described. Given this lack of rigor, ambiguity exists in the interpretations that scorers make about what the scoring criteria mean. This typically leads to a set of unreliable ratings. For example, if teachers are to rate students on the extent to which students are "controlling," some teachers may view this as a positive quality and some may view it as a negative quality. Clearly, an inadequately clarified scoring form can lead to all sorts of "noise" in the scores provided by teachers.

Procedural Flaws

Among common problems with scoring students' responses to performance tests, we usually encounter demands on teachers to rate too many qualities. Overwhelmed scorers are scorers rendered ineffectual. Teachers who opt for a large number of evaluative criteria are teachers who have made a decisively inept opt. Care should be taken that no more than three or four evaluative criteria are to be employed in evaluations of students' responses to your performance assessments. Generally speaking, the fewer evaluative criteria used, the better.

Teachers' Personal-Bias Errors

If you recall Chapter 4's consideration of bias, you'll remember that bias is clearly an undesirable commodity. Teachers, albeit unintentionally, are frequently biased in the way they score students' responses. Several kinds of personal-bias errors are often encountered when teachers score students constructed responses. The first of these, known as *generosity error,* occurs when a teacher's bias leads to higher ratings than are warranted. Teachers with a proclivity toward generosity errors see good even where no good exists.

At the other extreme, some teachers display *severity errors.* A severity error, of course, is a tendency to underrate the quality of a student's work. When a pupil's product deserves a "good," a teacher suffering from this personal-bias error will award it only an "average" or even a "below average."

Parent Talk ....

The vice president of your school's Parent Advisory Council has asked you to tell him why so many of your school's teachers are now assessing students with performance tests instead of the more traditional paper-and-pencil tests.

• • • *If I were you, here's how I'd respond:*

"The reason that most of us are increasingly relying on performance tests these days is that performance tests almost always measure higher-level student skills. With traditional tests, too many of our teachers found they were assessing only the students' abilities to memorize facts.

"In recent years, educators have become far more capable of devising really *demanding* performance tests that require students to display genuinely high-level intellectual skills—skills that are way, way beyond memorization. We've learned how to develop the tests *and* how to score students' responses using carefully developed scoring rules that we refer to as *rubrics*.

"Please stop by my classroom and I'll show you some examples of these demanding performance tests. We're asking more from our students, and we're getting it."

• • • *Now, how would you respond to the vice president of the Parent Advisory Council?*

Another sort of personal-bias error is known as *central-tendency error*. This describes a tendency for teachers to view everything as being "in the middle of the scale." Very high or very low ratings are avoided by such folks. They prefer the warm fuzziness of the mean or the median. They tend to regard midpoint ratings as inoffensive and therefore dispense midpoint ratings almost thoughtlessly.

A particularly frequent error arises when a teacher's overall impression of a student influences how the teacher rates that student with respect to an individual criterion. This error is known as *halo effect*. If a teacher has a favorable attitude toward a student, that student will receive a host of favorable ratings (deserved or not) on a number of individual criteria. Similarly, if a teacher has an unfavorable attitude toward a student, the student will receive a pile of unfavorable ratings on all sorts of separate criteria.

One way to minimize halo effect, at least a bit, is occasionally to reverse the order of the high and low positions on the scoring scale so that the teacher cannot *unthinkingly* toss out a whole string of positives (or negatives). What you really need to do to avoid halo effect when you're scoring students' responses is to remember that it's always lurking in the wings. Try to score a student's responses on each criterion using that specific criterion, not a contaminated general impression of the student's ability.

What Do Classroom Teachers Really Need to Know about Performance Assessment? ....

Performance assessment has been around for a long, long while. Yet, in recent years, a growing number of educators have become strong supporters of this form of assessment because it (1) represents an alternative to traditional paper-and-pencil tests and (2) is often more authentic—that is, reflective of tasks that people need to perform in the real world. One of the things you need to understand about performance assessment is that it differs from more conventional assessment chiefly in the degree the assessment task matches the behavior domain to which you wish to make inferences. Because performance tasks coincide more closely with such domains than do paper-and-pencil tests, more accurate inferences can often be derived about students. Another big plus for performance tests is they establish assessment targets that, because such targets often influence the teacher's instruction, have a positive impact on instructional activities.

You need to realize, however, that because performance tasks require a fair chunk of time from students, the teacher is often faced with making rather shaky generalizations on the basis of relatively few student performances. It's also important for you to recognize that the development of defensible performance tests is difficult cerebral work. It takes rigorous thinking to identify suitable tasks for performance tests, then isolate appropriate evaluative criteria and spell out the scoring scale for each criterion. And, of course, once the test and its associated scoring procedures are in place, you still have to score students' performances, an operation that invariably takes much more time than is required to score a ream of responses to selected-response tests.

The chapter's final admonitions regarding the numerous biases that teachers bring to the scoring of students' responses to performance tests should serve as a reminder. If you employ performance tests frequently in your classrooms, you'll need to be careful at every step of the process—from the original conception and berthing of a performance test down to the bias-free scoring of students' responses. In Chapter 12, you'll see how performance tests can be used to improve the quality of your instructional procedures.

Chapter Summary ....

Although Chapter 8 dealt specifically with performance assessment, a number of the points made in the chapter apply with equal force to the scoring of any type of constructed-response item such as those used in essay tests or short-answer tests. After defining performance tests as a measurement procedure in which students create original responses to an assessment task, it was pointed out that performance tests differ from more conventional tests primarily in the degree the test situation approximates the real-life situation to which inferences are made.

Drawing on an analysis supplied by Mehrens (1992), three influences spurring the recent interest in performance assessment are (1) dissatisfaction with selected-response tests, (2) the influence of cognitive psychology, and (3) the sometimes harmful instructional impact of conventional tests.

The identification of suitable tasks for performance assessments was given considerable attention in the chapter because unsuitable tasks will surely lead to unsatisfactory performance assessments. Seven evaluative criteria were supplied for performance test tasks: (1) generalizability, (2) authenticity, (3) multiple foci, (4) teachability, (5) fairness, (6) feasibility, and (7) scorability. Particular emphasis was given to selecting tasks about which defensible inferences could be drawn regarding students' generalized abilities to perform comparable tasks.

The significance of the skill to be assessed via a performance task was stressed. Next, *evaluative criteria* were defined as the standards by which the acceptability of a student's performance is judged. The evaluative criteria constitute the most important features of a *rubric* that's employed to score student responses. The significance of selecting suitable evaluative criteria was emphasized. Once the criteria have been identified, a numerical scoring scale, usually consisting of three to six score points, is devised for each evaluative criterion. The scoring criteria are applied to student performances in the form of ratings for student products or observations for student behaviors.

The chapter was concluded with an identification of four kinds of scoring errors that are often seen when teachers evaluate students' responses to performance tests. The four errors consisted of generosity bias, severity bias, central-tendency bias, and halo effect.

Self-Check

For this chapter's self-check, you'll need to respond to a bit of performance testing yourself. More specifically, you are now asked to generate a scoring guide for a fairly straightforward task requiring students to describe, in a letter to a foreign pen pal, "how a U.S. president is elected." The task is one of several such tasks in which the student is asked to describe an important procedure in U.S. government to a foreign pen pal.

Now, focusing on students at a grade level with which you are familiar, please develop a first-draft scoring guide consisting of one or more evaluative criteria and a scale for each criterion.

Pondertime

1. Do you think that the extra effort associated with performance assessment is worth it? Why?

2. What do you personally consider to be the greatest single strength of performance assessment? How about the greatest single weakness?

3. Are there any sorts of topics or instructional objectives for which you think performance assessment most appropriate?

4. What do you think the likelihood is that performance assessment will be widely used by the classroom teachers you know? Why?

5. Do you believe performance assessment is more likely to be used by individual teachers in their classrooms rather than for large-scale, statewide "educational accountability" assessments? Why?

6. Do you prefer *holistic* or *analytic* scoring of students' responses to performance tests? And, pray tell, why?

Self-Check Key

Not knowing what sort of scoring guide you would come up with, it's pretty difficult to provide very specific feedback to help you discern how suitable your scoring guide is. Although the level of detail embodied in the scoring rubric presented in Figure 8.5 may be greater than what you provided, the central features of that guide should be embodied in your draft scoring guide. In other words, you should have (1) identified evaluative criteria, (2) described the criteria, and (3) provided a point scale for each criterion with as much specificity as your energy permitted.

If you're using this text in connection with a formal class, perhaps you can get a classmate to exchange scoring guides with you for a robust co-critiquing session. If you're married or engaged in a meaningful relationship, ask your partner to look over your scoring guide and see if that person understands how to score students' responses to the pen pal assignment. If you currently aren't involved in a significant relationship, I do *not* suggest that you try to curry favor with a prospective paramour by calling on that person to mess around with your scoring guide. Instead, try dinner and a movie.

Additional Stuff

Airasian, Peter W. *Classroom Assessment* (2nd ed.). New York: McGraw-Hill, 1994.

Blum, Robert E., and Judith Arter (Eds.). *A Handbook for Student Performance Assessment in an Era of Restructuring*. Alexandria, VA: Association for Supervision and Curriculum Development, 1996.

Burger, Susan E., and Donald L. Burger. "Determining the Validity of Performance-Based Assessment." *Educational Measurement: Issues and Practice*, 13, no. 1 (Spring 1994) 9–15.

Crocker, Linda. "Assessing Content Representativeness of Performance Assessment Exercises." *Applied Measurement in Education*, 10, no. 1 (1997), 83–95.

Fitzpatrick, R., and E. J. Morrison. "Performance and Product Evaluation." In E. L. Thorndike (Ed.), *Educational Measurement*. Washington, DC: American Council on Education, 1971, 237–270.

Herman, Joan L., Pamela R. Aschbacher, and Lynn Winters. *A Practical Guide to Alternative Assessment*. Alexandria, VA: Association for Supervision and Curriculum, 1992.

Jorgensen, Margaret. *Assessing Habits of Mind: Performance-Based Assessment in Science and Mathematics*. Columbus, OH: ERIC Clearinghouse for Science, Mathematics, and Environmental Education, The Ohio State University.

Linn, Robert L., and Elizabeth Burton. "Performance-Based Assessment: Implications of Task Specificity." *Educational Measurement: Issues and Practice*, 13, no. 1 (Spring 1994): 5–8, 15.

Mehrens, William A. "Using Performance Assessment for Accountability Purposes." *Educational Measurement: Issues and Practice*, 11, no. 1 (Spring 1992): 3–9.

Snow, R. E., and D. F. Lohman. "Implications of Cognitive Psychology for Educational Measurement." In R. L. Linn (Ed.), *Educational Measurement*. New York: American Council on Education and Macmillan, 1989, 263–331.

Stecher, Brian M., and Stephen P. Klein. "The Cost of Science Performance Assessments in Large-Scale Testing Programs." *Educational Evaluation and Policy Analysis*, 19, no. 1 (Spring 1997): 1–14.

Stiggins, Richard J. *Student-Centered Classroom Assessment* (2nd ed.). Upper Saddle River, NJ: Prentice Hall, 1997.

Swanson, David B., Geoffrey R. Norman, and Robert L. Linn. "Performance-Based Assessment: Lessons from the Health Professions." *Educational Researcher*, 24, no. 5 (June/July 1995): 5–11, 35.

U.S. Congress, Office of Technology Assessment. *Testing in American Schools: Asking the Right Questions*. OTA-SET-519. Washington, DC: U.S. Government Printing Office, 1992.

Wiggins, Grant. "Assessment: Authenticity, Context, and Validity." *Phi Delta Kappan* (November 1993): 200–214.

Nonprint Stuff

Northwest Regional Laboratory. *Developing Assessments Based on Observation and Judgment* (Videotape #NREL-3A). Los Angeles: IOX Assessment Associates.

Pollock, Jane. *Designing Authentic Tasks and Scoring Rubrics* (Audiotape #295238S62). Alexandria, VA: Association for Supervision and Curriculum Development, 1997.

Popham, W. James. *The Role of Rubrics in Classroom Assessment* (Videotape #ETVT-18). Los Angeles: IOX Assessment Associates.

Popham, W. James. *A Parent's Guide to Performance Assessment* (Videotape #ETVT-26). Los Angeles: IOX Assessment Associates.

Popham, W. James. *Performance Assessment: How Authentic Must It Be?* (Videotape #ETVT-27). Los Angeles: IOX Assessment Associates.

Wiggins, Grant, and Richard Stiggins. "Tape 1—Traditional Tests" (Videotape #614237S62) in *Redesigning Assessment Series*. Alexandria, VA: Association for Supervision and Curriculum Development.

Wiggins, Grant, and Richard Stiggins. "Tape 3—Performance Assessment" (Videotape #614-227Z35) in *Redesigning Assessment Series*. Alexandria, VA: Association for Supervision and Curriculum Development.

9

Portfolio Assessment

"*A*ssessment should be a part of instruction, not apart from it" is a point of view that most proponents of portfolio assessment would enthusiastically endorse. Portfolio assessment, a relatively recent entry in the educational measurement sweepstakes, has captured the attention of large numbers of educators because it represents a clear alternative to more traditional forms of educational testing.

A *portfolio* is a systematic collection of one's work. In education, portfolios refer to systematic collections of students' work. Although the application of portfolios in education has been a relatively recent phenomenon, portfolios have been widely used in a number of other fields for many years. Portfolios, in fact, constitute the chief method by which certain professionals display their skills and accomplishments. For example, portfolios are traditionally used for that purpose by photographers, artists, journalists, models, architects, and so on. An important feature of portfolios is that they must be updated as a person's achievements and skills grow.

Portfolios have been warmly embraced by those educators who regard traditional assessment with less than enthusiasm. In Table 9.1, for example, a chart presented by Tierney, Carter, and Desai (1991) indicates what those three proponents of portfolios believe are the differences between assessment using portfolios and assessment based on standardized testing.

Classroom Portfolio Assessment versus Large-Scale Portfolio Assessment ....

Classroom Applications

Most advocates of portfolio assessment believe that the real payoffs for such assessment approaches lie in the individual teacher's classroom, because the relationship between instruction and assessment will be strengthened as a conse-

Table 9.1 **Differences in Assessment Outcomes between Portfolios and Standardized Testing Practices**

Portfolio	Testing
Represents the range of reading and writing students are engaged in	Assesses students across a limited range of reading and writing assignments which may not match what students do
Engages students in assessing their progress and/or accomplishments and establishing ongoing learning goals	Mechanically scored or scored by teachers who have little input
Measures each student's achievement while allowing for individual differences between students	Assesses all students on the same dimensions
Represents a collaborative approach to assessment	Assessment process is not collaborative
Has a goal of student self-assessment	Student assessment is not a goal
Addresses improvement, effort, and achievement	Addresses achievement only
Links assessment and teaching to learning	Separates learning, testing, and teaching

Source: Material from *Portfolio Assessment in the Reading-Writing Classroom*, by Robert J. Tierney, Mark A. Carter, and Laura E. Desai, published by Christopher-Gordon Publishers, Inc. © 1991, used with permission of the publisher.

quence of students' continuing accumulation of work products in their portfolios. Ideally, teachers who adopt portfolios in their classrooms will make the ongoing collection and appraisal of students' work a central focus of the instructional program rather than a peripheral activity whereby students occasionally gather up their work to convince a teacher's supervisors or students' parents that good things have been going on in class.

Here's a description of how an elementary teacher might use portfolios to assess students' progress in social studies, language arts, and mathematics. The teacher, let's call him Phil Pholio, asks students to keep three portfolios, one in each of the subject fields. In each portfolio, the students are to place their early and revised work products. The work products are always dated so that Mr. Pholio, as well as the students themselves, can see what kinds of differences in quality take place over time. For example, if effective instruction is being provided, there should be discernible improvement in the caliber of students' written compositions, solutions to mathematics problems, and analyses of social issues.

Three or four times per semester, Mr. Pholio holds 15- to 20-minute portfolio conferences with each student about the three different portfolios. The other, non-conferencing students take part in small-group and independent learning activities while the portfolio conferences are conducted. During a conference, the participating student plays an active role in evaluating his or her own work. Toward the close of the school year, students select from their regular portfolios a series of work products that not only represent their best final versions but also indicate how those final products were created. These selections are placed in a display portfolio that is then featured at a spring open-school session designed for parents. Parents who visit the school are urged to take their children's display portfolios home. Mr. Pholio also sends home portfolios to parents who are unable to attend the open-school event.

There are, of course, many other ways to use portfolios effectively in a classroom. Phil Pholio, our phictitious (sic) teacher, employed a fairly common approach, but a variety of alternative procedures could also work quite nicely. The major consideration is that the teacher uses portfolio *assessment* as an integral aspect of the *instructional* process. Because portfolios can be tailored to a specific student's evolving growth, the diagnostic value of portfolios for teachers is immense.

Who Is Evaluating Whom?

Roger Farr (1994), a leader in language arts instruction and assessment, contends that the real payoff from proper portfolio assessment is that students' *self-evaluation* capabilities are enhanced. Thus, during portfolio conferences the teacher encourages students to come up with personal appraisals of their own work. The conference, then, becomes far more than merely an opportunity for the teacher to dispense an "oral report card." On the contrary, students' self-evaluation skills are nurtured not only during portfolio conferences but also throughout the entire school year. For that reason, Farr strongly prefers the use of *working* portfolios instead of *showcase* portfolios because he believes that self-evaluation is nurtured more readily in connection with ongoing reviews of products not intended to impress external viewers.

For self-evaluation purposes, it is particularly useful to be able to compare earlier work with later work. Fortunately, even if a teacher's instruction is downright abysmal, students grow older and, as a consequence of maturation, tend to get better at what they do in school. If a student is required to review three versions of a student's written composition (a first draft, a second draft, and a final draft), self-evaluation can be fostered by encouraging the student to make comparative judgments of the three compositions based on appropriate evaluative criteria. As anyone who has done much writing knows, written efforts tend to get better with time and revision. Contrasts of later versions with earlier versions can prove illuminating from an appraisal perspective and, because students' self-evaluation is so critical to their future growth, from an instructional perspective, as well.

Does Self-Evaluation Equal Self-Grading? . . . .

After a midsummer, schoolwide three-day workshop on the Instructional Payoffs of Classroom Portfolios, the faculty at Rhoda Street Elementary School have agreed to install student portfolios in all classrooms for one or more subject areas. Maria Martinez, an experienced third-grade teacher in the school, has decided to try out portfolios only in mathematics. She admits to her family (but not to her fellow teachers) that she's not all that certain she'll be able to use portfolios properly with her students.

Because she has attempted to follow the guidelines of the National Council of Teachers of Mathematics, Maria stresses mathematical problem solving and the integration of mathematical understanding with content from other disciplines. Accordingly, she asks her students to place in their mathematics portfolios versions of their attempts to solve quantitative problems drawn from other subjects. Maria poses these problems for her third-graders, then requires them to prepare an initial solution strategy and to revise that solution at least twice. Students are directed to put all solutions (dated) in their portfolios.

Six weeks after the start of school, Maria sets up a series of 15-minute portfolio conferences with her students. During the three days that the portfolio conferences are held, students who are not involved in a conference move through a series of learning stations in other subject areas where they typically engage in a fair amount of peer critiquing of each others' responses to various kinds of practice exercises.

Having learned during the summer workshop that the promotion of students' self-evaluation is critical if students are to get the most from portfolios, Maria devotes the bulk of her 15-minute conferences to students' personal appraisals of their own work. Although Maria offers some personal appraisals of most students' work, she typically allows the student's self-evaluation to override her own estimates of a student's ability to solve each problem.

Because it will soon be time to give students their 10-week grades, Maria doesn't know whether to base the grades on her own judgments or on students' self-appraisals.

If you were Maria, what would you decide to do?

Large-Scale Applications

It is one thing to use portfolios for classroom assessment; it is quite another to use portfolios for large-scale assessment programs. Several states and large school districts have attempted to install portfolios as a central component of a large-scale accountability assessment program—that is, a program in which student performances serve as an indicator of an educational system's effectiveness. To date, the results of efforts to employ portfolios for accountability purposes have not been encouraging.

In large-scale applications of portfolio assessments for accountability purposes, students' portfolios are judged either by the students' regular teachers or by a cadre of specially trained scorers (often teachers) who carry out the scoring at a central site. The problem with specially trained scorers and central-site scoring is that it typically costs much more than can be afforded. Some states, therefore, have opted to have all portfolios scored by students' own teachers who then relay such scores to the state department. The problem with having regular teachers score students' portfolios, however, is that such scoring tends to be too unreliable for use in accountability programs. Not only have teachers usually not been provided with thorough training about how to score portfolios but there is also a tendency for teachers to be biased in favor of their own students. As you can see, the scoring of portfolios in large-scale assessment programs constitutes a nontrivial problem.

One of the most visible of the statewide efforts to use portfolios on every pupil has been a performance assessment program in the state of Vermont. Because substantial national attention has been focused on the Vermont program, and because it has been evaluated independently, many policymakers in other states have drawn on the experiences encountered in the Vermont Portfolio Assessment Program. Unfortunately, independent evaluators of Vermont's statewide efforts to use portfolios found that there was considerable unreliability in the appraisals given to students' work. And, if you harken back to Chapter 2's dip into the importance of reliability, it's tough to draw valid inferences about students' achievements if the assessment of those achievements are not made with consistency.

But, of course, this is a book about classroom assessment, not large-scale assessment. (I knew that!) It certainly hasn't been shown that portfolios do *not* have a place in large-scale assessment. What has been shown, however, is that there are significant obstacles that must be surmounted if portfolio assessment is going to make a meaningful contribution to large-scale educational accountability testing.

Key Ingredients in Classroom Portfolio Assessment ....

Although there are numerous ways to install and sustain portfolios in a classroom, you probably need to consider the following:

1. *Make sure your students "own" their portfolios.* In order for portfolios to represent a student's evolving work accurately, and to foster the kind of self-evaluation that is so crucial if portfolios are to be truly educational, students must perceive portfolios to be collections of their own work and not merely temporary receptacles for products that you ultimately grade. You will probably want to introduce the notion of portfolio assessment to your students (assuming that portfolio assessment isn't already a schoolwide operation and that your students aren't already familiar with the use of portfolios) by explaining the distinctive functions of portfolios in the classroom.

2. *Decide on what kinds of work samples to collect.* Various kinds of work samples can be included in a portfolio. Obviously, such products will vary from subject to subject. In general, a wide variety of work products is preferable to a limited range of work products. Ideally, you and your students can collaboratively determine what goes in the portfolio.

3. *Collect and store work samples.* Students need to collect the designated work samples as they are created, place them in a suitable container (a folder or notebook, for example), then store the container in a file cabinet, storage box, or some suitably safe location. You may need to work individually with your students to help them decide whether particular products should be placed in their portfolios.

4. *Select criteria by which to evaluate portfolio work samples.* Working collaboratively with students, carve out a set of criteria by which you and your students can judge the quality of their portfolio products. Because of the likely diversity of products in different students' portfolios, the identification of evaluative criteria will not be a simple task. Yet, unless at least rudimentary evaluative criteria are isolated, the students will find it difficult to evaluate their own efforts and, thereafter, to strive for improvement. The criteria, once selected, should be described with the same sort of clarity we saw in the previous chapter regarding how to use rubrics when evaluating students' responses to performance test tasks.

5. *Require students to evaluate continually their own portfolio products.* Using the agreed-on criteria, be sure that your students try to evaluate their own work. Students can be directed to evaluate their work products holistically, analytically, or using a combination of both approaches. Such self-evaluation can be made routine by requiring each student to complete brief evaluation slips on 3×5 cards on which they identify the major strengths and weaknesses of a given product, then suggest how the product could be improved. Be sure to have your students date such self-evaluation sheets so they can keep track of modifications in their self-evaluation skills. Each completed self-evaluation sheet should be stapled or paper-clipped to the work product being evaluated.

6. *Schedule and conduct portfolio conferences.* Portfolio conferences take time. Yet, these interchange sessions between teachers and students regarding students' work are really pivotal in making sure that portfolio assessment fulfills its potential. The conference should not only evaluate your students' work products but should also help them improve their self-evaluation abilities. Try to hold as many of these conferences as you can. In order to make the conferences time efficient, be sure to have students prepare for the conferences so that you can start right in on the topics of most concern to you and the student.

7. *Involve parents in the portfolio assessment process.* Early in the school year, make sure your students' parents understand what the nature of the portfolio assessment process is that you've devised for your classroom. Insofar as

is practical, encourage your students' parents/guardians periodically to review their children's work samples as well as their children's self-evaluation of those work samples. The more active that parents become in reviewing their children's work, the stronger the message will be to the child that the portfolio activity is really worthwhile. If you wish, you may have students select their best work for a showcase portfolio or, instead, simply use the students' working portfolios.

These seven steps reflect only the most important activities that teachers might engage in when creating assessment programs in their classrooms. There are obviously all sorts of variations and embellishments that are possible.

Purposeful Portfolios

There are numerous choice-points you'll encounter if you embark on a portfolio assessment approach in your own classroom. The first one ought to revolve around *purpose*. Why are you contemplating a stroll down the portfolio pathway?

Assessment specialists typically identify three chief purposes for portfolio assessment. The first of these is *documentation of student progress* wherein the major function of the assembled work samples is to provide the student, the teacher,

and the student's parents with evidence about the student's growth—or lack of it. These are the *working* portfolios that Farr and Tone (1994) advocate because they provide meaningful opportunities for self-evaluation by students. Stiggins (1997) believes that portfolios fulfilling this function can be described as *time-sequence portfolios.*

A second purpose of portfolios is to provide an opportunity for *showcasing student accomplishments.* Stiggins describes portfolios that showcase students' best work as *celebration portfolios* and he argues that celebration portfolios are especially appropriate for the early grades where "we do too little personal assessment just for the fun and memories" (1997, p. 458). In portfolios that are intended to showcase student accomplishments, students typically select their best work and reflect thoughtfully on its quality.

One midwest teacher I know always makes sure that students include the following elements in their showcase portfolios:

- A letter of introduction to portfolio reviewers
- A table of contents
- Identification of the skills or knowledge being demonstrated
- A representative sample of the student's best work
- Dates on all entries
- The evaluative criteria (or rubric) being used
- The student's self-reflection on all entries

The inclusion of student self-reflections about ingredients of portfolios is a pivotal ingredient in showcase portfolios. Some portfolio proponents contend that a portfolio's self-evaluation by the student helps the learner to learn better and permits the reader of the portfolio to gain insights about how the learner learns.

A final purpose for portfolios is *evaluation of student status*—that is, the determination of whether students have met previously determined quality levels of performance. Spandel and Culham (1995) describe such collections of student work as *passportfolios* because such portfolios really function as official permits to move on to the next instructional task or level. McMillan (1997) points out that when portfolios are used for this purpose, there must be greater standardization about what should be included in a portfolio and how the work samples should be appraised. Typically, teachers select the entries for this kind of portfolio and considerable attention is given to scoring so that the rubrics employed to score the portfolios will yield consistent results even if different scorers are involved. For evaluation portfolios, there is usually less need for self-evaluation of entries—unless such self-evaluations are themselves being evaluated by others.

Well, we've peeked at three purposes underlying portfolio assessment. Can one portfolio perform all three functions? My answer is a somewhat shaky *yes.* But if you were to ask me whether one portfolio can perform all three functions *well,* you'd get a rock-solid *no.* The three functions, though related—somewhat like second cousins—are fundamentally different.

That's why your very first decision if you're going to install portfolios in your classroom is to decide on the *primary purpose* of the portfolios. You can then determine what the portfolios should look like and how students should prepare them.

Scripture tells us that "no man can serve two masters." (The authors of that scriptural advice, clearly insensitive to gender equality, were not implying that females are more capable of double-master serving.) Similarly, one kind of portfolio cannot blithely satisfy multiple functions. Some classroom teachers rush into portfolio assessment because they've heard about all of the enthralling things that portfolios can do. But one kind of portfolio cannot fulfill all three functions. Pick your top-priority purpose, then build your portfolio assessment to satisfy that purpose.

Work-Sample Selection

For a teacher just entering the portfolio party, another key decision hinges on the identification of the work samples to be put into the portfolios. All too often, teachers who are novices at portfolio assessment will fail to think divergently enough about the kinds of entries that should constitute a portfolio's chief contents. In Table 9.2 you'll find some examples for mathematics and language arts that will suggest the considerable range of work samples that might be included.

But divergency is not necessarily a virtue when it comes to the determination of a portfolio's contents. You shouldn't search for varied kinds of work samples simply for the sake of variety. What's important is that the particular kinds of work samples to be included in the portfolio will allow you to derive valid inferences about the skills and/or knowledge you're trying to have your students master. It's far better to include a few kinds of *inference-illuminating* work samples than to include a galaxy of work samples, many of which do not contribute to your inferences about students' knowledge or skills.

Appraising Portfolios

As indicated earlier in the chapter, students' portfolios are almost always evaluated by the use of a scoring rubric. The most important ingredients of such a rubric are its evaluative criteria—that is, the factors to be used in determining the quality of a particular student's portfolio. If there's any sort of student self-evaluation to be done, and such self-evaluation is almost always desirable, then it is imperative that students have access to, and thoroughly understand, the rubric that will be used to evaluate their portfolios.

I realize that we've already spent some time dealing with rubrics and evaluative criteria, especially in Chapter 8's treatment of performance assessment. But I'm going to ask you, as a favor (note how inordinately polite I'm being), to wait until you get through with Chapter 12's description of Instructionally Illuminat-

Table 9.2   **Illustrative Entries for Mathematics and Language Arts Portfolio**

Mathematics[1]	Language Arts[2]
A solution to an open-ended question done as homework	Projects, surveys, reports, and units from reading and writing
A mathematical autobiography	Favorite poems, songs, letters, and comments
Papers that show the student's correction or errors or misconceptions	Interesting thoughts to remember
A photo or sketch made by the student of a student's work with manipulatives or with mathematical models of multidimensional figures	Finished samples that illustrate wide writing: persuasive, letters, poetry, information, stories
	Examples of writing across the curriculum: reports, journals, literature logs
A letter from the student to the reader of the portfolio, explaining each item	Literature extensions: scripts for drama, visual arts, written forms, webs, charts, time lines, murals
A report of a group project, with comments about the individual's contribution	Student record of books read and attempted
	Audiotape of reading
Work from another subject area that relates to mathematics, such as an analysis of data collected and presented in a graph for social studies	Writing responses to literacy components: plot, setting, point of view, character development, links to life, theme, literary links and criticism
A problem made up by the student	Writing that illustrates critical thinking about reading
Artwork done by the student, such as string designs, coordinate pictures, and scale drawings or maps	Notes from individual reading and writing conference
Draft, revised, and final versions of student work on a complex mathematical problem, including writing, diagrams, graphs, charts	Items that are evidence of development of style: organization, voice, sense of audience, choice of words, clarity
A description by the teacher of a student activity that displayed understanding of a mathematical concept or relation	Writing that shows growth in usage of traits: growing ability in self-correction, punctuation, spelling, grammar, appropriate form, and legibility
	Samples in which ideas are modified from first draft to final product
	Unedited first drafts
	Revised first drafts
	Evidence of effort: improvement noted on pieces, completed assignments

Sources: [1]Reprinted with permission from *Mathematics Assessment: Myths, Models, Good Questions, and Practical Suggestions,* by Jean Kerr Stenmark, p. 37, copyright ©1991 by the National Council of Teachers of Mathematics, Reston, VA.

[2]Tierney, R. J., Carter, M. A., & Desai, L. E. (1991). *Portfolio Assessment in the Reading-Writing Classroom.* Norwood, MA: Christopher-Gordon Publishers, pp. 72–74. Used with permission of the publisher.

ing Assessment to form your final views on portfolio rubrics. In that chapter, you'll see how rubrics can be deliberately designed so that they increase the likelihood of successful instruction. Chapter 12's treatment of rubrics is highly pertinent to the type of rubrics that you ought to employ if you use portfolio assessment in your own classroom. In short, before becoming concretely close-minded (and that's somewhat solid) about what your portfolio rubrics ought to look like, hold off a bit until you've wrapped up Chapter 12. Please!

The Pros and Cons of Portfolio Assessment ....

What you need to keep in mind is that portfolio assessment's greatest strength is that it can be tailored to the individual student's needs, interests, and abilities. Yet, portfolio assessment suffers from the drawback faced by all constructed-response measurement. Students' constructed responses are genuinely difficult to evaluate, particularly when those responses vary from student to student.

As we saw with Vermont's Portfolio Assessment Program, it is quite difficult to come up with consistent evaluations of different students' portfolios. Sometimes the scoring guides devised for use in evaluating portfolios are so terse and so general as to be almost useless. They're akin to Rorschach inkblots in which different scorers see in the scoring guide what they want to see. In contrast, some scoring guides are so detailed and complicated that they simply overwhelm scorers. It is difficult to devise scoring guides that embody just the right level of specificity. Generally speaking, most teachers are so busy that they don't have time to create elaborate scoring schemes. Accordingly, many teachers (and students) find themselves judging portfolios using fairly broad evaluative criteria. Such general criteria tend to be interpreted differently by different people.

Another problem with portfolio assessment is that it takes time—loads of time—to carry out properly. Even if you're very efficient in reviewing your students' portfolios, you'll still have to devote many hours both in class (during portfolio conferences) and outside of class (if you also want to review your students' portfolios by yourself). Proponents of portfolios are convinced that the quality of portfolio assessment is worth the time such assessment takes. You at least need to be prepared for the required investment of time if you decide to prance down the portfolio assessment path. And teachers need to receive sufficient training to learn how to do portfolio assessment well. Any teachers who set out to do portfolio assessment by simply stuffing student stuff into folders built for stuff stuffing will end up wasting their time and their students' time. Meaningful staff development is a must if portfolio assessment is to work well.

On the plus side, however, most teachers who have used portfolios agree that portfolio assessment provides a way of documenting and evaluating growth that is happening in a classroom in ways that standardized or written tests cannot. Portfolios have the potential to create authentic portraits of what students learn. I agree with Stiggins when he points out that "to merge effectively with instruction, portfolios must have a story to tell" (1997, p. 455). Fortunately, that story can be made compatible with improved student learning.

Most of the teachers I've talked with who use portfolio assessments are primarily enamored with two payoffs. They believe that the *self-evaluation* it fosters

Parent Talk . . . .

Suppose that Mr. and Mrs. Holmgren, parents of your student, Harry, stopped by your classroom during a back-to-school night to examine their son's portfolio. After spending almost 30 minutes going through the portfolio and skimming the portfolios of several other students, they speak to you—not with hostility, but with genuine confusion. Mrs. Holmgren sums up their concerns nicely with the following comments: "When we stopped by Mr. Bray's classroom earlier this evening to see how our daughter, Elissa, is doing, we encountered a series of extremely impressive portfolios. Elissa's was outstanding. To be honest, Harry's portfolio is a lot less polished. It seems that he's included everything he's done in your class, rough drafts as well as final products. Why is there this difference?

• • • *If I were you, here's how I'd respond to Harry's parents:*

"It's really good that you two could take the time to see how Harry and Elissa are doing. And I can understand why you're perplexed by the differences in Elissa's and Harry's portfolios. You see, there are *different* kinds of student portfolios, and different portfolios serve different purposes.

"In Mr. Bray's class, and I know this because we often exchange portfolio tips with one another, students prepare what are called *showcase* portfolios. In such portfolios, students pick their very best work to show Mr. Bray and their parents what they've learned. I think Mr. Bray actually sent his students' showcase portfolios home about a month ago so you could see how well Elissa is doing. For Mr. Bray and his students, the portfolios are collections of best work that, in a very real sense, celebrate students' achievements.

"In my class, however, students create *working* portfolios in which the real emphasis is on getting students to make progress and to evaluate that progress *on their own.* When you reviewed Harry's portfolio, did you see how each entry is dated and how he prepared a brief self-reflection of each entry? I'm more interested in Harry's seeing the improvement that he makes than in anyone seeing polished final products. You, too, can see the striking progress he's made over the course of this school year.

"I'm not suggesting that my kind of portfolio is better than Mr. Bray's. Both have a role to play. Those roles, as I'm sure you'll see, are quite different."

• • • *Now, how would you respond to Mr. and Mrs. Holmgren?*

in students is truly important in guiding students' learning over time. They also think the *personal ownership* that students experience regarding their own work, and the progress they experience, makes the benefits of portfolio assessment outweigh its costs.

Because portfolio assessment in education is a fairly new approach in the measurement and instruction game, there have been a number of excellent volumes written about portfolios in the past few years. I urge you to dig deeper into such portfolio writings if you are interested in installing portfolios in your own classroom. It's really impossible to treat the innards of the portfolio process properly in a single chapter such as this. The books listed in the Additional Stuff section at the end of the chapter do a first-rate job in helping you learn how to deal with the particulars of portfolio assessment so that you get most of the dividends of this approach to assessment with only a mild taste of its deficits.

What Do Classroom Teachers Really Need to Know about Portfolio Assessment? ....

As noted at the beginning to this four-chapter excursion into item types, the more familiar that you are with different kinds of test items, the more likely you will be to select an item type that best provides you with the information you need in order to draw suitable inferences about your students. Until recently, portfolios haven't been viewed as a viable assessment option by many teachers. These days, however, portfolio assessment clearly is a legitimate contender in the measurement derby.

You need to realize that if portfolio assessment is going to constitute a helpful adjunct to your instructional program, portfolios will have to become a central, not tangential, part of what goes on in your classroom. The primary premise in portfolio assessment is that a particularized collection of a student's *evolving* work will allow both the student and you to determine the student's progress. You can't gauge the student's evolving progress if you don't have frequent evidence of the student's efforts.

It would probably be educationally unwise to select portfolio assessment as a one-time measurement approach to deal with a short-term instructional objective. Rather, it makes more sense to select some goal of interest, such as the student's ability to write original compositions, then monitor that aspect of the student's learning throughout the entire school year. It is also important for you to realize that although portfolio assessment may prove highly valuable for classroom instruction and measurement purposes, at this juncture there is insufficient evidence that it can be used appropriately for large-scale assessment.

A number of portfolio assessment specialists believe that the most important dividend from portfolio assessment is the increased abilities of students to evaluate their own work. If this becomes one of your goals in a portfolio assessment approach, you must be certain to nurture such self-evaluation growth deliberately via portfolios instead of simply using portfolios as convenient collections of work samples for you to appraise.

The seven key ingredients in portfolio assessment that were identified in the chapter represent only one way of installing this kind of assessment strategy. Variations of those seven suggested procedures are not only possible, but to be encouraged. The big thing to keep in mind is that portfolio assessment offers your students and you a way to particularize your evaluation of each student's growth over time. And, speaking of time, it's only appropriate to remind you that it takes substantially more time to use a portfolio assessment approach properly than to score a zillion true-false tests. If you opt to try portfolio assessment, you'll have to see whether, *in your own instructional situation,* it yields sufficient educational benefits to be worth the investment you'll surely need to make in it.

Chapter Summary ....

After defining portfolios as systematic collections of students' work, contrasts were drawn between portfolio assessment and more conventional standardized testing. It was suggested that portfolio assessment was far more appropriate for an individual teacher's classroom assessment than for large-scale accountability assessments.

An emphasis on self-assessment was suggesting as being highly appropriate for portfolio assessment, particularly in view of the way that portfolios can be tailored to an *individual* student's evolving progress. Seven steps were then suggested as key ingredients for classroom teachers to install and sustain portfolio assessment in their classroom: (1) establish student ownership, (2) decide on what work samples to collect, (3) collect and score work samples, (4) select evaluative criteria, (5) require continual student self-evaluations, (6) schedule and conduct portfolio conferences, and (7) involve parents in the portfolio assessment process.

Three different functions of portfolio assessment were identified—namely, documentation of student progress, showcasing student accomplishments, and evaluation of student status. Teachers were urged to select a primary purpose for portfolio assessment.

The chapter was concluded with an identification of plusses and minuses of portfolio assessment. It was emphasized that portfolio assessment represents an important measurement strategy now available to today's classroom teachers.

Self-Check

The self-check for this chapter will be somewhat different because it has been stressed that teachers who install portfolio assessment systems in their own classes will undoubtedly devise procedures that mesh with their own subject-matter emphases and the abilities and interests of the students they teach. Nonetheless, to give you a bit of practice in using the seven key ingredients of class-room performance assessments that were cited in the chapter, you'll be reading a pair of scenarios about fictitious teachers who are installing and operating portfolio assessment programs in their mythical classrooms. Your task, as a compliant self-checker, is to read each scenario, then decide if one or more of the seven key ingredients are missing or have been violated. If you want to review the seven ingredients before you tackle these two self-check exercises, there are no prohibitions to your returning to pages 185 through 187.

Scenario One

Having decided to adopt a portfolio assessment approach for the composition segment of her junior high school English classes, Maria Flores introduces her students to the new assessment scheme by asking a commercial-artist friend of hers to speak to each class. The artist brings his own portfolio and shows the students how the portfolio allows prospective clients to judge his work. Ms. Flores tells her students that her friend's portfolio is called a "showcase portfolio" and that students will be preparing both a showcase portfolio to periodically involve their parents in reviewing work products, as well as "working portfolio" to keep track of *all* of their composition drafts and final products. Ms. Flores and her friend emphasize that both kinds of portfolios must be owned by the students, not the teacher.

Because all of their drafts and final versions are to be collected, students simply place copies of all such products in folders and, when finished, in a designated file drawer. Early in the academic year, Ms. Flores works with each of her classes to decide collaboratively on the criteria to be used on judging the composition efforts for a given class. Although there are slight differences in the criteria decided on for each class, the criteria for all classes are fairly similar.

Ms. Flores makes sure to review all students' portfolios at least once a month. Typically, she devotes one preparation period a day to a different class's portfolios. Because the portfolios are readily available in a file cabinet in her classroom, Ms. Flores finds it convenient and time efficient to evaluate students' progress in this manner. She provides a brief evaluation (dated) for students to consider when they work with their portfolios.

At least twice every term, Ms. Flores selects what she considers to be the students' best finished works from their working portfolios. She places such work products in a showcase portfolio. Students are directed to take these showcase portfolios home to let their families see what kinds of compositions they have been creating. Parents are enthusiastic about this practice. A number of parents have told the school principal that Ms. Flores's "take-home" portfolio system is the way they would like to see other aspects of their children's performances evaluated.

Now, please critique Ms. Flores's efforts in relation to the seven key ingredients of portfolio assessment supplied in the chapter.

Scenario Two

A third-grade teacher, Gary Gately, has just completed a summer staff-development workshop on portfolio assessment. He and a number of the teachers at his school have decided to try out performance assessment in at least limited parts of their instructional and assessment programs. Gary has decided to use portfolios with his students' mathematics work.

He introduces students to the activity by stressing the importance of their personal ownership of the portfolios and the significance of their personal evaluations of the kinds of mathematics work they put in their portfolios. Gary suggests to the class that students include only problem-solution mathematics work in their portfolios. Thus, all drill work and simple computational work is not to be put in the portfolios. The students discuss this suggestion and readily agree.

Gary works with students for two full days to decide on the evaluative criteria that they, and he, will use to evaluate the mathematics work in the portfolios. They decide that the major criteria will be (1) selection of proper solution strategies, (2) accurate completion of selected solution procedures, and (3) arrival at the correct solution to the problem.

Students routinely collect their work and place it for safekeeping in specially marked cardboard boxes that Gary has placed on the "Portfolio Shelf." Every two months, Gary holds an individual portfolio conference with each student during which he supplies the student with an evaluation of the portfolio's work.

It is clear to Gary that his students' ability to solve mathematics problems has improved substantially. Although it took students several weeks to get used to the process, they now seem to thoroughly enjoy Gary's version of portfolio assessment in mathematics.

Conjure up a critique of Gary Gately's approach to portfolio assessment.

Pondertime

1. What do you personally believe is the most important strength of portfolio assessment? What about the most important weakness of this form of assessment?

2. Three purposes of portfolio assessment were described in the chapter: documentation of student progress, showcasing student accomplishments, and evaluation of student status. Which of these three purposes do you believe to be most meritorious? And, of course, why?

3. What subjects, if any, do not lend themselves to some form of portfolio assessment?

4. If it is true that portfolios need to be personalized for particular students, is it possible to devise one-size-fits-all criteria for evaluating classroom portfolio work products? Why or why not?

5. How can the substantial time demands of portfolio assessment be effectively addressed by classroom teachers?

Self-Check Key

Scenario One

Ms. Flores's approach to portfolio assessment had much to commend it. Indeed, if the approach is really working, she probably shouldn't tinker with it. There were, however, two ingredients that Ms. Flores overlooked that some proponents of portfolio assessment consider important. First, she didn't push students very hard in the direction of self-evaluation. Second, she didn't hold any one-on-one portfolio conferences. During such conferences, of course, Ms. Flores could nurture students' self-evaluation skills. For a first try at performance assessment, however, our fictitious Ms. Flores did a rather nifty job.

Scenario Two

Gary missed out on only two of the chapter's seven key ingredients. He didn't involve parents in the process and, although he made some early noise about promoting self-evaluation on the part of the students, he really didn't push students' self-evaluation during the portfolio conferences or apart from those conferences.

Additional Stuff

Calfee, Robert C., and Pam Perfumo. "Student Portfolios: Opportunities for a Revolution in Assessment." *Journal of Reading*, 36, no. 7 (April 1993): 532–537.

Cole, Donna J., Charles W. Ryan, and Fran Kick. *Portfolios across the Curriculum and Beyond.* Thousand Oaks, CA: Corwin Press, 1995.

Farr, Roger C., and Bruce Tone. "Portfolio and Performance Assessment: Helping Students Evaluate Their Progress as Readers and Writers." *Growing to Meet Your Needs.* New York: Harcourt Brace College, 1994.

Grace, Cathy. "The Portfolio and Its Use: Developmentally Appropriate Assessment of Young Children." *ERIC Digest.* Urbana, IL: ERIC Clearinghouse, 1992.

Graves, Donald H., and Bonnie S. Sunstein (Eds.). *Portfolio Portraits.* Portsmouth, NH: Heinemann, 1992.

Mandel Glazer, Susan, and Carol Smullen Brown. *Portfolios and Beyond: Collaborative Assessment in Reading and Writing.* Norwood, MA: Christopher-Gordon, 1993.

McMillan, James H. Classroom *Assessment: Principles and Practice for Effective Instruction.* Boston: Allyn and Bacon, 1997.

Mumme, Judy. *Portfolio Assessment in Mathematics.* Santa Barbara, CA: University of California, 1991.

Reckase, Mark D. "Portfolio Assessment: A Theoretical Estimate of Score Reliability." *Educational Measurement: Issues and Practice,* 14, no. 1 (Spring 1995): 12–14, 31.

Spandel, Vicki, and Ruth Culham. *Writing From the Inside Out: Revising for Quality.* Portland, OR: Northwest Regional Educational Laboratory. Distributed through IOX Assessment Associates, Los Angeles.

Stiggins, Richard J. *Student-Centered Classroom Assessment* (2nd ed.). Upper Saddle River, NJ: Prentice-Hall, 1997.

Tierney, Robert J., Mark A. Carter, and Laura E. Desai. *Portfolio Assessment in the Reading-Writing Classroom.* Norwood, MA: Christopher-Gordon, 1991.

Viadero, Debra. "RAND Urges Overhaul in Vermont's Pioneering Writing Test." *Education Week* (November 10, 1993): 1.

Nonprint Stuff

American Educational Research Association. *Portfolio Assessment: Rhetoric Meets the Reality of Data* (Cassette Recording No. RA 3-25.33). Chicago: Teach 'Em, April 14, 1993.

Farr, Roger. *Portfolios and Language Arts: A First Look* (Videotape #RDVT-38A). Los Angeles: IOX Assessment Associates.

Farr, Roger. *Portfolio Conferences: What They Are and Why They Are Important* (Videotape #RDVT-39A). Los Angeles: IOX Assessment Associates.

Farr, Roger. *Developing Language Arts Performance Assessments: A Conversation with Dr. Roger Farr* (Videotape #RDVT-40A). Los Angeles: IOX Assessment Associates.

Northwest Regional Laboratory. *Using Portfolios in Assessment and Instruction* (Videotape #NREL-13A). Los Angeles: IOX Assessment Associates.

Wiggins, Grant, and Richard Stiggins. "Tape 2—Portfolios" (Videotape #614-226Z35) in *Redesigning Assessment Series.* Alexandria, VA: Association for Supervision and Curriculum Development.

10

....

Affective Assessment

*A*ffective variables, most educators concede, are important. Students' attitudes toward learning, for example, play a major role in how much learning those students subsequently pursue. The values that students have regarding truthfulness and integrity shape their daily conduct. And students' self-esteem, of course, influences almost everything they do. There's little doubt that the affective status of students should concern all educators.

In truth, however, few classroom teachers give explicit attention to influencing their students' attitudes and values. Even fewer classroom teachers actually try to assess the affective status of their students. Certainly, a teacher may observe a student's sour demeanor and conclude that he's "out of sorts" or she's "a mite depressed," but how many times have you heard about a teacher who tried to gather *systematic* evidence regarding students' attitudes and values? Unfortunately, systematic assessment of affect is pretty uncommon.

This chapter will address the issue of affective assessment by providing you with general insights regarding the assessment of students' attitudes and values. Thereafter, the chapter will give you some practical, step-by-step procedures for gauging students' status regarding a number of educationally important values and attitudes.

Why Assess Affect? ....

One question you might be asking yourself is, Why assess attitudes at all? Many teachers, particularly those who teach older students, believe that their only educational mission is to increase students' knowledge and skills. Affect, such teachers believe, simply doesn't fall into their proper sphere of influence. However, students who learn to do mathematics like magicians yet abhor mathematics certainly aren't apt to apply the mathematics they've learned. Students who can compose outstanding essays but believe they are "really rotten writers" won't spend much time volitionally whipping out essays.

The Importance of Affect

I'd like to get my own bias regarding this issue out on the table so you don't think I'm trying to subliminally influence you. I personally regard affective variables as far more significant than cognitive variables. How many times, for example, have you seen people who weren't all that "gifted" intellectually still succeed because they were highly motivated and hard working? Conversely, how many times have you seen truly able people simply veer away from challenges because they did not consider themselves worthy? Day in and day out, we see the enormous impact that people's affective status has on them. Affect is every bit as important as cognitive ability.

Have you ever seen a group of kindergarten students troop off to school loaded with enthusiasm and gumption, only to encounter those same students a few years later and see that a fair number were disenchanted with school and down on themselves? Well, I have. And what's going on with such children is surely taking place in the affective realm. When most kindergartners start school, they are enthused about school and themselves. However, after failing to measure up for a year or two, many of those formerly upbeat children carry around decisively lowered self-concepts. They've tried and been found wanting. Such negative attitudes about self and school will typically influence all of a child's subsequent education. Yet, because few teachers try to assess their students' affective status, most teachers don't know what their students' attitudes and values really are. That situation, I believe, needs to change.

Spurring Affectively Focused Instruction

Even if there were no such thing as externally imposed "educational accountability" whereby students' performances on high-stakes tests serve as indicators of educational effectiveness, what's on achievement tests would still influence what teachers teach. When I was a high school teacher, I knew what kinds of items I had on my final exams. (That is, I knew in the second year of teaching, after I'd whipped out my first-year final exams only minutes before my students needed to take those exams.) Because I wanted my students to do well on my final exams, I made reasonably sure that I spent at least some instructional time on the content covered by the final examinations.

It's the same with affective assessment. Let's say you've installed a fairly straightforward pretest-posttest evaluation design to assess any meaningful changes in your students' responses to an attitude inventory regarding how much they are interested in the subject(s) you're teaching. Your recognition that there will be a formal pretest-posttest assessment of students' subject-matter interest will, as surely as school buses run late, influence you to provide instruction so that your students will, in fact, become more positive about the subject(s) you're teaching.

In other words, the presence of affective postinstruction measurement will incline you to include affectively focused activities in your instruction. In a sense,

Where Went Wonder? . . . .

Lance Larson has decided to try to get an accurate reading of his kindergarten students' attitudes toward school. Although he has worked with kindergartners for the past four years, only recently has Lance become convinced of the importance of student affect.

Because he is working with very young children, most of whom can't read when they arrive at Mission Elementary School, Lance uses an orally administered, anonymously completed inventory for which he reads a question to the students and they are to respond by circling either a smiling face or a frowning face. Students respond to one question, and then another, after Lance tells them to "Answer by the bird," "Answer by the star," and so on.

At the end of the first week of school, students' responses to Lance's inventory indicated that they really liked school. In fact, 100% of the children responded that they couldn't wait to find out what new things they would learn at school each day. However, three months later, a readministration of the inventory showed that students' attitudes toward school seemed to have taken a nosedive. Well over half of his kindergartners indicated that they no longer looked forward to coming to school. Almost 75%, in fact, indicated that they were often bored in class. Lance was alarmed.

If you were Lance, what would you decide to do?

you're saying to yourself—and anyone else you care to have understand your instructional planning—that affective outcomes are important enough for you to formally assess. You can be assured that what's important enough to be assessed, even if it's measured in your classroom and nowhere else in the world, is likely to influence your instruction. As I confessed earlier, I think that affectively focused instruction deals with the kinds of outcomes that are the most important we teach.

Monitoring Students' Status

In addition to serving as an end-of-instruction goal, affective assessment devices, if administered regularly, help teachers determine if modifications in the instructional program are warranted. For example, let's say that you're a physics teacher and you want to get a fix on how enthused your students are about continuing their study of physics in college. Ideally, you'd like a fair number of your students to get fairly ecstatic over the raptures of future physics coursework. Suppose that each month you employed a brief self-report attitudinal inventory focused on the likelihood of students' pursuing future physics instruction. For illustrative purposes, let's assume that in September, 60% of your students registered an interest in taking college physics courses and that in October, 65% indicated interest. In November, however, interest in future physics courses nosedived so that only

25% of your students signified any interest in college physics. That's a clear message to you that something went on in late October or early November that really turned off your budding Nobel Laureates. A review of your instructional program during that period and some serious effort on your part to generate more interest in postsecondary physics would seem to be warranted. As you can see, periodic monitoring of your students' affective status can assist you in seeing what sorts of shifts in your instructional program might be needed.

In review, there are a number of reasons that classroom teachers should devote at least a segment of their assessment program to the measurement of students' affect. If you don't believe that your students' attitudes and values are important, of course, you'll not agree with the views I've expressed. But if you do think that student affect is significant, you'll want to learn what kinds of affective variables to assess and how to assess them. That's coming up shortly.

The Other Side of the Argument

Before turning to the nuts and bolts of affective assessment, I need to point out that a good many citizens do not share my view regarding the importance of affective assessment and instruction. Particularly in the past few years we have seen the emergence of a vocal group of individuals who have taken strong positions against schools' offering anything other than traditional academic (cognitive) education. Usually representing religious or conservative constituencies, these critics have argued that it is the job of the family and church to promote values in children, and that any attempt by the schools to systematically modify students' attitudes or values should cease.

In several states we have witnessed heated attacks on outcomes-based education (an approach to education in which heightened attention is given to the consequences of an educational program rather than the procedures employed to deliver the program). A major argument voiced by those who argue against outcomes-based education is that it may foster attitudes and values that are unacceptable to certain religious or political groups.

I agree with these critics that if any attention to affective outcomes is to be given, it must be focused only on those affective consequences that would be close to universally approved. For example, I regard the promotion of students' positive attitudes toward learning as an affective aspiration that almost everyone would support. Similarly, I can't really imagine that there are too many people who wouldn't want the schools to nurture students' self-esteem. Yet, I would hate to see educators dabbling with any controversial attitudes or values—that is, those that a meaningful number of parents wouldn't want their children to possess.

If you decide to devote some of your classroom assessment/instruction time to effective targets, you'll clearly need to consider carefully the legitimacy of the targets you select. And even if you do so, you should recognize that there will be some people who may disapprove of such affective education regardless of the ease with which you select your affective objectives (Droegemueller, 1993).

Which Affective Variables Should Be Assessed? . . . .

A Closer Look at Affect

Before discussing the sorts of variables that you, as a classroom teacher, might wish to assess, let's spend just a moment looking at the nature of *affect* itself. The reason that such affective variables as students' attitudes and values are important to us is that those variables typically influence students' future behavior. If you think about this for a bit, you'll realize that we don't really care all that much, in the abstract, whether students' attitudes toward learning are positive. The reason that we want to promote positive attitudes toward learning is because students who have positive attitudes toward learning today will be disposed to pursue learning in the future.

The affective status of students lets us see how students are predisposed to behave subsequently. If we find that students believe healthy bodies are important, those students will be predisposed to maintain their own bodily health in the future. If we find that students have positive attitudes toward persons from other ethnic groups, then in the future such students will be predisposed to behave appropriately toward persons from other ethnic groups. As seen in Figure 10.1, current affective status predicts future behavior.

Do attitudes predict future behavior perfectly? Of course not. But suppose there are 100 third-graders who display very negative attitudes toward violence as a way of settling disputes, and that there are 100 third-graders who believe that violence is an altogether suitable way of resolving disputes. Probabilistically, in the future there are likely to be fewer violent dispute-resolution behaviors from the first 100 third-graders than from the second. Affective assessment, therefore, allows teachers to get a far-better-than-chance fix on the behavioral dispositions of their students. That's why affective assessment is so important.

As you know, schools have historically focused on cognitive variables. And that's probably the way it's always going to be. Thus, if you are interested in giving some attention to affect in your own classroom, you'll need to select your affective foci judiciously. That's what we'll deal with next. We'll look at attitudes first, then consider values.

Figure 10.1   **The Relationship between Current Affect and Future Behavior Wherein an Individual's Affective Status Reveals That Individual's Future Behavior**

Potential Attitudinal Targets

There are all sorts of possible attitudinal foci for a teacher's instruction. Here are a few of the attitudes that are most commonly endorsed by teachers as reasonable attitudinal targets:

- *Subject-approaching attitudes.* Students should regard the subject matter taught (for example, mathematics) more positively at the end of instruction than they did when instruction began. At the very least, students should be no more negative toward the subject being taught as a consequence of instruction.
- *Positive attitudes toward learning.* Students should regard the act of learning positively. Students who are positive today about learning will tend to be tomorrow's learners.
- *Positive attitudes toward self.* Self-esteem is the attitude on which most people's personal worlds turn. Although children's self-esteem is probably influenced more by parents and nonschool events than by teachers, what happens in the classroom can have a significant impact on children's self-esteem.
- *Positive attitudes toward self as a learner.* Self-esteem as a learner is an affective variable over which educators have substantial influence. If students believe they are capable of learning, they will tend to learn.
- *Appropriate attitudes toward those who differ from us.* The more tolerant and accepting that students are toward members of other ethnic, gender, national, or religious groups, the more likely that those students will behave properly toward such individuals in the future.

There are numerous other subject-specific kinds of attitudes that teachers will want to foster. For example, many teachers who deal with language arts will want to enhance students' heightened confidence as writers—that is, students' more positive attitudes toward their own composition capabilities. Science teachers will want to foster students' curiosity. Health education teachers will wish to promote students' accurate perceptions of their vulnerability to health risks such as sexually transmitted diseases. Depending on your own instructional responsibilities, you'll discover that there are usually several attitudinal assessment contenders that you'll want to consider.

Potential Value Targets

There are all sorts of values to which people subscribe that the schools should have nothing to do with. Most educators agree that political values and religious values, for example, should not be dealt with instructionally in the schools. Whether students turn out to be liberals or conservatives is really none of a teacher's business. And, historically, there's been a long tradition of separating church and state. Teachers, therefore, certainly shouldn't be advocating acceptance of particular religions or rejection of others. Well, then, what sorts of values are sufficiently meritorious and noncontroversial so that they could serve as the targets for classroom attention? Here are a few to consider:

- *Honesty.* Students should learn to value honesty in their dealing with others.
- *Integrity.* Students should firmly adhere to their own code of values—for example, moral or artistic.
- *Justice.* Students should subscribe to the view that all citizens should be the recipients of equal justice from governmental law enforcement agencies.
- *Freedom.* Students should believe that democratic nations must provide the maximum level of freedom to its citizens.

Although these kinds of values may seem to be little more than lofty, flag-waving endorsements of goodness, you may still wish to consider them and similar values for potential effective assessment in your own classroom. If there really are significant values that you would like your students to embrace, and those values fall properly in the sphere of what schools should be about, then the possibility of including such values in a classroom assessment program may have real appeal for you.

Don't try to assess too many affective variables. You'd be surprised how quickly you can become overwhelmed with the time required to gather such data, and the time needed to make sense of the data you collect. This is another "less is more" setting in which you should try to get a fix on only a few of the affective dimensions you regard as most important for your students.

How Should Affect Be Assessed in Classrooms? ....

The assessment of affect can be carried out at varying levels of complexity and sophistication. To illustrate, in psychological experiments designed to get a fix on children's honesty, researchers have utilized trained accomplices who create elaborate situations where a child can or cannot cheat, then the researchers observe the child's behavior through one-way mirrors in order to draw inferences about the child's tendencies to be honest or dishonest in situations where the attractiveness of the temptations vary. I know few teachers who have the time or inclination to engage in very elaborate assessment of their students' affective status, although I suspect that those teachers would know how to use one-way mirrors advantageously.

As a practical matter, the classroom assessment of student affect must be relatively easy to pull off, or it simply isn't going to happen. Teachers are too busy to carry out the galaxy of responsibilities that they face each day. Accordingly, in this chapter I'm only going to set out for you a single, readily accomplishable procedure to assess your students' attitudes and values. If you wish to consider more elaborate and time-demanding ways of measuring your students' affect, there are several excellent volumes cited in the Additional Stuff section at the end of the chapter. The books by Anderson (1981) and by Webb and others (1981) are particularly thought provoking.

Self-Report Assessment

You can get a decent fix on students' affective status by asking them to complete self-report assessment devices. If you set up the assessment situation so that students can respond in a truly anonymous fashion, the data derived from self-report instruments can really be useful to you. Just as importantly, the use of straightforward self-report devices won't be so onerous that you become disenchanted with such measurement. Anderson (1981) has provided a compelling argument in favor of self-report affective measurement by educators. If you really have trouble accepting the proposition that self-report assessment is the measurement scheme to use when assessing your students' affective status, you might want to review the reasons that Anderson considered when he arrived at his advocacy of self-report affective assessment in schools.

Likert Inventories

Because of its reading applicability to a variety of affective assessment targets, the approach to attitudinal measurement introduced many years ago by Likert (1932) is the most widely used. Likert inventories will handle almost all of your affective assessment requirements, hence that approach is the only one you'll be learning about here. It is, by all odds, the most serviceable affective measurement strategy you'll encounter.

You've probably responded to Likert inventories many times in your life. They consist of a series of statements to which you register your agreement or disagreement. For example, you are given a statement such as "Reading this book about classroom assessment represents one of the finest professional experiences of my career." You then choose from a set of options to decide whether you agree or disagree with the statement. The usual options, at least for adults, are *strongly agree, agree, uncertain, disagree,* and *strongly disagree.* (I am altogether confident that you would have opted for the *strongly agree* response regarding the previous illustrative statement about this book's impact on your professional life.)

Clearly, depending on the age of the students you're teaching, you'll need to make adjustments in the statements used and in the number and/or phrasing of the response options. For example, with very young children you might need to use brief statements containing very simple words. You might even have to read the statements aloud. Older students might be able to handle the five-choice agreement scale just described, but for younger students you'll most likely want to drop down to three response options (for instance, *agree, don't know,* and *disagree*) or even two response options (perhaps *yes* and *no*). You'll be the best judge of the language level that should be used with the students you teach. In general, err in the direction of less-demanding rather than more-demanding language.

Building a Likert Inventory

Let's look, then, at a simple series of steps you should follow to create a Likert inventory for your own classroom:

1. *Choose the affective variable you want to assess.* Decide what attitude or value you want to assess, then try to get as clearheaded as possible about what the affective variable really means.
2. *Generate a series of favorable and unfavorable statements regarding the affective variable.* For example, if you were interested in students' attitudes regarding reading, you might construct a positive statements such as "I like to read on my own when I have free time" or negative statements such as "People who read for fun are stupid." Try to generate a few more statements than you ultimately plan to use. For students in secondary schools, a 10-item Likert inventory takes little time to complete. For students at lower grades, you'd probably want to use fewer items, perhaps 5 or 6. Try to construct an approximately equal number of positive and negative statements.
3. *Get several people to classify each statement as positive or negative.* Corral a few colleagues or family members to look at your generated statements and classify each statement as positive or negative. Toss out any statement that isn't unanimously classified as positive or negative.
4. *Decide on the number and phrasing of the response options for each statement.* The original Likert inventory had the following five options: SD = Strongly Disagree, D = Disagree, NS = Not Sure, A = Agree, and SA = Strongly Agree. As noted, younger children should employ fewer and, possibly, more simple options.
5. *Prepare the self-report inventory, giving students directions regarding how to respond and stipulating that the inventory must be completed anonymously.* If students haven't previously completed such inventories, they'll need good, clear directions. It is helpful to include an illustration or two of how students might respond. Sample statements about generally known topics, such as foods or movies, work well for such illustrations.
6. *Administer the inventory either to your own students or, if possible (as a tryout), to other students.* If another teacher is willing, try out your inventory with stu-

dents similar to your own. Based on the responses of those students, you can then improve the inventory before giving it to your own students. If you must use your own students, you can still improve the inventory for use later in the year with the same students or, perhaps, next year with another set of students.

7. *Score the inventories.* Assign points for each student's response to each item based on the *direction* of the statement. For instance, if you are using five response options, you would give five points to *strongly agree* responses to positive statements and also five points to *strongly disagree* responses to negative statements. Thus, for a 10-item inventory the scores could range from 10 to 50. Generally speaking, the higher the score, the more appropriate students' affective status appears to be.

8. *Identify and eliminate statements that fail to function in accord with the other statements.* If you know how to compute correlation coefficients, simply compute the correlation between students' responses to each item (1, 2, 3, 4, or 5, for example) and their total scores on the inventory (10 to 50). Eliminate those statements whose correlations to the total score are not statistically significant. (This is referred to as "Likert's criterion of internal consistency.") If you don't know how to compute correlation coefficients, simply "eyeball" students' responses and try to detect statements to which students are responding differently than to the rest of the statements. Dump those statements. (This is referred to as "Likert's criterion of internal consistency for people who don't know diddly about computing correlations.") Then rescore the inventories without the rejected items.

It's really just that simple to bang out a Likert inventory for your own purposes. For each affective variable of interest, you need a different inventory (or at least a different set of items). You can certainly measure several affective variables with different sets of items on the same inventory. The more experience you accumulate in creating Likert inventories, the easier it gets. After a short while, you'll really become quite skilled in whipping out such affective assessment devices.

If you're really under time pressure, and I know of few teachers who aren't, you can even skip some of the eight steps I just listed. For instance, you don't really need to get other people to classify your statements as positive or negative (Step 3) if you don't have the time to do so. And although you'd like to have a formal tryout of the inventory (Step 6), you may not have time to do it. What I'm really trying to suggest is that if you're faced with a choice between (a) skipping some desirable procedural steps and *using* an affective inventory or (b) *not using* an affective inventory because you don't have time to carry out all the recommended procedural steps—do some step skipping!

I'm not trying to suggest that Likert-type inventories are the only way of getting an estimate of your students' affect. There are other fairly straightforward self-report assessment schemes that you may wish to consider. For example, if you were interested in improving your fifth-grade students' attitudes toward mathematics, you might simply give them a list of a number of subjects, one of which was mathematics, then ask students to rank-order the subjects on the basis of which subject they most preferred to study. What you'd hope for, of course, is a preinstruction to postinstruction shift showing that students rank-ordered mathematics more positively after instruction. This rank-the-subject approach, you will note, is also a self-report affective measurement strategy.

The Importance of Genuine Anonymity

In order for you to draw accurate inferences about your students' affective state based on their responses to self-report inventories, it is clearly necessary for students to *respond truthfully* to your affective inventories. Unfortunately, many students tend to provide what are referred as *socially desirable* responses to affective self-report devices. In other words, many students are inclined to respond in the way that they think you want them to respond. Students are particularly apt to provide socially desirable responses if they believe the teacher can trace their responses. Consequently, to increase the likelihood that students will respond honestly to your affective inventories, it is imperative that you not only make all students' responses anonymous but that you also employ as many procedures as possible so that most students regard their responses as truly untraceable.

Among the more simple but effective anonymity-enhancement procedures you might want to consider are these:

1. *Directions.* Make sure the directions for your affective inventories stress the importance of honest answers and that students do not put their names on their inventories.
2. *Response restrictions.* Set up your inventories so that the *only* form of student response is to be check marks, circling of preferred answers, and so on. Prohibit students from writing any words whatsoever on their inventories. Because students believe that the teacher may figure out who supplied which inventory by recognizing students' handwriting, don't permit any handwriting whatsoever on affective inventories.
3. *Collection.* Install a procedure whereby students deposit their completed inventories in a collection box, or have a student (not one thought to be your "pet") collect the completed inventories. Announce *before* students start to fill out the inventories that one of these collection methods will be employed.

As you can see, you must try to make sure your students really don't think there's any way to trace their responses back to them. Even under those circumstances, this doesn't ensure that students will respond truthfully. However, well-conceived anonymity-enhancement techniques increase the odds that students will respond honestly.

Parent Talk ....

"You're messing with my child's head," was the first comment you heard from Mrs. Jillian, Paul's mother, when she telephoned you at school during your after-school planning period. Mrs. Jillian then continued by saying she had heard from Paul that you were getting students to fill out "attitude tests" that try to find out "whether kids have the right attitudes." Mrs. Jillian concluded by asking, "How dare you delve in Paul's value and attitudes! Isn't that something his dad and I should be influencing?"

• • • *If I were you, here's how I'd respond to Mrs. Jillian:*

"I agree completely with you, Mrs. Jillian, about whose right it is to influence Paul's values and attitudes. That responsibility is yours and Mr. Jillian's. But I have a hunch you may not have a clear picture of what I'm trying to do in Paul's class. Let me explain.

"As you may know, children at Paul's age often become disinterested in certain subjects, especially mathematics and science. What I've been trying to do is determine ways that I can help improve or sustain my students' interest in science and mathematics. I've been administering *anonymous* attitude inventories related to math and science on a pretest and posttest basis—that is, in the fall and in the spring. But I'm using the results of those anonymous inventories not to influence the attitudes or values of Paul or any other child. What I'm trying to do is figure out how my own teaching can engender more interest, from the entire class, in science and mathematics.

"I would *never* try to influence a value or attitude that falls within your family's purview. But I'm sure you'd like Paul, and the other students in his class, to regard science and mathematics positively, not negatively. Whether the children eventually pursue careers related to science or mathematics will, of course, be up to them and their families."

• • • *Now, how would you respond to Mrs. Jillian?*

When to Assess Affect

When should classroom teachers assess their students' affective status? Well, for openers, it seems important to set up at least a preinstruction and a postinstruction measure of students' attitudes and/or values. Thus, for elementary teachers teaching students in self-contained classrooms, an affective assessment at the start of the school year and, again, at its close will allow teachers to discern any meaningful changes in students' affect. Ideally, however, teachers can engage in occasional "affective dip sticking" to monitor students' affect. For example, every couple of months, a teacher might measure students' self-esteem as learners as well as their attitudes regarding learning. If these occasional assessments suggest that inappropriate affective changes are occurring, the teacher may wish to modify affect-related aspects of the instructional program.

In the next section of the chapter, you'll discover that you can often *sample* your students' affective status rather than measure all students' affective status. Thus, some of the suggested affective dip sticking might be carried out only with a portion of your students.

What Kind of Inferences Are at Stake in Affective Assessment? . . . .

When teachers use cognitively oriented tests, they typically make inferences about individual students. If, for instance, Harvey Haley earns a high score on a mathematics test, the teacher makes an inference about Harvey's possession of certain mathematics skills and knowledge. Teachers need to make inferences about individual students in order to make decisions about how to provide suitable instruction for those students.

Teachers also aggregate students' individual scores on achievement tests to arrive at group-focused inferences. For instance, if most students in a history class performed poorly on a start-of-the-term achievement pretest, yet most students topped a comparable posttest administered near the term's conclusion, the teacher would conclude that the students, as a group, had learned substantially more about history.

It's different with affect. Whereas cognitive tests (and, in most cases, psychomotor tests) are measures of students' *optimum performance,* affective inventories strive to measure students' *typical performance.* Remembering that when students complete most affective devices, those results don't count toward the students' grade, and that self-report assessment offers students a wonderful opportunity to distort their responses, there's a strong likelihood that at least some students won't respond honestly. As a consequence, inferences about the affective status of *individual* students (based on a student's responses to an affective inventory) are risky.

Besides, instructional decisions about individual students based on affective assessment devices are rare. If Harry Helms knows history well, but happens to hate it, few teachers would give Harry a low grade in history based on his disdain for "ancient folks' activities."

In contrast, however, teachers often make instructional decisions about what goes on in class based on aggregated affective data. Assuming that there will be a small number of students who supply inaccurate responses, it is still reasonable to assume that the total collectivity of students' responses will permit meaningful *group-focused inferences.* And that's the kind of inferences you should be making when you use affective assessment instruments. These assessment devices are simply too crude to permit individual-focused inferences. In aggregate, however, you ought to be able to make some very solid judgments about how your students, as a group, are affectively disposed. That is why, in some cases, you can collect affective data from only, say, half your class yet still make a fairly accurate inference about the group based on responses from the sample.

What Do Classroom Teachers Really Need to Know about Affective Assessment? . . . .

The most important thing that you need to know about affective assessment is that if you don't measure your students' affective status in a systematic fashion, you're far less likely to emphasize affect instructionally. Moreover, without systematic affective assessment, you're not apt to have a very decent fix on the affective consequences, possibly unintentional, that you're having on your students.

If you do decide to engage in some affective measurement in your own classes, you'll be much better off if you rely on fairly straightforward self-report instruments rather than trying to employ some exotic affective measurement strategies that are both time consuming and, at the same time, yield inferences of arguable validity. You also need to know that affective assessment devices are usually too imprecise to allow you to make inferences about individual students. Group-focused inferences are as far as you should go in the affective realm.

Chapter Summary . . . .

The chapter was initiated by your congenial author's unabashed endorsement of the instructional importance of affect and, as a consequence, the importance of assessing students' affective status. It was suggested that the use of affective assessment in classrooms would incline teachers to address affective goals instructionally. It was also argued that if teachers monitor their students' affective status, instructional modifications can be made if inappropriate or insufficient affective shifts in students are occurring. Affective variables were described as important predictors of individuals' future behaviors because people's affective status reveals their behavioral dispositions. It was also pointed out, however, that there are vocal groups whose members oppose instructional attention to affect.

Regarding the kinds of affective variables to assess in one's classroom, a series of potential attitudinal and value foci were presented. Teachers were urged to select only a few, highly meaningful affective variables rather than so many as to induce affective overwhelm.

Self-report assessment procedures were recommended as the most practical way to gather affective data in classrooms. Likert inventories were suggested as a highly efficient data-gathering device for affective variables. An eight-step procedure for developing Likert inventories was described. Anonymity was identified as an indispensable component of appropriate affective assessment. Several anonymity-enhancement procedures were described. It was also suggested that affective assessments be made prior to and at the conclusion of instruction as well as in the form of occasional affective dip sticking.

Finally, the nature of affective inferences was explored. It was argued that the imprecision of affective assessment devices should incline teachers to make group-focused inferences rather than inferences about individual students.

Self-Check

For this chapter's self-check exercises, you'll be presented with descriptions of fictitious teachers engaged in some form of affective assessment. Based on what you've read in the chapter (which should be *every single word and punctuation mark*), critique the actions of the teachers described in the following scenarios.

Scenario One

Molly Muggins, having read a chapter such as the one you've just about finished, has jumped into affective assessment with both feet. She measures her third-grade students' attitudes toward reading, writing, mathematics, science, and social studies every month. Molly's students are asked to complete the following sentence for each of the five subjects: "My current opinion of (*name of subject*) is:

_____

_____

_____

The monthly affective assessment takes only about 10 minutes. Molly has identified certain students who have particularly negative reactions toward particular subject areas. She intends to work individually with these students in an attempt to foster more positive attitudes.

What do you think of Molly's affective assessment efforts?

Scenario Two

Having decided to employ a Likert inventory for his affective assessments, Alex Allen, an English teacher, decided to focus on his students' confidence as writers. He then authored 10 positive statements such as "When I have to write something, I know I can," and 10 negative statements such as "If I'm called on to do a written report, I really panic." Alex mixed up the order of the 20 statements, then asked three other English teachers to classify each statement as positive or negative. Because three supposedly negative statements and two supposedly positive statements were classified differently by his three co-workers, Alex tossed out those five statements.

He decided to use a five-point response scale—namely, *strongly agree, agree, uncertain, disagree,* and *strongly disagree.* Alex then developed directions for his inventory, which he entitled You and Composition. The directions explained the response procedures and made it clear that there were no right or wrong answers. The directions also indicated that students were to respond anonymously and to deposit their completed inventories in a specially provided collection box. Because he had mixed up the 15 remaining statements (8 positive and 7 negative), he made sure that his scoring key coincided with the proper positive and negative statements.

One of the other English teachers in his school offered Alex the opportunity to try out his undeveloped affective assessment instrument to see how it worked. Alex jumped at the chance and administered the inventory to 31 of the other teacher's students. In looking over the results, Alex identified 2 negative and 3 positive statements that didn't seem to function like the rest of the statements. Accordingly, he dumped those statements and ended up with a 10-item Likert inventory that he intends to use with his class both before he gets into a major unit on composition and, a month later, when the unit has been completed.

What do you think of Alex's efforts to create a Likert inventory?

Scenario Three

Carl Klevins, a woodshop instructor, is immensely interested in affect. Because fewer and fewer students are signing up for his woodshop classes, Carl strives to promote subject-approaching tendencies on the part of his students. "I want my students, boys and girls alike, to become truly enthralled with the feel of sawdust in their pockets and the sound of other students using the woodshop's lathe." Carl spends at least five minutes per week jotting down in his notebook the behaviors that indicate to him certain students are responding positively to woodshop activities.

What do you think of Carl's way of getting a fix on his students' attitudes?

Pondertime

1. Some citizens are adamantly opposed to having the schools engage in any kind of systematic effort to influence students' attitudes or values. What do you suppose might be the reasons for their resistance to affective instruction and, most probably, to affective assessment as well?

2. Suppose you were a classroom teacher who was limited to only two affective variables to assess. Identify such affective variables that should be assessed, irrespective of the subject matter involved.

3. Throughout the chapter, a strong preference for self-report assessment devices was registered in contrast to more elaborate exotic assessment schemes. Do you agree with that position? Why or why not?

4. Can you think of procedures, other than those cited in the chapter, to enhance students' perceptions that their responses are truly anonymous?

5. Although the chapter suggested that group-focused inferences should be made from affective assessment devices, can you think of any defensible ways that teachers could get a decent fix on an individual student's attitudes and values? If so, how?

Self-Check Key

Scenario One

Molly messed up on a monthly basis. By requiring students to write out their responses, anonymity was blown. It's not even clear that students weren't supposed to put their names on their responses. In addition, Molly appears to be making individually focused inferences about how much certain subjects are liked. At best, even if she cleaned up her measurement act, Molly should only draw group-focused inferences. Molly's affective assessment efforts were not stellar.

Scenario Two

Alex was pretty much on target the whole way through. Indeed, he so compliantly adhered to the eight steps suggested on pages 207–208 for creating Likert inventories that you might conclude he had read the chapter.

Scenario Three

There are some teachers who can make extremely insightful judgments about students' unobservable affective status based on certain observable acts of students. Unfortunately, there are probably just as many teachers who are likely to make the wrong inferences about students' affect based on their observed behaviors. One of the more vexing difficulties to be coped with when using observation-based assessments of affect is that people often see what they want to see in a given situation. Teachers are no different. Thus, although we're glad to see Carl's attentiveness to affect, his assessment approach leaves a load to be desired.

Additional Stuff

Anderson, Lorin W. *Assessing Affective Characteristics in the Schools*. Boston: Allyn and Bacon, 1981.

Droegemueller, Lee. *The New Religious Right*. Paper presented to Education Policy Fellows, Arizona State University, April 9, 1993.

Kohn, Alfie. "How Not to Teach Values: A Critical Look at Character Education." *Phi Delta Kappan*, 78, no. 6 (February 1997): 428–439.

Likert, R. "A Technique for the Measurement of Attitudes." *Archives of Psychology*, 140, 1932.

Linn, Robert L., and Norman E. Gronlund. *Measurement and Assessment in Teaching* (7th ed.). Upper Saddle River, NJ: Prentice Hall, 1995.

McMillan, James H. *Classroom Assessment: Principles and Practice for Effective Instruction*. Boston: Allyn and Bacon, 1997.

Popham, W. James. "Educational Assessment's Lurking Lacuna: The Measurement of Affect." *Education and Urban Society*, 26, no. 4 (August 1994): 404–416.

Popham, W. J. *Educational Evaluation* (3rd ed.). Boston: Allyn and Bacon, 1993, 150–193.

Popham, W. James. "Appraising Two Techniques for Increasing the Honesty of Students' Answers to Self-Report Assessment Devices." *Journal of Personnel Evaluation in Education*, 7, no. 1 (June 1993): 33–41.

Webb, Eugene J., Donald T. Campbell, Richard D. Schwartz, Lee Sechreat, and Janet Belew Grove. *Nonreactive Measures in the Social Sciences* (2nd ed.). Boston: Houghton Mifflin, 1981.

Nonprint Stuff

Popham, W. James. *Improving Instruction: Start with Student Attitudes* (Videotape #ETVT-19). Los Angeles: IOX Assessment Associates.

Popham, W. James. *Assessing Student Attitudes: A Key to Increasing Achievement* (Videotape #ETVT-20). Los Angeles: IOX Assessment Associates.

11

· ·

Improving Teacher–Developed Assessments

*I*f you've ever visited the manuscript room of the British Museum, you'll recall seeing handwritten manuscripts authored by some of the superstars of English literature. It's a moving experience. Delightfully, the museum presents not only the final versions of famed works by such authors as Milton and Keats but also the early drafts of those works. It is somewhat surprising and genuinely encouraging to learn that those giants of literature didn't get it right the first time. They had to cross out words, delete sentences, and substitute phrases. Many of the museum's early drafts are genuinely messy, reflecting all sorts of rethinking on the part of the author. Well, if the titans of English literature had to revise their early drafts, is it at all surprising that teachers usually need to spruce up their classroom assessments?

This chapter is designed to provide you with several procedures by which you can improve the assessment instruments you develop. Although I can promise you that if you use the chapter's recommended procedures, your tests will get better, they'll probably never make it to the British Museum—unless you carry them in when visiting.

There are two general improvement strategies to be described in the chapter. First, you'll learn about *judgmental* improvement procedures in which the chief means of sharpening your tests is human judgment—your own and that of others. Second, you'll be considering *empirical* test-improvement procedures that are based on students' responses to your assessment procedures. Ideally, if time permits and your motivation abounds, you can use both forms of test-improvement procedures for your own classroom assessment devices.

Judgmentally Based Improvement Procedures ....

Human judgment, although it sometimes gets us in trouble, is a remarkably useful tool. Judgmental approaches to test improvement can be carried out quite systematically or, in contrast, rather informally. Judgmental assessment-improvement strategies differ chiefly according to who is supplying the judgments. There are three sources of test-improvement judgments you should consider—those supplied by (1) yourself, (2) your colleagues, and (3) your students. We'll consider each of these potential judgment sources separately.

Judging Your Own Assessment Instruments

Let's suppose you've created a 70-item combination short-answer and multiple-choice examination for a U.S. government class and, having administered it, you want to improve the examination for next year's class. We'll assume that during item development you did a reasonable amount of in-process sharpening up of the items so that they represented what, at the time, was your best effort. Now, however, you have an opportunity to revisit the examination to see if its 70 items are all that marvelous. It's a good thing to do.

Let's consider another form of assessment. Suppose you have devised what you think are pretty decent directions for your students to follow when preparing portfolios or when responding to tasks in a performance test. Even if you regard those directions as suitable, it's always helpful to review such directions after a time to see if you can now detect shortcomings that, at the time you originally prepared the set of directions, escaped your attention.

As you probably know from other kinds of writing, it is almost always the case that if you return to one of your written efforts after it has had time to "cool off," you're likely to spot deficits that, in the heat of the original writing, weren't all that apparent to you. However, beyond a fairly casual second look, you'll typically be able to improve your assessment procedures even more if you approach this test-improvement task more systematically. To illustrate, you could use specific review criteria when you judge your earlier assessment efforts. If a test item or a set of directions falls short on any criterion, you should obviously do some modifying. Presented here are five review criteria that you might wish to consider if you set out systematically to improve your classroom assessment procedures:

- *Adherence to item-specific guidelines and general item-writing commandments.* When you review your assessment procedures, it will be useful to review briefly the general item-writing commandments supplied earlier (in Chapter 6) as well as the particular item-writing guidelines provided for the specific kind of item(s) you've developed. If you now see violations of the principles set forth in either of those two sets of directives, fix the flaws.

- *Contribution to score-based inference.* Recall that the real reason teachers assess students is in order to arrive at score-based inferences about the status of students. Therefore, it will be helpful for you to reconsider each aspect of a previously developed assessment procedure to see whether it does, in fact, really contribute to the kind of inference about your students that you wish to draw.
- *Accuracy of content.* There's always the possibility that previously accurate content has now been superseded or contradicted by more recent content. Be sure to check that the content you included earlier in the assessment instrument is still accurate and that your answer key is still correct.
- *Absence of content lacunae.* This review criterion gives me a chance to use one of my favorite words, the plural form of *lacuna,* which, incidentally, means a *gap.* Although *gap* would have done the job in this instance, you'll admit that *gap* looks somewhat tawdry when stacked up against *lacuna.* (This, of course, is a norm-referenced contrast.) Hindsight is a nifty form of vision. Thus, when you take a second look at the content coverage represented in your assessment instrument, you may discover that you originally overlooked some important content. This review criterion is clearly related to an earlier review criterion regarding the assessment's contribution to the score-based inference that you want to make. Any meaningful lacunae in content will obviously reduce the accuracy of your inference.
- *Fairness.* Although you should clearly have tried to eradicate any bias in your assessment instruments when you originally developed them, there's always the chance that you overlooked something. Undertake another bias review just to make certain you've been as attentive to bias elimination as you possibly can be.

I can personally attest to a case of bias blindness when I authored a textbook on educational evaluation in the seventies. Recognizing that a number of women at that time were beginning to take offense at authors' use of masculine pronouns when referring to unnamed individuals (for example, "The student lost *his* lunch"), I had assiduously written the textbook so that all the illustrative people were plural. I never had to use *his* or *her* because I could always use *their.* After churning out the last chapter, I was smugly proud of my pluralization prowess. Yet, having been so attentive to a pronoun issue that might offend some women, I blithely included a cartoon that showed scantily clad females cavorting before male members of a school board. Talk about dumb! If only I'd taken a serious second look at the book before it hit the presses, I might have spotted my insensitive error. As it was, because the cartoon appeared in all copies of the first edition (not the second!), I received more than a few heated, and quite deserved, complaints from readers.

It's not being suggested that you fill out an elaborate rating form for each of these five review criteria—with each criterion requiring a numerical rating.

Rather, I'm recommending that you seriously think about these five criteria before you tackle any judgmental review of a previously developed assessment
instrument.

Collegial Judgments

If you are working with a colleague whose judgment you trust, it's often helpful
to ask that person to review your assessment procedures. To get the most mileage
out of such a review, you'll probably need to provide your co-worker with at least
a brief description of review criteria such as the five previously cited ones—that
is, (1) adherence to item-specific guidelines and general item-writing commandments, (2) contribution to score-based inference, (3) accuracy of content, (4) absence of content lacunae, and (5) fairness. You will need to describe to your colleague the key inference(s) you intend to base on the assessment procedure. It will
also be useful to your colleague if you identify the decisions that will, thereafter,
be influenced by your inferences about students.

I've found that collegial judgments are particularly helpful to teachers who
employ many performance tests or who use portfolio assessments. Most of the
empirically based improvement procedures you'll be learning about later in the
chapter are intended to be used with more traditional sorts of items such as those
found in multiple-choice exams. For portfolio assessment and performance tests,
judgmental approaches will often prove more useful.

Remember, if *you* are the creator of the portfolio assessment or performance
tests you're setting out to improve, you're apt to be biased in their favor. After all,
parents usually adore their progeny. What you need is a good, hard, *nonpartisan*
review of what you've been up to assessment-wise.

To do a thorough job of helping you review your assessment approaches, of
course, your colleague will need to put in some time. In fairness, you'll probably
obliged to toss in a *quid pro quo* or two whereby you return the favor by reviewing
your colleague's tests (or by resolving a pivotal personal crisis in your colleague's
private life). If your school district is large enough, you might also have access to
some central-office supervisorial personnel who know something about assessment. Here's a neat opportunity to let them earn their salaries—get them to review your assessment procedures. It is often asserted that another pair of eyes can
help improve almost any written document. This doesn't necessarily mean that
the other pair of eyes see accurately while yours are in need of contact lenses. You
should listen to what other reviewers say, but be guided by your own judgments
about the virtues of their suggestions.

Student Judgments

When teachers set out to improve assessment procedures, a rich source of data is
often overlooked because teachers typically fail to secure advice from their students. Yet, because students have experienced test items in a most meaningful

context, more or less as an executionee experiences a firing squad, student judgments can provide useful insights. Student reactions can help you spot shortcomings in particular items and in other features of your assessment procedures such as a test's directions or the time you've allowed for completing the test.

The kinds of data secured from students will vary, depending on the type of assessment procedure being used, but questions such as those on the item-improvement questionnaire in Figure 11.1 can profitably be given to students after they have completed an assessment procedure. Although the illustrative questionnaire in Figure 11.1 is intended for use with a selected-response type of test, only minor revisions would be needed to make it suitable for a constructed-response test, a performance test, or a portfolio assesment system.

It is important to let students finish a test prior to their engaging in such a judgmental exercise. (Note, once more, the possessive pronoun modifying the gerund *engaging.* You are, obviously, reading some grammatically top-drawer stuff here.) If students are asked to *simultaneously* play the roles of test takers and test improvers, they'll probably botch up both tasks. No student should be expected to serve two such functions, at least at the same time.

Simply give students the test as usual, collect their answer sheets or test booklets, and provide them with new, blank test booklets. *Then* distribute a questionnaire, such as the one seen earlier. In other words, ask students to play examinees and item reviewers, but to play these roles consecutively, not simultaneously.

Now, how do you treat students' reactions to test items? Let's say you're a classroom teacher and a few students come up with a violent castigation of one of your favorite items. Do you automatically buckle by scrapping or revising the item? Of course not; teachers are made of sterner stuff. Perhaps the students were miffed about the item because they didn't know how to answer it. One of the best ways for students to escape responsibility for a dismal test performance is to assail the test itself. Teachers should anticipate a certain amount of carping from low-scoring examinees.

Figure 11.1   **An Illustrative Item-Improvement Questionnaire for Students**

Item-Improvement Questionnaire for Students
1. If any of the items seemed confusing, which ones were they?
2. Were there any items that had more than one correct answer? If so, which ones?
3. Were there any items that had no correct answers? If so, which ones?
4. Were there words in any items that confused you? If so, which ones?
5. Were the directions for the test, or for particular subsections, unclear? If so, which ones?

Yet, after allowing for a reasonable degree of complaining, student reactions can sometimes provide useful insights for teachers. A student-castigated item may, indeed, deserve castigation. To overlook students as a source of judgmental test-improvement information, for either selected-response or constructed-response items, would clearly be an error.

To review, then, judgmentally based test-improvement procedures can rely on the judgments supplied by you, your colleagues, or your students. In the final analysis, you will be the decision maker regarding whether to modify your assessment procedures. Nonetheless, it is typically helpful to have others react to your tests.

Empirically Based Improvement Procedures ....

In addition to judgmentally based methods of improving your assessment procedures, there are improvement approaches based on the empirical data that students supply when they respond to the assessment instruments you've developed. Let's turn, then, to the use of student-response data in the improvement of assessment procedures. A variety of empirical item-improvement techniques have been well honed over the years. We will consider these more traditional item-analysis procedures first, turning later to a few more recent wrinkles for using student data to improve a teacher's classroom assessments procedures.

Most of the procedures that are employed to improve classroom assessments on the basis of students' responses to those assessments rely on numbers. And I recognize that there are some readers of this book (*you* may be one) who are definitely put off by numbers. I sometimes believe that there is a secret cult among prospective teachers who have taken a "tremble pledge"—that is, a vow to tremble when encountering any numerical value larger than a single digit (a number larger than 9). If you are one of these mathphobics, I beg you to stay calm because the numbers you'll be encountering in this and later chapters will really be Simple-Simon stuff. Tremble not. It'll be pain free. Just work through the easy examples and you'll survive with surprising ease.

Difficulty Indices

One useful index of an item's quality is its *difficulty*. The most commonly employed item-difficulty index, often referred to simply as a *p value*, is calculated as follows:

$$\text{Difficulty } p = \frac{R}{T}$$

where R = the number of students responding correctly (right) to an item.
  T = the total number of students responding to the item.

To illustrate, if 50 students answered an item, and only 37 of them answered it correctly, then the p value representing that item's difficulty would be

$$\text{Difficulty } p \ = \ \frac{37}{50} \ = \ .74$$

It should be clear that such p value can range from 0 to 1.00, with higher p values indicating items that more students answered correctly. For example, a p value of .98 would signify an item that was answered correctly by almost all students. Similarly, an item with a p value of .15 would be one that most students (85%) missed.

The p value of an item should always be viewed in relationship to the student's chance probability of getting the correct response. For example, if a binary-choice item is involved, *on the basis of chance alone* students should be able to answer the item correctly half of the time, and thus the item would have a p value of .50. On a four-option multiple-choice test, a .25 p by chance alone would be expected.

Sometimes slight variations of the basic item-difficulty formula are employed so that, for example, we compute a difficulty index where we dump the decimal point:

$$\text{Difficulty } = \ \frac{\text{Right}}{\text{Total}} \times 100$$

In this instance, of course, multiplying the ratio between correct and total item responses by 100 gets rid of the decimal point so that difficulty indices range from 0 to 100. Other folks may prefer to use percentages, so that an item's difficulty value can range from 0% to 100%. However, in all of these indices, what we are isolating is the proportion of total student responses that are correct. Item p values can prove serviceable in empirically shaping up your items because they let you know how tough an item is for your students.

Educators sometimes err by referring to items with high p values (for instance, p values of .80 and above) as "easy" items, while items with low p values (of, say, .20 and below) are described as "difficult" items. Those descriptions may or may not be accurate. Even though we typically refer to an item's p value as its *difficulty* index, the actual difficulty of an item is tied to the instructional program surrounding it. If students are well taught, they may perform excellently on a complex item that, by anyone's estimate, is a tough one. Does the resulting p value of .95 indicate the item is easy? No. The item's complicated content has simply been taught effectively. For example, almost all students in a pre-med course for prospective physicians might correctly answer a technical item about the central nervous system that almost all "people off the street" would answer incorrectly. A p value of .96 based on the pre-med students' performances would not render the item intrinsically easy.

Item-Discrimination Indices

For norm-referenced tests, one of the most powerful indicators of an item's quality is the item discrimination index. In brief, an *item-discrimination index* typically tells us how frequently an item is answered correctly by those who perform well on the total test. Fundamentally, an item-discrimination index reflects the relationship between students' responses for the total test and their responses to a particular test item. One approach to computing an item-discrimination statistic is to calculate a correlation coefficient between students' total test scores and their performance on a particular item.

A *positively discriminating item* indicates that an item is answered correctly more often by those who score well on the total test than by those who score poorly on the total test. A *negatively discriminating item* is answered correctly more often by those who score poorly on the total test than by those who score well on the total test. A *nondiscriminating item* is one for which there's no appreciable difference in the correct response proportions of those who score well or poorly on the total test. This set of relationships is summarized in the following chart. (Remember that < and > signify *less than* and *more than*, respectively.)

Type of Item	Proportion of Correct Responses on Total Test
Positive Discriminator	High Scorers > Low Scorers
Negative Discriminator	High Scorers < Low Scorers
Nondiscriminator	High Scorers = Low Scorers

In general, teachers would like to discover that their items are positive discriminators because a positively discriminating item tends to be answered correctly by the most knowledgeable students (those who scored high on the total test) and incorrectly by the least knowledgeable students (those who scored low on the total test). Negatively discriminating items indicate that something is awry, because the item tends to be missed more often by the most knowledgeable students and answered correctly more frequently by the least knowledgeable students.

Now, how do you go about computing an item's discrimination index? The following four steps can be employed for the analysis of classroom assessment procedures:

1. *Order the test papers from high to low by total score.* Place the paper having the highest total score on top, and continue with the next highest total score sequentially until the paper with the lowest score is placed on the bottom.
2. *Divide the papers into a high group and a low group, with an equal number of papers in each group.* Split the groups into upper and lower halves. If there is an

Parent Talk ....

Suppose a parent of one of your students called you this morning, before school, to complain about his son's poor performance on your classroom tests. He concludes his grousing by asking you, "Just how sure you are that the fault is in Tony and not in your tests!"

• • • *If I were you, here's how I'd respond to the parent:*

"I'm glad you called about your son's test results, because I'm sure we both want what's best for Tony, and I want to be sure that I'm making the instructional decisions that will be best for him.

"The way I use my classroom tests is to try to arrive at the most accurate conclusion I can about how well my students have mastered the skills and knowledge I'm trying to teach them. It's very important, therefore, that the conclusions I reach about students' skill levels are valid. So, every year, I devote systematic attention to the improvement of each of my major exams. You'll remember that it was on the last two of these exams that Tony scored so badly.

"What I'd like to do is show you the exams I've been giving my students and the data I use each year to improve those exams. Why don't we set up an after-school or, if necessary, an evening appointment for you and your wife to look over my classroom assessments and the evidence I've been compiling over the years to make sure my tests help me make valid inferences about what Tony and the rest of my students are learning."

• • • *Now, how would you respond to this parent?*

odd number of papers, simply set aside one of the middle papers so that the number of papers in the high and low groups will be the same. If there are several papers with identical scores at the middle of the distribution, then randomly assign them to the high or low distributions so that the number of papers in the two groups is identical. The use of 50% groups has the advantage of providing enough papers to permit reliable estimates of upper and lower group performances.

3. *Calculate a* p *value for each of the high and low groups.* Determine the number of examinees in the high group who answered the item correctly, then divide this number by the number of examinees in the high group. This provides you with p_h. Repeat the process for the low group to obtain p_l.

4. *Subtract* p_l *from* p_h *to obtain each item's discrimination index* (D). In essence, then, $D = p_h - p_l$.

To Catch a Culprit: Teacher or Test ·

Susan Stevens teaches sixth-grade social studies in Exeter Middle School. During the seven years that she has taught at Exeter, Susan has always spent considerable time in developing what she refers to as "creditable classroom assessments." She really has put in more than her share of weekends working to create crackerjack examinations.

This last spring, however, Susan completed an extension course on educational testing. In that course she learned how to compute discrimination analyses of her test items. As a consequence, Susan has been subjecting all of her examinations to such analyses this year.

On one of her examinations that contained mostly selected-response items, Susan discovered to her dismay that 4 of the test's 30 items turned out to have negative discriminators. In other words, students who performed well on the total test answered the 4 items incorrectly more often than students who didn't do so well on the total test. To her surprise, all 4 negatively discriminating items dealt with the same topic—that is, relationships among the legislative, judicial, and executive branches of the U.S. government.

Susan's first thought was to chuck the 4 items because they were clearly defective. As she considered the problem, however, another possibility occurred to her. Because all 4 items were based on the same instructional content, perhaps she had confused the better students with her explanations.

If you were Susan and wanted to get to the bottom of this issue so you could decide whether to overhaul the items or the instruction, how would you proceed?

Suppose you are in the midst of conducting an item analysis of your midterm examination items. Let's say you split your class of 30 youngsters' papers into two equal upper-half and lower-half papers. All 15 students in the high group answered item 42 correctly, but only 5 of the 15 students in the low group answered it correctly. The item discrimination index for item 42, therefore, would be $1.00 - .33 = .67$.

Now, how large should an item's discrimination index be in order for you to consider the item acceptable? Ebel (1979) offered the experienced-based guidelines in Table 11.1 for indicating the quality of norm-referenced test items. If you consider Ebel's guidelines as approximations, not absolute standards, they'll usually help you decide whether your items are discriminating satisfactorily.

An item's ability to discriminate is highly related to its overall difficulty index. For example, an item that is answered correctly by all students has a total p value of 1.00. For that item, the p_h and p_l are also 1.00. Thus, the item's discrimination index is zero ($1.00 - 1.00 = 0$). A similar result would ensue for items in

Table 11.1   **Guidelines for Evaluating the Discriminating Efficiency of Items**

Discrimination Index	Item Evaluation
.40 and above	Very good items
.30–.39	Reasonably good items, but possibly subject to improvement
.20–.29	Marginal items, usually needing improvement
.19 and below	Poor items, to be rejected or improved by revision

Source: Ebel, 1979.

which the overall p value was zero—that is, items that no examinee had answered correctly.

   With items that have very high or very low p values, it is thus less likely that substantial discrimination indices can be obtained. Later in the chapter we will see that this situation has prompted proponents of criterion-referenced tests (who often hope that almost all postinstruction responses from students will be correct) to search for alternative ways to calculate indices of item quality.

Distractor Analyses

For a selected-response item that, perhaps on the basis of its p value or its discrimination index, appears to be in need of revision, it is necessary to look deeper. In the case of multiple-choice items, we can gain further insights by carrying out a *distractor analysis* in which we see how the high and low groups are responding to the item's distractors.

   Presented in Table 11.2 is the information typically used when conducting a distractor analysis. Note that the asterisk in Table 11.2 indicates that choice B is the correct answer to the item. For the item in the table, the difficulty index (p) was .50 and the discrimination index (D) was −.33. An inspection of the distrac-

Table 11.2   **A Typical Distractor-Analysis Table**

Item No. 28	Alternatives				
($p = .50, D = −.33$)	A	B*	C	D	Omit
Upper 15 students	2	5	0	8	0
Lower 15 students	4	10	0	0	1

tors reveals that there appears to be something in alternative *D* that is enticing the students in the high group to choose it. Indeed, while over half of the high group opted for choice *D*, not a single student in the low group went for choice *D*. Alternative *D* needs to be reviewed carefully.

Note also that alternative *C* is doing nothing at all for the item. No student selected choice *C*. In addition to reviewing choice *D*, therefore, choice *C* might be made a bit more appealing. It is possible, of course, particularly if this is a best-answer type of multiple-choice item, that alternative *B*, the correct answer, needs a bit of massaging as well. For multiple-choice items in particular, but also for matching items, a more intensive analysis of examinee responses to individual distractors can frequently be illuminating. In the same vein, careful scrutiny of examinees' responses to essay and short-answer items can typically supply useful insights for revision purposes.

Item Analysis for Criterion-Referenced Tests

When teachers use criterion-referenced tests, they typically hope that most students will score well on those tests after instruction has occurred. In such instances, because postinstruction *p* values may approach 1.0, traditional item-analysis approaches will often yield low discrimination indices. Accordingly, several alternative approaches to item analysis for criterion-referenced tests have been devised in recent years.

Two general item-analysis schemes have been employed thus far, depending on the kinds of criterion groups available. Both of these item-analysis schemes are roughly comparable to the item-discrimination indices used with norm-referenced tests. The first approach involves the administration of the criterion-referenced test to *the same group of students* both prior to and following instruction. A disadvantage of this approach is that the teacher must wait for instruction to be completed before securing the item-analysis data. Another problem is that the pretest may be *reactive,* in the sense that its administration sensitizes students to certain items so that the students' posttest performance is actually a function of the instruction *plus* the pretest's administration.

Using the strategy of testing the same groups of students prior to and after instruction, we can employ an item discrimination index calculated as follows:

$$D_{ppd} = p_{post} - p_{pre}$$

where p_{post} = proportion of students answering the item correctly on posttest.

p_{pre} = proportion of students answering the item correctly on pretest.

The value of D_{ppd} (discrimination based on the pretest-posttest difference) can range from –1.00 to +1.00, with high positive values indicating that an item is sensitive to instruction.

For example, if 41% of the examinees answered item 27 correctly in the pretest and 84% answered it correctly on the posttest, then item 27's D_{ppd} would be .84 – .41 = 43. A high positive value would indicate that the item is sensitive to the instructional program you've provided to your students. Items with low or negative D_{ppd} values would be earmarked for further analysis because such items are not behaving the way one would expect them to behave if instruction were effective. (It is always possible, particularly if many items fail to reflect large posttest-minus-pretest differences, that the instruction being provided was not all that wonderful.)

The second approach to item analysis for criterion-referenced tests is to locate two *different groups of students,* one of which has already been instructed and one of which has not. By comparing the performance on items of instructed and uninstructed students, you can pick up some useful clues regarding item quality. This approach has the advantage of avoiding the delay associated with pretesting and posttesting the same group of students and also of avoiding the possibility of a reactive pretest. Its drawback, however, is that you must rely on human judgment in the selection of the "instructed" and "uninstructed" groups. The two groups should be fairly identical in all other relevant respects (for example, in intellectual ability) but different with respect to whether or not they have been instructed. The isolation of two such groups sounds easier than it usually is. Your best bet would be to prevail on a fellow teacher whose students are studying different topics.

If you use two groups—that is, an instructed group and an uninstructed group—one of the more straightforward item discrimination indices is D_{uigd} (discrimination based on uninstructed versus instructed group differences). This index is calculated as follows:

$$D_{uigd} = p_i - p_u$$

where p_i = proportion of instructed students answering an item correctly.
p_u = proportion of uninstructed students answering an item correctly.

This index can also range in value from –1.00 to +1.00. To illustrate its computation, if an instructed group of students scored 91% correct on a particular item, while that same item was answered correctly by only 55% of an uninstructed group, then D_{uigd} would be .91 – .55 = 36. Interpretations of D_{uigd} are similar to those used with D_{ppd}.

As suggested earlier, clearly there are advantages associated with using both judgmental and empirical approaches to improving your classroom assessment procedures. Practically speaking, classroom teachers have only so much energy to expend. If you can spare a bit of your allotted energy to spiff up your assessment instruments, you'll usually see meaningful differences in the quality of those instruments.

What Do Classroom Teachers Really Need to Know about Improving Their Assessments? ....

You ought to know that teacher-made tests can be improved as a consequence of judgmental and/or empirical improvement procedures. Judgmental approaches work well with either selected-response or constructed-response kinds of test items. Empirical item improvements have been used chiefly with selected response tests, hence are more readily employed with such test items. You should realize that most of the more widely used indices of item quality, such as discrimination indices, are intended for use with test items in norm-referenced assessment approaches, and may have less applicability to your assessment procedures if you employ criterion-referenced measurement strategies. Finally, you must understand that because educators have far less experience in using (and improving) performance assessments and portfolio assessments, there isn't really a delightful set of improvement procedures available for those assessment strategies—other than good, solid judgment.

Chapter Summary ....

A focus on two strategies for improving assessment procedures was seen in this chapter. It was suggested that, with adequate time and motivation, teachers could use judgmental and/or empirical methods of improving their assessments.

Judgmentally based improvement procedures were described for use by teachers, teachers' colleagues, and students. Five review criteria for evaluating assessment procedures were presented for use by teachers and their colleagues: (1) adherence to item-specific guidelines and general item-writing commandments, (2) contribution to score-based inferences, (3) accuracy of content, (4) absence of content lacunae, and (5) fairness. A set of possible questions to ask students about test items was also provided.

Two empirical item-improvement indices described in the chapter were p values and item discrimination indices. A step-by-step procedure for determining item discrimination values was described. Designed chiefly for use with norm-referenced tests, item discrimination indices do not function well when large numbers of students respond correctly to the items involved. Distractor analyses have proven highly useful in the improvement of multiple-choice items because the effectiveness of each of an item's alternatives can be studied. Finally, two indices of item quality for criterion-referenced test items were described. Although roughly comparable to the kind of item discrimination indices widely used with norm-referenced tests, the two indices for criterion-referenced test items can be used in settings where many students perform well on examinations.

Self-Check

For the first five exercises on this chapter's self-check, see if you can determine whether the item-improvement scheme described is primarily a *judgmental* or an *empirical* item-improvement approach.

1. A mathematics teacher (wouldn't you know?) improves her test items by modifying those that fail to correlate highly with students' total test scores.

2. At the end of his major examinations, a chemistry teacher requires his students to critique a blank copy of test they just completed in order to identify any confusing items.

3. Because he has learned that very difficult or very easy items don't discriminate among students, a sixth-grade teacher discards any test items having p values less than .10 or more than .90.

4. Groups of high school science teachers interested in "alternative assessment in the sciences" regularly exchange newly developed performance tests with one another for purposes of evaluation and to secure test-improvement suggestions. Accompanying each performance test is a set of information indicating how students appraised the test after completing it.

5. An art teacher rejects the idea that his fellow art teachers' appraisals of test items are meritorious, hence scrutinizes all of his criterion-referenced test items using a discrimination index based on pretest-to-posttest differences in p values.

For the last five self-check exercises, you'll be presented with a brief description of a teacher's actions or a set of data from an analysis of a classroom assessment item. Then you'll be asked a parenthetical question. See how well you can answer each question.

6. A music teacher has analyzed her History of Music final examination and discovered that for 5 of the 35 short-answer items, the p values were .95 or above.

   (Should this music teacher delete the five items the next time she uses the test?)

7. Here's a distractor analysis for a multiple-choice item in a social studies teacher's geography test:

Item No. 10	Alternatives			
$(p = .50, D = .50)$	A	B	C	D*
Upper 12 students	2	0	1	9
Lower 12 students	1	6	2	3

(Is there anything present in these data to suggest serious item deficits?)

8. A teacher reports to her principal that almost all of her items she has studied based on the D_{uigd} index have values well in excess of .50.

(Should the teacher toss these items out?)

9. Now check out this distractor analysis from a multiple-choice item in a physical education instructor's examination on Sports Safety Rules:

Response Options						Item No. 27
A	B*	C	D	F	Omit	$(p = .62, D = .15)$
1	15	1	1	2	0	Top 20 students
2	12	2	1	3	0	Bottom 20 students

(If the teacher is using the test to select the very best students, is this item acceptable?)

10. Mr. Philips, a health education teacher, analyzes his tests using empirical data from students' performances. He tries to reuse items that have discrimination indices below .20 and p values between .23 and .75. If he gets a negatively discriminating item, he is elated.

(Is Mr. Philips making sensible decisions?)

Pondertime

1. Why is it difficult to generate discrimination indices for performance assessments consisting of only one or two fairly elaborate tasks?

2. If you found that there was a conflict between judgmental and empirical evidence regarding the merits of a particular item, which form of evidence would you be inclined to believe?

3. Why do you suppose that relatively few classroom teachers attempt systematically to improve their assessment procedures?

4. Why is it usually true that when teachers review tests they've written earlier, the teachers can often spot deficits not previously discerned?

5. Why is it that a number of teachers who employ criterion-referenced assessment strategies tend to place little emphasis on traditional item discrimination indices?

Self-Check Key

1. Empirical

2. Judgmental

3. Empirical

4. Judgmental

5. Empirical

6. Not necessarily. The students' high performances may simply indicate superb instruction.

7. No, the item is a pretty tough one, but it discriminates well. The distractor analysis suggests that the three distractors (Choices *A, B,* and *C*) appear to be doing their jobs. It seems to be an okay item.

8. Again, a negative answer wins here. The whopping difference between the performance of instructed versus uninstructed students attests to the teacher's potent instruction.

9. The physical education teacher appears to be using the test in order to make norm-referenced interpretations (selecting "the very best students"). In that case, the discrimination index (.15) is too low.

10. Unfortunately, Mr. Philips is shooting for lower discrimination indices than he should. There's nothing wrong with choosing middle difficulty items, but he should be distressed, not jubilant, when his items discriminate negatively. Such negative discriminators arise when more of the most capable students miss an item while more of the least capable answer it correctly. Unless Mr. Philips is truly perverse, he should be chagrined when such items are encountered in his tests.

Additional Stuff

Airasian, Peter W. *Classroom Assessment* (2nd ed.). New York: McGraw-Hill, 1994.

Crocker, Linda. "Assessing Content Representativeness of Performance Assessment Exercises." *Applied Measurement in Education,* 10, no. 1 (1997): 83–95.

Downing, Steven M., and Thomas M. Haladyna. "Test Item Development: Validity Evidence from Quality Assurance Procedures." *Applied Measurement in Education,* 10, no. 1 (1997): 61–82.

Ebel, R. L., and D. A. Frisbie. *Essentials of Educational Measurement* (5th ed.). Englewood Cliffs, NJ: Prentice Hall, 1991.

Linn, Robert L., and Norman E. Gronlund. *Measurement and Assessment in Teaching* (7th ed.). Upper Saddle River, NJ: Prentice Hall, 1995.

Stiggins, Richard J. *Student-Centered Classroom Assessment* (2nd ed.). Upper Saddle River, NJ: Prentice Hall, 1997.

12

Instructionally Oriented
Assessment

*T*eachers test a child in order to make better decisions about how to educate the child. At least, they ought to.

In this chapter I will attempt to synthesize much of the content that you've encountered in the previous 11 chapters. More specifically, I'm going to describe two ways that the quality of a teacher's instruction can be markedly improved as a consequence of classroom assessments. One of those assessment-based strategies for improving instruction is fairly well known by teachers—even if it's not all that widely employed. The second assessment-based strategy for improving instruction, on the other hand, is understood by relatively few teachers. It is the second instructional improvement strategy, therefore, that will receive the greatest attention. This chapter, in short, deals with *how testing can help teaching*.

The two assessment-based strategies for instructional improvement that will be the focus of this chapter are presented below:

Strategy One: Making instructional decisions in light of assessment results. A teacher makes instructional decisions after assessing students to determine their status regarding the teacher's educational objectives.

Strategy Two: Planning instruction to achieve the objective(s) represented by a test. A teacher deliberately designs instruction to promote students' attainment of the knowledge, skills, and/or affect operationalized by an assessment.

Let's now consider each of these two ways of strengthening instruction.

Instructional Decisions and Assessment Results ....

If you were to ask a flock of teachers how assessment results might improve the quality of their teaching, a fair number of the teachers would respond that better classroom decisions can ordinarily be made if teachers have a more accurate idea of their students' current learning levels. We considered such decisions way back in Chapter 1. Unfortunately, too many teachers think that the chief role of classroom tests is for the assignment of students' grades. But any teacher who uses tests *dominantly* to determine whether students get high or low grades should receive a solid F in classroom assessment. Surely, classroom tests have helped teachers dispense grades since the Middle Ages. But classroom tests can do so much more. If teachers use classroom assessments properly, students' performances on those tests can help teachers make far better instructional decisions. Let's see how such assessment-based decision making works.

Assessment, Inferences, and Decisions

Most teachers have a ton of experience with classroom tests. As participants in the testing game, they've often been on the receiving end of assessment when they, themselves, were students. Or, after they finally arrived at the grown-up side of the teacher's desk, they've dispensed numerous tests to their own students. Because of all this testing, many teachers have become so inured to assessment that they've actually forgotten the reason teachers test in the first place. Accordingly, let's take a brief look at *why* teachers assess students.

Ordinarily, a teacher assesses a student to determine the student's status with respect to an educational objective that the teacher wants the student to master. Putting it another way, the teacher wants to know the student's level of learning in relationship to some sort of outcome that the teacher intends to promote. Usually, the outcome is *cognitive* in nature—for instance, the student's mastery of a skill or a body of knowledge. The desired outcome could, however, be *affective*—for example, when the teacher attempts to promote particular attitudes or interests. And, of course, in certain subjects, such as the arts or physical education, teachers are concerned with promoting their students' *psychomotor* prowess.

So, whether the intended educational outcome is cognitive, affective, or psychomotor, teachers often need to determine their students' status with respect to that outcome. In Figure 12.1, you'll see an intended instructional outcome represented as a thick-walled circle. To give Figure 12.1 a touch of class, I have labeled the circle as *a target instructional domain*. If you prefer a less pretentious but equally accurate descriptor, think of the circle in Figure 12.1 as "the stuff the teacher wants to teach."

Figure 12.1   **The Cognitive, Affective, or Psychomotor Outcome That the Teacher Intends to Promote Instructionally**

To give you an idea of the kinds of target instructional domains Figure 12.1 is intended to exemplify, here are a few illustrative instructional domains that teachers frequently pursue:

Cognitive

- Students will become skilled in solving age-appropriate mathematical word problems.
- Students will become knowledgeable regarding the key historical events leading to the U.S. Revolutionary War.

Affective

- Students will become more confident in their ability to make oral presentations to their peers.
- Students' enjoyment of volitional reading will increase dramatically.

Psychomotor

- Students will substantially increase the speed and accuracy of their keyboarding skills.
- Students will become more proficient in shooting basketball "jump shots" despite being closely guarded by an opposing player.

If you spend a moment or two reviewing these illustrative intended outcomes, you'll realize that each of these target instructional domains is really quite substantial. Consider, for example, the cognitive domain dealing with the student's ability to solve mathematical word problems. We could conjure up an almost unlimited number of such problems, and students would really have to be skilled to solve those problems. That's a hefty instructional domain. Similarly, the affective domain dealing with students' confidence in being able to make oral presentations to peers covers a ton of oral-communication terrain, ranging from confidence in giving one-minute impromptu speeches or presidential State of the Union addresses. And, when it comes to the psychomotor domain of shooting jump shots while being closely guarded, there are myriad places on the basketball court from which such shots can be launched, and there are at least half a myriad ways that a closely guarding opponent can closely guard a jump-shooter.

Putting it simply, almost any really significant target instructional domain is so substantial that teachers, as a practical matter, will be unable to determine a student's status by *exhaustively* assessing the domain. It would take too long. If students were actually assessed regarding *all* components of teachers' target instructional domains, those students would surely be drawing social security checks before they earned their high school diplomas.

As a practical solution, therefore, teachers *represent* target instructional domains by *sampling* from those domains. That's really what a classroom assessment ought to be—a representative sample of a target instructional domain. In Figure 12.2, you'll see represented the original target instructional domain you first met in Figure 12.1, as well as a classroom assessment that can be used to help teachers ascertain a student's status with regard to the target instructional domain. Note that Figure 12.2's thick-walled target instructional domain is being represented by a thin-walled classroom assessment. Because it's far too time consuming, for example, to test a student's knowledge of *all* the "key historical events leading to the U.S. Revolutionary War," a teacher's classroom test must *sample* that content. The thin-walled, content-sampling classroom test, therefore, only *represents* the target instructional domain.

Teachers should never be interested in a student's performance on a classroom test in and of itself. The student's assessment performance should be regarded as a *proxy* for the student's status with respect to the target instructional domain that's represented by the test. It is the student's test performance that allows teachers to draw an *inference* about the student's instructional-domain status. This inference is then used by the teacher to make instructional decisions. Such a decision chain is shown in Figure 12.3. It is the assessment-based inference about students' status with respect to the target instructional domain that should influence the teacher's decisions about instruction. And that, of course, is why we fussed so much about the *validity* of assessment-based inferences in Chapter 3.

Now, as noted before, many teachers regard tests chiefly as tools by which to determine students' grades. And, of course, there ought to be a relationship be-

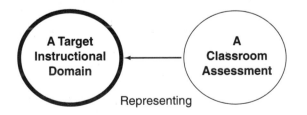

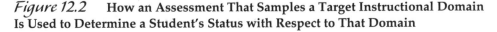

Figure 12.2   **How an Assessment That Samples a Target Instructional Domain Is Used to Determine a Student's Status with Respect to That Domain**

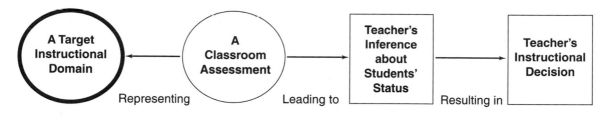

Figure 12.3   **The Assessment-Inference-Decision Chain That Should Guide Classroom Teachers**

tween students' grades and the way those students perform on tests. What I'm suggesting, however, is that tests-as-grade-determiners are far less important than tests-as-instruction-determiners.

If teachers want to approach classroom assessment *exclusively* in terms of the contribution that students' performances make to improved *instructional* decisions, there will still be plenty of assessment results available to use for grading purposes. When grading time comes, teachers will still have access to oodles of test results that can be translated into grades. But the role of test-as-grade-determiners ought to be a decisively secondary role. The foremost function of classroom assessment should be to help teachers make better instructional decisions.

What Kinds of Instructional Decisions Are Abetted by Assessment Results?

If teachers do accept the proposition that students' performances on assessments should inform a teacher's instructional decisions, they'll usually discover there are three major categories of decisions that can be made better if students' assessment performances are considered. Those three kinds of instructional decisions are listed in Table 12.1.

What to Teach?   As seen in Table 12.1, one important kind of instructional decision that's almost certain to be made better on the basis of students' assessment results is what to teach in the first place. Kids come to school in all sorts of sizes, loaded with different amounts of smarts and with dissimilar skills. At any grade level, it is folly to assume that this year's crop of students will be a mirror image of last year's crop. And, given such anticipatable crop variation, this year's students will often need to be taught different stuff than last year's students.

One of the best ways for teachers to make a decision about what they should be teaching is to *preassess* students at the very beginning of a school year or school term. A teacher should find out what skills and knowledge students have when they walk through the classroom door. Based on the results of such preassessments, a teacher can then determine what instructional activities are really

Table 12.1   **Categories of Instructional Decisions Enhanced by a Consideration of Students' Assessment Performances**

Decision Category	Typical Assessment Strategy	Decision Options
• What to teach in the first place?	Preassessment prior to the start of instruction	Whether to provide instruction for specific instructional objectives?
• How long to keep teaching toward a particular instructional objective?	En route assessments of students' progress	Whether to continue or cease instruction for an objective, either for an individual student or for the whole class?
• How effective was an instructional sequence?	Comparing students' posttest to pretest performances	Whether to retain, discard, or modify a given instructional sequence the next time it's used?

needed and what instructional activities would be redundant. The teacher can dump any plans for redundant instruction and focus instruction, instead, on educational objectives that are suitable for *those particular students*.

If teachers fail to preassess their incoming students, teachers' judgments about what instruction is needed are apt to be wrong. Some teachers, of course, can make sensible judgments about their students' entry behavior based on observations of students during the first few days of class. That, too, is a form of preassessment. Not all classroom assessment obliges students to make marks on paper. But, without any *systematic* form of preassessment, many teachers will make mistakes about what they should be teaching.

How Long to Teach?   The second kind of decision that can be beneficially influenced by students' assessment results concerns the duration of instruction. How long should the teacher continue to teach toward a given instructional objective? In some instances, that decision will be made for a whole class. For instance, a planned three-week instructional unit on How a Bill Becomes a Law might be appropriately wrapped up in only two weeks if the students display, on an en route progress-monitoring quiz, that they've really mastered the particulars of the bill-to-law sequence.

The teacher's decision to halt instruction on a particular objective might also be made on a student-by-student basis. For instance, suppose an English teacher were promoting her students' abilities to compose paragraphs that not only "glisten" from a communication perspective, but are also "devoid of mechanical muck-ups." If, via occasional en route assessments during class, the teacher spots individual students who have already mastered this paragraph-composition skill, she may choose to send those students down some sort of enrichment road while keeping the rest of her students on the paragraph path. Progress-monitoring assessments, because they typically provide teachers with better evidence than might be obtained from the teacher's casual observations, will help teachers decide more accurately when to terminate instruction that's focused on a particular educational objective.

How Effective Was Instruction?   A third type of assessment-influenced instructional decision deals with the effectiveness of an instructional sequence. Most teachers want to know whether the instructional scheme that they devised did, in fact, "work." If the instructional sequence was a winner, then the next time the teacher tackles the objective for which the instruction was devised, essentially the same instructional approach ought to be followed. If, however, there's assessment evidence to indicate that the instruction was only so-so or, worse, downright dismal, then major alterations are warranted when that instructional sequence is next needed.

The most straightforward way for teachers to discover whether their instructional sequences are effective is to rely on comparisons between assessments of students made both prior to and following instruction. Although, from a ritzy research perspective, there may be difficulties associated with simple pretest-to-posttest contrasts, from an in-the-busy-classroom perspective, such contrasts usually help teachers arrive at sensible conclusions about the effectiveness of their instruction.

Suppose, for example, that prior to a one-month teaching unit about narrative essays, only 20% of the students could write such essays properly, but, at the close of the unit, almost 80% of the students could churn out satisfactory narrative essays. This would be pretty compelling evidence that whatever the teacher was doing instructionally seemed to work. In contrast, if the end-of-unit posttest showed that there were *still* only 20% of the students who could write a satisfactory narrative essay, the teacher ought to think seriously about revamping what appears to be a cruddy instructional approach.

Because, in the classroom, *testing time* takes away from *teaching time,* teachers may sometimes want to take advantage of *item sampling,* a time-saving assessment strategy. In an item-sampling approach, a classroom assessment is subdivided into different parts so that different students can complete different parts of the assessment. For instance, if there were a 20-item pretest that usually took students about 20 minutes to complete, the teacher might split the 20-item test into four 5-item subsections, then have one-fourth of the students in the class complete each of the four subsections. The pretest now requires only 5 minutes of class time instead of 20 minutes. To get a fix on the total class performance, the teacher simply lumps the subpart scores together and computes the average percent-correct score for the entire 20-item test. The average performance of the class, estimated via item sampling, will almost always give teachers a reasonably accurate picture of how the entire class would have scored on the total test if students had taken all the items. Because students' *posttest* performances are often used for grading purposes, item sampling is less frequently employed at posttest time because each student, to be graded accurately, ordinarily needs to complete all the assessment items. But, for preassessment guidance regarding the status of an entire class, item sampling is a time-saver.

In review, we've now described several sorts of instructional decisions that can be made more appropriately if teachers have access to students' assessment results. Those decisions involved what to teach, how long to teach it, and whether it was taught effectively. Students' test results, of course, are not the *only* factor that teachers should consider when making instructional decisions. But teachers who rely on assessment results to help them make better instructional decisions will, in fact, almost always make better instructional decisions.

Planning Instruction to Achieve Assessment–Operationalized Objectives . . . .

We now turn to the second of our two assessment-based strategies for improving the quality of classroom instruction. As indicated earlier, it's an improvement strategy with which few teachers are familiar. This second strategy requires a substantial rethinking about the role of educational assessment. Let's get that rethinking underway.

At What Cost Boosting? ....

The new superintendent in Little Lakes Unified School District was appointed by the district's school board on the basis of her promise to "boost our standardized test scores." Subsequently, Rebecca Rowe, an English teacher in Placid Waters High School, was on the receiving end of a strident message from her principal. "Get those standardized test scores up in language arts or else!" was the last sentence spat out by Mrs. Grinch as she left Rebecca's classroom.

Rebecca does want to see her students learn more, but after consulting the Teacher's Manual for the standardized test used by the district, she is baffled about how to devise more effective instructional plans. The descriptions of what the language arts section of the test measures, Rebecca believes, are far too vague for her purposes.

One of her colleagues points out to Rebecca that in the school counselor's office a teacher can review the actual forms of the standardized test because the same test is given each spring and then stored in each school. The colleague suggests that student familiarity with the content of some actual test items is bound to do a bit of "mandated score-boosting."

If you were Rebecca and were faced with this situation, what would your decision be?

Tests as Instructional Influencers

Historically, teachers have used classroom tests at or near the close of an instructional sequence. And, of course, teachers would like their students to perform well on any end-of-instruction tests. If students are successful on end-of-instruction classroom tests, it usually means that students have learned well and, accordingly, that teachers have taught well. More often than not, teachers' classroom tests have been constructed only *after* instruction is over or when instruction is nearing its conclusion (for instance, at the end of a semester, a school year, or a short-duration teaching unit). Obviously, classroom assessments that are devised *after* instruction is over will have scant impact on what the teacher teaches. The teacher's instruction, or at least the vast majority of it, is a "done deal" by the time the test is constructed.

Classroom assessments, therefore, have typically had little impact on instructional planning. At least that was true until the "era of educational accountability" arrived in the 1970s and 1980s. During that period, legislators in most states enacted a string of laws requiring students to pass basic skills tests in order to receive high school diplomas or, in some cases, to be advanced to higher grade levels. Thus was born what educators have come to call "high-stakes" tests, because there were important consequences for the students who were required to take those tests.

There was another sense in which statewide tests became "high stakes." In schools where all, or almost all, students passed the tests, teachers and administrators were applauded. But in schools where many students failed the tests, teachers and administrators were blamed. The stakes associated with statewide testing were elevated even more when newspapers began, in the 1980s, to publish annual statewide test scores of all districts and all schools in the state. Each school and district was *ranked* in relation to the state's other schools and districts. There were, of course, numerous winners as well as an equal number of losers.

As noted in Chapter 1, what was being measured by the tests began to influence the nature of what was taught in classrooms. The phrase *measurement-driven instruction* became widely used during the eighties to depict an educational reform strategy in which it was hoped that the content of high-stakes tests would have a substantial and positive influence on the content of classroom instruction.

Because of this heightened attention to student performance on important statewide and districtwide tests, we also saw clearly identifiable attention being given to the evidence of student success on teacher-made *classroom* tests. Many educational administrators and policymakers concluded that if students' performances on statewide tests reflected a school's educational effectiveness, then even at the classroom level, good test results would indicate that good teaching was taking place, while bad test results would indicate the opposite. Greater and greater emphasis was given to "evidence of effectiveness" in the form of improved student performance on whatever types of classroom tests were being employed. Increasingly, *evidence* of student learning—evidence in the form of student performance on classroom tests—is being used in the personnel appraisals of teachers. Teachers' competence is being determined, at least in part, by how well a teacher's students perform on the teacher's classroom tests.

Given this ever-increasing administrative reliance on student test results as one indicator of a teacher's instructional effectiveness, it was only natural that many teachers tried to address instructionally whatever was to be tested. Tests had clearly begun to influence teaching. And it was increasingly recognized by teachers not only that the content of their tests *could* influence their teaching but, perhaps, the content of those tests *should* influence their teaching.

If testing should influence teaching, why not construct classroom assessments *prior* to instructional planning? In that way, any planned instructional sequence could mesh more effectively with the content of the test involved. Moreover, why not build classroom assessments with the instructional implications of those assessments deliberately in mind? In other words, why not build a classroom assessment not only before any instructional planning, but in such a way that the assessment would beneficially inform the teacher's instructional planning? Such an approach, as you might have already guessed, is the essence of the second assessment-based strategy to improve instructional quality. A contrast between a more traditional educational approach in which instruction influences assessment and the kind of assessment-influenced instruction being described here can be seen in Figure 12.4.

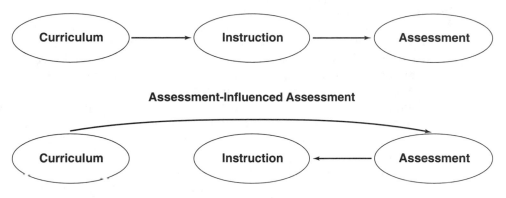

Figure 12.4   **Traditional Instruction-Influenced Assessment versus Assessment-Influenced Instruction, Both of Which Are Governed by Curricular Considerations**

In a traditional approach to instructional design, an approach in which instruction influences assessment, the teacher (1) is guided by the curriculum that's been adopted by the state and/or district, (2) plans instructional activities to promote the educational objectives set forth in that curriculum, and (3) assesses students. In an assessment-influenced approach to instructional design, also indicated in Figure 12.4, the teacher still (1) starts with the educational objectives set forth in the curriculum, (2) then moves to create assessments based on those goals, and (3) only thereafter plans instructional activities intended to promote students' mastery of the knowledge, skills, and/or attitudes that are to be assessed. In both approaches, curriculum is the starting point. Educational objectives, or content standards, still govern the entire process. But in the two contrasting approaches, the sequence of instructional planning and assessment development is reversed.

Dividends of Assessment Illumination

Assessment-illuminated instruction rests on the assumption that, in many instances, what is to be assessed *will* influence the teacher's instructional decisions. Consequently, if the assessment can be created prior to the teacher's instructional planning, the resultant clarity provided to the teacher will help the teacher make more appropriate instructional choices.

When teachers develop their classroom assessments *before* instructional plans are made, teachers are meaningfully *clarifying* the curricular objectives that are being pursued. In other words, the assessment serves as the operational definition of whether an objective has been achieved. That clarity provides far more insight for teachers when, subsequently, they make their instructional plans.

It is important to remember that, as indicated earlier, classroom assessments *represent* the knowledge and/or skills being promoted. Teachers should *never* teach toward the classroom test itself. Instead, teachers should teach toward the knowledge, skills, and/or attitudes that are sampled by the classroom test. But, when teachers construct classroom assessments prior to instructional decision making, those teachers will have a markedly better understanding of what the objectives really are. And, of course, the more clear-headed that teachers are about curricular *ends,* the more skillfully they can select suitable instructional *means* to accomplish those ends.

With increased clarity regarding the nature of the curricular objectives being promoted, there are all sorts of derivative instructional-planning benefits. Here are a few of the most salient dividends that you, as a teacher or teacher-in-preparation, will receive:

- *More accurate task analyses.* Because you'll know more clearly what the terminal results of an instructional sequence are supposed to be, you can better pinpoint the enabling or en route knowledge/skills that your students must acquire before mastering what's being taught.
- *More on-target practice activities.* Because you'll know better what kinds of end-of-instruction outcomes are being sought for your students, you can make sure to select guided-practice and independent-practice activities that are more accurately aligned with the target outcomes.
- *More lucid expositions.* Because you'll understand more clearly what's to be assessed at instruction's conclusion, during the instruction you can provide clearer explanations to your students about the content involved and where the instructional activities are heading.

Instructional planning will benefit from early development of classroom assessments most fundamentally because you will, as a consequence of prior assessment development, better understand what it is hoped that your students will be able to do when instruction has been concluded.

Constructing Assessments with Instruction in Mind

Because the nature of assessment instruments will often influence a teacher's instructional plans, why not *deliberately* construct those assessment instruments so that appropriate instructional decisions are more likely? If teachers wish to derive the maximum instructional dividends from their classroom assessments, they must construct their assessment devices with specific attention being given to how students can be *taught* to do whatever that assessment device is measuring. Putting it another way, teachers must constantly be "thinking instructional possibilities" as they create their classroom assessments. Whether it's a selected-response test, a constructed-response test, or a self-report affective inventory, teachers must continually ask themselves, "Can I teach what this assessment instrument measures?"

When classroom assessments are skillfully crafted, with instructional implications in mind, the resulting assessment devices will almost certainly illuminate a teacher's instructional decision making more beneficially than will a classroom assessment device churned out with little attention given to instruction. This can be seen in Table 12.2, where it is suggested that instructional-planning dividends are most substantial when classroom assessments are created *before* such planning takes place and if those assessments are deliberately generated *with instruction in mind.*

Yet, you might be thinking, it's easier to *say* that assessment instruments ought to be created with instructional considerations in mind than it is to actually *create* such instruments. You're right. And that's the topic with which we'll conclude this chapter—namely, how to build instructionally illuminating assessment instruments. In turn, we'll consider how to create instructionally beneficial constructed-response tests (such as essay exams), selected-response tests (such as multiple-choice exams), and affective assessments (such as self-report attitudinal inventories).

Constructed-Response Assessments

Constructed-response assessments, as we saw in Chapter 7, can range from the most rudimentary "fill-in-the-blank" quizzes all the way to very complex performance tests in which students must create elaborate written and/or oral responses to an intellectually demanding assignment. Stripping away the frills, in each constructed-response test there is a *task* for students to perform and a *scoring scheme* to determine the adequacy of a student's performance.

Table 12.2   **Instructional-Planning Dividends Associated with the Timing of When Classroom Assessments are Developed**

Timing of Classroom Assessment Development	Instructional Planning Dividends
• Developed at or near the end of instruction	None
• Developed prior to teaching, but with no special consideration given to instruction	Substantial
• Developed prior to teaching, with primary consideration given to the assessment's instructional implications	*Really* Substantial

The less elaborate that the students' tasks are, the less elaborate the scoring scheme needs to be. For example, if students are given a test where they are being asked only to fill in the dates that certain historical events occurred (a decidedly dismal chore), there's really no need for a more elaborate scoring approach than "Did they come up with the correct dates?"

For more demanding tasks, however, students' responses are generally evaluated on the basis of a scoring rubric. A rubric, as seen in Chapter 8, has three essential features. It (1) identifies the evaluative criteria to be employed when judging a student's response to the task, (2) describes for each criterion how to judge qualitative differences in students' performances, and (3) indicates whether the evaluative criteria are to be applied holistically or analytically.

Whether a rubric's evaluative criteria are applied holistically or analytically, those criteria are the rubric's most important feature—at least from an instructional perspective. Fundamentally, the evaluative criteria in a rubric identify those factors that can be used to distinguish among differences in the quality of students' responses. Evaluative criteria *that can be addressed instructionally* will guide the teacher's planning so appropriate instruction is more likely to ensue. Evaluative criteria generated without keeping instruction in mind will render effective instruction less likely. Let's spend a moment to explore how a rubric's evaluative criteria can help or hurt a teacher's instructional decision making.

Think back to Figure 12.2, where it was shown that a classroom assessment is intended to represent the student's mastery of a target instructional domain. (If you don't have keen visual recollective powers, you are hereby granted permission to go back to Figure 12.2 and take a peek.) In reality, almost all significant constructed-response tests are focused on the measurement of students' *skills* rather than their *knowledge* (knowledge usually being more efficiently assessed via selected-response tests). Therefore, a demanding performance test is usually intended to provide the teacher with a valid inference about the student's mastery of the skill that the performance test samples.

It is important to remember that a constructed-response performance test only *samples* the skill the teacher is attempting to have students master. If teachers forget this significant truth, they'll usually find that their scoring rubrics will lead them in an instructionally dysfunctional direction. Let's see why.

Task-Specific Rubrics.   Some rubrics are created so that their evaluative criteria are linked only to the particular task embodied in a specific performance test. I call these *task-specific rubrics.* Such a rubric does little to illuminate instructional decision making because it implies that students' performances on the constructed-response test's specific task are what's important. They're not! What's important is the student's ability to perform well on the *class of tasks* that can be accomplished by using the skill measured in the assessment. If students are taught to shine only on the single task represented in a performance test, but not on the full range of comparable tasks, students lose out. If students learn to become good problem solvers, they'll be able to solve all sorts of problems—not merely the one problem embodied in a particular performance test.

So, to provide helpful instructional illumination—that is, to assist the teacher's instructional decision making—a rubric's evaluative criteria dare not be task specific. Instead, they must be rooted in the skill itself. Let me illustrate by considering an evaluative criterion frequently employed in rubrics that are used to judge students' written communication skills—namely, the evaluative criterion of *organization*. Presented here is a task-specific criterion that might be used in a scoring rubric to judge the quality of a student's response to the following task:

> "Compose a brief narrative essay, of 400 to 600 words, describing what happened during yesterday's class session when we were visited by the local firefighters who described a fire-exit escape plan for the home."

> ***A task-specific evaluative criterion for judging the organization of students' narrative essays:*** Superior essays will (1) commence with a recounting of the particular rationale for home fire-escape plans the local firefighters provided, then (2) follow up with a description of the six elements in home-safety plans in the order those elements were presented, and (3) conclude by citing at least three of the life-death safety statistics the firefighters provided at the close of their visit. Departures from these three organizational elements will result in lower evaluations of essays.

Suppose you're a teacher who has generated or been given this task-specific evaluative criterion. How would you organize your instruction? If you really tried to gain instructional guidance from this evaluative criterion, you'd be aiming your instruction directly at a particular task—in this case, a narrative account of the firefighters' visit to your class. You'd have to teach your students to commence their narrative essays with a rationale when, in fact, using a rationale for an introduction might be inappropriate for other sorts of narrative essays. Task-specific evaluative criteria do not help teachers plan instructional sequences that promote their students' abilities to *generalize* the skills they acquire. Task-specific criteria are just what they are touted to be—specific to one task.

During recent years, I've had an opportunity to review a number of rubrics that classroom teachers are trying to employ. From an instructional perspective, most of these rubrics don't pass muster. Many of the rubrics are task specific. Such task-specific rubrics may make it easier to score students' constructed responses. For *scoring* purposes, the more specific that evaluative rubrics are, the better. But task-specific rubrics do *not* provide teachers with the kinds of *instructional* insights that rubrics should.

Hypergeneral Rubrics.   Another variety of scoring rubric that will not help teachers plan their instruction is what I refer to as a *hypergeneral rubric*. Such a rubric is one in which the evaluative criteria are described in exceedingly general and amorphous terms. The evaluative criteria are so loosely described, in fact, that teachers' instructional plans really aren't benefited. For example, using the previous example of a task calling for students to write a narrative essay, a hypergeneral evaluative criterion for organization might resemble the following one:

> *A hypergeneral evaluative criterion for judging the organization of students' narrative essays:* Superior essays are those in which the essay's content has been arranged in a genuinely excellent manner, whereas *inferior* essays are those that display altogether inadequate organization. An *adequate* essay is one that represents a lower organizational quality than a superior essay, but a higher organizational quality than an inferior essay.

You may think I'm putting you on when you read the illustrative hypergeneral evaluative criterion just given. But I'm not. I've seen many such hypergeneral scoring rubrics. These rubrics ostensibly clarify how teachers can score students' constructed responses, but really these amorphous rubrics do little more than loosely redefine such quality descriptors as *superior, proficient,* and *inadequate.* Hypergeneral rubrics provide teachers with no genuine benefits for their instructional planning because such rubrics do not give the teacher meaningfully clarified descriptions of the criteria that are to be used in evaluating the quality of students' performances.

Skill-Focused Rubrics.   Well, because I've now denigrated task-specific rubrics and sneered at hypergeneral rubrics, it's only fair for me to trot out the type of rubric that really can illuminate a teacher's instructional planning. Such scoring rubrics can be described as *skill-focused* because they really are conceptualized around the skill that is (1) being measured by the constructed-response assessment and (2) being pursued instructionally by the teacher. It is my conviction, based on discussions with many teachers who have used a variety of scoring rubrics, that teachers who create a skill-focused scoring rubric prior to their instructional planning will almost always devise a better instructional sequence than will teachers who don't.

For an example of an evaluative criterion that you'd encounter in a skill-focused rubric, look over the following illustrative criterion for evaluating the organization of a student's narrative essay:

> *A skill-focused evaluative criterion for judging the organization of students' narrative essays:* Two aspects of organization will be employed in the appraisal of students' narrative essays—namely, *overall structure* and *sequence.* To earn maximum credit, an essay must embody an overall structure containing an introduction, a body, and a conclusion. The content of the body of the essay must be sequenced in a reasonable manner—for instance, in a chronological, logical, or order-of-importance sequence.

Now, when you consider this evaluative criterion from an instructional perspective, you'll realize that a teacher could sensibly direct instruction by (1) familiarizing students with the two aspects of the criterion—that is, overall structure and sequence; (2) helping students identify essays in which overall structure and sequence are, or are not, acceptable; and (3) supplying students with gobs of guided and independent practice in writing narrative essays possessing the desired overall structure and sequence. And the better that students become in being able to employ this double-barreled criterion in their narrative essays, the better those students will be at responding to a task such as the illustrative one we just saw about the local firefighters' visit to the classroom. This skill-focused evaluative criterion for *organization,* in other words, can generalize to a wide variety of narrative-writing tasks, not just an essay about visiting fire-folk.

And even if teachers do not create their own rubrics—for instance, if rubrics are developed by a school district's curriculum or assessment specialists—those teachers who familiarize themselves with skill-focused rubrics in advance of instructional planning will usually plan better instruction than will teachers who aren't familiar with a skill-focused rubric's key features. Skill-focused rubrics make clear what a teacher should emphasize instructionally when the teacher attempts to promote student mastery of the skill being measured.

Let me set out five rubric rules that I encourage you to follow if you're creating your own skill-focused scoring rubric—a rubric that you must generate *before* you plan your instruction.

Rule 1: Make sure the skill to be assessed is significant. It takes time and trouble to generate scoring skill-focused rubrics. It also takes time and trouble to score students' responses by using such rubrics. Make sure that the skill being promoted instructionally, and scored via the rubric, is worth all that time and trouble. Skills that are scored with skill-focused rubrics should represent demanding accomplishments by students, not trifling ones.

Rule 2: Make certain all of the rubric's evaluative criteria can be addressed instructionally. This second rule calls for you always to "keep your instructional wits about you" when generating a rubric. Most importantly, you must scrutinize every potential evaluative criterion to make sure you can actually teach students to master it. This doesn't oblige you to adhere to any particular instructional approach. Regardless of whether you are wedded to the virtues of direct instruction, indirect instruction, constructivism, or any other instructional strategy, what you must be certain of is that students can be *taught* to employ appropriately *every* evaluative criterion used in the rubric.

Rule 3: Employ as few evaluative criteria as possible. Because people who start thinking seriously about a skill will often begin to recognize a host of nuances associated with that skill, they sometimes feel compelled to set forth a veritable litany of evaluative criteria. But for instructional purposes, as for most other purposes, less almost always turns out to be more. Try to focus your instructional attention on three or four evaluative criteria; you'll become overwhelmed if you try to promote students' mastery of a dozen evaluative criteria.

Rule 4: Provide a succinct label for each evaluative criterion. The instructional yield of a skill-focused rubric can be increased simply by giving each evaluative criterion a brief explanatory label. Later in this chapter you'll meet an illustrative skill-focused rubric for oral communication that contains four evaluative criteria—namely, *delivery, organization, content,* and *language.* These one-word, easy-to-remember labels will help remind you *and your students* of what's truly important in judging mastery of the skill being assessed.

Rule 5: Match the length of the rubric to your own tolerance for detail. I've spent a fair amount of time worrying about this particular rule because much of my early experience in generating skill-focused rubrics dealt with the creation of lengthy scoring rubrics for high-stakes statewide or districtwide assessments. Such detailed rubrics were intended to constrain scorers so their scores would be in agreement. But I've discovered that many classroom teachers consider fairly long, rather detailed rubrics to be altogether off-putting. Whereas those teachers might be willing to create and/or use a one-page rubric, they would regard a six-page rubric as reprehensible. More recently, therefore, I've been recommending much shorter rubrics—rubrics that never exceed one or two pages.

You see, I'm most interested in the *impact* on instructional planning that a rubric has. And rubrics that aren't created by teachers because "they're too much work" or rubrics that aren't used by teachers because "they're *way* too long" will obviously have no impact on teachers' instructional planning. If it's a choice between (1) a rubric that will yield high interscorer agreement or (2) a rubric that will have a positive impact on instructional planning, I opt for the latter. For my purposes, then, I now recommend rubrics that are as terse as possible yet still provide reasonable clarity about the evaluative criteria in those rubrics.

Of course, not all teachers are put off by very detailed rubrics. Some teachers, in fact, find that abbreviated rubrics just don't do an adequate job for them. Such detail-prone teachers would rather work with rubrics that spell out, with all sorts of specifics, just what's involved when differentiating between quality levels regarding each evaluative criterion. I've come to the conclusion, therefore, that rubrics should be built to match the detail preferences of the teachers involved. Thus, let's suppose teachers are creating their own rubrics. Then teachers who believe in brevity should create brief rubrics, and teachers who desire detail should create lengthier rubrics. If school districts (or publishers) are supplying rubrics to teachers, I recommend that *two* versions of each rubric be provided—a short version and a long version. Let teachers decide on the level of detail that best meshes with their own tolerance/need for detail.

So, with these five rubric rules in mind, what would a skill-focused rubric look like? To give you an example, I've supplied one in Figure 12.5. It's an abbre-

Figure 12.5   **An Illustrative Skill-Focused Scoring Rubric (Analytic) for Oral Communication**

Task

During regular class sessions, students will be required to present a specified oral communication (namely, an impromptu, extemporaneous, or extensively prepared speech) to their peers.

Evaluative Criteria

Each oral communication will be judged on the basis of four evaluative criteria—namely, *delivery, organization, content,* and *language.* Each evaluative criterion is based on two or three factors that are considered when the criterion is applied. These factors are identified below (and explained, if necessary) for each evaluative criterion.

The stringency with which these criteria are applied should vary depending on the nature of the oral communication involved (e.g., lower expectations would be employed when judging impromptu speeches than when judging extensively prepared speeches). Consideration should also be given to the age of the students involved.

When considering each evaluative criterion's factors, the notions of "adequate" and "superior" performances should be used. *Adequate* student performance refers to a level of quality consonant with what would be expected of a student who is making suitable developmental or instructional progress. In a sense, therefore, adequate performance on any factor signifies, roughly, that the student is performing at grade-level expectations. *Superior,* then, means the student's performance is clearly at a level of quality higher than grade-level expectations. For each of the four criteria, 1 to 3 points can be awarded. Any given speech, therefore, can receive a total score of 4 to 12 points. Although intended to be used analytically, the rubric can be employed holistically by disregarding per-criterion point allocations.

Delivery

The delivery rating for an oral communication is based on the following three factors: *volume, rate,* and *articulation* (that is, pronunciation and enunciation).

- In *advanced* speeches (3 points), all three delivery factors are at least adequate and two or three factors are superior.

- In *proficient* speeches (2 points), all three delivery factors are at least adequate.

- In *partially proficient* speeches (1 point), fewer than three delivery factors are adequate.

(continued)

Figure 12.5   **Continued**

Organization

The organization rating for an oral communication is based on the following two factors: *sequence* and *relationship* among ideas in the communication (that is, the clarity of the order and connection among the speech's points).

- In *advanced* speeches (3 points), both organization factors are superior.
- In *proficient* speeches (2 points), both organization factors are at least adequate.
- In *partially proficient* speeches (1 point), fewer than two organization factors are adequate.

Content

The content rating for an oral communication is based on the following three factors: *amount* of content, *relevance* of the content to the assigned speech topic, and *adaptation* of the content to the listeners and situation.

- In *advanced* speeches (3 points), all three content factors are at least adequate and two or more are superior.
- In *proficient* speeches (2 points), all three content factors are at least adequate.
- In *partially proficient* speeches (1 point), fewer than three content factors are adequate.

Language

The language rating for an oral communication is based on the following two factors: *grammar* and *word choice*.

- In *advanced* speeches (3 points), both language factors are superior.
- In *proficient* speeches (2 points), both language factors are at least adequate.
- In *partially proficient* speeches (1 point), fewer than two language factors are adequate.

viated version (I lean toward lean) of an analytic oral communications rubric originally developed by the Massachusetts Department of Education. It is the kind of skill-focused rubric that can guide teachers' instructional planning because there are four instructionally addressable evaluative criteria around which a teacher can organize instructional activities. If teachers in any subject, at any grade level, become familiar with the ingredients of Figure 12.5's illustrative skill-focused rubric, they will almost always plan better instructional sequences intended to promote students' oral communication skills. And that, of course, is the payoff of instruction-illuminated instructional design.

Selected-Response Assessments

In contrast to constructed-response assessments when rubrics must be employed to evaluate students' performances, selected-response assessments provide options from which students make choices. As indicated in Chapter 6, the most common examples of selected-response tests used by teachers are multiple-choice tests and binary-choice tests. If selected-response tests are to be employed as part of an assessment-illuminated instructional design strategy, then those tests must also be created *prior* to instructional planning, and they must also be created with their instructional implications clearly in mind.

Fundamentally, we can distinguish between two kinds of educational objectives that selected-response tests can be used to assess. First, selected-response tests can assess a student's *knowledge*—that is, the student's recollection of memorized information such as facts or dates of significant events. Memorized information, as you saw in Chapter 5, resides at the lowest level of Bloom's cognitive taxonomy of educational objectives. For any of the five higher levels of Bloom's taxonomy (comprehension, application, analysis, synthesis, and evaluation), the student is required to employ a *skill*—a skill not fundamentally unlike the kinds of skills measured by constructed-response performance tests. Let's look briefly at how to create selected-response tests that illuminate instructional planning when teachers are trying to promote students' knowledge or skills.

Assessing Knowledge via Selected-Response Tests.   Knowledge, even though it resides at the lowest level of Bloom's taxonomy, is a good thing. We want our students to know lots of content. But if the *only* thing that teachers did was to pour knowledge into students' heads, of course, that would be unacceptable. We want our students to possess not only knowledge but also a host of higher-level cognitive skills. Because selected-response tests can be efficiently employed to measure students' knowledge, such tests are often used for just that purpose. The question, therefore, is, How can selected-response assessments of knowledge be constructed so that they are instructionally illuminating? The answer is straightforward. To make selected-response assessments of knowledge instructionally illuminating, *the domain of knowledge being sampled by the test must be fully explicated* prior to the test's creation.

Let me use a simple example. If Mrs. Jones, an elementary school teacher, is trying to promote her students' ability to remember the correct spelling of the new words systematically introduced by the language arts textbook during the school year, Mrs. Jones needs to list *all* the eligible words at the time she generates her selected-response test of students' spelling abilities. There might, for example, be 500 words on the total list, and the selected-response test itself might contain a sample of only 20 or 25, but Mrs. Jones needs to identify, prior to her instructional planning, the complete domain of knowledge (in this case, the eligible spelling words) that students should learn.

It is the same story for any body of information to be memorized. Whether it's a set of dates of historical events, definitions of vocabulary words, or rules for a complex game, when teachers create their selected-response tests in advance of instruction, they need to set forth exactly what's involved in the total domain of knowledge that's being assessed. Then the assessment itself is easily created by sampling (representatively, if possible) from the domain. The delineation of the full knowledge domain prior to instruction will, of course, enable teachers to plan their instruction more accurately so that attention is given to the content of the entire domain, not merely the content that's actually assessed.

Assessing Skills via Selected-Response Tests.   As indicated before, when students are asked to display higher-than-lowest-level cognitive behavior, it is possible to identify criteria that can be used to distinguish between correct and incorrect responses. For example, suppose that the teacher is building a test to measure students' abilities to distinguish between newspaper advertisements that are reasonable versus those advertisements that employ one or more unscrupulous advertising ploys. What the teacher needs to do when developing the test is to list all

Parent Talk ....

Suppose one of your better students, Mary Ruth Green, brings in a note from her parents, expressing concern that your classes seem to be organized to "teach to the test, not educate students." Mr. and Mrs. Green ask you to call them at home so they can, using their speaker phone, both discuss this concern with you.

• • • *If I were you, here's what I'd say on the phone to Mary Ruth's parents:*

"Thanks for raising this issue. It's an important concern, and because we all want what's best for Mary Ruth, I'm pleased to be able to explain how we're using tests in my class.

"Actually, I do use tests to influence my instruction. But the tests really only *represent* the skills and knowledge I'm trying to get Mary Ruth and her classmates to learn. I use the tests to help me plan my instruction and to make an interpretation about whether students are mastering what the test represents. In that way, I'll know whether more instruction is needed on particular topics.

"Please be assured, I am definitely not teaching to particular test items. All of the items on my tests, in fact, have never been seen before by the students. But those items do reflect the knowledge and skills my class is supposed to promote.

"You'll also realize that half of Mary Ruth's grade is based on the portfolio assessment system we use. I think the portfolio work samples, when blended with the test results, give me an even better picture of my students' progress."

• • • *Now, how would you respond to Mr. and Mrs. Green?*

of the reprehensible advertising ploys, then make sure that the test items give students an opportunity to determine whether a given advertisement is reasonable or embodies one of the unscrupulous ploys. There are a good many ways that teachers could create selected-response items for such a test. But let's imagine the teacher creates a 10-item exam in which each item first presents an actual advertisement, and is then followed by five choices. For example, an actual advertisement might be followed by the five choices given here:

The above advertisement (choose the best answer):
a. is reasonable.
b. contains an *ad hominem* argument.
c. includes deceptive statistics.
d. invokes unknown authority.
e. None of the above.

Notice that in order to answer this kind of item correctly, the student needs to be able to recognize *all* of the unscrupulous advertising ploys because, for any given item, the advertisement provided may be unreasonable, but it might not include one of the ploys given. (The advertising ploys would typically vary with each item.) Yet, because the teacher listed, prior to the test's creation, all the disdainful advertising ploys, not only will the items be easier to construct but also the teacher's instructional planning will be better.

For selected-response assessments that require students to apply skills, it is important for the teacher to isolate the key factors constituting those skills (much as we saw in the way that the evaluative criteria should be spelled out for skill-focused scoring rubrics). The teacher then systematically represents those factors (by formal inclusion or exclusion) in the choices from which students are making their selections for each test item.

More than two decades ago, I developed a statewide selected-response test of a student's ability to comprehend the main idea of a reading passage. After the student had been given an age-appropriate selection to read, there were four multiple-choice statements of the selection's main idea presented. The student had to choose one. One of the wrong answer alternatives was always fundamentally *irrelevant* to the reading selection's content. (Relevancy, as an evaluative criterion, can be taught.) One wrong answer alternative always contained content that was *inaccurate* in terms of the reading selection's content. (Accuracy, as an evaluative criterion, can also be taught.) One wrong answer alternative was always *too narrow* or *too broad* in relation to the reading selection. (Appropriate scope—that is, the absence of excessive narrowness or broadness—can also be taught.) One answer, the correct alternative, always properly represented the reading selection's main idea by being relevant, accurate, and of an appropriate scope. By incorporating relevancy, accuracy, and appropriate scope in the test items' answer options, the test communicated to teachers that those concepts should be addressed instructionally.

And that, of course, is what teachers need to do when building selected-response tests in advance of instruction. They need to make sure that whatever knowledge or skills are involved will be clearly identified in advance of item generation, then fully employed in the creation of the assessment's selected-response options. Instructional planning directed toward the promotion of those skills or that knowledge will, then, be more likely to be effective because the skills or knowledge can be directly addressed during the instructional sequence.

Affective Assessments

Finally, we should consider how to make classroom affective assessments helpful when teachers plan their instruction. For me, the chief instructional dividend of formally assessing students' affect is that the very *commitment* to formal affective assessment inclines teachers to give more direct attention to affective instruction than otherwise would have been the case.

To illustrate, let's say Mr. Hovens, a third-grade teacher, decides to promote students' *confidence* in their abilities to use mathematics. Suppose Mr. Hovens develops a 10-item self-report inventory that students are to complete anonymously at the beginning and at the end of the school year. Each of the inventory's 10 items asks students to agree or disagree with statements such as "If I'm in a store and I have to figure out how much something costs when it's not marked, I usually can do it." Students respond to each item by circling responses ranging from "very confident" to "not at all confident." Now the very fact that Mr. Hovens is going to administer the affective inventory on a pretest and posttest basis will almost certainly sensitize Mr. Hovens to the importance of the affective variable being assessed—and will invariably incline him to devote meaningful instructional attention to that affect.

Also, as with the other kinds of assessments we've been considering, the construction of affective assessments prior to instructional planning will almost certainly lead teachers to more defensible instructional-design decisions. By clarifying what a teacher intends to promote in the affective realm, the teacher really gets a better understanding of what's involved in that affective variable. Such clarity, of course, contributes to better instructional planning.

What Do Classroom Teachers Really Need to Know about Instructionally Oriented Assessment? ....

The view of classroom assessment given in this chapter represents what, for many teachers, is a decisively different way of thinking about assessment. What teachers really need to do in connection with this "different" view of classroom assessment is decide whether they want to employ it. At bottom, instructionally oriented assessment is really quite simple. To implement such an approach, teachers merely need to (1) develop their assessments prior to instructional planning and (2) make certain the content of those assessments can be addressed instructionally.

I don't want to suggest that the adoption of an instructionally oriented approach to classroom assessment is fools-play. It surely isn't. To adopt this assessment approach, teachers must be consistently clear-headed about how they're going to proceed instructionally. And it's tough to be consistently clear-headed. Time spans during which one can think sloppily are so appealing. But clear-headed planning of classroom assessments that clarify the teacher's instructional aims will bring about what all teachers want—better learning for students.

For most classroom teachers, viewing assessments as bona fide *instructional allies* will require a meaningful reconceptualization of the way they view the relationship between teaching or testing. Tests should not be regarded merely as instructional afterthoughts. Tests, if they are worth the considerable effort we often put into their creation, really ought to help teachers teach better.

Chapter Summary ....

In this chapter an attempt was made to support the virtues of instructionally oriented assessment—that is, assessment conceived chiefly as a vehicle to improve the caliber of teachers' instructional decision-making. Two ways of enhancing a teacher's instructional efforts were described. First, attention was given to *making instructional decisions in light of assessment results.* That approach, well known to most teachers (although not practiced by many), calls for teachers to make instructional decisions only after ascertaining their students' status with respect to the educational objectives being pursued. Three general kinds of instructional decisions were identified as those likely to benefit from results-influenced decision making—namely, what to teach, how long to keep teaching it, and whether the teaching was effective.

Attention was then given to *planning instruction to achieve the objective(s) represented by a test.* Such an assessment-illuminated instruction calls for classroom assessments to be created before instructional plans are made so that greater clarity can be obtained by teachers regarding their instructional intentions. For such assessment-illuminated instructional design to yield optimal benefits, however, classroom assessments must be constructed with instruction clearly in mind. Ways of creating assessments so that what they measure is more instructionally addressable were described for constructed-response, selected-response, and affective assessments.

Self-Check

This is a particularly important chapter because it suggests how you can use classroom assessment to do the very thing that most people originally went into teaching to do—namely, teach students well. Because of the chapter's significance, I'm going to ask to tackle two tasks that will require you to enlist the assistance of another person.

First, I want you to describe to someone else, orally and without notes, the overall message of this chapter about instructionally oriented assessment. Ideally, the person you'd choose would be a teacher or a teacher-in-training, but any human being whose vital signs are still positive will do. After the person has listened to your scintillating summary, ask that individual to explain it back to you—to see how well you did.

Next, and this is really tough, I'd like you to build a classroom test, constructed response or selected response, that can illuminate instructional *planning*. Then briefly describe how you'd plan successful instruction to promote what the test is measuring. Having done so, again I'd like to you snare an educationally knowledgeable person and have that individual look over your test and your instructional plans to give you some feedback about the likelihood that your instruction will promote the cognitive, psychomotor, or affective objective you're hoping to accomplish.

If you choose a performance test, of course, you'll need to whomp up a rubric for scoring students' responses to the performance test's task. Keep the objective modest in scope so that this self-check doesn't become a life's endeavor. You still have three chapters to go!

Pondertime

1. The chapter identified two major strategies—that is, making instructional decisions in light of assessment results and planning instruction to achieve the objective(s) represented by a test—to link assessment and instruction. Which of the two strategies do you prefer? Why?

2. How can teachers teach toward what's measured by a classroom test without teaching directly to the test's items?

3. How widely do you think the use of test results to make instructional decisions actually is? Why do you think this is so?

4. What, to you, are the most important things to keep in mind when developing classroom tests that are intended to support teaching?

Self-Check Key

For this chapter's two tasks, you're really going to have to rely on your own judgments about how well you did. Did the person (or persons) you involved seem to know what you'd done? Is that person still speaking to you? (If not, there are numerous other persons available. They're everywhere!)

Additional Stuff

Arter, Judy. *Assessing Student Performance* (Professional Inquiry Kit, #196214S62). Alexandria, VA: Association for Supervision and Curriculum Development, 1996.

Brookhart, Susan M. "A Theoretical Framework for the Role of Classroom Assessment in Motivating Student Effort and Achievement." *Applied Measurement in Education,* 10, no. 2 (1997): 161–180.

Glaser, Robert. "Criterion-Referenced Tests: Part I. Origins." *Educational Measurement: Issues and Practice,* 13, no. 4 (Winter 1994): 9–11.

Glaser, Robert. "Instructional Technology and the Measurement of Learning Outcomes: Some Questions." *Educational Measurement: Issues and Practice,* 13, no. 4 (Winter 1994): 6–8.

Millman, Jason. "Criterion-Referenced Testing 30 Years Later: Promise Broken, Promise Kept." *Educational Measurement: Issues and Practice,* 13, no. 4 (Winter 1994): 19–20, 39.

Pallrand, George J. "The Relationship of Assessment to Knowledge Development in Science Education." *Phi Delta Kappan,* 78, no. 4 (December 1996): 315–318.

Popham, W. James. "The Instructional Consequences of Criterion-Referenced Clarity." *Educational Measurement: Issues and Practice,* 13, no. 4 (Winter 1994): 15–18, 30.

Shepard, Lorrie A., Roberta J. Flexer, Elfrieda H. Hiebert, Scott F. Marion, Vicky Mayfield, and Timothy J. Weston. "Effects of Introducing Classroom Performance Assessments on Student Learning." *Educational Measurement: Issues and Practice,* 15, no. 3 (Fall 1996): 7–18.

Smith, Mary Ann. "The National Writing Project After 22 Years." *Phi Delta Kappan,* 77, no. 10 (June 1996): 688–692.

Stiggins, Richard J. *Student-Centered Classroom Assessment* (2nd ed.). Upper Saddle River, NJ: Prentice Hall, 1997.

Nonprint Stuff

Association for Supervision and Curriculum Development. *ASCD Conference on Teaching & Learning: Assessment* (On Video: Stock #496274S62). Alexandria, VA: Author, 1996.

Hunter, Madeline. *Teaching and Testing: A Conversation with Madeline Hunter* (Videotape #ETVT-36). Los Angeles: IOX Assessment Associates.

Kline, Everett, and Grant Wiggins. *Curriculum and Assessment Design* (Audiotape #295191S62). Alexandria, VA: Association for Supervision and Curriculum Development, 1995.

Northwest Regional Laboratory. *Seeing With New Eyes* (Videotape #NREL-17). Los Angeles: IOX Assessment Associates.

Popham, W. James. *Creating Challenging Classroom Tests: When Students SELECT Their Answers* (Videotape #ETVT-23). Los Angeles: IOX Assessment Associates.

Popham, W. James. *Creating Challenging Classroom Tests: When Students CONSTRUCT Their Responses* (Videotape #ETVT-24). Los Angeles: IOX Assessment Associates.

Popham, W. James. *Improving INSTRUCTION through Classroom Assessment* (Videotape #ETVT-25). Los Angeles: IOX Assessment Associates.

Popham, W. James. *Assessing Mathematics Learning* (Videotape #STVT-26). Los Angeles: IOX Assessment Associates.

13

Making Sense Out of Standardized Test Scores

*C*lassroom teachers need to be able to interpret the results not only of their own assessment procedures but also of the various kinds of standardized tests that are frequently administered to students. Teachers need to be able to interpret such test results not only to base classroom instructional decisions on those results but also to be able to respond accurately when students' parents raise such questions as, "What does my child's grade-equivalent score of 7.4 really mean?" or "When my child's achievement test results are at the 97th percentile, is that good or bad?"

This chapter focuses on the task of making sense out of students' performances on standardized achievement and aptitude tests. One of the kinds of tests under consideration will be the achievement tests (for instance, in mathematics or reading) that are developed and distributed by commercial testing companies. Achievement tests are also developed and administered by state departments of education in connection with statewide assessment programs in such subjects as social studies, sciences, mathematics, reading, and writing. These state tests often employ reporting procedures akin to those used with commercially distributed standardized achievement tests.

And, even though I've desperately tried to avoid numbers larger than 9, in this chapter you'll encounter a few that are larger. Don't be dismayed. Simply go through the examples, one step at a time, and you'll emerge from the chapter a finer human being. The numbers in this chapter will be easier to deal with than might be thought at first glance.

Finally, although today's teachers encounter aptitude tests less frequently than did teachers a decade or two ago, we'll also deal with how to interpret students' performances on the kinds of academic aptitude tests administered by national testing companies. The chapter is intended to help you personally understand how to interpret such test scores and, thinking ahead to your future interactions with score-perplexed parents, to help you explain to parents how to derive meaning from their children's test reports.

Standardized Tests ....

A *standardized* test is a test, either norm referenced or criterion referenced, that is administered, scored, and interpreted in a standard manner. Almost all *nationally* standardized tests are distributed by commercial testing firms. Most such firms are for-profit corporations, although there are a few not-for-profit measurement organizations, such as the Educational Testing Service (ETS), that distribute nationally standardized tests. Almost all nationally standardized tests, whether focused on the measurement of students' aptitude or achievement, are norm-referenced assessment devices.

Standardized achievement tests have also been developed in a number of states under the auspices of state departments of education. These statewide tests (clearly intended to be administered, scored, and interpreted in a standardized fashion) have usually been installed to satisfy a legislative mandate aimed at achieving a form of educational accountability. In some instances, important decisions about individual students are made on the basis of a student's test performance. In many states, for example, if a student does not pass a prescribed statewide basic skills examination by the end of high school, the student is not awarded a diploma, even though all other curricular requirements have been satisfied. In other cases, even though no contingencies for individual students depend on how a student performed on a test, results of student tests are publicized on a district-by-district or school-by-school basis. The test results thus serve as an indicator of local educators' effectiveness, at least in the perception of many citizens. These state-sired standardized achievement tests are generally criterion-referenced assessment devices. Educational aptitude tests are not developed by state departments of education.

Although standardized tests have traditionally consisted almost exclusively of selected-response items, in recent years the developers of standardized tests have attempted to incorporate an increasing number of constructed-response items in their tests. Standardized tests, because they are intended for widespread use, are developed with far more care (and cost) than is possible in an individual teacher's classroom. Even so, the fundamentals of test development that you've learned about in earlier chapters are routinely employed when standardized tests are developed. In other words, the people who create the items for such tests attempt to adhere to the same kinds of item-writing and item-improvement precepts you've learned about. The writers of multiple-choice items for standardized tests worry, just as you should, about inadvertently supplying examinees with clues that give away the correct answer. The writers of short-answer items for standardized tests try to avoid, just as you should, the inclusion of ambiguous language in their items.

Which Test to Believe ....

Each spring in the Big Valley Unified School District, students in grades 5, 8, 10, and 12 complete nationally standardized achievement tests in reading and mathematics as well as a nationally standardized test described by its publishers as "a test of the student's cognitive aptitude." Because William White teaches eighth-grade students in his English classes, he is given the task of answering any questions about the test results raised by his eighth-graders' parents.

He is faced with one fairly persistent question from most parents, particularly those parents whose children scored higher on the aptitude test than on the achievement test. For example, Mr. and Mrs. Wilkins (Wanda's parents) put the question like this: "If Wanda scored at the 90th percentile on the aptitude test and only at the 65th percentile on the achievement test, does that mean she's not putting in enough study time? Putting it another way," they continued, "should we really believe the aptitude tests results or the achievement test's results? Which is Wanda's 'true' test performance?"

If you were William, and had to decide how to answer the questions posed by Wanda's parents, what would your answers be?

There are, of course, staggering differences in the level of effort associated with the construction of standardized tests and the construction of classroom tests. A commercial testing agency may assign a fleet of item writers and a flock of item editors to a new test-development project, whereas you'll be fortunate if you have a part-time teacher's aide to proofread your tests to see if there are typographical errors.

Group-Focused Test Interpretation ....

Although the bulk of this chapter will be devoted to a consideration of score-reporting mechanisms used to describe an individual student's performance, you'll sometimes find that you need to describe the performance of your students as a group. To do so, you'll typically compute some index of the group of scores' *central tendency*, such as when you determine the group's *mean* or *median* performance. For example, you might calculate the *mean raw score* or the *median raw score* for your students. A *raw score* is simply the number of items that a student answers correctly. The *mean*, as you probably know, is the arithmetic average of a set of scores. For example, the mean of the scores 10, 10, 9, 8, 7, 6, 3, 3, and 2 would be 6.4 (that is, summing the nine scores and then dividing by nine). The *median* is the midpoint of a set of scores. For the nine scores in the previous example, the median would be 7 because that score divides the group into two equal parts. Means and medians are useful ways to describe the point at which the scores in a set of scores are centered.

In addition to describing the central tendency of a set of scores (via the mean and/or median), it is also helpful to describe the *variability* of the scores—that is, how spread out the scores are. One simple measure of the variability of a set of students' scores is the *range*. The range is calculated by simply subtracting the lowest student's score from the highest student's score. To illustrate, suppose the highest test score by students in your class was a 49 correct out of 50 earned by Hortense (she always tops your tests; it is surprising she missed one). Suppose further that the lowest score of 14 correct was, as usual, earned by Ed. The range of scores would be 35—that is, Hortense's 49 minus Ed's 14.

Because only two scores influence the range, it is less frequently used as an index of test score variability than is the *standard deviation*. A standard deviation is a kind of average. More accurately, it's the average difference between the individual scores in group of scores and the mean of that set of scores. The larger the size of the standard deviation, the more spread out are the scores in the *distribution*. (That's a ritzy term to describe a set of scores.) Presented here is the formula for computing a standard deviation for a set of scores:

$$\text{Standard Deviation (S.D.)} = \sqrt{\frac{\Sigma\,(X - M)^2}{N}}$$

where: $\Sigma\,(X - M)^2$ = the sum of the squared raw scores (X)
– the mean (M)
N = number of scores in the distribution

Here's a step-by-step description of how you compute a standard deviation using this formula. First, compute the mean of the set of scores. Second, subtract the mean from each score in the distribution. (Roughly half of the resulting values, called *deviation scores,* will have positive values and half will have negative values.) Third, square each of these deviation scores. This will make them all positive. Fourth, add the squared deviation scores together. Fifth, divide the resulting sum by the number of scores in the distribution. Sixth, and last, take the square root of the results of the division you did in the fifth step. The square root that you get is the standard deviation. Not too tough, right?

To illustrate the point that larger standard deviations represent more spread in a distribution of scores than smaller standard deviations, take a look at the two fictitious sets of scores on a 10-item short-answer test presented in Figure 13.1. Both sets of scores have a mean of 5.0. The distribution of scores at the left is much more homogeneous (less spread out) than the distribution of scores at the right. Note that the standard deviation for the more homogeneous scores is only 1.1, whereas the standard deviation of the more heterogeneous scores is 3.2. The larger the standard deviation, therefore, the more distant, on average, will be the distribution's scores from the distribution's mean.

You may have occasions to describe the scores of an entire group of the students you teach. Those descriptions might portray your students' performances on standardized tests or on teacher-made tests. If you get at all comfortable with means and standard deviations, those two indices usually provide a better picture

Figure 13.1　**Two Fictitious Sets of Tests Scored with Equal Means but Different Standard Deviations**

More Homogenous Scores:	*More Heterogeneous Scores:*
3, 4, 4, 5, 5, 5, 5, 6, 6, 7	0, 1, 2, 4, 5, 5, 6, 8, 9, 10
Mean = 5.0	*Mean = 5.0*
$S.D. = \sqrt{\dfrac{12}{10}} = 1.1$	$S.D. = \sqrt{\dfrac{102}{10}} = 3.2$

of a score distribution than do the median and range. But if you think means and standard deviations are statistical gibberish, then go for the median (midpoints are easy to identify) and range (ranges require only skill in subtraction). With group-based interpretations out of the way, let's turn now to interpreting individual students scores from the kinds of standardized tests commonly used in education.

Individual Student Test Interpretation.......................

Two overriding frameworks are generally used to interpret students' test scores. Test scores are interpreted in *absolute* or *relative* terms. When we interpret a student's test score *absolutely*, we infer from the score what it is that the student can or cannot do. For example, based on a student's performance on test items dealing with mathematics computation skills, we make an inference about the degree to which the student has mastered such computation skills. The teacher may even boil the interpretation down to a dichotomy—namely, whether the student should be classified as having mastered or not having mastered the skill or knowledge being assessed. A mastery versus nonmastery interpretation represents an *absolute* interpretation of a student's test score. Classroom teachers often use this absolute interpretive approaches when creating tests to assess a student's knowledge or skills based on a particular unit of study.

When we interpret a student's test score *relatively*, we infer from the score how the student stacks up against other students who are currently taking the test or have already taken the test. For example, when we say that Johnny's test score is "above average" or "below average," we are making a relative test interpretation because we use the average performance of other examinees to make sense out of Johnny's test score.

As pointed our earlier, this chapter focuses on how teachers and parents can interpret scores on standardized tests. Because almost all standardized test scores require relative interpretations, the three interpretive schemes to be considered in the chapter are all relative score-interpretation schemes. Because the vast majority of standardized tests, whether achievement tests or aptitude tests, provide relative interpretations, teachers need to be especially knowledgeable about relative score-interpretation schemes.

Percentiles

The first interpretive scheme that we'll consider, and by all odds the most commonly used one, is based on *percentiles,* or, as they are sometimes called, *percentile ranks.* Percentiles are used most frequently in describing standardized test scores because percentiles are readily understandable to most people.

A percentile compares a student's score with those of other students in a *norm group.* A percentile indicates the percent of examinees in the norm group that the student outperformed. A percentile of 60, for example, means that the student performed better than 60% of the examinees in the norm group.

Let's spend a moment describing what a norm group is. As indicated, a percentile compares a student's score with scores earned by those in a norm group. This comparison with the norm group is based on the performances of a group of individuals who have already been administered a particular examination. For instance, before developers of a new standardized test publish their test, they will administer that test to a large number of students who then become the norm group for the test. Typically, different norm groups of students are assembled for all the grade levels for which percentile interpretations are made.

Figure 13.2 shows a graphic depiction of a set of 3,000 examinees' scores such as might have been gathered during the norming of a nationally standardized achievement test. Remember, we refer to such examinees as the norm group. The area under the curved line represents the number of examinees who earned

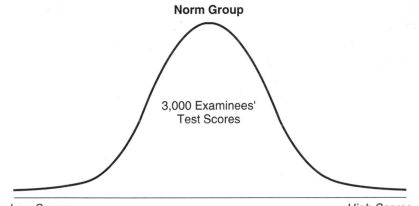

Norm Group

3,000 Examinees'
Test Scores

Low Scores   *High Scores*

Figure 13.2   **A Typical Norm Group**

scores at that point on the baseline. You'll notice that, for a typical norm group's performance, most examinees score in the middle while only a few examinees earn very high or very low scores.

In fact, if the distribution of test scores in the norm group is *perfectly* normal, then, as you see in Figure 13.3, over two-thirds of the scores (represented by the area under the curved line) will be located relatively close to the center of the distribution—that is, plus or minus one standard deviation (S.D.) from the mean.

Not all norm groups are national norm groups. Sometimes test publishers, at the request of local school officials, develop local norms. These local norms can be either state norms or school-district norms. Comparisons of students on the basis of local norms is sometimes seen as being more meaningful than are comparisons based on national norms.

In many instances, local norms are different from national norms because the students in a particular locality are not representative of the nation's children as a whole. If there is a difference between local and national norms, then there will be a difference in a student's percentile scores. A student's raw score—that is, the number of test items answered correctly—might be equal to the 50th percentile based on *national* norms but be equal to the 75th percentile based on *local* norms. That kind of situation would occur if the students in the local group hadn't performed as well as students in the nation at large. National and local norms provide decisively different frameworks for interpreting standardized test results. When reporting test scores to parents, make sure you communicate clearly whether a child's percentiles are based on national or local norms.

It's also true that some norm groups have been more carefully constituted than others. For example, certain national norm groups are more representative of the nation's population than are other national norm groups. There are often large differences in the representativeness of norm groups based on such variables as

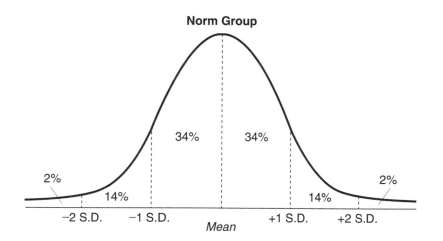

Figure 13.3   **A Normally Distributed Set of Norm-Group Scores**

gender, ethnicity, geographic region, and socioeconomic status of the students in the groups. In addition, many standardized tests are renormed only every 5 to 10 years. It is important to make sure that the normative information on which percentiles are based is both representative and current.

Grade-Equivalent Scores

Let's turn from percentiles to look at a *grade equivalent*, or, as they're often called, *grade-equivalent scores*. Grade-equivalent scores constitute another effort to provide a relative interpretation of standardized test scores. A *grade equivalent* is an indicator of student test performance based on grade level and months of the school year. The purpose of grade equivalents is to transform scores on standardized tests into an index that reflects a student's grade-level progress in school. A grade-equivalent score is a *developmental* score in the sense that it represents a continuous range of grade levels.

Let's look at a grade-equivalent score of 4.5:

A Grade-Equivalent Score:

Grade → 4.5 ← Month of School Year

The score consists of the grade, a decimal, and a number representing months. The number to the left of the decimal point represents the grade level, in this example, the fourth grade. The number to the right of the decimal point represents the month of the school year, in this example, the fifth month of the school year.

Many test publishers, using statistical schemes, convert raw scores on standardized tests to grade-equivalent scores. These grade-equivalent scores often appear on students' score reports. Grade-equivalent scores are most appropriate for basic skills areas such as reading and mathematics where it can be assumed that the degree of instructional emphasis given to the subject is fairly uniform from grade to grade.

The appeal of grade-equivalent scores is that they appear to be readily interpretable to both teachers and parents. However, many teachers and parents actually have an incorrect understanding of what grade-equivalent scores signify. To see why these scores are misunderstood, it's necessary to understand a bit about where they come from in the first place.

To determine the grade-equivalent scores that should be hooked up with particular raw scores, test developers typically administer the same test to students in several grade levels, then establish a trend line reflecting the raw score increases at each grade level. The test developers then estimate at other points along this trend line the grade equivalent for any raw score.

Let's illustrate this important point. In Figure 13.4, you will see the respective performance of students at three grade levels. The same 80-item test has been given to students at all three grade levels: grades 4, 5, and 6. A trend line is then established from the three grades where the test was actually administered. The result of that estimation procedure is seen in Figure 13.5.

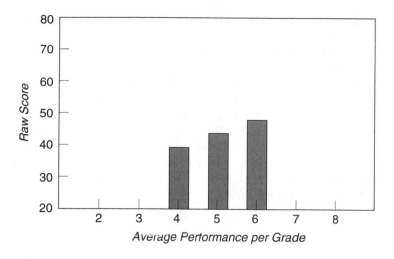

Figure 13.4   **Student Performances at Three Third-Grade Levels**

In order for these estimated grade-equivalent scores to be accurate, several assumptions must be made. First, it must be assumed that the subject area tested is emphasized equally at each grade level. It must also be assumed that student mastery of the tested content increases at a reasonably constant rate at each grade level over an extended period of time. And, as implied earlier, the assumption that the mastery of the test's content increases gradually over time is particularly difficult to support in subject areas other than reading and mathematics.

The implied precision associated with a grade-equivalent score of 6.2, therefore, is difficult to defend. A 6.2 grade-equivalent score suggests a degree of accu-

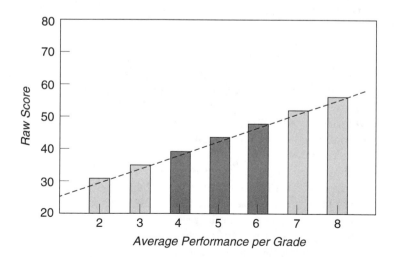

Figure 13.5   **A Trend Line Used to Estimate Average Performance of Students at Nontested Grades**

racy that is simply not warranted. An unskilled interpreter of norm-referenced test results may think that a 6.2 grade-equivalent score indicates the student's raw score represents a performance equal to that of a sixth-grade pupil in the second month of the sixth-grade year. Remember that most grade-equivalent scores are created on the basis of estimation, not real test-score data. Because substantial sampling and estimation errors are apt to be present, grade-equivalent scores should always be taken with several grains of salt.

Now that you understand grade-equivalent scores to be, at best, rough estimates, let's return to the potential misinterpretations that teachers and parents often make regarding grade-equivalent scores. Let's say a third-grade student makes a grade-equivalent score of 5.5 in reading. What does this grade-equivalent score mean? Here's a wrong answer: "The student can do fifth-grade work." Here's a *really* wrong answer: "The student should be promoted to the fifth grade." The right answer, of course, is that the third-grader understands reading skills that the test covers about as well as an average fifth-grader does at midyear. A grade-equivalent score should be viewed as the applicable place where a student is along a developmental continuum, not as the grade level in which the student should be placed.

If standardized tests are used in your school district, and if those tests yield grade-equivalent scores, it is important to provide parents with an accurate description of what a grade-equivalent score means. Parents who have not been given an accurate definition of such scores frequently think that a high grade-equivalent score means their child is capable of doing work at the grade level specified. Some parents even use high grade-equivalent scores as a basis for arguing that their child should be advanced to a higher grade. Because many parents have a misconception of what a grade-equivalent score means, they may have an inflated estimate of their child's level of achievement. The high frequency of parental (and teacher) misinterpretations is the reason that some districts have, as a matter of policy, eliminated grade-equivalent scores when reporting standardized test results.

Remember, if a fourth-grade student gets a grade equivalent of 7.5 in mathematics, it is *not* accurate to say that the fourth-grader is doing well in seventh-grade mathematics. It is more appropriate to say that a grade-equivalent score of 7.5 is an estimate of how an average seventh-grader might have performed *on the fourth-grader's mathematics test*. Obtaining a 7.5 grade-equivalent score doesn't mean that the fourth-grader has any of the mathematics skills taught in the fifth, sixth, or seventh grade because those mathematics skills were probably not even measured on the fourth-grade test.

But what happens when grade-equivalent scores are *below* the actual grade level tested? Let's say a fifth-grader earns a mathematics grade-equivalent score of 2.5. It doesn't make much sense to say that the fifth-grader is doing fifth-grade mathematics work as well as a second-grader, because second-graders obviously aren't given fifth-grade mathematics work. About the best you can say is that in mathematics achievement, the fifth-grader appears to be lagging several years behind grade level.

Scale Scores

Let's move, now, to the last of our three score-interpretation schemes: scale scores. A scale score constitutes yet another way to give relative meaning to a student's standardized test performances. Scale scores are being used with increasing frequency these days to report results of national and state-level standardized programs.

Although scale scores are sometimes not used in reporting standardized test results to parents, scale-score reporting systems are often employed in describing group test performances at the state, district, and school levels. Because of the statistical properties of scale scores, they can be used to permit longitudinal tracking of students' progress. Scale scores can also be used to make direct comparisons among classes, schools, or school districts. The statistical advantages of scale scores are considerable. Thus, we see scale-score reporting systems used with more frequency in recent years. As a consequence, you need to become familiar with the main features of scale scores because such scores are likely to be used when you receive reports of your students' performances on standardized tests.

A *scale* that is used for test scores typically refers to numbers that are assigned to examinees on the basis of their test performance. Higher numbers (higher scores) reflect increasing levels of achievement or ability. Thus, such a scale might be composed of a set of raw scores where each additional test item correctly answered yields one more point on the raw-score scale. Raw scores, all by them-

selves, however, are difficult to interpret. A student's score on a raw-score scale provides no idea of the student's *relative* performance. Therefore, measurement specialists have devised different sorts of scales for test interpretation purposes.

Scale scores are *converted raw scores* that use a new, arbitrarily chosen scale to represent levels of achievement or ability. Shortly, you'll be given some examples to help you understand what is meant by converting scores from one scale to another. In essence, a scale-score system is created by devising a brand-new numerical scale that is often very unlike the original raw-score scale. Students' raw scores are then converted to this brand-new scale so that, when score interpretations are to be made, those interpretations rely on the converted scores based on the new scale. Such converted scores are called *scale scores*.

For example, in Figure 13.6, you see a range of raw score points from 0 to 40 for a 40-item test. Below the raw-score scale, you see a new, converted scale ranging from 500 to 900. For a number of reasons, to be described shortly, it is sometimes preferable to use a scale-score reporting scheme rather than a raw-score reporting scheme. Thus, a student who achieved a raw score of 30 items correct might be assigned a scale score of 800, as shown in Figure 13.7.

One of the reasons that scale scores have become popular in recent years is the necessity to develop several equidifficult forms of the same test. For example, a basic skills test must sometimes be passed before high school diplomas are awarded to students. Those students who initially fail the test are, typically, given other opportunities to pass it. The different forms of the test that are used for such

Figure 13.6   **A Raw-Score Scale and a Converted-Score Scale**

Raw-Score Scale				
0	10	20	30	40

Converted-Score Scale				
500	600	700	800	900

Figure 13.7   **An Illustration of a Raw-Score Conversion to a Scale Score**

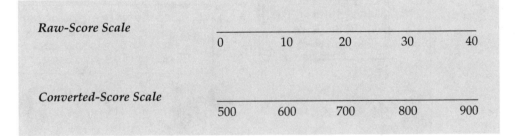

Raw-Score Scale			✕	
0	10	20	30	40

↓

Converted-Score Scale			✕	
500	600	700	800	900

retake purposes should, for the sake of fairness, represent assessment challenges for examinees that are equivalent to those represented by the initial form of the test. However, because it is next to impossible to create test forms that are absolutely identical, scale scores can be used to help solve the problem. Scores on two test forms of differing difficulty levels can be statistically adjusted so that, when placed on a converted score scale, the new scale scores represent students' performances as if the two test forms had been equidifficult.

Most of the more popular types of scale-score systems are based on what measurement specialists refer to as *item response theory*, or *IRT*. IRT scale-score reporting systems are distinctively different from raw-score reporting systems because IRT scale-score schemes take into consideration the difficulty and other technical properties of every single item on the test. Thus, some test publishers have produced IRT-based scale scores for their tests that range from 0 to 1,000 across an entire K–12 grade range. For each grade level, there is a different average scale score. For example, the average scale score for third-graders might be 585 and the average scale score for the tenth-graders might be 714.

These IRT-based scale scores can, when constructed with care, yield useful interpretations if one can reference them back to some notion of relative performance such as percentiles. If average scale scores are provided at different grade levels, this also can aid in the interpretation of scale scores. Without such relative interpretation crutches, however, scale scores cannot be meaningfully interpreted by either educators or parents.

Mistakes are often made in interpreting scale scores because educators assume that all scale scores are somehow similar. For example, when initially administered over 40 years ago, the mean scale score on the verbal section of the Scholastic Assessment Test was 500. This does not signify that the mean score on the Scholastic Assessment Test today is 500 or that other tests using scale scores will always have mean scores of 500. Scale-score systems can be constructed so that the mean score is 50, 75, 600, 700, 1,000, or any number the scale constructor has in mind.

Contrasting the Three Interpretive Options

We've now considered three types of score interpretation schemes—percentiles, grade-equivalent scores, and scale scores. It's time to review and summarize what's really important about these three ways of making sense out of standardized test scores.

We first considered percentiles. A *percentile* indicates a student's standing in relationship to that of a norm group. If a student's test score is equal to the 25th percentile, the student's performance exceeds the performances of 25% of the individuals in the norm group. One advantage of percentiles is that they're easy to interpret. And, for the most part, people's interpretations of percentiles are accurate. A disadvantage of percentiles is that the defensibility of the interpretation is totally dependent on the nature of the normative data on which the percentiles are based. Unrepresentative or out-of-date norm data yield percentile interpretations that are not accurate. As pointed out earlier, because percentile interpretations are so widely used, it's imperative for teachers to be knowledgeable in using such interpretations.

Percentiles

Advantage: readily interpretable
Disadvantage: dependent on quality of norm group

Next we considered grade-equivalent scores. A *grade equivalent* indicates the nature of a student's test performance in terms of grade levels and months. Thus, a grade equivalent of 3.7 would indicate that the student's test score was estimated to be the same as the average performance of a third-grader during the seventh month of the school year. One advantage of grade-equivalent scores is that, because they are based on grade levels and months of the school year, they can be readily communicated to parents. A significant disadvantage associated with grade equivalent scores, however, is that they're frequently misinterpreted.

Grade Equivalents

Advantage: readily communicable
Disadvantage: often misinterpreted

Finally, scale scores were described. *Scale scores* are interpreted according to a converted numerical scale that allows us to transform raw scores into more statistically useful scale-score units. A student who gets a raw score of 35 correct out of 50 items, for example, might end up with a converted scale score of 620. An advantage of scale scores is that they can be used to create statistically adjusted equidifficult test forms. Scale-score schemes based on *item response theory (IRT)* do this by weighting individual test items differently based on an item's difficulty and other technical properties. A disadvantage of scale-score reporting schemes is that they're impossible to interpret all by themselves. Unless we mentally reference scale scores back to percentiles or average grade-level scale scores, such scores are essentially uninterpretable.

Scale Scores

Advantage: useful in equalizing difficulties of different test forms
Disadvantage: not easily interpretable

It should be clear to you that each of these three score-interpretation schemes has some potential virtues as well as some potential vices. You probably realize, even if you understand the general nature of each of these three interpretation schemes, it may be necessary to secure additional technical information to interpret each reporting scheme with confidence. Such information is usually found in the technical manuals that accompany standardized tests. For example, what was the nature of the norm group on which percentiles were based? What

Parent Talk ....

Suppose that one of your students' parents, Mr. Lopez, visits your classroom during a back-to-school evening and raises a series of questions about his daughter, Concepción. Most prominently, Mr. Lopez is concerned with Concepción's scores on the nationally standardized achievement tests administered each spring in your district. Mr. Lopez is troubled by spring-to-spring changes in Concepción's percentiles. As he says, "For the last three springs, her percentile scores in language arts have been the 74th, the 83rd, and the 71st. What's going on here? Is she learning, then unlearning? What accounts for the differences?"

• • • *If I were you, here's how I'd respond to Mr. Lopez:*

"You are certainly wise to look into what appears to be an inconsistent measurement of Concepción's standardized achievement test scores. But what you need to understand, Mr. Lopez, is that these sorts of tests, even though they are nationally standardized, developed by reputable testing firms, and widely used, are not all that precise in how they measure students. Many parents, of course, recognize that their children's test scores are often reported numerically in the form of national percentiles. But this does *not* signify that a given child's national percentile is unerringly accurate.

"The kinds of year-to-year shifting that you've seen in Concepción's language arts percentiles are quite normal because a given year's test result is not all that accurate. Assessment specialists even admit the *anticipated* amount of flip-flop in students' scores when they talk about each test's 'standard error of measurement.' It's something like the sampling errors we hear about for national surveys—you know, 'plus or minus so many percentage points.' Well, measurement error is similar to sampling error. And let me assure you that Concepción's scores will, quite understandably, vary from spring to spring.

"What we do see in her language arts performances over the last three years is a consistently high, well above average achievement level. When her performance is compared to that of a representative, nationally normed sample, Concepción is doing very well, indeed."

• • • *Now, how would you respond to Mr. Lopez?*

sort of mathematical operations were used in generating a scale-score reporting scheme? To interpret particular standardized test's results sensibly, teachers sometimes need to do a bit of homework themselves regarding the innards of the reporting scheme that's being used.

The Instructional Yield from Standardized Achievement Tests

Nationally standardized norm-referenced achievement tests, as noted previously, are developed and sold by commercial testing companies. The more tests those companies sell, the more money those companies make. Accordingly, the representatives of commercial testing companies usually suggest that their standardized achievement tests will not only yield valid norm-referenced interpretations about the students who take the tests but will also provide classroom teachers with a galaxy of useful information for instructional decision making. In my experiences, the *instructional* payoffs of standardized achievement tests are more illusory than real. More often than not, claims for the instructional dividends of norm-referenced achievement tests reflect the zeal of a testing firm's sales force, not the reality of how teachers can actually use the results of standardized tests.

Are standardized achievement tests better than no tests at all? Of course they are. But will standardized tests provide the instructionally sensible, fine-grained diagnostic data that teachers need for accurate decisions? My answer, based on many years of using these tests, is decisively negative.

What Do Classroom Teachers Really Need to Know about Interpreting Standardized Test Scores? ....

Because results of standardized tests are almost certain to come into your professional life, at least in some form, you need to have an intuitive understanding of how to interpret those results. The most common ways of describing a set of scores is to provide an index of the score distribution's central tendency (usually the mean or median) and an index of the score distribution's variability (usually the standard deviation or the range). There will probably be instances in which you either have to describe the performances of your students or to understand the descriptions of the performances of other groups of students (such as all students in your school or your district).

To make accurate interpretations of standardized test scores for your own students, and to help parents understand how to make sense of their child's standardized test scores, you need to comprehend the basic meaning of percentiles, grade-equivalent scores, and scale scores. You really ought to know what the major advantage and disadvantage of each of those three score-interpretation schemes is. You'll then be in a position to help parents make sense out of their children's performances on standardized tests.

Chapter Summary ·

Standardized tests were defined as assessment instruments that are administered, scored, and interpreted in a standard manner. Standardized tests are used to assess students' achievement and aptitude. These tests of student achievement are developed by large testing companies as well as by state departments of education (usually to satisfy a legislatively imposed educational accountability requirement). Although most standardized tests feature the use of selected-response items, many developers of such tests attempt to incorporate increasing numbers of constructed-response items in their assessment devices.

For describing a distribution of test scores, two indices of central tendency—the mean and the median—were described as well as two indices of variability—the range and the standard deviation.

Three ways of interpreting results of standardized tests were discussed: percentiles, grade-equivalent scores, and scale scores. The nature of each of these interpretation procedures was described as well as strengths and weaknesses of the three interpretation procedures.

Self-Check

It's time for a good, old-fashioned true-false test to sharpen your conversance with all these exotic notions about score interpretations. Give the following true-or-false statements your best shot:

(T or F)   **1.** Most standardized aptitude tests have been developed by state departments of education to implement legislatively enacted accountability laws.

(T or F)   **2.** One of the shortcomings of the range as an index of variability is that it is derived from only two raw scores.

(T or F)   **3.** If a distribution of test scores was particularly heterogeneous, it would have a larger standard deviation than if it were particularly homogeneous.

(T or F)   **4.** Because norm groups for nationally standardized tests must be carefully and representatively constituted, they can be effectively used for up to 15 years before renorming is required.

(T or F)   **5.** Locally devised norms based on the performance of local examinees are almost always lower than nationally devised norms based on the performance of examinees nationally.

(T or F)   **6.** Percentiles are the most commonly used way of describing students' performances on standardized tests.

(T or F)   **7.** Whereas percentiles represent a *relative* scheme for interpreting standardized test results, grade-equivalent scores represent an *absolute* scheme for interpreting standardized test results.

(T or F)   **8.** To install a grade-equivalent interpretation scheme, measurement experts typically gather normative data from students at all grade levels for which grade-equivalent scores are to be computed.

(T or F)   **9.** For grade-equivalent scores to function properly, it is assumed that the subject area tested is emphasized about equally at each grade level tested.

(T or F)   **10.** A grade-equivalent score of 6.2 for a fifth-grader indicates that the fifth-grader is performing six months and two weeks ahead of expectations.

(T or F)   **11.** Scale scores, although increasingly used to describe results in standardized tests, are difficult to interpret by themselves.

(T or F)   **12.** Scale-score interpretations of standardized aptitude tests are almost always based on a mean score of 500.

(T or F)   **13.** One advantage of the scale scores derived from item response theory is that their use permits the presentation of equidifficult challenges to examinees when different test forms are used.

(T or F)   **14.** Although grade-equivalent scores are readily communicable, they are often misinterpreted.

(T or F)   **15.** A percentile score for a student on a nationally standardized examination is based chiefly on the percent of test items that the student answered correctly.

Pondertime

1. If you had to use only *one* of the three individual student interpretation schemes treated in the chapter (percentiles, grade-equivalent scores, and scale scores), which one would it be? Why did you make that choice?

2. It is sometimes argued that testing companies and state departments of education adopt scale-score reporting methods simply to make it more difficult for everyday citizens to understand how well students perform. (It's easier for citizens to make sense out of "65% correct" than "an IRT scale score of 420.") Do you think there's any truth in that criticism?

3. In recent years we have seen a marked reduction in the number of available standardized *aptitude* tests in contrasts to the number of available *achievement* tests. Why do you suppose that is?

4. If you were trying to explain to a group of parents how to make sense out of percentile, grade equivalents, and scale scores, how would you go about it so that the parents would really grasp the rudiments of these three score-interpretation procedures?

5. Twenty years ago, it was much less difficult to get district educational officials to require their students to participate in the renorming of standardized tests than it is today. What factors account for that difference?

Self-Check Key

1. F
2. T
3. T
4. F
5. F
6. T
7. F
8. F
9. T
10. F
11. T
12. F
13. T
14. T
15. F

You'll note that there are seven true statements and eight false statements. (Yes, your author also follows the guidelines given in Chapter 6 for binary-choice items.)

Notice that the 15 items you just completed deal largely with knowledge. Yet, I'll wager that the readers who performed well on this little excursion into knowledge assessment also have a pretty fair general understanding of the content addressed in the chapter. That's the reason many teachers, over the years, have been willing to use selected-response sorts of tests as stand-ins for higher-level constructed-response assessments. I'm not recommending such a practice, because I really believe that loftier assessment targets spur loftier instructional approaches. I simply wanted you to see why large numbers of teachers may be inclined to reject many of the "new-fangled" assessment approaches currently being touted. Such teachers tend to believe that the old-fashioned selected-response tests allow them to get a sufficiently accurate enough fix on their students' abilities.

Additional Stuff

Airasian, Peter W. *Classroom Assessment* (2nd ed.). New York: McGraw-Hill, 1994.

Ebel, R. L., and D. A. Frisbie. *Essentials of Educational Measurement* (5th ed.). Englewood Cliffs, NJ: Prentice Hall, 1991.

Flanagan, Dawn P., Judy L. Genshaft, and Patti L. Harrison (Eds.). *Contemporary Intellectual Assessment: Theories, Tests, and Issues.* New York: Guilford, 1997.

Linn, Robert L., and Norman E. Gronlund. *Measurement and Assessment in Teaching* (7th ed.). Upper Saddle River, NJ: Prentice Hall, 1995.

McMillan, James H. *Classroom Assessment: Principles and Practice for Effective Instruction.* Boston: Allyn and Bacon, 1997.

Mehrens, W. A., and I. J. Lehmann. *Measurement and Evaluation in Education and Psychology* (4th ed.). New York: Holt, Rinehart and Winston, 1991.

Popham, W. James. *Modern Educational Measurement: A Practitioner's Perspective* (2nd ed.). Englewood Cliffs, NJ: Prentice Hall, 1990.

Popham, W. James, and Kenneth A. Sirotnik. *Understanding Statistics in Education.* Itasca, IL: F. E. Peacock, 1992.

Sternberg, Robert J. "Myths, Countermyths, and Truths about Intelligence." *Educational Researcher,* 25, no. 2 (March 1996): 11–16.

Wainer, Howard, and David Thissen. "How Is Reliability Related to the Quality of Test Scores? What Is the Effect of Local Dependence on Reliability?" *Educational Measurement: Issues and Practice,* 15, no. 1 (Spring 1996): 22–28.

Nonprint Stuff

Association for Supervision and Curriculum Development. *Reporting Student Progress* (Videotape #495249T87). Alexandria, VA: Author, 1996.

Northwest Regional Laboratory. *Understanding Standardized Tests* (Videotape #NREL-10A). Los Angeles: IOX Assessment Associates.

Popham, W. James, and Sarah J. Stanley. *Making Sense Out of Standardized Test Scores* (Videotape #ETVT-33A). Los Angeles: IOX Assessment Associates.

Popham, W. James, and Sarah J. Stanley. *A Parent's Guide to Standardized Tests* (Videotape #ETVT-34A). Los Angeles: IOX Assessment Associates.

14

··

Appropriate and Inappropriate Test–Preparation Practices

*T*his chapter deals with an important assessment-related issue that never really troubled teachers a decade or two ago. Unfortunately, it is a problem that today's classroom teachers have to confront seriously. Faced with growing pressures to increase students' scores on achievement tests, some teachers have responded by engaging in test-preparation practices that are highly questionable. In recent years, for example, a number of reports have been made of teachers and administrators who deliberately coached students with actual copies of a supposedly "secure" examination (Cannell, 1989). There are even reports of educators' erasing students' incorrect answers and substituting correct answers in their place. Such acts, of course, stem from the increasing emphasis on student test performance as the chief indicator of an educational program's success.

High-Stakes Assessment Arrives ··························

The preoccupation with student test scores as the definitive indicator of educational effectiveness first surfaced in the 1980s. Although attention had been given to the quality of student test performances prior to that decade, it was in the 1980s

Sections of this chapter are based on an essay by the author originally published in the Winter 1991 issue of *Educational Measurement: Issues and Practices,* pp. 12–15. Copyright 1991 by the National Council on Measurement in Education. Adapted by permission of the publisher.

Was It Really Wrong? ···

Judy Jameson is a tenth-grade history teacher in Grant High School. All tenth-graders are given language arts and mathematics tests that must be passed if the students are to receive a state-sanctioned diploma from the district.

The test administration takes place during a two-day period in the school cafetorium and is supervised by Grant High teachers. During those two days, on three occasions Judy overheard Mr. Pelkins respond to students who raised their hands for clarification. Mr. Pelkins did not merely clarify; he told the student what the correct answer was to the test item. After some subtle inquiries, Judy learned that each of the students that Mr. Pelkins had helped was currently in his tenth-grade general mathematics class.

Judy is now trying to decide whether she should do anything about Mr. Pelkins's conduct and, if so, what?

If you were Judy, what would your decision be?

that attentiveness to student test performance became pervasive. In large measure, the focus on pupils' test scores stemmed from increasing incredulity on the part of citizens that public education was performing properly. Taxpayers, and their elected representatives, registered serious doubts that educational tax dollars were being well spent. Spawned by such doubts, the era of educational accountability became a reality in the 1980s when state after state enacted laws requiring students to be assessed by annually administered achievement tests. Students' performances on such tests were used not only to determine the quality of statewide schooling but also (because of the widespread practice of publishing such test scores in local newspapers) to mirror the effectiveness of individual school districts and schools.

In every sense of the expression, these legislatively mandated achievement tests were *high-stakes tests* because there were significant contingencies associated with the test results. The contingencies were experienced either by the students who took the tests or by the educators who administered the tests. To students, the tests were significant because test scores were often linked to high school graduation or to grade-level promotion. To educators, because of the manner in which test results were publicized by the local media, high test scores were viewed as indicating an effective instructional program and, of course, low test scores were seen to indicate the opposite. Because of these contingencies, teachers and administrators found themselves frequently called on to raise test scores. Candid educators will agree that pressures to boost students' test scores are still widespread.

Discussions with classroom teachers regarding what sorts of test-preparation practices they regard as appropriate and inappropriate have led to one inescapable conclusion: Most teachers have not devoted serious thought to the appropriateness of their test-preparation practices. Given the relatively recent arrival of high-stakes testing in education, it is not surprising that scant attention has been given to the appropriateness of various test-preparation practices. Yet, because no decrease in the pressures on educators to promote higher test scores seems likely, it is apparent that teachers need to consider seriously what sorts of test-preparation practices are, indeed, appropriate.

Although it is anticipated that instructional specialists and measurement experts will sharpen the issues associated with this increasingly important issue, few writers have given serious attention to the topic. Among the exceptions are Mehrens and Kaminski (1989), who have supplied a thought-provoking analysis on the topic of test preparation.

Assessment Results as Inference Illuminators

Before addressing topics related to test preparation, it is important to remember the function of educational achievement tests. An educational achievement test is employed in order for us to make a reasonable inference about a student's status with respect to a domain of knowledge and/or skills it represents. Ideally, of course, an achievement test will sample the assessment domain representatively so that the level of a student's performance on the achievement test will serve as a reasonably accurate reflection of the student's status with respect to the assessment domain. The nature of this relationship is illustrated in Figure 14.1 where it is indicated that a student who answered correctly 80% of the items in an achievement test would be expected to have mastered about 80% of the content in the domain of knowledge and/or skills that the test was measuring. The relationship between a student's test performance and that student's mastery of the assessment domain represented by the achievement test, as will be seen later, is a key factor in establishing the appropriateness of test-preparation practices.

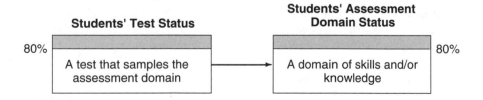

Figure 14.1   **The Inference-Illuminating Relationship between a Test and the Assessment Domain It Samples**

Two Evaluative Standards ....

Two standards can be employed by teachers who wish to ascertain the appropriateness of given test-preparation practices. Taken together, the two standards provide teachers with guidance regarding the suitability of particular test-preparation activities. Here, then, is the first standard—the standard of *professional ethics*.

Professional Ethics

No test-preparation practice should violate the ethical norms of the education profession.

This first standard obliges teachers to avoid any test-preparation practice that is unethical. Ethical behaviors, of course, are rooted not only in fundamental morality but also in the nature of a particular profession. For example, physicians should be governed not only by general ethical principles dealing with honesty and respect for other people's property but also by ethical principles that have evolved specifically for the medical profession. Similarly, teachers should not engage in test-preparation practices that involve violations of general ethical canons dealing with theft, cheating, lying, and so on. In addition, however, teachers must take seriously the ethical obligations that they undertake because they have agreed to serve *in loco parentis*. Teachers who serve "in place of the parent" take on an ethical responsibility to serve as models of ethical behavior for children.

It should also be noted that when teachers engage in test-preparation practices that, if brought to the public's attention, would discredit the education profession, such practices may be considered professionally unethical. This is because, in the long term, such practices erode public confidence in our schools and, as a result, financial support for the schools. Consequently, this erosion of public support renders the education profession less potent.

Thus, according to the standard of professional ethics, teachers should not engage in test-preparation practices that involve such behaviors as violating state-imposed security procedures regarding high-stakes tests. A growing number of states have enacted regulations so that teachers who breach state test-security procedures can have their credentials revoked. Accordingly, teachers should not engage in test-preparation practices that are unethical because there are potential personal repercussions (for example, loss of credentials) or professional repercussions (for example, reduced citizen confidence in public schooling). Most importantly, teachers should avoid unethical test-preparation practices because such practices are *wrong*.

Let's look, then, at the second of our two standards—the standard of *educational defensibility*.

Educational Defensibility

No test-preparation practice should increase students' test scores without simultaneously increasing students' mastery of the assessment domain tested.

This second standard emphasizes the importance of engaging in instructional practices that are in the educational best interests of students. Teachers should not, for example, artificially increase students' scores on a test while neglecting to increase students' mastery of the domain of knowledge and/or skills that the test is supposed to reflect.

An appropriate test-preparation practice raises not only students' prepreparation-to-postpreparation performance on a test but also raises students' prepreparation-to-postpreparation mastery of the assessment domain being tested. This

Appropriate Test Preparation

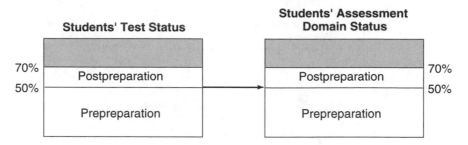

Figure 14.2   **Appropriate Test Preparation Based on the Criterion of Educational Defensibility**

situation is illustrated in Figure 14.2 where you can see that a 20% prepreparation-to-postpreparation jump in students' mastery was seen both on the test and on the assessment domain it represents.

Conversely, an inappropriate test-preparation practice raises students' prepreparation-to-postpreparation performance on the test, but not students' mastery of the assessment domain itself. This situation is illustrated in Figure 14.3 where students' test performances increase, but their assessment domain mastery doesn't.

The result of such inappropriate test-preparation practices is that a deceptive picture of students' achievement is created. The test results no longer serve as an accurate indicator of students' status with respect to an assessment domain. As a consequence, students who in reality have not mastered a domain of content may fail to receive appropriate instruction regarding such content. The students will have been instructionally shortchanged because inappropriate test-prepara-

Inappropriate Test Preparation

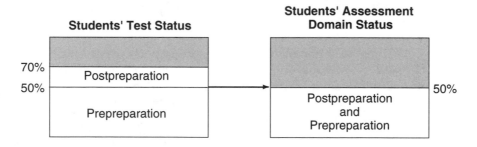
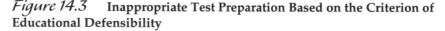

Figure 14.3   **Inappropriate Test Preparation Based on the Criterion of Educational Defensibility**

tion practices led to an inflated estimate of their content mastery. Such test-preparation practices, because they rob students of needed instruction, are educationally indefensible.

Five Test–Preparation Practices . . . .

We can now turn to a consideration of five common test-preparation practices. These five practices are not exhaustive in the sense that there are no other conceivable test-preparation procedures. The five practices do, however, capture most of the important test-preparation options available to teachers. Some of these involve special instruction rather than regular classroom instruction. *Special instruction* consists of extra preparation sessions, during or outside class, that are devoted exclusively to the readying of students for tests. In contrast, *regular classroom instruction*, although its focus may be relevant to the content of a test, occurs as part of the teacher's ongoing instructional program. The five test-preparation practices are the following:

1. *Previous-form preparation* provides special instruction and practice based directly on students' use of a previous form of the actual test. For example, if the currently published form of a nationally standardized achievement test is being used on a statewide basis as part of an educational accountability system, the teacher gives students guided or independent practice with earlier, no longer published, versions of the same test.
2. *Current-form preparation* provides special instruction and practice based directly on students' use of the form of the test currently being employed. For example, the teacher gives students guided or independent practice with actual items copied from a currently used state-developed high school graduation test.
3. *Generalized test-taking preparation* provides special instruction that covers test-taking skills for dealing with a variety of achievement-test formats. For example, the teacher shows students how to make calculated guesses for certain types of items or how to allocate test-taking time judiciously.
4. *Same-format preparation* provides regular classroom instruction dealing directly with the content covered on the test, but employs only practice items that embody the same format as items actually used on the test. For example, if a mathematics achievement test includes addition problems formatted only in vertical columns, the teacher provides practice with addition problems formatted solely in that manner.
5. *Varied-format preparation* provides regular classroom instruction dealing directly with the content covered on the test, but employs practice items that represent a variety of test-item formats. For example, if the achievement test uses subtraction problems formatted only in vertical columns, the teacher provides practice with problems formatted in vertical columns, horizontal rows, and in story form.

Parent Talk ···

> Mrs. Stern is the mother of Sarah, one of your most talented students. Mrs.
> Stern, it is rumored, will be running for election to your district's school board
> in the fall. Accordingly, whenever Mrs. Stern raises questions about Sarah's ed-
> ucation, you always try to be especially responsive. You are no dummy.
>
>   When Sarah arrived at school this morning, she gave you a brief note from
> her mother. The note said, "Why is so much time spent in our school, and in
> your class, 'teaching to the test' this year? Shouldn't our children be learning
> more than what's on a test?"

• • • *If I were you, here's how I'd respond to Mrs. Stern in person or with a note (if
in person, I might reply on bended knee):*

"You're right on target to be raising this issue, Mrs. Stern, but I want you to understand an important difference between teaching to the test, in the sense that you
teach to the students to do well on particular test items, versus teaching to the test, in
the sense that you teach the students to master the skills and/or knowledge represented by the test.

"What I do in my class is the latter, and that's also what most of my colleagues
do. In other words, we teach directly toward the important skills and knowledge
that our tests measure. Those are the key kinds of skills and the significant bodies of
knowledge that you and I both want Sarah to acquire. But the classroom assessments
we use only sample a student's mastery of such knowledge or skills.

"So it would be instructionally unwise for us to teach toward *particular* test
items. We want Sarah and her classmates to master skills and knowledge so they can
apply what they've learned in many settings, not merely on a specific test.

"Putting it simply, we do *not* teach toward a set of test items, but we *do* teach
toward the skills and knowledge that our tests represent."

• • • *Now, how would you respond to Mrs. Stern?*

Applying the Two Standards ····························

When these five test-preparation practices are scrutinized according to the standards of professional ethics and educational defensibility, only two turn out to be
appropriate.

Previous-form preparation violates the educational defensibility standard because students' test scores are apt to be boosted via such special preparation sessions without concomitant rises in students' mastery of the content domain being
tested. In addition, because in the public's view this kind of test-preparation practice may be seen as an improper instance of coaching students *merely* for test-score
gains, it may be viewed by some as professionally unethical. Previous-form
preparation, therefore, is inappropriate. (This same judgment would apply to the

use of commercial test-preparation materials that are based chiefly on specially created "parallel" forms of a currently used test.)

Current-form preparation clearly loses out on both standards. Not only is it educationally indefensible but such preparation also constitutes an outright example of cheating. Current forms of the test must be stolen or surreptitiously copied in order to be used in such potentially improper score-boosting special sessions. Teachers who are caught readying their students via current-form preparation should, in fact, be caught.

Generalized test-taking preparation turns out to be an appropriate form of test preparation because such special instruction on how to take tests is, characteristically, rather brief and not seriously deflective of a student's ongoing education. More importantly, because such test-taking preparation readies students to cope with a number of different sorts of tests, students will be less apt to be intimidated by a previously unencountered type of test item. In a very real sense, therefore, generalized test-taking preparation sessions allow students' test performances to be more accurately reflective of their true state of knowledge and/or skill. Such preparation, *if not excessively lengthy*, is clearly appropriate.

Same-format preparation, although it may be ethical, is not educationally defensible. If students in their regular classroom instruction are allowed to deal *only* with the explicit item format used on a test, then those students will be far less likely to generalize what they have learned. Test scores may rise, but comparable content mastery is not apt to rise. Although many administrators may, because of powerful pressures to boost scores, endorse this form of test-preparation practice, it should be resisted because it is educationally unsound.

Varied-format preparation, in contrast, satisfies both of our two evaluative standards. Students during their regular classroom instruction are given practice not only with content as it is conceptualized on the test but also with content conceptualized in other ways. Rises in test scores will, in general, be accompanied by rises in mastery of the assessment domain being tested because students' generalized mastery of the content is being fostered.

Of the five test-preparation variants, then, only varied-format preparation and generalized test-taking preparation satisfy both evaluative standards. This can be seen in Table 14.1.

Table 14.1   **Per-Standard Indicator of the Appropriateness of Five Test-Preparation Practices**

Test-Preparation Practice	Standard Satisfied?	
	Professional Ethics	*Educational Defensibility*
Previous Form	No	No
Current Form	No	No
Generalized Test Taking	Yes	Yes
Same Format	Yes	No
Varied Format	Yes	Yes

What Do Classroom Teachers Really Need to Know about Test-Preparation Practices? ....

As a classroom teacher, you may find that your own test-preparation practices may not coincide perfectly with one of the five practices described. You'll probably discover that if you are preparing your students specifically for some sort of high-stakes test, however, your approach will be reasonably close to one of the five practices treated in the chapter. More important than the five preparation practices, of course, are the two evaluative standards. You should review with care your own preparation activities linked to high-stakes tests. The two evaluative standards provided here—professional ethics and educational defensibility—will prove useful in such a review.

Chapter Summary ....

This chapter dealt with an important assessment-related issue—namely, how teachers should prepare their students for significant tests. After a recounting of why it is that classroom teachers are under substantial pressure to boost their students' test scores, two evaluative standards were supplied by which test-preparation practices can be judged. The two standards were (1) *professional ethics*, which indicates that no test-preparation practice should violate the ethical norms of the education profession, and (2) *educational defensibility*, which indicates that no test-preparation practice should increase students' test scores without simultaneously increasing students' mastery of the assessment domain tested. Five test-preparation variants were then described: (1) previous-form preparation, (2) current-form preparation, (3) generalized test-taking preparation, (4) same-format preparation, and (5) varied-format preparation. Having applied the two evaluative standards to the five test-preparation practices, it was concluded that the only two practices satisfying both standards were generalized test-taking preparation (if brief) and varied-format preparation.

Self-Check

To see how skillfully you can use the chapter's two standards for evaluating teachers' test-preparation practices, you'll now be given five written descriptions of fictitious teachers' test-preparation activities. Your task is to decide, for each description, whether either, neither, or both of the two evaluative standards (professional ethics and educational defensibility) have been violated by the preparation activity described. Having done that, decide personally whether you think the preparation activities described were appropriate or inappropriate.

Description One

Mrs. Gordon makes sure that she has her sixth-grade students practice in the fall for the nationally standardized achievement tests that are required in the spring by the district's school board. Fortunately, she has been able to make photocopies of most of the test's pages during the past several years, so she can organize a highly relevant two-week preparation unit wherein students are given actual test items to solve. At the close of the unit, students are supplied with a practice test on which about 60% of the test consists of actual items copied from the nationally standardized commercial test. Mrs. Gordon provides students with an answer key after they have taken the practice test so that they can check their answers.

Any violations? _____ If so, which? _____

What's your opinion of this preparation? _____

Description Two

Mrs. Hillard knows that the criterion-referenced reading test administered to all state eighth-graders contains a set of six fairly lengthy reading selections, each of which is followed by about 10 multiple-choice items dealing with such topics as (1) the main idea of the selection as a whole or the main idea of its constituent paragraphs, (2) the meaning of selection's technical terms that can be arrived at from contextual clues, and (3) the defensibility of inferential statements linked to the selection.

Mrs. Hillard routinely spends time in her eighth-grade language arts class trying to improve her students' reading comprehension capabilities. She has the students read passages similar to those used in the statewide criterion-referenced test, then gives her students a variety of practice tests, including written multiple-choice, true-false, and oral short-answer tests in which, for example, individual students must state what they believe to be the main idea of a specific paragraph in the passage.

Any violations? _____ If so, which? _____

What's your opinion of this preparation? _____

Description Three

Because there is a statewide reading comprehension test that must be passed by all high school students before they receive state-sanctioned diplomas, Mr. Gillette, a tenth-grade English teacher, spends about four weeks of his regular class sessions getting students ready to pass standardized tests. He devotes one week to each of the following topics: (1) time management in examinations, (2) dealing with test-induced anxiety, (3) making calculated guesses, and (4) trying to think like the test's item writers. Mr. Gillette's students seem appreciative of his efforts.

Any violations? _____ If so, which? _____

What's your opinion of this preparation? _____

Description Four

Because she is eager for her students to perform well on their twelfth-grade senior mathematics tests (administered by the state department of education), Mrs. Williamson gives students answer keys for all of the test's selected-response items. When her students take the test in the school auditorium, along with all of the school's other twelfth-graders, she urges them to use the answer keys discreetly and only if necessary.

Any violations? _____ If so, which? _____

What's your opinion of this preparation? _____

Description Five

Mr. Phillips prepares his sixth-grade social studies students to do well on a state-administered social studies examination by having all of his students practice with test items similar to those on the examination. Mr. Phillips tries to replicate the nature of the state examination's items without ever using exactly the same content as is apt to appear on that examination. He weaves in his test-preparation activities as part of his regular social studies instruction. Most students really don't know that they are receiving examination-related preparation.

Any violations? _____ If so, which? _____

What's your opinion of this preparation? _____

Pondertime

1. Can you think of standards, other than the two described in the chapter, that should be used in evaluating a classroom teacher's test-preparation practices? If so, what are they?

2. How about test-preparation practices? Can you think of any others that are meaningfully different from the five described in the chapter? If so, using the chapter's two evaluative standards or any new ones that you might prefer, how appropriate are such test-preparation practices?

3. In the chapter it was concluded that only two of the five described test-preparation practices were winners. Do you agree? If not, why not? If you do agree, why?

4. Do you think it is appropriate for teachers to devote any explicit preparation to having their students perform well on high-stakes tests? Why or why not?

5. How do you think classroom teachers can best be prepared to deal with the test-preparation issue in an appropriate fashion?

Self-Check Key

1. Mrs. Gordon has violated both evaluative standards by engaging in what most people regard as downright cheating. Hopefully, you didn't consider this teacher's preparation efforts to be all that wonderful.

2. Mrs. Hillard is clearly engaged in a version of varied-format preparation. She is violating neither of the two evaluative standards. Indeed, because of the likelihood that she is promoting her students' generalized reading comprehension abilities during her regular language arts evaluation, she is engaging in solidly appropriate test preparation.

3. Mr. Gillette's month-long test-preparation marathon was simply too long. Although both of the two evaluative standards appear to have been satisfied, the lengthy test-preparation activities really are costing students a full month of English instruction. To be absurd, let's say Mr. Gillette spent his entire, year-long instructional efforts on generalized test-preparation schemes such as described in this chapter. Such an approach would clearly be depriving students of an English course. In that sense, particularly if parents discovered that Mr. Gillette's students were learning nothing about English, there would surely be some negative repercussion and, as a consequence, an erosion of confidence in the schools. Thus, the professional ethics standard might have been violated. But even if neither of the two evaluative standards had been violated, Mr. Gillette's month-long test-preparation extravaganza was simply too, too long.

4. Mrs. Williamson is engaged in dishonest test preparation that loses out on both evaluative standards. Before you think that this is a silly and obvious example, you should know that several teachers have been fired and had their teaching licenses revoked because of precisely the kind of behavior depicted in this scenario.

5. Mr. Phillips satisfied the professional ethics standards but lost out on the educational defensibility standard. Irrespective of whether his students know they were being prepared, and without regard to the inclusion of the test preparation as part of his regular instruction, Mr. Phillips's students aren't likely to be able to generalize the social studies mastery they'll display on the state examination to other settings in which they'll need to possess such mastery.

Additional Stuff

Angoff, William, and Eugene G. Johnson. "The Differential Impact of Curriculum on Aptitude Test Scores." *Journal of Educational Measurement,* 27, no. 4 (Winter 1990): 291–305.

Cannell, J. J. *How Public Educators Cheat on Standardized Achievement Tests.* Albuquerque, NM: Friends for Education, 1989.

Kilian, Lawrence J. "A School District Perspective on Appropriate Test-Preparation Practices: A Reaction to Popham's Proposal." *Educational Measurement: Issues and Practice,* 11, no. 4 (Winter 1992): 13–15, 26.

Kumar, V. K., L. Rabinsky, and T. N. Pandy. "Test Mode, Test Instructions and Retention." *Contemporary Educational Psychology*, 4 (1979): 211–218.

Mehrens, W. A. "Facts about Samples, Fantasies about Domains." *Educational Measurement: Issues and Practice*, 10, no. 2 (Summer 1991): 23–25.

Mehrens, W. A., and J. Kaminski. "Methods for Improving Standardized Test Scores: Fruitful, Fruitless, or Fraudulent." *Educational Measurement: Issues and Practices*, 8, no. 1 (1989): 14–22.

Phillips, S. E. "Legal Defensibility of Standards: Issues and Policy Perspectives." *Educational Measurement: Issues and Practice*, 15, no. 2 (Summer 1996): 5–13, 19.

Popham, W. J. "The Perils of Responsibility-Sharing." *Educational Measurement: Issues and Practice*, 11, no. 4 (Winter 1992): 16–17.

Powers, Donald E. "Coaching for the SAT: A Summary of the Summaries and an Update." *Educational Measurement: Issues and Practice*, 12, no. 2 (Summer 1993): 24–30.

Rogers, W. Todd, and David J. Bateson. "The Influence of Test-Wiseness on Performance of High School Seniors on School Leaving Examinations." *Applied Measurement in Education*, 4, no. 2 (1991): 159–183.

Schmeiser, Cynthia B. "Ethical Codes in the Professions." *Educational Measurement: Issues and Practice*, 11, no. 3 (Fall 1992): 5–11.

Nonprint Stuff

American Educational Research Association. *Effects of Classroom Performance Assessments on Instruction* (Cassette Recording No. RA 3-16.27). Chicago: Teach 'Em, April 13, 1993.

Hunter, Madeline. *Teaching and Testing: A Conversation with Madeline Hunter* (Videotape #ETVT-36A). Los Angeles: IOX Assessment Associates.

Popham, W. James, and Sarah J. Stanley. *Test Preparation Practices: What's Appropriate and What's Not* (Videotape #ETVT-31A). Los Angeles: IOX Assessment Associates.

15

Evaluating Teaching and Grading Students

*T*his chapter is the one right before the index. If you possess modest powers of inference, and have ever read another book containing an index, you are likely to conclude that this is the book's last chapter. You are correct. And, if you have reveled in reading the initial 14 chapters of the book, you'll surely greet this last-chapter news with sadness. If, on the other hand, you've found Chapters 1 through 14 less than scintillating, your burden will soon be over. In either case, this final chapter will deal with two important uses to which classroom teachers can put the results of assessments—evaluating teaching and grading students.

Distinction Drawing

Just so we're all on the identical page of music, let's make certain that you and I are employing the same meaning when we use the two terms around which this final chapter is fashioned. In casual conversation, you'll sometimes find educators using the terms *evaluation* and *grading* interchangeably, but these two words really stand for distinctively different education-related activities.

There was a time when educators really didn't distinguish between *evaluation* of students and *grading* of students, but those days have passed. Because program evaluation has become such a prominent part of educational practice, when most educators encounter the term *evaluation* these days, they think about the evaluation of an educational program such as a newly installed cooperative learning scheme.

When classroom teachers engage in *evaluation*, those teachers are typically arriving at conclusions about the quality of their own instructional efforts. In that sense, therefore, you should think about evaluation as "program evaluation." Because the program under consideration in most classrooms is the instructional program provided to students by the teacher, then *evaluation* will be used in this chapter to signify the attempt on the part of teachers to determine how well they're doing instructionally. Evaluation, then, can be roughly equated with "teacher evaluation" because when teachers' evaluate their instructional endeavors, they're really evaluating the quality of the instructional program they put together as well as the way they delivered that program. The focus of *evaluation* in this chapter, therefore, is on *teachers*.

In contrast, the focus of *grading* is on *students*. When a teacher grades a student, the teacher is assigning some kind of symbol (we'll discuss several options later), such as a letter grade of A, B, C, D, or F, that signifies "how well the student has done." Although in most classrooms there's surely a relationship between the quality of the teacher's instructional program and the grades that students receive, those two notions are really independent. For example, Mrs. Bevins, a third-grade teacher, could evaluate her own language arts program very negatively because her instruction seemed to confuse many students. Nevertheless, Mrs. Bevins would still award grades of A to several students who, despite the confusing language arts instruction, nevertheless seemed to grasp the language arts concepts being considered.

Teachers' judgments about their own instructional effectiveness, as well as their decisions about what grades to assign individual students, can be greatly influenced by assessment results. Both grading and evaluation, of course, can be illuminated by other sources of information. Neither of those two activities should be ruled by test results.

Evaluation of Teaching and the Use of Assessment Data ....

There are two types of evaluation that bear on teachers' appraisals of their instructional efforts. *Formative evaluation* refers to the appraisal of the teacher's instructional program for purposes of improving that program. For example, suppose you're teaching a three-week social studies unit on International Cooperation to a class of fifth-graders for the first time and you want to improve the unit so that the next time you offer it, the unit will be more effective. That's a task for formative evaluation, and students' assessment results will surely help you. Summative evaluation, in contrast, is not improvement focused. *Summative evaluation* refers to appraisals of teachers' competencies in order to make more permanent decisions about those teachers such as (1) continuation of employment or (2) awarding of tenure. When teachers are evaluated summatively, they're almost always evaluated by some type of external evaluator—for example, an administrator or supervisor.

Classroom teachers, therefore, usually do their own formative evaluations because they wish to spruce up their instruction. For summative evaluation, classroom teachers may be called on to supply evidence (such as students' test results) to supervisors who will then use that evidence.

A Preinstruction versus Postinstruction Paradigm

Whether for formative evaluation or summative evaluation, the classic pretest-posttest paradigm presented in Figure 15.1 will prove serviceable for gauging instructional impact. If you assess your students prior to teaching them, then assess your students after you've taught them, any difference between their preinstruction and postinstruction performances ought be chiefly attributable to what went on in between—your teaching.

There are certain problems associated with the classic pretest-posttest scheme for discerning instructional impact, of course, but as a general paradigm for figuring out whether your instruction is making any dents in your students, the approach represented in Figure 15.1 isn't all that bad. One of the difficulties with the pretest-posttest model that you need to watch out for is the possibility that the pretest will be *reactive;* that is, it will sensitize your students to "what's important" so that they behave atypically when taught about what was on the test. In other words, the effects measured by the posttest will really be a function of your instruction *plus* the pretest. However, if the posttest results for Topic X truly turn out to be what you want when you use a reactive pretest, then you might decide to toss in a pretest every time you teach Topic X.

Different Students, Different Results

For purposes of summative evaluation, such as when you are being evaluated by school district officials for purposes of continued employment, there's a really difficult problem to consider, and that is the extent to which pretest-to-posttest assessment results for students will be influenced by the caliber of the students you happen to be teaching. If you're teaching a ninth-grade geography class and have

Figure 15.1   **A Classic Preinstruction versus Postinstruction Paradigm for Determining Instructional Impact**

been blessed with a group of bright, motivated, and well-informed students, it is certain that the pretest-to-posttest gains you obtain will be quite different from the gains you might see if you were teaching a collection of dull, unmotivated students whose conception of geography stops at the boundaries of the schoolyard.

Yet, even though those who would use your students' performance as evidence of your effectiveness must take into consideration the particular students you teach and the education context in which you instruct those students, it would be unreasonable to say that teachers should not be evaluated, *at least in part,* by the learning they are able to produce in their students. Thus, in addition to other sources of information regarding your instructional efforts (such as classroom observations), evidence of student growth, typically based on a contrast of pretest and posttest performances, should be considered as a reflection of your instructional prowess. It is *imperative,* however, that those who use student-assessment data for purposes of summative evaluation do so in the context of the situation in which the teacher teaches—the most important feature of which are the specific students being taught.

For your own formative evaluation purposes, there's somewhat less need to get caught up with the "dissimilar students" problem. After all, you'll know your own students and will be able to judge whether you have a group of fast-thinking wizards whose pretest-to-posttest gains will be astounding or a group of slow-thinking students whose progress will be substantially less electrifying.

To the extent that you're using gain scores (that is, posttest-minus-pretest scores), you should be aware of another technical problem that will sometimes get in your way. If your students do *very* well on the pretest, it's more difficult for them to show gains than if they'd scored lower prior to instruction. When students score very high on tests, they tend to "top out" because of what is called a *ceiling effect.* Sometimes, in fact, if your students score really poorly on a pretest, they'll be likely to score higher on the posttest *by chance alone.* (If you want to intimidate your colleagues during faculty meetings, that is called a *regression effect,* wherein extremely low-scoring [or high-scoring] students tend to regress toward the mean when retested. By casually asserting that your "students' progress, of course, might be attributable to a regression effect," you'll surely awe a few of your fellow teachers.)

What to Assess

Whether you use your students' assessment results yourself for the formative evaluation of your own teaching or, in contrast, supply those results to others who will use such evidence for summative evaluation, you still have to decide what to assess. Think back, if you can remember that long ago, to Chapter 5's discussion of what to assess. Remember that the key factor governing what you should assess in your classroom is always the educational decision(s) that you need to make. For purposes of formative evaluation, you'll have to think through for yourself what kinds of evidence you'll need in order to tinker with or to fundamentally overhaul your instructional activities. Surely you'll want to know how much your students have learned.

You should also seriously consider the assessment of students' *affect*. Affective assessment is of little utility for decisions about individual students because, as seen in Chapter 10, such measurement is too imprecise for defensible inferences about particular students. However, for judging the effectiveness of your instructional efforts, group-based inferences about students' pretest-to-posttest shifts in affect are useful.

Because you'll not be using affective results to make decisions about individual students, and because affective measures when used as pretests turn out to be particularly reactive, you might consider using a data-gathering scheme such as the one shown in Figure 15.2 where it can be seen that half of the class (Half-Class A) completes Affective Inventory I prior to instruction and Affective Inventory II after instruction, whereas the other half of the class (Half-Class B) does the opposite. Because you can accurately estimate the affective impact of your instruction from a 50% sample of your students, it is really not necessary to assess all of them. The pretest-to-posttest contrasts to be made are displayed in Figure 15.2 by the gray lines. As can be seen, Half-Class A's pretest performance is contrasted with Half-Class B's posttest performance, and vice versa. Note that potential reactivity has been reduced because no student is completing, as a posttest, the affective inventory that was completed as a pretest.

In sum, students' assessment results are clearly important when teachers evaluate themselves or when others evaluate teachers. Although there are other important sources of evidence to be used in appraising a teacher's instructional efforts, what happens to students as a consequence of instruction is, unarguably, a significant source of evidence.

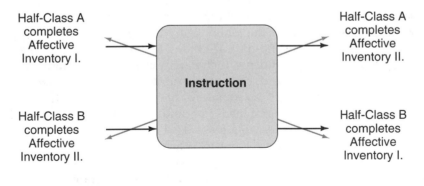

Half-Class A completes Affective Inventory I.

Half-Class B completes Affective Inventory II.

Instruction

Half-Class A completes Affective Inventory II.

Half-Class B completes Affective Inventory I.

⟷ = Appropriate comparisons

Figure 15.2   **A Data-Gathering Design to Reduce the Reactivity of Pretesting**

Evaluating Teaching via Standardized Achievement Tests

There's a widespread belief among parents and educational policymakers that the best way to evaluate the instructional effectiveness of teachers or schools is to use students' performances on standardized achievement tests. Despite the prevalence of this view, however, it is absolutely *inappropriate* to evaluate instructional quality on the basis of students' standardized achievement test results. Yet, because many teachers don't understand why it is that students' performances on standardized tests don't provide an accurate indication of instructional quality, many parents and members of school boards continue to believe that scores on standardized achievement tests provide a good indication of how well teachers have been teaching.

In an appendix at the close of this chapter, I've included a brief essay I wrote for parents about why standardized achievement tests should not be used as a way of judging teaching. I encourage you to read that essay and master its essentials well enough so that you could, if called on to do so, explain to a group of colleagues or a group of parents why standardized achievement test scores do *not* give us a good picture of how successful a school or teacher has been.

Assessment-Based Grading ....

Teachers give grades. One supposes that when the original blueprints for "teacher" were drawn, there must have been a mandatory grade-giving component included somewhere. Other than tradition, however, why is it that teachers dispense grades to students so regularly?

The answer's fairly simple. A teacher needs to let students know (1) how well they're doing, as when a teacher assigns interim grades on various assignments during the course of the school year; and (2) how well they've done, as when a teacher dishes out end-of-year-grades. Metaphorically, a teacher sets out a multiple-course meal for students, then determines whether those students have eaten each course and the overall meal nutritiously. For teachers to find out whether they've taught well, as we saw earlier in the chapter, the extent of students' learning must be determined. For students to find out how well they've learned, the extent of their learning must also be determined.

Although, as we shall see, there are other factors to be considered in grading students than simply how well the students performed on classroom assessments, there's little argument that a *major* consideration in the grade a student receives should be the quality of the student's assessment performances. In this section of the chapter, we'll be looking at different ways that those assessment results can be incorporated into students' grades.

Deciding on Grading Criteria and Weighting the Criteria

It is all too common, unfortunately, for teachers to give little serious thought to grading until they are confronted, face to face, with the need to give grades. (As a beginning high school teacher, I believe that I decided how to give my initial set of first-semester grades a full 30 seconds before assigning those grades.) A more appropriate approach to grade giving would be to think out—well in advance of the press of grade-giving demands—just what criteria should be used in awarding grades to students and, beyond that, just how much weight should be assigned to each criterion.

It may well be that several of the grading criteria you use will be based on students' assessment performances—but on different types of tests. For instance, final examination results are apt to be weighted more heavily than midterm examination results, which, in turn, are likely to be weighted more heavily than results on weekly quizzes. If a portfolio system is employed in the class, it is likely that substantial weight would be given to the evidence of students' capabilities reflected by the contents of their portfolios. In a similar vein, if students are required to respond to fairly elaborate performance test tasks, then surely the resulting student performances would be deemed more important by the teacher than other, less demanding assessment activities. In short, you'll weight differently the importance of students' performances on various kinds of assessments based on your judgments about the significance of the various assessments.

Beyond assessment-based evidence, however, there are other criteria that teachers often employ when dispensing grades. For example, class participation,

Should Level-of-Effort Be Rewarded? . . . .

Karl Kramer teaches second-graders at Twelfth Street Elementary School. He's been doing so for six years. During the past year, however, Karl has seriously been reconsidering his whole approach to grading. That reconsideration was stimulated by three students who in the past would have been placed in some form of special needs program but now have been mainstreamed into Karl's second-grade class.

Although the three students, Marie, Floyd, and James, are having difficulty with much of the content treated in class, all three are obviously trying particularly hard to succeed. In fact, if Karl were to grade on effort alone, the three students would probably get the highest grades in class.

In the past, Karl has given no credit for student effort when grades were awarded. Now, however, he finds that he's rethinking that decision.

If you were Karl, what would you do?

homework-completion rates, and classroom cooperation are used by some teachers as criteria to be employed in the grading process. What is being suggested here is simply that, before you are faced with time-induced pressures to award grades, you should give serious thought to (1) identifying the factors you'll consider when grading and (2) deciding how much those factors will count.

In Table 15.1, you'll find an illustrative grading scheme devised along the lines being recommended here. The fictitious illustration in Table 15.1 depicts what might have been decided on by a high school government teacher. Note that there are six criteria, the first four of which are based on students' assessment performances. In the opinion of the fictitious teacher whose grading criteria are set forth in Table 15.1, a full 85% of students' grades should be based on the results of classroom assessments. Note that students' results on the one-week performance test count more than their results on the midterm examinations. Remember, this is a fictitious example for illustrative purposes only. As a teacher, *you* will decide what grading criteria to use and how much to weight each one.

Grade Descriptors

When teachers award grades, there are several options available to them. For final, end-of-term or end-of-year grades, it is necessary to adhere to whatever grade-descriptor system has been adopted by the district. Thus, if the district's policy is to use grades of A, B, C, D, or F, then the district's teachers must use those grades even if, during the course of the year, the teachers employed a different grade-descriptor scheme in class. Although many school districts, or schools within those districts, have grading policies that are quite general, some grading policies are particularly restrictive—setting forth specific limits on the percentages of particular grades that can be awarded by teachers.

Table 15.1   **An Illustrative Set of Grading Criteria for a High School Government Class**

Grading Criteria	Contribution to Final Grade
1. Final examination	30%
2. Midterm examination	20%
3. One-month performance test	25%
4. Periodic weekly quizzes	5%
5. Homework-completion rate	10%
6. Classroom participation	10%

Generally speaking, there are three major options available to teachers when they describe how well a student has performed. Teachers can use (1) letter grades, (2) numerical grades, or (3) verbal descriptors. Most of us are familiar with *letter grades* because such grades have been widely used for a long, long time. A grade of A is yummy and a grade of F is sucko. In some districts, teachers are also allowed to add pluses or minuses to letter grades, thus transforming a grading scale that has 5 points (A, B, C, D, or F) to one with 15 points. A grade of F–, we assume, reflects genuinely abysmal rock-bottom performance. A *numerical grading system* is usually organized around some chosen number of points such as 100, 50, or 10. Students are then given a number of points on each classroom assessment so that when students see their grade for the assessment, they realize they have earned, for example, "7 points out of a possible 10." *Verbal descriptors* are used instead of numerical or letter grades when teachers rely exclusively on phrases such as "excellent," "satisfactory," and "needs improvement." The number of such phrases used—that is, the number of possible verbal-descriptor grades that might be employed—is up to the teacher. If verbal-descriptor grades are used throughout an entire district, the choice of verbal descriptors is typically decided by district officials.

Counting Scores versus Giving Grades

It's delightfully easy to score a 20-item true-false test. All you have to do is count up the number of correct answers that a student made, then divide that sum by 20. What you get as a consequence of such fairly low-level arithmetic is a "percent correct." And when you pass back students' test papers with a percent correct on each paper, most of your students have a pretty good idea of what that means. Those students who earned percent-correct scores of 95 or 100 are elated; those who earned scores of 55 or 60 are less enthused. (They would be particularly morose if they realized that on a true-false test they could get a 50% correct by chance alone.)

However, when a teacher calculates students' percent-correct scores for any type of selected-response assessment device, the teacher is not giving students grades. Rather, the teacher is simply calculating the proportion of correct answers chosen by the student. To give a student a *grade,* the teacher needs to take another step and indicate *how good* a given percent correct is. Remember, a teacher grades students to let them know how well they're doing. And even though most students realize that if they scored nearly 100% correct on a test, they've done pretty well, it's also possible that, on a particularly tough test, a 75% correct score would be a very fine performance. That's why teachers have to assign grades.

Although teachers who use selected-response assessment devices can delay the necessity to make grading decisions by dispensing a series of percent-correct scores throughout the school year, teachers who use constructed-response tests are usually faced with the need to make grading decisions somewhat earlier. For example, if your students have churned out an original sonnet for you as part of their midterm examinations, it's pretty tough to assign such sonnets a percent-correct score. But it is possible. Some teachers go through a complex series of grade-avoidance gyrations even for constructed-response tests by establishing a maximum number of points attainable, then giving students feedback in such forms as "27 points earned out of 40." As with teachers who rely on percent-correct scores on selected-response tests, this simply delays the moment of truth when grades will, indeed, have to be awarded.

I am not suggesting that teachers who provide *en route* feedback to their students in the form of percent correct or proportion of points earned are displaying abject cowardice. As a high school teacher and a college professor, I've used such systems myself many times. I'm only trying to point out that score counting is not grade giving, and that teachers ultimately have to give their students grades.

Grade-Giving Options

Let's look at four common grade-giving approaches. Each of these approaches can be used not only for end-of-term or end-of-year grades but also for grading the assessment performances of students during the school year. In other words, these four grading approaches can be applied whether you are assigning Johnny an end-of-term grade in your science class or a grade on his two-week experiment on Psychological Depression in Earthworms.

You're probably already familiar with the four grading approaches to be described because, when you were a student, you most likely encountered them all:

- *Absolute grading.* When grading *absolutely*, a grade is given based on a teacher's idea of what level of student performances is truly necessary to earn, for instance, an A. Thus, if an English teacher has established an absolute level of proficiency needed for an A grade, and in a given class no student performs at the A-level of proficiency, then no student gets an A. Conversely, if the teacher's absolute grading standards were such that *all* students had performed beyond the A-level requirements, then the teacher would shower all students with A grades. An absolute system of grading has much in common with a criterion-referenced approach to assessment.

    The major argument in favor of an absolute approach to grading is that there are, indeed, legitimate levels of expectation for students which, although judgmentally devised by teachers, must be satisfied in order for specific grades to be awarded. And, of course, it is always the case that people form their absolute expectations based on seeing how folks usually perform. Thus, there's a sense in which *absolutes flow from relatives*.

- *Relative grading.* When teachers grade *relatively*, a grade is given based on how students perform in relation to one another. Thus, for any group of students, there will always be the *best* and the *worst* performances. Those students who outperform their classmates will get high grades irrespective of the absolute caliber of the students' performances. Conversely, because some students will always score relatively worse than their classmates, such low scorers will receive low grades no matter what. This system of grading is somewhat analogous to a norm-referenced approach to assessment.

As noted earlier, there is a sense in which even a teacher's *absolute* expectations regarding the level of performance needed to achieve an A, B, C, D, or F are derived from years of working with students and discerning how well they're usually capable of performing. But a relative grading system uses the students *in a given class* as the normative group, not all the students whom the teacher has taught in the past.

The chief argument for a relative system of grading is that because the quality of the teacher's instructional efforts may vary, and the composition of a given group of students may vary, some type of class-specific grading is warranted. Teachers who use a relative-grading approach tend to appreciate its flexibility because grading expectations change from class to class.

- *Aptitude-based grading.* When grading on *aptitude*, a grade is given to each student based on how well the student performs in relation to that student's academic potential. To illustrate, if a particularly bright student outperformed all other students in the class, but still performed well below what the teacher believed the student was capable of, the student might be given a B, not an A. In order to grade on aptitude, of course, the teacher needs to have an idea of what students' academic potentials really are. To gain an estimate of each student's academic aptitude, teachers either have to rely on the student's prior performance on some sort of academic aptitude test or, instead, must form their own judgments about the student's academic potential. Because academic aptitude tests are being administered less frequently these days, in order to use an aptitude-based grading approach, teachers will generally need to arrive at their own estimate of a student's potential.

  The main argument in favor of aptitude-based grading is that it tends to "level the playing field" by grading students according to their innate gifts and thereby encourages students to fulfill their potential. A problem with this grading approach, as you might guess, is the difficulty of deciding on just what each student's academic potential really is.

- *Pass/fail grading.* When teachers grade on a *pass/fail* basis, they are essentially establishing a specific level of proficiency required for a "pass," then dividing students into two groups—the passers and the failers. Pass/fail grading is employed more frequently in postsecondary education than in grades K–12 because the grade-point average (GPA) that a student earns in, say, high school is often employed as a predictor of how well the student will perform in college. Pass/fail grading systems, because they separate students into only two groups, are insufficiently discriminating to contribute all that much to diversity on students' GPAs, hence are not often employed prior to college. The passing standard that a teacher employs in such systems can be based on an absolute or a relative orientation.

From a teacher's perspective, pass/fail grading is reasonably simple for making decisions about most students. What gets sticky, of course, is the need to make tough judgment calls about those students who are "just barely" passers or "just barely" failers.

As indicated earlier, any of these four grading approaches can be used to assign grades for individual efforts of students, such as their performances on a short essay examination, or for arriving at a student's total-year grade. For instance, thinking back to Chapter 9's treatment of portfolio assessment, it would be possible to use any of the four grading approaches in order to arrive at students' portfolio grades—grades that might be dispensed in letter, numerical, or verbal form.

Typical Grade-Communication Mechanisms

When teachers give in-class grades to students, those grades are usually written on the students' completed examinations, term projects, or whatever documents have been graded. When teachers communicate to students' parents, on the other hand, there are three fairly standard grade-communication mechanisms employed.

First, there is the time-honored and oft-maligned *report card.* Report cards are intended to relay to the student's parents an estimate of how well a student is performing. Some report cards can be relatively terse documents with room for only a grade-per-subject and nothing else. In contrast, others can be elaborate documents with all sorts of information provided to parents. The more elaborate versions of report cards, of course, take far more time for teachers to complete. The nature of report cards typically depends on the preferences of district officials. Individual teachers often don't have all that much say in the composition of the districtwide report card.

A second form of grade reporting to parents consists of *interim reports*—brief written communications to parents regarding their children's progress in school. In some instances, interim reports are little more than short notes indicating such things as a student's areas of strength and weakness as well as what the child should be working on at home. District policy may or may not govern the form and frequency of interim reports.

The third form of grade reporting to parents relies on *parent/teacher conferences.* Such conferences, used more frequently with parents of younger children, allow the teacher to communicate more fully to parents regarding a child's progress and to give parents an opportunity to raise questions about the quality of their child's performance. Again, district policy may or may not prescribe the

Parent Talk ....

Imagine that one of your students' parents, Mrs. Aquino, wants to discuss her daughter's grade in your class. Specifically, she wants to know, "What goes into Mary's grade?"

• • • *If I were you, here's how I'd respond to Mrs. Aquino:*

"I'm delighted you want to look into how Mary is graded in my class. What I'd like you to do is look over my classroom information system that I've been able to get up and running this year on my lap-top computer. Why don't you come in to my class before or after school and I'll show you how I arrive at each of the components contributing to Mary's grade. I'll also show you how I've tried to weight the grade-determination importance of certain tests and other assignments that Mary and her classmates complete.

"What you need to understand, Mrs. Aquino, is that any grade given to any student is almost always a teacher-judgment based on an amalgam of different sorts of evidence. And, to be honest, because teachers' judgments are involved, and teachers are altogether human, there will invariably be some errors teacher's in grading.

"But I assure you that I and the other teachers in our school are trying to do the fairest and most accurate job we can when we grade our students. Why don't you visit and we can review what goes into Mary's grade?"

• • • *Now, how would you respond to Mrs. Aquino's concerns?*

number and nature of such grade-focused conferences. Many elementary teachers, although they realize that parent/teacher conferences consume much time, appreciate the opportunity that such conferences provide to offer parents a richer description of their children's progress than is possible with alternative grade-reporting systems.

Grading's Inherent Imprecision

Wouldn't it be nice if teachers never made mistakes when they grade students? But, as you probably know all too well from having been the recipient of too-low or too-high grades during your own years as a student, teachers make grading errors. Certainly, teachers don't want to make mistakes in the grades they give to their students; however, grading is a judgment-based enterprise in which flawed decisions will surely be made.

Fortunately, in the long haul, such errors tend to balance one another out. Do you recall from Chapter 8 that there are three kinds of rater bias—namely, generosity bias, severity bias, and central-tendency bias? It is true that many teachers are biased in the same three ways when they grade students. Thus, over the years, a given student will probably be on the receiving end of some undeserved high grades and some unwarranted low grades. What you need to remember is that if you do the best job you can in dispensing grades to your students—that is, if you assign grades carefully and with the kind of deliberateness suggested in this chapter—you'll have done your grading as well as you can. Human judgment, as potent as it is, is not flawless. And it certainly isn't flawless when it comes to grading students.

Standard Setting in High-Stakes Tests

You should be aware that the same kinds of judgmentally based choices that you have to wrestle with as an individual teacher must also be faced by those who must set the "cut-score" or "passing standard" on high-stakes tests. To illustrate, on all of the statewide graduation tests that must be passed before students receive state-sanctioned diplomas, a cut-score must be established that distinguishes between those students who should receive diplomas and those who shouldn't receive diplomas. Because of the high visibility of these diploma-sanctioned tests, and the important consequences for individual students, considerable attention is usually given to the establishment of a test's passing standard.

The most common method of setting a passing standard for high-stakes tests was devised by a measurement specialist named William Angoff. Angoff's procedure calls for a standard-setting committee to be established, then have its members render individual judgments about the difficulty of every item in the test on the basis of the proportion of qualified students who would answer each item correctly. For example, committee members might be asked, "How many students out of a 100 who are *just barely qualified* to receive a high school diploma would answer this item correctly?" These per-item difficulty estimates are then summed and discussed by committee members after having seen how difficult each item actually was for a group of students similar to those with whom the test is to be used. Frequently, for instance, a p value for each item based on a tryout of the test is provided to the standard-setting committee. The committee then learns of the consequences of setting a given passing standard; that is, the committee members are told how many students (total students as well as for ethnic groups) would fail if the passing standard were set at particular points. Finally, after one or more days of item judging and group deliberation, a passing standard is set for the high-stakes test involved.

Having moderated a good many of these standard-setting sessions, I want you to realize the even with all the whistles and bells of the high-stakes standard-setting process, most members of the standard-setting committee walk out the door at the end of the day every bit as uncertain they made a good decision as you do when you're deciding whether to give Hortense an "excellent" or a "satisfactory." Grading is a gunky, gunky game.

What Do Classroom Teachers Really Need to Know about Assessment-Based Evaluation of Teaching and Grading of Students? . . . .

If there ever were two education-related activities in which the results of student assessments play a vital role, those two activities are the evaluation of one's teaching and the grading of one's students. When teachers evaluate the quality of their own efforts, a significant source of data should be the nature of students' performances on classroom assessment devices. When teachers give grades to students, a salient factor should be the quality of students' performances on classroom assessments.

You should realize that when you use students' test results as indicators of your own instructional prowess, a major determiner of how well your students perform will be the particular students with whom you're working. Even using a straightforward pretest-posttest evaluation paradigm doesn't circumvent the problem created because of the dissimilarity of different teachers' students. For purposes of formative evaluation, disparities in students' entry behaviors don't pose all that much of a problem. For purposes of summative evaluation, however, disparities in the abilities and motivation levels of different teachers' students should induce caution in the evaluative use of students' test results. Judgments about the caliber of growth attained by a given teacher must be made in the context of the particular instructional situation in which the teacher is functioning.

Regarding grading, you should know that you need to give careful attention to the isolation of grading criteria and to the weighting of those criteria. However, when you get down to it—that is, when you get down to the dispensing of actual grades—you're more than likely to miss on certain students. Yet, given the inescapably judgmental basis of grading, that's as good as it's going to get.

Chapter Summary . . . .

Having drawn a distinction between *evaluation* as an activity focused on determining the effectiveness of the teacher and *grading* as an activity focused on letting students know how well they are performing, the chapter then tackled the topic of evaluation. *Formative evaluation* was contrasted with *summative evaluation*. Formative evaluation focuses on the improvement of the teacher's instructional endeavors, whereas summative evaluation focuses on such decisions as continuation of the teacher's employment. A preinstruction versus postinstruction paradigm was recommended as a straightforward way of employing assessment results to help determine the effectiveness of instruction. The use of affective assessment devices was urged, in addition to cognitively oriented assessment instruments, when ascertaining a teacher's impact on students.

Turning to grading of students, it was recommended that teachers explicate their grading criteria and assign weights to each criterion. Four schemes for arriving at grades were described: ability grading, relative grading, aptitude-based grading, and pass/fail grading. Letter, numerical, and verbal reporting methods were also described, as were several mechanisms for communicating a student's grades to the student's parents. The chapter was concluded with an attempt to offer teachers solace for their task of judgmentally awarding grades to students.

Self-Check

We'll close out this chapter with a fairly short set of self-check exercises. They're also rather easy. Clearly, because this is the final set of these little practice activities, I want to send you forth in an upbeat mood. Check out the five activities described below in the first set of practice exercises and decide whether each is dominantly *evaluation* (E) or *grading* (G) as these two operations were defined in the chapter. These are, as you know by now, binary-choice items.

(E or G)   **1.** Molly Muggins uses her algebra students' final examination results to determine whether she needs to alter the way she teaches the unit on simultaneous equations.

(E or G)   **2.** Bertram Billings decides which students will receive "exemplary" or "acceptable" labels on their Parent Communication Reports based on students' performances on classroom tests (25%) and, chiefly, on their writing portfolios (75%).

(E or G)   **3.** Sarah Selmo uses her third-grade students' pretest-to-posttest results when conferencing with her principal, who must decide whether to recommend Sarah for tenure in the district.

(E or G)   **4.** Hillary Harris lets her students evaluate all major ingredients in their portfolios, then combines these student evaluations with her own evaluations of the portfolios so that interim progress reports, varying from 1 to 10, can be sent to students' parents.

(E or G)   **5.** William Wimzy bases each student's entire course grade on the student's accomplishments in carrying out an elaborate performance test administered during the final three weeks of the school year.

Now, for the last five self-check exercises of the book, grapple with five additional binary-choice items. You've already had some true-false items at the end of an earlier chapter, so as a change of pace please judge each of the following five statements (based on the chapter's contents), as TT (terribly true) or FF (fervently false).

(TT or FF)   **6.** The focus of summative evaluation is on more "terminal" decisions about teachers, whereas formative evaluation focuses chiefly on improving the teacher's instructional effectiveness.

(TT or FF)   7. With the application of sufficient forethought and quantitatively oriented evidence, the assignment of students' grades can be transferred into a largely error-free enterprise.

(TT or FF)   8. Absolute grading practices are roughly comparable to criterion-referenced assessment, whereas relative grading practices are somewhat akin to norm-referenced assessment.

(TT or FF)   9. Generally speaking, students' assessment results should play a rather minor role in the awarding of grades or in the evaluation of a teacher's instructional effectiveness.

(TT or FF)   10. Chapter 15, positioned as it is in advance of the book's index yet close to the book's back cover, is this book's final chapter.

Pondertime

1. Assuming that a teacher was committed to the use of students' test results in the evaluation of teaching, do you think that those test results would be more useful in *formatively* oriented teacher evaluation or in *summatively* oriented teacher evaluation? And why, pray tell, do you think that?

2. In this chapter there was a fairly elaborate data-gathering design presented (with arrows and everything!) to help teachers reduce the reactive effects of pretesting. Do you think that the approach to data gathering seen in Figure 15.2 should be used more frequently with cognitive or affective assessment instruments? Realistically, how often do you think most classroom teachers would be inclined to use this rather elaborate data-gathering scheme?

3. When teachers evaluate themselves (or when supervisors evaluate teachers), various kinds of evidence can be used in order to arrive at an evaluative judgment. If you were a teacher who was trying to decide on the *relative worth* of the following types of evidence, where would you rank the importance of students' test results?
   a. Systematic observations of the teachers' classroom activities
   b. Students' anonymous evaluations of the teacher's ability
   c. Students' pretest-to-posttest gain scores on achievement tests
   d. A teacher's self-evaluation

   Would your ranking of the importance of these four types of evidence be the same in all instructional contexts? If not, what factors would make you change your ratings?

4. Assume that you are a high school English teacher who is wrestling with the task of arriving at a "grading philosophy." You have narrowed your grading approaches to three—namely, *relative* grading, *aptitude-based* grading, and *absolute* grading. Which of these three strategies do you think is the most defensible one you can use to bestow grades on your deserving and/or undeserving students?

5. How important do you think a student's performance on classroom assessment devices ought to be in the awarding of grades? What other factors, if any, should be given serious consideration in the grading of students?

6. If you were devising an assessment scheme to determine how well a reader of this book had mastered its contents, what sort of a procedure would you employ? Would you, for instance, recommend a selected-response test, a performance test, a portfolio, or perhaps selective cranial surgery?

Self-Check Key

1. E
2. G
3. E
4. G
5. G
6. TT
7. FF
8. TT
9. FF
10. TT (Wasn't that easy?)

Additional Stuff

Airasian, Peter W. *Classroom Assessment* (2nd ed.). New York: McGraw-Hill, 1994.

Airasian, Peter W., and Arlen R. Gullickson. *Teacher Self-Evaluation Tool Kit*. Thousand Oaks, CA: Corwin Press, 1997.

Frary, Robert B., Lawrence H. Cross, and Larry J. Weber. "Testing and Grading Practices and Opinions of Secondary Teachers of Academic Subjects: Implications for Instruction in Measurement." *Educational Measurement: Issues and Practice*, 12, no. 3 (Fall 1993): 23–30.

Guskey, Tom (Ed.). *Communicating Student Learning* (Yearbook). Alexandria, VA: Association for Supervision and Curriculum Development, 1996.

Krumboltz, John D., and Christine J. Yeh. "Competitive Grading Sabotages Good Teaching." *Phi Delta Kappan*, 78, no. 4 (December 1996): 324–326.

Mandel Glazer, Susan. "Want to Change Your Testing? Here's How to Begin." *Teaching K–8* (August–September 1993): 152–154.

McMillan, James H. *Classroom Assessment: Principles and Practice for Effective Instruction*. Boston: Allyn and Bacon, 1997.

Popham, W. James. "Using Participant-Satisfaction Forms to Evaluate Staff Development Program." *NASSP Bulletin*, 81, no. 586 (February 1997): 112–116.

Popham, W. James. *Educational Evaluation* (3rd ed.). Boston: Allyn and Bacon, 1993.

Standards for Educational and Psychological Testing. Washington, DC: American Psychological Association, 1985.

Stanley, Sarah J., and W. James Popham (Eds.). *Teacher Evaluation: Six Prescriptions for Success*. Alexandria, VA: Association for Supervision and Curriculum Development, 1988.

Stiggins, Richard J. *Student-Centered Classroom Assessment* (2nd ed.). Upper Saddle River, NJ: Prentice Hall, 1997.

Wilson, Ben, and James A. Wood. "Teacher Evaluation: A National Dilemma." *Journal of Personnel Evaluation in Education*, 10, no. 1 (March 1996): 75–82.

Wright, S. Paul, Sandra P. Horn, and William L. Sanders. "Teacher and Classroom Context Effects on Student Achievement: Implications for Teacher Evaluation." *Journal of Personnel Evaluation in Education*, 11, no. 1 (April 1997): 57–67.

Nonprint Stuff

Association for Supervision and Curriculum Development. *Reporting Student Progress* (Videotape #495249T87). Alexandria, VA: Author, 1996.

Northwest Regional Laboratory. *Developing Sound Grading Practices* (Videotape #NREL-9A). Los Angeles: IOX Assessment Associates.

Popham, W. James. *Making the Grade: Helping Parents Understand What's Important* (Videotape #ETVT-22). Los Angeles: IOX Assessment Associates.

Appendix ....

Standardized Test Scores: Do They Really Show How Good Schools Are?

Parents want their children to go to a good school. That's normal. And to determine how good a school is, parents often rely on the scores that the school's students earn on standardized tests. That's understandable. But it's also wrong.

One of the most widely held parental beliefs is that students' standardized test scores provide an accurate indication of how effective a school's teachers are. That belief, although widespread, is mistaken.

Nonetheless, many parents use newspapers' school-by-school rankings on standardized tests to decide if a school is good enough. They even go so far as to use test scores when purchasing a new home. (Realtors often trot out high test scores to clinch a sale.) And once a child is enrolled in a particular school, many parents use test results to keep track of how well the school is doing.

So, because thousands of parents make judgments each year about a school's effectiveness based *chiefly* on the school's standardized test scores, more parents need to understand what standardized tests *can* and *cannot* do. One thing that standardized tests cannot do is show how good schools are.

Source: W. James Popham, University of California, Los Angeles.

What Are Standardized Tests?

Technically, any test that's administered, scored, and interpreted in a standard manner can be described as a "standardized" test. But when most people talk about standardized tests, they're referring to the nationally standardized tests that are created and distributed by commercial test publishers.

There are two fundamentally different types of standardized tests likely to be encountered by parents: *aptitude* tests and *achievement* tests. An aptitude test is a *predictor* test. Scholastic aptitude tests are used to make predictions about how well students will perform in some future academic setting. The most widely used of these scholastic aptitude tests are those that predict how well high school students will perform in college. Of these, the SAT (Scholastic Assessment Test) and the ACT assessment are the best known. But *school-by-school* comparisons on the ACT or SAT are not readily available to parents. And these standardized *aptitude* tests aren't even administered until students arrive at junior or senior high school. Such aptitude tests, therefore, provide little guidance to parents about school effectiveness.

A standardized *achievement* test, however, is not a predictor test. Instead, a standardized achievement test measures knowledge and skills that a student possesses in a particular content area such as mathematics, language arts, or social studies.

Standardized achievement tests are designed for children at all grade levels. In many school districts, all children are required to take a standardized achievement test every spring, usually starting at about third grade. Because standardized achievement tests are employed to measure students' knowledge and skills, they are thought by parents to be suitable indicators of a school's effectiveness.

There are only five major standardized achievement tests currently used in the United States. Those five tests are the California Achievement Tests, Comprehensive Tests of Basic Skills, Iowa Tests of Basic Skills, Metropolitan Achievement Tests, and Stanford Achievement Tests. Students' scores on these five nationally standardized achievement tests are often *incorrectly* used by parents to judge a school's educational effectiveness and sometimes, even more incorrectly, to judge a particular teacher's instructional skill.

Purpose of Standardized Tests

Since the beginning of standardized achievement testing, the purpose of such tests has been to *compare* an individual test taker's performance to the performance of students in a norm group. A norm group is a large and representative number of students who have previously completed the test. So, when parents learn that their child scored "at the 77th percentile" on a nationally standardized achievement test, this indicates that their child outperformed 77 percent of the students in the national norm group.

Educators "refer" a student's test score to the norm group's performance in order to interpret the score's meaning. Hence, standardized achievement tests are frequently described as *norm-referenced tests*.

Given the *comparative* function of standardized achievement tests (comparing a test taker's performance to the performances of students in the test's norm group), it is essential that such tests "spread out" examinees' performances. What the developers of standardized tests yearn for is plenty of high, low, and middle scores on their tests. That "spread" of scores is needed not only for the norm group's performance but also for all other student performances.

The more diverse the students' test scores are, the better. If there is not sufficient score diversity, then fine-grained comparisons of a particular test taker's performance with the norm group's performances aren't possible. If students' test scores are "all bunched up," meaningful comparisons can't be made.

This point is illustrated in the two distributions of test scores (shown below) where the number of students' scores is represented by the area under the curved lines. In the top distribution, there is sufficient spread of test scores; in the bottom distribution, the spread of test scores is insufficient.

Suppose the developers of a standardized achievement test in seventh-grade social studies set out to create a new test. The test developers will try to include test items drawn from the broad array of social studies content that a typi-

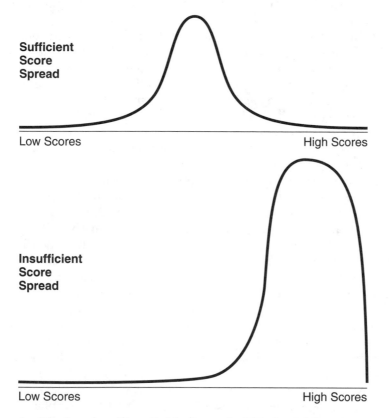

Sufficient Score Spread

Low Scores   High Scores

Insufficient Score Spread

Low Scores   High Scores

An Ideal and an Unsuitable Spread of Students' Scores on Standardized Achievement Tests

cal seventh-grade student might be expected to possess. But there's so much social studies content to be dealt with in the seventh grade, the test developers can't cover it completely. Instead, they must *sample* from the content that's apt to be covered by teachers.

The test developers' content sampling doesn't really have to be all that precise. If the test items deal with content that a seventh-grader might be expected to know, and if the items yield a spread of scores for students, then the test will function in the way that standardized achievement tests are supposed to function.

If a standardized achievement test permits comparisons between a particular student's score and the scores of students in the test's norm group, then the test will be doing its job. But that job is *not* to evaluate teachers or schools. Let's briefly consider three reasons that standardized tests shouldn't be used for such purposes.

Unrecognized Content Mismatches.   The first drawback in using standardized test scores as indicators of educational quality stems from substantial mismatches between what's actually tested and what's actually taught. If an instructor teaches Content *X*, but a standardized test measures Content *Y*, it's pretty clear that the Content *Y* test won't reveal how well Content *X* has been taught. Let's see how such curricular mismatches arise.

Nationally standardized achievement tests are built and distributed by large corporations whose financial success depends directly on the number of tests sold. Unfortunately, from a sales perspective, there is enormous diversity in what's taught in different parts of our nation. Unlike some countries where there is a national curriculum, the curricular decisions in the United States are made at the state and school-district level. Curriculum, as a consequence, is carved up differently in different states and school districts. For example, what is emphasized in fifth-grade language arts may vary quite substantially in such diverse school districts as Duluth, Des Moines, and Detroit.

Given this curricular diversity, testing companies face severe sales reductions if they specify *precisely* what their tests are measuring. Suppose a school administrator is considering the purchase of a nationally standardized achievement test and sees that what is being taught locally does not mesh well with what the national test is measuring. The administrator will realize that the district won't look good on tests that aren't well aligned with the district's curriculum. How likely, then, do you think the administrator will be to purchase the test?

Accordingly, because of so many national curricular differences, the publishers of standardized tests typically describe their tests in very *general* terms thereby picking up the classic Rorschach dividend of allowing potential purchasers to see in an inkblot label what they want to see. For instance, a given district's educators are instructionally stressing reading comprehension. A potentially purchasable standardized achievement test is described by its sales representative as measuring reading comprehension. The district's educators assume the test will be aligned with the district's instructional emphases. The odds are that the district's educators are wrong.

Over the past decade or so, analyses of the content of standardized achievement tests indicate that there is frequently an enormous mismatch between what a standardized achievement test measures and what is being taught in a particular school. Sometimes, as much as half of what is being *tested* is not even supposed to be *taught* by a school. If half of what's tested by a standardized test is not taught in a school, should we be surprised if the school's students don't perform well on that standardized test?

From a parent's perspective, the most troubling point of the mismatch between the content tested and the content taught is that many *educators* are unaware of such mismatches. Far too many teachers, just as parents, assume that the standardized achievement test used in their school covers the content they routinely teach. A careful analysis of the tested content, however, almost always reveals that those teachers are mistaken.

Mismatches between what's tested and what's taught will obviously lead to inaccurate judgments by parents trying to base a judgment about educational quality on students' standardized achievement test scores. Thus, *teaching/testing mismatches* is the first strike against the use of standardized achievement test scores as indicators of educational quality.

Failing to Test Important Content.   There's a second problem with using standardized test scores to evaluate educational quality. That difficulty stems from the overriding purpose of standardized achievement tests—namely, to spread out students' scores so that those scores can be compared with the performances of the norm group's students, usually in the form of percentiles.

But, as noted earlier, to make these percentile comparisons as precise as test publishers would like, students' scores must be substantially spread out. For purposes of spreading out students' scores on a standardized achievement test, any given test item should be answered correctly by between 40 and 60 percent of the test takers. If items are answered correctly by a much larger proportion of students, for instance, 80 to 100 percent of the students, those items will not do their share in spreading out students' overall test scores. Test developers, therefore, try to avoid including such items in standardized tests. And when the test is revised every 5 to 10 years or so, the test's revisers certainly try to discard such items.

Now for the rub. Think about what's covered by the test items on which students perform well. Those items usually measure things that the teacher thought important enough to stress instructionally. The better the teacher teaches important content, the better the students perform on test items measuring such content. But the better the students perform on those items, the more likely the items will be discarded from future forms of the test!

There is a systematic tendency to remove from routinely revised standardized achievement tests the very items that cover the most important content teachers teach. From the test developer's perspective, it isn't important to measure the most significant content that teachers teach. Instead, it's important to spread out student scores so that comparisons with the norm group's performance are possible.

But if you're a teacher who is stressing important content, how fair is it if your instructional skill is evaluated on the basis of an achievement test that deliberately fails to measure the most important content you're teaching? That's strike two against the use of standardized test scores to measure instructional effectiveness.

Item-Focused Instruction.   The final problem with using standardized achievement test scores to evaluate schools or teachers is that these tests are revised only every 5 to 10 years. And, more often than not, the tests themselves are actually stored in the schools where they are administered each year by the school's teachers. So, even if a teacher is not malevolently trying to "teach kids the actual test items," there's still a familiarization factor that, over the years, can *artificially* boost a school's test scores.

To illustrate, think about a sixth-grade teacher who, for several years, has administered a standardized social studies achievement test in which two items deal with the invention of the steam engine. Isn't it natural for the teacher, in future years, to devote just a bit of attention to steam engines and their origins? After all, the teacher might think, "If this content is important enough to be included on a *national* test, shouldn't I be spending a bit of instructional time teaching my students about that content?"

As a consequence of teachers' familiarity with a standardized test's content, and the resultant instructional emphases given to that content, there is almost always an increase in students' test scores over the span of several years when the same form of a standardized achievement is reused. Parents, however, should place little confidence in such familiarity-induced improvements. Students are often being taught the content measured by a given test's *items,* not how to master the *knowledge* and *skills* supposedly measured by the test. And that's strike three!

What Standardized Tests Can Tell Parents

If standardized achievement tests should never be used to evaluate schools or teachers, what are such tests good for? The answer is that standardized achievement tests give parents an approximate idea of how their child stacks up against students in a national norm group. It is an *approximate* reflection of the student's comparative achievement, because standardized achievement tests embody far less measurement precision than parents often assume.

Even though these tests are commercially distributed, printed professionally, and ultimately end up in the form of numerical scores—sometimes even with *decimals*—they're really not all that precise. If you were to readminister the same test to children after the delay of only a few days, you'd be surprised at how much the students' scores would change.

But even recognizing this imprecision of measurement, if parents find out that one of their children is scoring at the 95th percentile on a standardized achievement test (that's good) and their other child is scoring at the 20th percentile (that's not so good), this information can guide parents in their interactions with their children's teachers.

Historically, standardized achievement tests have been created to permit comparisons among students with respect to their relative mastery of a content sample in a specific subject. And, given the brevity of most standardized achievement tests, most of those content samples are pretty skimpy. But even if parents recognize that the content sample in a standardized test is pretty slim, there's still some virtue in finding out how a child's achievement compares with that of a national norm group.

Measuring Mileage with a Tablespoon

If parents understand the nature of standardized achievement tests and what their historic function has been, they will be far less likely to appraise a school's quality, or a teacher's skill, on the basis of standardized test scores. Suppose you're baking cupcakes for a school's money-raising event. Would you use a measuring cup to tell when your oven has reached a temperature of 400 degrees? Of course not. Measuring cups were designed for another purpose. It's the same situation when parents try to determine a school's success by using a measurement tool built for a decisively different purpose.

If you consider the content of standardized achievement tests carefully, you'll find that those tests measure many things students have learned at home rather than things they've learned at school. It's not too outlandish to assert that standardized achievement tests measure what students come to school with, not what they've been taught there.

The subtitle of this essay raises a key question about standardized achievement test scores: "Do they really show how good schools are?" Think of that question as a one-item quiz. By this time, you really ought to know the answer.

Index